CW00709212

# China's State Enterprise Reform

The Chinese economic reform process of the last quarter of a century has engendered significant changes in the structure and management of work organizations. Central to the process has been the 'corporatization' and 'marketization' of the *danwei*, or state-owned enterprises (SOEs). This book examines the history of post-Mao state-enterprise reform and extends this to discuss the major social consequences of such large-scale corporate restructuring. Drawing on the academic literature on China's economic transition and extensive primary research data from large SOEs in the Chinese steel industry, it assesses the extent to which the aims of reducing government interference in the running of SOEs, developing a sense of enterprise, and achieving cost reductions and productivity improvements through large-scale workforce reductions have been achieved within a climate of reform-induced labour unrest and incipient political instability.

**John Hassard** is Professor of Organizational Analysis at Manchester Business School and Senior Research Associate at the Judge Business School, Cambridge University.

**Jackie Sheehan** is Associate Professor of Contemporary Chinese Studies and Deputy Director of the Institute for Contemporary Chinese Studies, University of Nottingham.

**Meixiang Zhou** is Programme Manager of the United Nations Development Programme, China.

**Jane Terpstra-Tong** is Lecturer in Management in the Faculty of Business Administration, University of Macau.

**Jonathan Morris** is Professor of Organizational Analysis at Cardiff University Business School.

# Routledge Contemporary China Series

# China's State Enterprise Reform

## From Marx to the market

**John Hassard, Jackie Sheehan,
Meixiang Zhou, Jane Terpstra-Tong
and Jonathan Morris**

Routledge
Taylor & Francis Group

LONDON AND NEW YORK

First published 2007
by Routledge
2 Park Square, Milton Park, Abingdon, Oxon OX14 4RN

Simultaneously published in the USA and Canada
by Routledge
270 Madison Ave, New York, NY 10016

*Routledge is an imprint of the Taylor & Francis Group,
an informa business*

© 2007 John Hassard, Jackie Sheehan, Meixiang Zhou,
Jane Terpstra-Tong and Jonathan Morris

Typeset in Times New Roman by
Florence Production Ltd, Stoodleigh, Devon
Printed and bound in Great Britain by
Biddles Ltd, King's Lynn

*British Library Cataloguing in Publication Data*
A catalogue record for this book is available from the British Library

*Library of Congress Cataloging in Publication Data*
China's state enterprise reform: from Marx to the market /
John Hassard . . . [et al.].
       p. cm. – (Routledge contemporary China series ; 19)
       Includes bibliographical references and index.
    1. Government business enterprises – China. 2. Government
ownership – China. 3. Privatization – China. 4. China – Economic
policy    I. Hassard, John, 1953–
HD4318.C4529 2007
338.6'20951–dc22                                    2006026305

ISBN10: 0–415–37172–4 (hbk)
ISBN10: 0–203–09971–0 (ebk)

ISBN13: 978–0–415–37172–8 (hbk)
ISBN13: 978–0–203–09971–1 (ebk)

# Contents

# Illustrations

## Tables

## Boxes

## Appendices

# Preface

As public ownership has been the prevalent form of ownership since socialist China was founded, we argue that the reform of state-owned enterprises (SOEs) has posed the major challenge to the government in seeking economic transition to a market-based economy. While most other aspects of Chinese economic reform (e.g. price management, product and factor markets, taxation, investment financing, trading regimes, the foreign exchange system, etc.) have made significant progress during the transition era, SOE restructuring has lagged behind and remains the government's biggest problem. Within the pages of this book we offer an explanation of this 'SOE problem' by developing a history of Chinese economic reform since 1978. The focus of the analysis is the various stages of economic experimentation designed to reform the traditional *danwei* system under which China's SOEs have operated. In making our arguments we draw upon the academic literature on public enterprise reform, empirical studies of Chinese SOE restructuring, and a range of economic, management and sociological theories.

Originally, in being state-owned, funded and operated, public enterprises in China were not responsible for either profits or losses. Any profit was remitted to the state and any losses were met from the state budget. Characteristically they were political and social as much as economic organizations. Above all, such public enterprises were responsible for workers' job provision and general welfare, including housing, medical care, education and pensions. Under the economic reform programme that has operated in China since 1978, however, efforts have been made to transform these public enterprises into more clearly bounded economic entities, notable being efforts to reduce their social welfare burdens. In the process, an attempt has been made to separate enterprise operations from government administration, with measures such as profit retention, tax for profit and management contracting marking early phases of reform, and corporatization, shareholding and privatization those of later periods. Within the early reform phases, essentially those established pre-1990, the emphasis was on changes to the *internal* governance of enterprises. Reform measures centred largely on personnel control rights and revenue distribution, with delegation of authority, profit sharing and employee ownership being experimented with under the main reform programme of the

# Acknowledgements

There are a number of people and organizations we would like to thank for their support while we have been researching and writing this book. We would like to thank Dr Xiao Yuxin (University of Aberdeen), a co-author of Chapter 6, for his friendship and companionship during many of our visits to China, and, in particular, for liaising with the steel companies researched in the course of this project. In the same vein we would like to thank Professor Chen Zhicheng (University of Science and Technology, Beijing) whose assistance in arranging site visits and meetings has also been invaluable, especially during the early years of research. Other academics who have greatly assisted us in our work are Professors She Yuanguan (University of Science and Technology, Beijing) and Paul Cook (University of Manchester). We would also like to thank Professor Malcolm Warner (University of Cambridge) for initially suggesting us as potential authors to our editor at Routledge, Peter Sowden. We are indebted to the many Chinese executives, managers and workers we have interviewed in the course of this research, as we are to the ministry officials and university researchers who have helped us similarly. Also, in China we have been assisted in the process of data collection by the State Council Development Research Centre. Our field investigations were supported by the Economic and Social Research Council (UK), the British Council, the Institute for Contemporary Chinese Studies (University of Nottingham) and the Chinese Academy of Social Sciences. We would also like to thank the staff of the Chongqing Hotel, Chongqing, for hosting our 'Tuesday Club' research meetings. Finally, kind thanks go to Sue Haffner of the Manchester Business School for her assistance in assembling the manuscript.

restructuring we take heed of the various social and political consequences to arise from them, most notably those resulting from recurrent rounds of enterprise downsizing.

John Hassard, Jackie Sheehan, Meixiang Zhou,
Jane Terpstra-Tong and Jonathan Morris

# Abbreviations

| | |
|---|---|
| ACFTU | All-China Federation of Trade Unions |
| AMC | asset management corporation |
| CCP | Chinese Communist Party |
| CMRS | Contract Management Responsibility System |
| CNOOC | China National Offshore Oil Corporation |
| COE | collective-owned enterprise |
| CRS | Contract Responsibility System |
| EBIT | earnings before interest and tax |
| ECE | Eastern and Central European countries |
| EPS | earnings per share |
| ERDCSETC | Enterprise Reform Division of China State Economic and Trade Commission |
| EVA | Economic Value Added |
| FCRS | Fiscal Contract Responsibility System |
| FDI | foreign direct investment |
| FDRS | Factory Director Responsibility System |
| FSU | former Soviet Union |
| GCS | Group Company System |
| GITIC | Guangdong International Trust Investment Company |
| HCRS | Household Contract Responsibility System |
| ILO | International Labour Organization |
| IPO | initial public offering |
| MBO | management buy-out |
| MES | Modern Enterprise System |
| NPLs | non-performing loans |
| PBC | People's Bank of China |
| ROE | return on equity |
| SASAC | State-owned Assets Supervision and Administration Commission |
| SCER | State Commission for Economic Restructuring |
| SCS | Shareholder Cooperative System |
| SDCE | State Development and Economic Commission |
| SESC | State Enterprise Supervisory Committee |

| SETC | State Economic and Trade Commission |
| SEZ | special economic zone |
| SOE | state-owned enterprise |
| TFP | total factor productivity |
| TISCO | Tangshan Iron and Steel Company Limited |
| TVEs | township and village enterprises |
| UNOCAL | Union Oil Company of California |
| WACC | Weighted Average Cost of Capital |
| WISCO | Wuhan Iron and Steel Company Limited |
| WSPC | Wuhan Steel Processing Company Limited |

# Introduction

This book presents arguments and findings relevant to understanding the historical context and contemporary status of state-enterprise reform in China. In so doing, we present evidence from a series of studies examining social and economic changes arising from attempts at economic liberalization. The various chapters of the book consider, *inter alia*: the relationship between public ownership and public enterprises; theoretical debates relevant to processes of economic transformation; the historical evolution of China's economic reform programme since 1978; issues of surplus labour, worker re-employment and industrial unrest; and contemporary case studies of reform measures within large-scale Chinese state enterprises.

The book is written mainly for students, researchers and teachers interested in modern Asian economies and, in particular, in the economic, social and political effects of state-enterprise reform in China. In recent years the nature of Chinese enterprise reform has been of concern to students and researchers in a number of academic fields, especially those of economics, management studies, finance and accounting, modern history, sociology and political science. The book will be valuable, therefore, on the one hand to students of Asian economies in transition, and on the other to researchers investigating the institutional reshaping of modern China.

Research for the book is based primarily on a series of year-on-year visits to China by the authors from 1993 to the time of writing in late 2005. In the main these visits have been to major SOEs, and notably to eight large iron and steel SOEs in various regions of China (details presented later). Our research has also involved visits to non-state enterprises, listed subsidiaries of state enterprises, universities whose staff are involved with research into state-enterprise reform, and meetings with ministry officials with expertise in SOE transformation. Although our analysis covers the whole period of Chinese economic reform, we offer particularly detailed assessment of events during the mid- to late 1990s when, arguably, economic experimentation in China was at its height.

## Themes and issues

The basic theme of the book is that, during the last quarter of a century or so, a significant change has taken place in many previously planned economies as they move toward 'marketization'. As a consequence, the transformation of public enterprises from state to market, primarily through privatization, has culminated in organizational change on a genuinely global scale (Cook and Kirkpatrick 1988, 1995, 2000; Sachs 1993; Hughes 1994; Shirley 1999; Sachs *et al.* 2000a and b; World Bank 1995, 2002; Hassard *et al.* 2005). Our primary focus is on such transitional change in China, whose reform process has been perceived as evolutionary and thus one which stands in marked contrast to the 'big bang' approach implemented in economies such as those of Central and Eastern Europe and the former Soviet Union (FSU). More than two decades of reform in China has generated rapid economic growth, dramatic rises in real income and improved living standards. As such, the contrast of the reform paths, measures and outputs of the Chinese economy and those of Eastern Europe and the FSU could not be more striking (Nolan 1995a, 2001; Qian 2000). As Walder has argued:

> as a gradual rather than abrupt transition to the market, China's public industry was protected rather than subject to privatization. China's reform path has confounded the widespread and deeply held belief that gradual reform and public ownership simply cannot work, not even as a transitional strategy.
>
> (1996: 1)

Indeed, according to World Bank figures, under a policy of gradualist change, China's real GDP per capita has grown by approximately 8 per cent per annum since the early 1980s, and its per capita income has nearly quadrupled during the same period (Jeffries 2001; Hassard *et al.* 2005).

Viewed as an unconventional economic model, China's gradualist approach to transition has attracted considerable attention from policy-makers and academics, notably as its strategies have become recognized as economically successful. As recent history reflects the sharply contrasting fortunes of the two main exemplars of transitional reform, the FSU and China, this experience has, in turn, served to query the efficacy of 'orthodox' transition theory, particularly in terms of policies related to accelerated privatization, price liberalization and political democratization (Nolan 2001). While the FSU states followed conventional theory and appeared to suffer both economically and socially, by adopting an unconventional strategy of gradualism China's reform became characterized by continuing high growth within a climate of stability (although we will question the extent of this stability in the chapters that follow).

Questions have been raised, therefore, regarding what should be done, in terms of economic theory, to accomplish efficiency in public enterprise transformation. In particular, the global debate over the mechanisms for transforming public to private enterprises still remains moot on questions of ownership change, the introduction of competition, and management reform. While some theorists advocate ownership transition through privatization (see Shirley 1997, 1999; Zhang, Weiying 1999; Shirley and Walsh 2000), others emphasize that market competition, not property rights, is the primary determinant of enterprise performance (see Yarrow 1986; Cook and Kirkpatrick 1988, 1995, 2000; Vickers and Yarrow 1988; Lin *et al.* 1998; Carlin *et al.* 2001), and still others stress management reform, which involves the perfecting of market-supporting institutions (Stiglitz 1994; Nolan 1995a, 2001; Farazmand 1996, 1999, 2004; Kolodko 1999; Qian 2000; Tsui and Lau 2002; Hassard *et al.* 2005). Although it is acknowledged that ownership, competition and management are all key actors in the transformation drama, there is much academic debate as to their preferred order of appearance and which should take the major role.

As SOEs continue to play a major part in its economy, SOE transformation has been central to China effecting successful marketization and, thus, to maintaining economic growth. As SOE reform has been of central concern not only economically but also socially, the question of how to transform SOEs has been one of the most difficult the Chinese Communist Party has faced since 'liberation' in the late 1940s. Transformation processes are accompanied by significant implications for work organization and labour management. In particular, political concerns over large-scale unemployment and the provision of social security remain at the centre of the economic stage (Solinger 2005). In order to minimize the costs of reform and maximize the benefits, it can be argued that attention must be paid to the interaction between the transformation process and the situation of labour, notably as the state enterprise's role as an employment provider is transformed absolutely through economic reform. The large number of lay-offs resulting from Chinese SOE transition is potentially the cause of significant social pressure, and notably so in relation to welfare provision, with such pressure generating significant effects in terms of labour unrest and associated political responses. However, relatively little research has addressed these issues, and especially the interaction between enterprise restructuring, surplus labour and social security. It is important, therefore, to investigate the implications for labour arising out of the transformation of SOEs in a transitional economy, for these serve to clarify, and provide insights into, the varying roles of competition, ownership and management.

As the transformation of Chinese public enterprises deepened in the 1990s and entered a phase of strategic industrial restructuring and reorganization, SOEs became subject to a range of dramatic changes under the guidance of marketization (Hassard and Sheehan 1997; Gao and Yang 1999; Hassard *et al.* 2005). In contrast to the massive SOE privatization practised in other economies, China employed a series of experimental methods of transformation in the move from a centrally planned to a market economy. The underlying notion was that if SOEs were transformed into market-oriented economic entities, they would experience improved efficiency and performance. But China has been confronted by problems stemming from such reform and incurred considerable social costs in the process (Shirk 1993; Wu 1999; Gao and Yang 1999; Zhang, Weiying 1999; Solinger 2001, 2002, 2005; Blecher 2002; Cai 2002; Hurst and O'Brien 2002). After a quarter of a century of reform, privatization, for example, mainly through shareholding and the clarification of property rights, has become increasingly accepted, and is being implemented dynamically as a national trend. Primarily, ownership change in China involves either the state as a controlling shareholder of key SOEs or SOE employees as shareholders, with the concept of ownership change through the reorganization of shareholding becoming popular and employee shareholding common in small- and medium-sized SOEs (Gao and Yang 1999; Cooper 2003a and b; Hassard *et al.* 2006). Yet, it is evident that not all SOEs have improved their performance according to expectations after the transformation of ownership. Many SOEs, in fact, have displayed relative decline after the implementation of a shareholding system or other kind of ownership change. In practice, ownership change in SOEs often appears to be at best self-determined or at worst chaotic, thus reflecting a general lack of regulatory instructions and criteria. Consequences of such actions include state asset-stripping and the inequitable distribution of reform costs and benefits. This has generated concern that ownership change is not, in itself, a generic panacea.

With regard to the nature and role of management in SOEs undergoing economic transformation, relatively little research has been carried out to date. What research exists tends to argue that poor management, at government and enterprise levels, continues to present a significant problem for the transformation process, even after ownership change and the introduction of competition (Walder 1996; Qian 1999; Tsui and Lau 2002; Hassard *et al.* 2005). Frequently such studies have addressed this issue from a corporate governance perspective emphasizing the efficient use of resources and the need for accountability in their stewardship (Shleifer and Vishny 1997; Estrin and Wright 1999; Buck *et al.* 1999; Stiglitz 1999; Zhang and Zhong 2000; Shirley and Walsh 2000). It can be argued, however, that the management of SOEs before and after privatization requires a broader appreciation than that offered by the corporate governance perspective. Consideration of the role of macro-state level institutional relations and regulations and micro enterprise-managerial mechanisms and structures are also necessary.

## Research aims and objectives

As noted, the shift from a planned to a market economy has taken different forms in different countries, with two broad types being identified – shock therapy and gradualism. Of these the Chinese case represents the latter (Nolan

1995a, 2001, 2003). Although the Chinese economy has traditionally been depicted as 'growing out of plan' (Naughton 1995a) the gradual reform of its SOEs has now reached a point where it has ostensibly turned away from the previously planned economic framework and towards a more market-oriented one. Nevertheless, SOEs remain challenged by politically related problems, for example, of ownership restrictions, management autonomy, surplus workers and the lack of a robust social security system (Hassard *et al.* 2005). Our research aims to provide insights into key factors accounting for the success or otherwise of such public-enterprise transformation, and deepen our understanding of the roles of ownership, competition and management. In doing so, we focus on how SOEs have responded strategically to the deployment of various mechanisms for transition, the research providing an integrated economic, institutional and managerial perspective. Although it has been suggested that SOE ownership change in a non-competitive market is unlikely to improve efficiency, we note how China has, nevertheless, promoted such privatization policies when competitive markets are relatively under-developed. This suggests perhaps that our knowledge of transition processes should not be restricted to conventional theories and concepts. Indeed, it can be argued that the exclusive use of economic theory to direct and explain the practice of transition shows the considerable limitations of that discipline. It seems that both management and political theories have roles to play in explaining and guiding processes of transition, yet to date they have received scant attention in the literature (see Shirk 1993; Nolan 1995a; Farazmand 1999; Qian 1999; Tsui and Lau 2002; Hassard *et al.* 2005). The everyday practice of transition suggests that mainstream economic theory faces serious challenges from new institutional and management perspectives in terms of the validity of theoretical explanation, the latter being geared, for example, to answering questions such as: 'Should the transformation of Chinese SOEs adopt a privatization approach before or after the creation of competitive markets?' and 'What role can management reform play in the transition process?'. Experience suggests that a more comprehensive approach be adopted in this area of study.

In addressing these issues, our book has three main objectives: the first is to carry out contemporary research into China's SOE reform and the transformation from plan-driven '*danwei*' towards market-driven economic entities. Although there is a growing body of literature on China's economic reform, which includes studies on the reform of state enterprises from an economic perspective, plus empirical studies from an industry-based view, there is currently only a small amount of research on the SOE transition from institutional and managerial perspectives. This book aims to fill this gap by presenting detailed research on Chinese SOE transformation through integrating economic, institutional and managerial perspectives.

Our second objective is to develop new insights into the transition mechanisms related to ownership change, the creation of competition and management reform. Particular attention is paid to identifying the relations between, and the interactions among, these three key reform mechanisms. In so doing, our research intends not only to develop new insights at the level of theory, but also to make suggestions at the levels of policy and practice.

And third, we wish to analyse the impact of SOE transformation on local government, management and, particularly, labour. We suggest that more attention should be paid to issues of social stability, especially in terms of how labour is affected by the new cost/benefit relations of state-enterprise economic reform. It is worth noting that one of the general reform goals is to raise the living standards of labour, thus generating national wealth whilst avoiding undue social disparity. The transformation of SOEs often alters traditional social responsibilities in terms of the provision of employee welfare and urban employment. In the Chinese case this can have a considerable impact on state employees. Such impacts on labour can potentially reach the level whereby social stability is seriously threatened. Our research aims to draw attention to the issue of a balance of economic growth and social stability in the process of economic transition.

## Research questions

Chinese economic reform can be divided into several distinct phases, with public-enterprise transformation constituting a crucial component of the process. Specifically, SOE reform started with the expansion of enterprise autonomy, progressed to the implementation of the CRS, subsequently became characterized by the operation of the MES, and recently has experimented with shareholding and notably the SCS. This evolutionary process is embodied in the shift from a planned to a market economy, from state to mixed ownership, and from social to economic objectives.

The Chinese economic reform process, therefore, raises a number of questions for researchers of business, management and economics. Our research addresses two in particular. The first is, 'how do ownership, competition and management influence the process of public enterprise transformation?'. In the process of SOE reform, an array of measures has been employed in the struggle to achieve the goals and objectives of reform. Debates centre on the differing priorities of ownership change, the introduction of competition, and management reform. Our research investigates the relationships between such mechanisms and their application in the reform process. It analyses the behaviour and performance of SOEs over a period when they are heavily affected by each of the three mechanisms. As a consequence, our study bears a proposition – neither competition, ownership nor management mechanisms alone are able to achieve the smooth transformation of a public enterprise for the purpose of improved performance and efficiency. In other words, the transition of public enterprises is more likely to be achieved through an integrated approach that involves ownership change, the introduction of competition and management improvement.

The second question is, 'what is the nature of the interaction between labour and the public enterprise during the transformation process?'. When the transformation of public enterprises is evaluated from the perspective of labour issues, the impact of economic reform on employees is a factor that needs to be addressed (Kikeri 1998; Cook and Kirkpatrick 2000; Sheehan *et al.* 2003). This is particularly so in the case of public enterprises, which have traditionally played such an important role in the provision of employee welfare and urban employment, and have contributed so greatly to social stability (Kolodko 1999; Hassard *et al.* 2005). During the reform era, Chinese public enterprises have acted as cushions to absorb much of the social and political impacts of economic transition. Prior to reform, Chinese public enterprises were responsible for employees' housing, medical care, children's education, pensions etc. In the process of reform, however, enterprises have divested themselves to a large extent of the burden of such cradle-to-grave welfare provision. In many sectors industrial workforces have been affected significantly by radical job reduction programmes. The tradition of job security that characterized work within the SOE has been sundered as, instead, millions of 'surplus' workers have been laid-off from public enterprises. Our book thus examines how public-enterprise transformation has impacted upon both enterprise managers and employees, and how the benefits and costs of economic transition can be balanced in order to achieve sustainable economic growth as well as social stability. Closely associated with our second research question, therefore, is an understanding of the relationship between public-enterprise transformation and the labour issue. More specifically, public-enterprise transformation may yield a range of unfavourable impacts on employees and employment in a society where a robust social security net is still lacking. In turn, the labour issue may affect public-enterprise transformation. This can be tested through investigation of changes in employment, wages and employee welfare, as well as the implementation of transition measures related to labour.

## Structure of the book

Our arguments are presented in a series of nine substantive chapters. In general the early chapters of the book (Part I, Chapters 1–4) are dedicated to issues of 'economic transition in theory and practice', those of the middle (Part II, Chapters 5–7) to 'reform programmes, surplus workers and labour unrest', and those toward the end (Part III, Chapters 8 and 9) to 'contemporary studies of enterprise restructuring'. The chapters in the first two-thirds of the book are devoted to the main decades of economic reform experimentation in China, the 1980s and 1990s, and those toward the end to events from 2000 to the time of writing in December 2005. Whereas the various chapters of the book combine to form a contemporary history of Chinese economic reform and enterprise restructuring, each is written as a dedicated statement on a particular theme, issue or case. In developing this approach we apologise for any overlap in content arising from the need to provide adequate context to the topics addressed in individual chapters. The nine substantive chapters can be summarized as follows:

In Chapter 1 ('Theorizing state-enterprise reform') we describe how public enterprises were widely established in industrial countries between the 1930s and 1950s and rapidly expanded among the developing countries in the 1960s and 1970s. They were built with state ownership for reasons of social and economic justice with the rationale that such SOEs could avoid problems resulting from market failure. However, from the late 1970s, and especially throughout the 1980s and 1990s, SOEs experienced widespread privatization and denationalization. Public-enterprise reform and privatization became seen as key policy instruments in the improvement of economic performance. In particular, privatization was seen as a key means to promote market forces and shift the balance between public and private sectors in the economy. We discuss the various reasons for the rise and fall of the public enterprises and describe how the globally phenomenal shift from state to private ownership was accompanied by a burgeoning literature debating whether competition or ownership change mattered more for improving economic efficiency. The combined force of the government failure, principal-agent, property rights and public choice theories concluded that enterprises operating under public ownership were less efficient compared to their private sector counterparts. By contrast, strong arguments against this ownership-solution viewpoint emerged from the competition-solution perspective, especially in addressing economic transition in developing countries. This view argued that the competitive environment is more important than ownership per se, and that ownership change was favoured only within a competitive market; i.e. where there is a lack of competitive product and capital markets, ownership change alone has very limited success. Increasingly, however, a third voice on transition suggested the need to reform the management of public enterprises, from both the macro-state and micro-enterprise levels, so as again to improve economic efficiency. Within the chapter we consider these three arguments and in so doing attempt to establish a framework for the analysis of economic reform in Chinese public enterprises.

In Chapter 2 ('Perspectives on China's reform path') we describe how the literature on transitional economies, such as those of Eastern and Central Europe and Asia, has polarized around two main policies – radical privatization and gradual reform. The former is concerned primarily with the change of ownership from public to private hands: the latter the introduction of competition and the improvement of management (including regulatory and institutional reform). We suggest that in this literature differences can be discerned between the Messianic tone of earlier writing on economic transformation (e.g. Kornai 1990; Sachs and Woo 1994) and the increasingly reflective or measured voice of later theory and evidence (e.g. Kolodko 1999; Carlin *et al.* 2001; Sachs *et al.* 2000a and b; Estrin 2002). We also note some striking differences in the policies and practices described in works that examine, on the one hand, the processes of transformation in Eastern and Central European (ECE) countries (notably Russia) (see Nolan 1995a; Bevan *et al.* 2001) and on the other, those of China (see Naughton 1994, 1995b; Rawski 1994; Walder 1996; Tsui and Lau 2002; Hassard *et al.* 2005). This chapter examines such theories, perspectives and evidence, but mainly in relation to debates on China's reform path and whether it is to be characterized as radical or gradual.

Chapter 3 ('Economic transformation: context and content') describes how from the establishment of New China in 1949 to the economic reform programme initiated in 1978, the nation was characterized as a socialist planned economy following the framework of the FSU. As a result: economic management and control was carried out by means of administrative commands passed down from the central bureaucracy to individual enterprises; resource allocation was determined by national plans, because state ownership was favoured at the expense of other forms of ownership; decision-making power was highly concentrated in state administrative departments and motivation often relied on politically driven, non-material or moral encouragement; distribution was characterized by egalitarianism and government administration was directly involved in the management and operation of enterprises; and enterprises were granted money by the government and fulfilled various assigned tasks – they were not responsible for profits or losses, for there was almost no market or private sector to speak of within a largely inefficient economy. We describe how by the time of Mao Zedong's death in September 1976, China's total factor productivity was extremely low, and that when Deng Xiaoping came to power subsequently the primary task was to grow the economy. Under such circumstances economic reform was initiated in late 1978 to stimulate the economy and improve efficiency. The strategic approach to reform was gradual, evolutionary and incremental. The chapter analyses this generic context and content of Chinese economic and enterprise reform prior to presenting empirical studies of state-enterprise transformation in later chapters.

In Chapter 4 ('Reforming China's state enterprises') we argue that although the share of the state sector in China's national economy continues to decline, it remains significant in terms of the nation's general economy. SOEs continue to provide much needed revenue to government and contribute significantly to urban employment. The reform of large SOEs, therefore, remains at the heart of China's economic reform programme. Widely regarded as the most difficult area of reform, we describe how it has been characterized by a complicated and uneven experimental process. Initially seeing an enterprise responsibility system adopted through implementation of a contracting system in the 1980s, subsequent experimentation has focused on 'corporatization' and the establishment of a 'modern enterprise' system. In the process of such transformation, SOEs have been confronted with difficulties arising from deteriorating profitability and increasing debts, which demand further reform of ownership and governance. Reforms in the 1990s turned on the establishment of corporatization and its aim to overcome the problems of the factory system. The government took steps to convert the great majority of large- and medium-sized SOEs into corporations that were expected to adapt to market conditions, with clarified property rights and strong internal management. In recent years, the SCS has been viewed as an effective way to deepen the current reform of SOEs, with the system spreading rapidly in small- and medium-sized state enterprises. We note, however, that problems have emerged in the process of corporatizing the SOEs, with one of the most enduring being the very definition of state-owned property. The current reform of SOEs aims to clarify property rights as well as resolve problems relating to the optimization of enterprise governance structures and the professional management of human resources. Although competition has been continually fostered since the beginning of the reform period – for example, through the encouragement of township and village enterprises (TVEs) and the introduction of international competition – this essentially relates to competition from outside the state sector rather than within. It can be argued that SOEs still need to be exposed more readily to market-based competition. We argue finally that the reform process has generated far-reaching impacts on labour, notably in terms of employment and welfare. On the one hand, millions of workers have been laid-off from SOEs since the mid-1990s as the state sector shrinks under the reform process. On the other, there remains the lack of a robust social safety net for unemployed workers. Under these circumstances, state enterprises will continue to play a role in employee welfare provision.

Chapter 5 ('Rise and fall of the Contract Responsibility System') represents the first of a series of chapters in which we move from theories of transition to empirical studies of reform. Initially we examine the reasons for the rise and fall of one of China's major enterprise reform programmes – the CRS – which governed relations between the enterprise and the state in China from the early 1980s until 1994–1995. We focus mainly on Beijing's Capital Iron and Steel Corporation (usually known by its shortened Chinese title of Shougang), since this was the flagship of the CRS experiment and exemplifies some of the problems that were ultimately perceived by the state to outweigh the benefits of the system. The chapter describes how the CRS operated at two main levels: enterprise-level contracting with the state (the state contract system) and internal contracting within the enterprise's businesses (the internal contract system). We outline how the CRS was introduced in the steel industry during the course of the 6th Five-Year Plan, 1980–1985, and was eventually adopted by 85 per cent of enterprises within the industry. It was modified several times during its existence in the light of enterprises' experiences in applying it. The main variations were a mid-1980s shift from profit remittance to taxation of profits (which proved unpopular with enterprises since it generally required them to turn over more money to the state and retain less for investment and development) and the subsequent return to the system of contracted profit remittance. The CRS was initially perceived as a great success at Shougang, with transnational and transbusiness diversification contributing to very high annual growth in profits of about 20 per cent during the period of the reform. Like other enterprises, Shougang was seen to have benefited from increased autonomy in investment and management. However, a number of problems were identified while the CRS was in force – problems that were regarded as sufficiently serious to warrant the gradual phasing-out of the system and the development of new reform models to tackle the deep problems of enterprise reform. Our discussion of these problems refers to the generality of Chinese steel makers that operated the CRS during the 1980s and early 1990s, as well as to the specific case of the Shougang Corporation.

In Chapter 6 ('Modern enterprises, group companies and surplus labour') we examine the progress made in those state-enterprise reforms developed in the early–mid-1990s under the rubric of the MES and GCS experiments. We describe the evolution of the MES/GCS programmes, provide case analysis of MES/GCS restructuring, and consider the main problem to emerge from the process – high levels of surplus labour. In so doing, we explore how economic, political and social forces serve both to compel and constrain organizational action, employing a case-study method to examine particular dynamics and outcomes. In the wake of our previous discussion of the CRS, we analyse the continuing confusion during the 1990s as to what the enterprise reform process in China entailed, beyond the emblematic 'capitalism with Chinese characteristics'. We argue that such confusion remained at two levels: at the theoretical were issues of how to conceptualize organizational transformation in the move from a planned to market economy, and we note from our earlier discussions how several schools of thought have attempted to grapple with this question. At the level of practice, the reform process appeared to be anarchic or chaotic, with a plethora of different measures and systems operating even within the same segment of the economy, and certainly between segments. We reinforce our argument by suggesting that the concept of a singular reform process has obscured the differences across and between enterprises. In attempting to make sense of the experience of MES/GCS reforms we produce a qualitative, multi-source case analysis of processes and practices, primarily in respect of a small sample of steel corporations. In so doing we have been influenced by the 'choice within constraints' theory of the 'new' institutionalism. Our use of institutional theory emphasizes the influences of systems in the corporate environment that serve to shape economic, social and organizational behaviour. In developing our analysis, however, we do not wish to offer unqualified support for a variant of institutionalism that would emphasize consistency and uniformity in the reform process. Instead, given the often chaotic nature of state-enterprise reform, we suggest an overtly political approach that reflects how, in everyday practice, the management of China's SOEs is both influenced by, and in turn influences, the network of relations established between the enterprise, the community, local government and the state.

Chapter 7 ('State capitalism, labour unrest and worker representation') examines how workers in China's SOEs have responded to the changing nature of those enterprises during the reform period. In particular it analyses the causes of the rising incidence of labour unrest among SOE employees since the second half of the 1990s, as drastic restructuring of the state sector took place and unemployment reached its highest levels in China for decades. We discuss how protests over lay-offs, bankruptcies, and unpaid pensions and wages reached the stage where parts of the reform programme were threatened with delay as local and national governments sought to contain workers' resentment. Yet, as is argued, sometimes these efforts to mollify workers succeed only in further stoking their anger at what they perceive as patronizing and token concessions that do not address their most important concerns. SOE workers have conventionally been viewed as a very privileged group within Chinese society, an elite section of the workforce amply compensated for its still relatively low wage levels by the benefits of the 'iron rice-bowl' system of lifelong job security and enterprise provision of social welfare. Lack of labour mobility and dependency on the enterprise for such things as subsidized housing, medical care, children's schooling etc., in turn, have been identified as major factors in SOE workers' relative political docility and loyalty to the ruling Chinese Communist Party. The general view that the Chinese industrial workforce has been notable for its passivity and the ease with which it could be controlled has, however, been challenged by other accounts that stress the relative frequency of unrest among Chinese workers and note the involvement of SOE workers in periodic protest movements which have questioned the legitimacy of the Party that claims to rule in their name. Even with reference to the pre-reform period, the depiction of SOE employees as a favoured elite unwilling to bite the hand that fed it was somewhat one-sided, and since 1978 the steady undermining of the 'iron rice-bowl' as reform has progressed has further reduced the effectiveness of what was never a completely reliable method of containing workers' grievances and assertions of collective interests. Moreover, outbreaks of worker unrest are not, we argue, simply the reaction of a previously privileged group to the loss of its exclusive benefits, for some SOE workers now explicitly reject the enterprise-based paternalism of the past. Rather than campaign for its reinstatement, they are, instead, organizing independently to press demands for the legal rights which they feel are due to them now that they have found themselves in an insecure, quasi-capitalist employment relationship in their enterprise. These rights include the right to adequate welfare and pensions and the right to organize their own trade unions.

Chapters 8 and 9 present detailed contemporary case studies of reform in two major Chinese steel enterprises – Wuhan Iron and Steel (Wugang), and Tangshan Iron and Steel (Tanggang). In Chapter 8 ('Restructuring Wuhan Iron and Steel') we suggest that, overall, Wugang seems to have benefited from the reform process in general and the MES in particular. Steel production facilities have been upgraded to among the best in China and crude steel production increased by 76 per cent from 1992 to 2003. Profitability in the last few years has been above the world average and the separation of non-steel business and social units is well under way. As such Wugang appears to be a model for what the state wants large state enterprises to do and how they should do it. We argue, however, that there remain worries regarding the way surplus labour is to be handled and the prospect of resistance resulting from those potentially to be laid-off and who consider their benefits to be infringed. Thus far Wugang seems to have met with only minor resistance from its workers despite the significant changes made in the restructuring process. We describe how from a reading of Wugang's annual reports one gets the impression that the company has successfully transferred surplus workers out of its steel business, thereby making its steel units look lean. However, most surplus labour has, in fact, been transferred to the non-steel business and remains within the group. It can be argued that the improvement in Wugang's steel business was obtained at the expense of its non-steel business, and that the overstaffing problem remains widespread in the non-steel units. The question remains of how long Wugang can sustain such shuffling around of its surplus labour, and, potentially linked to that, of how long the company can avoid significant and overt industrial unrest. If Wugang fails to resolve its redundancy problem satisfactorily in the years to come, this will most likely intensify resistance from workers. Reform at Wugang was constrained by its paternalistic responsibility inherited from the old planned economy together with political concerns over maintaining stability during the transition. As a result, settlement of redundant workers was, and continues to be, a key issue of Wugang's reform efforts, especially in the current phase aimed at separating-off the non-core business units and social service units.

In our final substantive chapter, Chapter 9 ('Restructuring Tangshan Iron and Steel'), we suggest that in terms of restructuring, Tanggang, did not progress as fast as Wugang. We describe how, by the end of 2003, its main accomplishments in restructuring were limited to incorporating a subsidiary, Tangshan Iron and Steel Company Ltd (TISCO) and listing it on a domestic stock exchange. With regard to separating-off its social service units, Tanggang has thus far failed to make substantial progress. We offer two reasons for this relatively slow pace of reform. First, in being provincially rather than centrally administered, the enterprise was not on the nation's top priority list. And second, Hebei's former mayor had been too politically conservative to fight for priority in reforming the province's steel industry. Tanggang did not apply drastic measures to lay off employees, even though it had a much worse redundancy problem than Wugang. Further, its proximity to Beijing reinforced the general stability concern of political and enterprise leaders, while allowing surplus workers to remain in the enterprise impaired Tanggang's productive efficiency and profitability. We note, however, that recently Tanggang appears to have been pressured into speeding-up its reform. This appears linked to the fact that the state has provisionally decided to move Shougang to Tangshan by 2010. As part of the preparation for the 2008

Beijing Olympics, environmentally unfriendly plants such as Shougang are being relocated – hence the merger between Shougang and Tanggang. The state plans to make Shougang and Tanggang the largest steel maker in the north, similar to Baosteel's position in the east. This merger development will likely put Tanggang back on the state's priority list, notably as Tanggang's reform progress will be a key issue in discussions of the enterprise's future cooperation with Shougang. The Hebei provincial government also continues to intervene in matters concerning the provision of low-cost loans for Tanggang as well as the enterprise's operational decisions. As such, it appears that Tanggang will continue to grow in a direction consistent with the state's industrial policy as long its 'state-owned' problems continue to attach to it, which may be for some considerable time.

# Part I

# Economic transition in theory and practice

# 1 Theorizing state-enterprise reform

## Introduction

SOEs were widely established in industrial countries between the 1930s and 1950s and rapidly expanded among developing nations in the 1960s and 1970s. They were built with state ownership for reasons of social and economic justice. The rationale was that SOEs could avoid problems resulting from market failure. However, from the late 1970s and especially throughout the 1980s and 1990s, SOEs worldwide experienced widespread denationalization and privatization, perhaps the most dramatic case being that of the United Kingdom under the Thatcher government.

This global phenomenon of the privatization of SOEs is defined, according to Cook and Kirkpatrick (1997: 2) as 'the transfer of productive assets from public to private ownership'. Faced with the challenges of government failure, SOE reform and privatization have been seen as key policy instruments in the improvement of economic efficiency (Cook and Kirkpatrick 1988, 2000; World Bank 1995, 1996; Yarrow and Jasinski 1996; Cook *et al.* 1998; Frydman *et al.* 1999; Shirley and Walsh 2000; Brown and Earle 2001; Estrin *et al.* 2001; Nolan 2003; Bhaumik and Estrin 2005). In particular, privatization is perceived as a means to promote market forces and shift the balance between the public and private sectors of the economy.

There are various reasons for the rise and fall of the SOEs. The global phenomenon of a shift from state to private ownership of public enterprises has been accompanied by a literature that carries with it a debate over whether it is competition or ownership change (from public to private) that matters most in the improvement of economic efficiency. The combined force of literature debating principal-agent, property rights and public choice theories concludes that enterprises operating under public ownership arc less efficient when compared with their private sector counterparts (Galal *et al.* 1994; World Bank 1995; Shirley and Walsh 2000).

In contrast, strong arguments against this ownership-solution viewpoint emerge from the writings of those advocating the competition-solution view, especially in relation to state-enterprise transition in developing countries. The competition-solution view argues that a competitive environment is more important than ownership per se and that a change in ownership is favoured only within a competitive market. In other words, where there is a lack of competitive product and capital markets, ownership change (privatization) alone has very limited success (see Yarrow 1986, 1999; Vickers and Yarrow 1988; Cook and Kirkpatrick 1988, 1997, 2000; Cook 1997; Carlin *et al.* 2001; Nolan 2003).

A third voice on SOE transformation has suggested that the foremost need is to reform the management practices related to public enterprises at both the state and enterprise levels. Among those who have argued for improved management rather than ownership change are Stiglitz (1993), Davey (1995), Korten (1995), Nolan (1995) and Farazmand (1999, 2001, 2004). This position was supported earlier by the World Bank, before the bank shifted, from the late 1980s, towards advocating ownership change (Cook 1997). (For example, the World Development Report for 1983 stated that 'the key factor determining the efficiency of an enterprise is not whether it is publicly or privately owned, but how it is managed' (World Bank 1983: 50).)

This chapter examines research evidence related to the arguments introduced above. First, in order to establish a basic framework for understanding the nature of SOE operations and sources of SOE problems, we analyse the main reasons and objectives for the establishment of public enterprises. Second, we examine debates concerning the mechanisms for improving public-enterprise performance, with this analysis focusing on our three main issues of ownership, competition and management reform. And third, we examine the literature on the labour effects associated with SOE transformation.

## Reasons for establishing SOEs

A considerable body of literature has suggested that the establishment of the SOE was essentially a remedy for market failure. Various forms of market failure prevented the economy from achieving efficient resource allocation. Economic analysis rationalized government intervention in productive activities as a response to such specific market imperfections. The establishment of public enterprises could provide a way for direct government participation (Yarrow and Jasinski 1996; Cook and Kirkpatrick 2000). These justifications were coupled with arguments that public enterprises facilitated economic independence and planned development. Where there is market failure, and the unregulated pursuit of profit does not lead to the maximization of economic efficiency, public enterprise can be established to correct the misalignment of public and private objectives.

Other reasons for the establishment of SOEs were explored by Cook and Kirkpatrick (1988, 2000) and Van De Walle (1989). First, it was considered that SOEs in general would provide government access to much-needed sources of revenue. 'Governments mistakenly believed that [SOEs] would generate large profits with which they would be able to finance investment in priority sectors of the economy' (Van De Walle 1989: 602). Second, there were ideological and political reasons. For example, public production could be made to appear more attractive in an ideological climate in which the private sector was held in low esteem and a large public role in the economy was seen as necessary for rapid and sustained development. It could also secure for the government valuable industrial information and the control of strategic industries. As such, public enterprise could be justified both for reasons of employment creation and national security. And third, SOEs could be used as a counterweight to the concentration of private economic power or as a remedy for short supply/risk aversion on the part of private entrepreneurs, or to strengthen the economic position of particular ethnic groups or geographical regions, or to overcome critical economic bottlenecks. Cook and Kirkpatrick (2000) state that public enterprises are often established by governments for reasons quite different from, and often incompatible with, profit-maximization. Public enterprises often operate in non-competitive markets; the absence of competition is one reason for creating them.

The mainstream public ownership literature discusses issues such as those outlined above, and especially the remedying of market failure, the redistribution of economic resources, and the political benefits to industrial concerns (see Yarrow and Jasinski 1996; Cook and Kirkpatrick 2000). Yarrow and Jasinski (1996) summarized the various objectives of public ownership as follows:

1 *Remedying market failures/inefficiencies.* Public ownership can provide one possible means for dealing with the perceived inefficiencies of certain types of market.
2 *Redistributing economic resources.* As with market failure, there may be a number of ways to achieve the desired redistribution of resources, for example by various combinations of taxes and subsidies. Such redistribution considerations often strongly influence the introduction of an enterprise or industry into the public sector. For instance, a public utility absorbs subsidies for one group of consumers from the profits made by another group of consumers.
3 *Creating political benefits.* The political benefits include prestige projects that can often be favoured by politicians in accordance with political needs and preferences. A public enterprise can receive patronage from politicians.
4 *Achieving strategic goals.* More often than not, for reasons of military or national security, or as a necessary counterweight to foreign ownership, governments have designated certain sectors of the economy to be of 'strategic' importance for economic development. Public ownership is one way of channelling resources to such strategic sectors.

## SOE problems

It is commonly argued that as a result of central planning, public enterprises regularly failed to meet strategic targets for efficiency and performance. Major reasons cited were that social welfare burdens and government intervention adversely affected the SOEs' ability to optimize economic effectiveness. As such, the divestiture of the government/state ownership of public enterprises has been the pervasive economic paradigm for nearly three decades. Subsequently, privatization has been implemented across the globe, which involves the extension of market principles to goods and services financed and/or produced by governments.

As a result, the phenomenon of public-enterprise transition (mainly through privatization) has been the principal theme of a considerable body of social and economic literature. A number of studies have claimed that public enterprises as a whole are less efficient than private firms and thus frequently cause resource misallocation (Alchian 1965; Killick 1983; Boardman and Vining 1989; World Bank 1995; Shirley and Walsh 2000). Shirley (1983) and Kikeri *et al.* (1994) summarized the common problems of public enterprises as follows: unclear, multiple or sometimes conflicting objectives (both social and economic); bureaucratic intrusion; over-centralization of decision-making; inadequate capitalization; lack of managerial skills; and excessive personnel costs.

The World Bank (1995) suggested that public enterprises had the following inherent problems of information and incentives: (i) *information asymmetry*, due to managers' information advantages. Under this condition, managers were able to use their knowledge of the enterprise to negotiate with government – the owner of the enterprise – for targets which frequently favoured themselves. (ii) *Inefficient incentives and impaired profit-orientation*, due to controlled prices and political intervention. Compared with private firms, penalties and rewards in/for SOEs were not employed properly, which resulted in resource waste and poor performance. (iii) *Deficits and loss-making*, notably the burden on government arising from loss-making SOEs absorbing too many state subsidies and thus contributing to the undermining of macroeconomic stability.

In the face of the problems associated with public ownership, a general perception that government strategic development planning had 'failed' emerged in many economies. Growing concern with the apparent inefficiency of state enterprises led to a variety of policy attempts to improve SOE performance and thus economic efficiency. Among them privatization has been an instrument widely implemented in developed, developing and transitional economies. In the 1980s and 1990s, reform of SOEs generally incorporated a policy priority for a dramatic shift from public ownership to private ownership and thus toward diminishing the government's role in economic strategy (Kikeri *et al.* 1994; World Bank 1997a; Cook *et al.* 1998; Overseas Economic Cooperation Fund (OECF) 1998; Cook and Kirkpatrick

2000; Shirley and Walsh 2000). Divestiture or privatization as a means to shrink the public sector featured prominently in these attempts, while other solutions embraced the introduction of competition and management reform.

The arguments reflected in the public-enterprise reform debate can therefore be classified into three groups: Group one emphasizes ownership change as a means to address the SOEs' problems, with policy priority being given to privatization (the 'ownership-solution' group). Group two stresses the importance of the competitive market in tackling SOE problems, with policy priority being given to promoting competition to foster a competitive market (the 'competition-solution' group). And Group three advocates the reform of management within the system, with policy priority being given to improving SOE management at both macro-state level and micro-enterprise level, in terms of developing institutions and internal firm management (the 'management-solution' group). The following sections examine the public ownership debate in relation to these three groups of literature.

## Ownership-solution literature

The ownership-solution literature advocates privatization – a shift of the majority of ownership from public to private hands (Nellis 1999) – as a measure to improve economic efficiency. It argues that ownership (property rights) is crucially important, given the assumption that the state will use public enterprises for political purposes rather than profit-maximization, and that this will have an adverse effect on enterprise performance in any market structure (Shirley and Walsh 2000). After Alchian's (1965) early study of SOEs, the conclusion of which was that they are inherently less efficient than private firms, the extensive ownership-solution literature has argued that private ownership is invariably superior to public ownership. The key reason is that public ownership has innate problems of information processing and incentivization, which can only be solved by private ownership. Shirley (1999: 117) supports this view, suggesting that '[the] literature, through comparing the performance of enterprises before and after privatization or a privatized firm with a counterfactual, has generally favoured private ownership in both competitive and, although more ambiguously, regulated monopoly markets' (see also Galal *et al.* 1994; Megginson *et al.* 1994; Martin and Parker 1997). Furthermore, Shirley and Walsh (2000) maintain, from examining 52 empirical studies from the early 1970s, that results across sectors and countries show clear support for private ownership, although the theoretical arguments on private versus public ownership are less clear cut.

The theoretical grounds of ownership change are rooted in theories of government behaviour and corporate governance, including public choice, property rights and principal-agent theories (Cook 1997; Shirley 1999). Public choice theory advocates that deductive models of how government agencies behave are developed with clear directions for policy analysis and normative recommendations (Dunleavy 1986). It is suggested that public managers, bureaucrats and politicians alike will use their control of SOEs to serve their own interests, rather than to enhance the state firm's efficiency (Shirley 1999). In the public sector, interests of income, power and prestige can be enhanced by increases in managers' budgets, whereas in the private sector, increased profits are the source of such rewards. It is assumed that under public ownership managers will constantly petition for ever-growing budgets and transfers. If SOEs are constantly requesting higher budgets (as the SOE interest groups are often budget-maximizers), while politicians can allocate funds to a variety of purposes besides transfers to SOEs, it is anticipated that SOE managers will have something to offer the politicians in return. Thus bribery (signally of politicians) and other forms of corruption are felt likely to take place within public ownership, often at the expense of efficiency. As Cook notes, 'this body of theory attributes poor performance of publicly-owned agencies to a divergence of "interests" between bureaucrats and politicians that run government and the public interest in general' (1997: 890). Similarly, Shleifer and Vishny (1994) suggest that SOE efficiencies can be reduced by political meddling resulting from public ownership.

Property rights theory argues that individuals respond to incentives and that the pattern of incentives is influenced by the property rights structure. The theory suggests that when a company has little or no right to be a residual claimant – that is, no individual or group has a clearly specified right to claim any residual benefits or surplus left after other claims are met – it will operate with low levels of efficiency (Demsetz and Lehn 1985; Grossman and Hart 1986). It is assumed that business people in private firms are profit-maximizers, with private property rights being exclusive and voluntarily transferable. In SOEs however it is virtually impossible to transfer state ownership rights from one individual or group to another. This inability to transfer ownership rights is viewed by privatization advocates to result in economic systems that are inherently less efficient than those based on private property. It is claimed that the owners of a private firm have more powerful incentives to monitor management behaviour (and thus to ensure enterprise efficiency) than the owners of state enterprises. The rule is: the greater the personal financial investment, the greater the interest in the operation of the firm. As in an SOE the manager has no wealth invested in the firm and no rights to share profits, he or she is therefore less motivated to pursue efficiency. As Shirley (1999: 116) argues 'since no one can clearly benefit from an SOE's efficient operation, no one will be strongly motivated to hold management accountable for performance'. According to this theory, private ownership with clarified property rights represents a solution to SOE problems of efficiency and effectiveness.

A third theoretical argument for ownership change comes from principal-agent theory, which again concerns the issue that the aim of decision-makers in privately owned firms should be the maximization of profit. In this theory, there exists a principal (e.g. the owner) and an agent (e.g. the manager) of a firm, with the central 'agency problem' being that the agent may not share the same objectives as the principal. The principal wants to induce the agent to act in the principal's interests, but the principal's control over the agent is always somewhat imperfect due to the lack of full information about the circumstances and behaviour of the agent, as well as the differences of interest between the principal and agent. Therefore, the principal faces monitoring problems and associated costs (Alchian and Demsetz 1972; Vickers and Yarrow 1988). According to this theory, the central issue for the principal is to lay down the optimal incentive scheme for the agent in order to solve the principal-agent dilemma and thus ensure the efficient operation of the firm. Principal-agent theory was thus

> originally developed for the private sector to explain the divergence often found between the goals of managers (agents) in private firms and shareholders/owners (principals) . . . [W]hen the functions of ownership and control/operation in a firm are separated, very often there are conflicts between the interests of the owner and the manager in relation to information asymmetry and ill-matched incentives and control.
>
> (Cook 1997: 890)

In sum, as managers have every incentive to exercise control in pursuit of their own objectives rather than profitability, agency problems may arise in which the owner's interests are impaired (Fama and Jensen 1983; Hart 1983). Principal-agent theory is therefore concerned precisely with problems of information and incentives (Vickers and Yarrow 1988).

To elaborate, the relationships between owners and managers of business firms are thus prime examples of principal-agent relationships. The manager (agent) is contracted to act on behalf of (private or public) shareholders (principals) in order to maximize the latters' interests. Therefore, a 'perfect' contract is needed to structure the manager's incentives to correspond exactly to the interests of the shareholders. However, in everyday reality it is impossible to draw a perfectly complete contract to meet this standard. Under public ownership the problems of information asymmetry in agency relation-ships make it even harder for the principal to hold the agent accountable for achieving the agreed targets (Laffont and Tirole 1986; Sappington 1991). Under state ownership, the populace as a whole is the principal, with a variety of agents acting on its behalf, including government ministers, members of parliament, managers of firms etc. All these agents are, in fact, a coalition – a group who work together and share some, but not all, goals. Also, the populace does not have an effective voice on issues of discretion and control. In such circumstances, the ownership-solution literature claims that private enterprises have fewer agency problems than public enterprises and, in particular, that it is less costly to monitor agents in private than public enterprises. In other words, private ownership is invariably economically superior to public ownership.

In the light of the above, the major policy implication is to strengthen monitoring by owners. Ownership change through privatization is thus viewed as the primary solution to SOE inefficiencies, for it is anticipated that in making government intervention more difficult enterprises will be freer to focus on profit-maximization (Shleifer and Vishny 1994; World Bank 1995; Boycko *et al.* 1996; Shirley 1999; Shirley and Walsh 2000). Shleifer and Vishny (1994) argue that, even in fully competitive markets, SOEs remain relatively inefficient because politicians encourage or even force them to pursue political as well as economic goals. Distortionary political interventions, such as encouraging over-employment, adversely affect the operational and administrative efficiency of SOEs. Under private ownership, such interventions are more costly and transparent, and therefore it is more difficult to influence private firms in this regard. Thus the ownership-solution group regards ownership as the key source of efficiency and argues that ownership matters more than competition for monitoring productive efficiency.

Empirical evidence is frequently used to demonstrate that private firms are more efficient than public firms and that ownership factors matter most. Boardman and Vining (1989, 1992) for example presented data showing that private firms are more efficient than SOEs even in the most competitive of industrial markets. Based on analysis of the 500 largest non-US industrial firms, they claim that state-owned and mixed-ownership firms are significantly less profitable and productive than privately owned companies, and that full privatization is needed because mixed-ownership firms are no more profitable than those wholly owned by the state. Boardman and Vining challenge the competition-solution notion that ownership does not affect efficiency in the case where markets are fully competitive, for they demonstrate empirically that private performance is superior in such markets. They believe that ownership has a greater impact, and that competitive markets are rooted in private property. Boardman and Vining argue that it is impossible to simulate competitive conditions under conditions of government financing or government production.

Elsewhere, Kikeri *et al.* (1994) provided empirical evidence that SOEs actually hamper market performance as they are more likely than private firms to set prices below marginal cost and to seek regulatory barriers to entry by exercising political influence. Similarly, Megginson *et al.* (1994) looked at firm performance before and after privatization and found that private ownership increased efficiency in all situations, although the effect is clearer in competitive markets. Nellis (1999) noted that politicians distort state-enterprise functions to meet political goals, while private firms produce advantages for management monitoring. And the World Bank (1995) supported these claims by documenting the political use and abuse of its sample SOEs and arguing that it is impossible to obtain the advantages of competitive markets in the context of government provision in the production of goods and services. As such they argue that in highly competitive markets private firms are inherently superior to public firms and thus that ownership does matter.

Analysing economic transition in 12 countries (including China) the World Bank (1995) also identified a number of 'components' for achieving public-enterprise reform. These included 'divestiture' (ownership transfer), 'competition creation' (involving liberalized trade), 'eased restrictions on entry, unbundled large enterprises, (and) hard budgeting' (by eliminating subsidies and more commercially based credit), 'financial sector reform' and 'changes in the relationship between SOEs and government'. The World Bank argued that 'the greater the participation of private agents in ownership and management, the better enterprise performance' (World Bank 1995: 6).

Similarly, Ros (1999) claimed that, although both ownership and market structure significantly affect efficiency, the ownership effect is slightly more robust across different measures of performance, while Nellis (1999: 24) noted that 'it is time to rethink privatization in transition economies, but it is not time to discard it. Privatization remains the generally preferred course of action where competitive markets are in place and the market-supporting institutions are functioning'. And on discussing a range of problems presented by privatization, Shirley and Walsh (2000) blamed flaws in the 'implementation process' rather than in the concept itself.

The ownership-solution group, therefore, criticizes the competition-solution advocates, stating that the concept of markets without property is a 'grand illusion' (Shirley and Walsh 2000). It is argued that under public ownership, government interference in SOEs overwhelms the effects of competition. In particular, inherent difficulties in the management of SOEs serve to negate the impact of competitive markets. Shirley and Walsh (2000) criticize studies which suggest that the performance of SOEs is to be improved under conditions of competition (e.g. Yarrow 1986) for failing to question whether such improved performance actually matches that of private (or privatized) firms, arguing that while market structure has a positive impact on performance, this impact fails to dominate the ownership effect.

## Competition-solution literature

In contrast, the competition-solution literature is based on theories arguing that market competition, not property rights, is the primary determinant of enterprise performance. This literature is rooted largely in public interest theories.

It is noted by some competition-solution writers that the *meaning* of competition needs to be comprehended adequately in order to understand its role in the improvement of efficiency. Cook (2001) points out that classical and neo-classical interpretations of competition differ significantly – neo-classical economics views competition as a state of affairs, a competitive equilibrium characterized by market structure, while classical economics relates competition to a process of business behaviour. Elsewhere, drawing on competition as a process, Schumpeterian theory puts the emphasis not so much on price competition, but the competition from new products, new technology, new sources of supply and new types of organization (see Cook 2001). And in behavioural and evolutionary approaches, competition is a process of change characterized by competitive order rather than a competitive equilibrium; it can lead to a variety of market structures that realize efficient outcomes.

The competition-solution group thus emphasizes that competition influences allocative, operational and internal efficiencies. Evidence suggests that these effects can be extended to public firms (Beato and Mas-Colell 1984; Cremer *et al.* 1987; Vickers and Yarrow 1988). As Vickers and Yarrow argue (1988: 27–28):

> public interest theories are based upon the assumption that, in their dealings with industry, government departments seek to maximize economic welfare . . . Given a welfare-maximizing government, and assuming for the moment that monitoring of management is equally effective under both types (public and private) of ownership, it is immediately obvious that public ownership has some potential advantages over the private alternative. In particular, it provides government with additional policy instruments to correct any deviations between social and private returns that arise from failures in goods and factor markets.
>
> (Vickers and Yarrow 1988: 28)

In this respect the influence of competition on operational efficiency again falls into the two categories of incentive effects and information effects. With regard to the former, competition in product markets creates incentive effects by threatening the managers of inefficient firms with diminished market share. As the World Bank (2002: 133) argues 'product market competition increases efficiency (and productivity, and the growth of productivity in the economy) by providing incentives for managers to reduce costs, innovate, reduce slack, and improve the institutional arrangements in production'. With respect to information effects, competition can provide owners with information about firm costs and management effort. Armed with this information, owners can evaluate management effort more accurately and design incentive systems more appropriately and effectively (Holmstrom 1982). Vickers and Yarrow (1988) cite the information effect of competition as an important influence on public-sector performance – in the presence of competition, prices will tend towards marginal cost and resources can be allocated to their highest value.

In relation to policy making for the improvement of enterprise performance and economic efficiency, the competition-solution group naturally gives priority to the creation of competitive markets rather than forms of ownership change. Yarrow (1986: 332) argues that 'it cannot be expected that one form of ownership will be superior to the other in all industries and in all countries. The competitive and regulatory environment is more important than the question of ownership *per se.*' Similarly, Kay and Thompson (1986) argue that although private ownership has an edge in fully competitive markets, focusing on ownership at the expense of competition yields sub-optimal results. Cook and Kirkpatrick (2000) extend the point about the need to create a competitive environment by stressing that such an environment must be based on mechanisms that ensure due levels of managerial autonomy and financial accountability.

Vickers and Yarrow (1988: 44) suggest that, in competitive markets, public ownership is not always the less efficient type of ownership, and that 'managerial incentive structures are determined via a complex set of interactions among factors that include the type of ownership, the degree of product market competition, and the effectiveness of regulation'. Vickers and Yarrow (1988) further argue that in the absence of vigorous product market competition, the relative advantage of incentive or monitoring efficiency under private or public ownership is less clear cut and that much will depend upon the effectiveness of regulation. Based on a comprehensive evaluation of British privatization between 1979 and 1987 – a period of approximately the first two Thatcher governments – Vickers and Yarrow conclude that 'the allocation of property rights does matter because it determines the objectives of the "owners" of the firm (public and private) and the systems of monitoring managerial performance' (1988: 3). Yet, they argue 'the degree of product market competition and the effectiveness of regulatory policy typically have rather larger effects on performance than ownership *per se*' (1988: 3). They also claim that 'public ownership and competition are perfectly compatible with each other' (Vickers and Yarrow 1988: 51).

Additionally, Jones *et al.* (1991) developed a theoretical model embracing a number of the determinants of the level and distribution of gains from public-enterprise reform. They argue that increased competition in the economy, widespread social insurance, fiscal stringency and financial market development can all increase the reform gains. Cook and Kirkpatrick's (1988) research on privatization in less developed countries echoes that gains in efficiency performance are more likely to result from an increase in market competition than from a change in ownership. They note further (Cook and Kirkpatrick 1997) that privatization is a policy instrument that can be used in developing countries to bring about improved economic efficiency, but it needs to be used in a selective and pragmatic manner alongside political capability and government commitment, not as an ideological crusade. The market environment and policy framework must also be liberalized if enterprise performance is to be significantly improved. Commander *et al.* (1999) echo that changes in ownership without adequate attention to market structure can result in longer-term negative effects, and that for successful restructuring to occur requires the imposition of hard budget constraints and increased competition. The World Bank (2002: 30) notes similarly that 'competition is an important force in promoting institutional change as well as economic development and growth'.

In terms of empirical evidence, Willig (1985) shows that competition can reveal information about managerial effort by increasing the level of sensitivity in relation to ratios of profits to costs. It is assumed that armed with better economic information, owners can devise incentive structures that align managers' interests more closely with their own. As to whether the effects of competition are stronger or weaker than the effects of ownership, Vickers and Yarrow (1988) cite the information effect of competition as an important influence on public-sector performance. This is supported by the findings in Cook and Kirkpatrick (1988) which suggest that competition-led instruments, such as market liberalization and deregulation, rather than privatization, are likely to yield more substantial gains in the context of developing countries. Shirley and Walsh (2000) cite two empirical studies (i.e. Peltzman 1971; Jones 1985) which suggest, in the absence of competition, SOEs will produce allocatively inefficient results. Earlier, Caves and Christensen (1980) found, in a comparison of public and private Canadian railroads, that, in the presence of competition, there is no significant difference between public and private efficiency. They conclude that 'public ownership is not inherently less efficient than private ownership – the inefficiency of government enterprises stems from their isolation from effective competition rather than their public ownership *per se*' (1980: 278).

Yarrow (1986) in particular acknowledges that competitive and regulatory environments shape the incentives of managers. His survey of pre- and post-privatization firm performance in Britain suggests that performance depended more on market structure than on ownership. Yarrow (1999) subsequently came to the conclusion that reforms emphasizing ownership over market structure are misguided. Cook and Kirkpatrick's (1988) study of developing countries suggests that improvements in economic performance are more likely to result from an increase in market competition than a change from public to private ownership in situations where institutions and regulation are relatively weak. Furthermore, ownership change, particularly through privatization, which is often undertaken for reasons of raising revenue by heavily debt-burdened governments, is not necessarily linked to the notion of promoting efficiency or competition. Thus, market competition (especially product market competition) is necessary for privatization to be fully realized. Cook and Kirkpatrick (1995) demonstrate that privatization of enterprises in non-competitive market environments, often in the circumstances of developing countries, will do little to improve economic performance.

Pendleton's study of the British bus industry also suggests that 'competition may be necessary to achieve the objectives of privatization' (1999: 788), while Carlin *et al.* (2001), from a survey of 3,300 firms in 25 transition countries, conclude that competition appears much more important than the effect of ownership per se in influencing performance. Cook (2001: 16) further stresses that 'given the lack of information and institutional weaknesses found in low-income countries, private monopolies are more likely to exploit their position by influencing the regulatory environment or by evading regulation'. He suggests that this is likely to undermine the potential gains to be made from privatization and deregulation. Besides, competition is claimed to be beneficial in addressing regulatory failure, although as Cook (2001) indicates, competition policies require a strong government to implement them. Elsewhere, Demsetz (1968) suggested a solution to such regulatory failure; that is, to foster competition through bidding for the right to operate as a monopoly. This solution received subsequent support from Kay and Thompson (1986) and Bishop and Kay (1989) who saw it as a way to introduce a form of competition into non-competitive markets.

The competition-solution literature, therefore, casts a critical eye over works advocating ownership-solution in relation to flaws in theory and empirical analysis (Vickers and Yarrow 1988; Cook 1997). Vickers and Yarrow (1988: 39) warn that 'many studies focus almost exclusively upon the ownership variable and fail to take proper account of the effects on performance of differences in market structure, regulation, and other relevant economic factors'. They warn also of the interacting effects of ownership, competition and regulation on incentive structure and firm performance. In concert, Cook (1997) questions the World Bank's advocacy of privatization, arguing that the property rights and principal-agent arguments used by the World Bank as the basis for ownership change policies have a number of theoretical weaknesses, even when applied to the private sector. Notably the two theories' assumption of the existence and operation of an efficient capital market does not apply to developing countries, particularly lower-income economies.

Earlier, Williamson (1963) noted how the profit-maximization hypothesis in the theory of the firm (which is reflected in the theoretical basis of the ownership-solution literature) has been subject to repeated criticism. Williamson cites the tendency for 'treating profit maximization as being the entire objective of the firm without regard for the conditions of competition in which the firm operates' (1963: 238). Yarrow (1999) supported this view that the application of principal-agent theory to explain the problems of modern firms, or guide privatization, is not fully satisfactory, claiming that a broader framework than profit-maximization is necessary to understand the performance of firms sheltered from the rigours of competition. And Cook and Minogue (1990) and Chang and Singh (1997) suggest that the ownership-solution advocates have paid insufficient attention to the fact that political economy dimensions also apply to the private sector.

The competition-solution advocates also show dissatisfaction with the empirical analysis of the ownership-solution advocates. Cook (1997) implies that it is inappropriate for ownership-solution advocates to transfer their findings from developed to developing and transition countries, and to derive general conclusions (e.g. a 'one size [privatization] fits all' policy) from a small number of empirical results. Notably, empirical evidence fails to support a basic notion of ownership change for improved performance (see Nolan 1995b; Bevan et al. 2001). Bevan et al.'s (2001: 36) study of 437 Russian enterprises, for example, arrived at the conclusion that 'private ownership and better performance are not correlated, though restructuring is positively associated with the competitiveness of the market environment'.

After discussing the views of the main advocates of ownership-solution and competition-solution respectively, it is worth noting that there is actually much common ground between them. Both groups generally admit that ownership and competition *matter* for the improvement of enterprise performance – disputes are mainly about which matters more. While the debates between these two groups extended into the late 1990s, the practical experiences of transition showed mixed results, with both groups facing pressure to consider a broader concept of transition. Evidence in their subtle adjustment of advocacy can be found in Shirley (1997: 854) who states that 'divestiture is less effective without competition, incentives fail if budgets are soft'. Shirley and Walsh (2000) document similarly that a number of empirical studies favour private ownership in a competitive market, yet claim, at the same time, that a competitive market is a condition for successful privatization. Shirley and Walsh (2000) conclude that further research is needed to model the institutional circumstances under which privatization will dominate state ownership and vice versa. This is also echoed in Sachs *et al.*'s (2000b) suggestion of a motto for a new privatization paradigm – 'while ownership matters, institutions matter just as much'. Sachs *et al.* point out that the notion of 'one size fits all' policy is problematic in transition economies. Privatization alone is not enough – it must be tailored by complementary reform in relation to institutions to support ownership functioning. Success factors include market competitiveness (removal of entry barriers), institutions to address agency issues, hard budget constraints and depoliticization of firm objectives. While Cook and Kirkpatrick (1997) suggest that privatization forms part of a broad programme of public-enterprise reform, Cook (2001: 31) stresses that it is one of the main instruments influencing competition policy, warning that 'weak regulation of competition is likely to undermine the potential gains to be made from privatization and deregulation'.

## Management-solution literature

It is suggested increasingly that there are limitations for economic discipline in incorporating the theoretical frameworks of ownership-solution and competition-solution into policy-making. In addition, over the years, evidence of the contrasting successes and failures of a number of developing and transition economies has become clear (Nolan 2003). For example, Russia and other FSU states are perceived to have experienced significant privatization failures (Nolan 1995a; Sachs *et al.* 2000a and b), whereas China's reform without radical privatization tends to be viewed in a positive light (Qian 1999). In this context, a sizeable body of literature has emerged incorporating the frameworks of institutional and management theory. This literature suggests there is more to organizational incentives than advocating privatization based on the assumption of profit-maximizing. It is felt similarly that viewing profit as the single argument affecting the relationship between owners and managers is naive and simplistic. It is argued instead that rapid ownership change is not the prime measure for the improvement of performance, as state enterprises which offer realistic incentives to managers can be efficient. In this respect, the reform of management regulation (including the government's role in the 'rule of law') and market-supporting institutions are major preconditions for improving performance and economic efficiency. Such reform includes state macro-management, in relation to institutions and government functional structures, as well as operational management at the micro enterprise level.

The management-solution literature rests on a broad concept of public enterprise reform by bringing into focus several institutional and management dimensions (see Shirk 1993; Stiglitz 1993, 1994, 1999; Davey 1995; Naughton 1995a; Nolan 1995a, 2003; Smyth 1998; Farazmand 1999, 2004; Kolodko 1999; Nolan and Wang 1999; Xu 2000). Researchers advocate management reform without the need for mass privatization. For improving efficiency and performance, they propose a shift in focus from ownership issues towards those related to institutions and management. Stressing the importance of management can be seen, in some ways, as reflecting interests in those institutional, behavioural and growth issues identified, for example, by Cyert and March (1963); Marris (1964); Williamson (1967, 1990); Crew (1975); Cyert (1988); Hodgson (1989) and Samuels (1995). Such theories agree that markets are organized by, and have effects on, the institutions which shape them, and that institutions matter in economic transformation. In so doing, theories of enterprise management place managers and managerial motivation in a central position, with profit-maximization as the unique goal of the firm being displaced. As Williamson (1967) suggested, since the managers of the firm are empowered and have substantial discretion, they often pursue goals other than profit. As such, management may choose a position between minimum and maximum profit bounds.

In *A Behavioral Theory of the Firm* (1963) Cyert and March famously argued that the profit-maximizing emphasis of neo-classical theory has been replaced by profit-satisfying under behavioural theory. It is assumed that modern firms are highly complex systems possessing significant problems of control and organization. As such they have to be managed rather than subjected uniquely to the market. Similarly, in *The Economic Theory of Managerial Capitalism* (1964) Marris stresses growth-maximization instead of neo-classical profit-maximization, based on the assumption of managerial discretion. Diversification (e.g. through acquisition) is emphasized as it is often difficult for the firm to grow at a rate faster than that of the industry. The firm will become interested in diversification when the growth rate in the original market becomes insufficient to sustain the firm's growth potential. In this way, the internal growth of the firm supplements the competitive control mechanism. In industries where barriers to entry are high, entry by the diversified firm may be the only possible strategy (Cyert 1988). Wildsmith (1973) comments that the predicted responses of managerial theories, while qualitatively different to those of the profit-maximizers, are closer to those found in reality. In modern corporations, especially large ones, where there can no longer be traditional owner-managers, other forms of control readily emerge.

There is an emerging literature on post-socialist transformation and transitional economies that draws on new institutional economics as the basis for analysis (Smyth 1998; Kolodko 1999; Hassard *et al.* 2004). Importance is increasingly attached to institutions in transforming economies in the recognition that 'not only ownership matters – institutions matter too' (Smyth 1998). The literature agrees that markets are organized by, and in turn have effects on, the institutions that form them (Williamson 1990; Samuels 1995; Levy and Spiller 1996).

Smyth (1998) offers a review of key institutional perspectives and evaluates their relevance to the debate on post-socialist transformation. In so doing he argues that the essence of the 'new economics' is appreciation of the primary role of institutions. Kolodko (1999) similarly claims that new institutional arrangements are of key importance for successful transformation. A market economy requires not only liberal regulation and private ownership, but also adequate institutions. According to Kolodko, market economies do not expand without well-designed institutions; in other words, without making adequate provision for institutional arrangements, liberalization and privatization are unable to establish a sound market economy.

It is argued, however, that unlike the ownership- and competition-solution approaches, the institutionally oriented management-solution approach is still in its infancy, and seeks a strong theoretical framework and empirical evidence in respect of transforming economies. Smyth (1998) notes that as the application of new institutional economics is very limited, the insights it offers remain too general for policy guidance. Farazmand (1999: 565) suggests that a new theory of public enterprise needs to be proposed in order to create economically efficient and socially just government: 'This theory of public enterprise management must serve as a bridge between the excesses of market/corporate inequality and injustice on the one hand and the authoritative/coercive functions of the modern state on the other.' Furthermore, Farazmand (ibid.) notes that 'such a theory of public enterprise management must be based on professional competence, effective account-ability and responsiveness measures, competitive productivity scales, and measurable organizational performance'.

In analysing transition in Russia, Nolan (1995a: 56) noted that 'there existed no theory of the transition from the command system', and that in analysing issues of large system change 'proper policy requires political economy, not merely the separate sciences of "economics", politics or sociology' (1995a: 5). As such, the theory used to guide the improvement of a market economy will not be the same one used to guide the transformation of a command (planned) economy. Nolan (1995a) criticizes the transition 'orthodoxy' which advocates rapid privatization by over-stressing the role of the market and argues that the theoretical and empirical basis of the orthodoxy's policy of economic reform is outmoded. He cautions against exaggerated claims of market-driven mass privatization and high-speed transition, insisting that 'the conclusions of the accumulated developments in Western economic theory are far from being so strongly supportive of the power of the "invisible hand" as the transition orthodoxy imagined' (1995a: 84). Nolan cautions that it is practically impossible to exercise rapid privatization of state assets, as successful privatization is hugely time-consuming and requires an established market economy. He argues further that in transition, SOEs can improve their performance without outright privatization, suggesting that:

> the essence of capitalism is much more the existence of contracts that encourage effective use of resources by the manager of those resources, than it is the direct interest of the manager of resources being stimulated by the fact that they own those resources . . . The vast bulk of managers within large companies are stimulated to effective performance by appropriate contracts and by non-pecuniary motivation, rather than by ownership.
>
> (1995a: 316)

With respect to the limitations of competition, Stiglitz (1993) states that because of politicians' desire to use SOEs for political purposes, they cannot credibly commit to encouraging competition. Besides, it is acknowledged that market competition is often imperfect and incomplete, even in the most economically advanced countries (Stiglitz 1988; Barr 1992). Stiglitz (1994) appears to favour China's strategy of improved economic efficiency through gradual reform, although his views on the controversies between privatization and 'government corporatization' (public-enterprise reform) are rather mixed. He admits that in many areas there is little justification for a significant governmental role, except as a part of the transition process, and that corporations under state ownership, but which pay attention to individual incentives, can be efficient. The important point is to promote a pragmatic rather than ideological position on public-enterprise transition. Stiglitz (1999) suggests that if the corporatization route is chosen as part of the transitional strategy, it is essential that hard budget constraints be imposed with due attention paid to incentives.

To return to an earlier point, the behavioural theory of the firm also proposes that managers may operate the firm in a fashion consistent with assumptions of self-interest rather than by attending exclusively to shareholders' best interests by maximizing profit (Williamson 1963). Noting that privatization is to be used in a selective and pragmatic manner, and that privatization alone is unlikely to be sufficient in significantly improving public enterprise performance, Cook and Kirkpatrick (1997: 27) have suggested that 'other forms of public enterprise reform, where ownership remains with the state but the contractual relationship between the enterprise and government is redefined, are needed'.

Davey (1995), Korten (1995), Thayer (1995) and Farazmand (1998, 1999, 2001, 2004) all call for the reform of public-enterprise management rather than privatization. They direct their harshest criticisms to the ownership-solution advocates, especially those promoting 'sweeping' privatization. While Thayer warns that privatization can promote corruption and contribute to rises in unemployment, Davey (1995) suggests one of the consequences of privatization is to turn a 'welfare state' into a 'police state', as privatization brings with it 'social problems' and can require increased state control to maintain social order. Writers critical of privatization argue that 'western values of efficiency and the British and American approach to large-scale privatization are generally not applicable to countries where the private sector is underdeveloped and corrupt, and itself in need of government support' (Farazmand 1999: 555). Farazmand (1999) notes further that warnings about the long-term negative consequences of sweeping privatization, as a pro-claimed marketplace panacea for the ills of public enterprises, have often been ignored by policy-makers and academic proponents of privatization. It is argued that advocates of such reform policy are, in general, ideologically oriented toward a conservative political economy, one favouring a strong marketplace and 'free' enterprise, small government with a limited role in the economy, and a supply-side economic system (Korten 1995; Farazmand 1999).

Similarly, for reasons of social and economic justice, the same set of researchers see sweeping privatization not as a simple economic policy, but rather as a global ideological strategy of capitalism designed to reverse the older strategy of state intervention in the economy. Their criticisms of privatization point to a variety of concerns such as market failure, the exploitative nature of the private sector, massive corruption (especially among contractors doing business with government), social problems, degraded citizenship values, deterioration of public infrastructures, and environmental destruction. As Farazmand (1996, 1997, 1998, 1999) forcibly states, privatization only benefits the globally dominant states (e.g. USA, UK), international donors (e.g. IMF, WTO, World Bank) and transnational and global corporations, which use it as a global strategic instrument of capital expansion, surplus value promotion and global corporate capitalism. As such, privatization will domestically put the poor at greater risk and globally result in underdeveloped countries being turned into subsidiaries of transnational corporations and global donors.

An alternative to such sweeping privatization is radical reform of public-enterprise management:

> What is needed is to ensure that public enterprise managers are adequately equipped with new skills of accountability, transparency, flexibility,

responsiveness and responsibility, efficiency and effectiveness. It is also necessary to promote a culture of respectful and dutiful treatment of citizens, consideration of citizens as human beings and partners in public management (not as clients or consumers), and to resist commodification of people and their values.

(Farazmand 1999: 563)

Farazmand argues that 'public enterprise management must also be based on professional competence, effective accountability, responsiveness measures, competitive, productivity scales, and measurable organizational performance' (1999: 566). In terms of flattening the organizational structure of public enterprise to promote information transparency and accuracy, and to balance incentives and control, reforms need to be taken to reorganize the managerial structure of public enterprises.

Empirical evidence to support the management-solution position has generally been less abundant than that for the frameworks of ownership- and competition-solution. Arguments supporting the management-solution theory are mainly grounded on the experience of a small number of countries. China and Vietnam, for example, were cases in the OECF (1998) report of developing countries that had improved their economic performance primarily through reform rather than mass privatization.

Of the empirical studies conducted since the early 1990s, Campbell and Pedersen (1996) document the role of institutions of post-communist European economies in the process of economic transformation, whereas Orru *et al.* (1997) present evidence on the emergence of new economic institutions in East Asia. Shirk (1993) offers empirical evidence on manage-ment and institutional changes by examining Chinese industrial SOE reform, focusing on reforms in management and finance. She argues that 'Chinese political institutions shaped industrial reform policies by establishing the incentives of political actors and the rules by which they made decisions', and as such 'the overall path of Chinese economic reform over the past decade can be best understood by focusing on the political institutions in which reform policies were made' (1993: 20–21). In arguing that Chinese economic reform policies were shaped by the institutional setting, Shirk concludes that two features of political institutions are necessary for economic reform, namely flexibility and authority. The former refers to the presence of choice-making institutions with internal rules and an enfranchisement formula that encourages (or can be modified to encourage) innovation. The latter refers to China's approach to the retention of authority by retaining the Chinese Communist Party's power to appoint government officials and SOE managers.

Levy and Spiller (1996) also develop an institutional model of privatiza-tion in their study of telecommunications, drawing upon evidence from Argentina, Chile, Mexico, the Philippines and the United Kingdom. Their model highlights the importance of an 'independent judiciary', a 'capable bureaucracy' (for making credible and efficient regulation for privatized firms), and 'checks and balances in the government'. Similarly, based on evidence from a number of transition countries, Sachs *et al.* (2000b: 556) argue that policy prescriptions 'should be less ideological and more tailored to the country's institutional conditions and stage of transition'. In their view, transfer of ownership, without the necessary institutional structures in place for owners to exercise authority, may even worsen levels of economic performance, as this may reflect the simple substitution of poor government control of management with weak private sector control, or even none at all.

Overall, the management-solution group suggests instruments for management improvement, including the maturation of institutions at the macro level, reorganization of the managerial structure of public enterprises, performance contracting, and the use of takeover and bankruptcy. It is assumed that these instruments exert pressure on enterprise managers to pursue efficient performance.

## SOE transformation and labour

As a precursor to our analysis in later chapters, we note that until recently labour employment (and related issues of social welfare) has been one of the least addressed issues in public-enterprise reform and restructuring. In the 1990s this lack of information on the employment impact of privatization increased the fears and concerns of government and workers alike (Kikeri 1998). Of the literature to emerge in this period, Commander (1998) described enterprise restructuring and its interaction with the labour market in Central European firms, while Van der Hoeven and Sziraczki (1998) examined lessons from privatization on labour issues by drawing on the experience of the Republic of Korea, India, Mexico, Bulgaria, the Czech Republic, Eastern Germany and Hungary. According to such research, there was widespread evidence to suggest that attempts to improve efficiency and profitability during public-enterprise transition led to the continuing reform of working practices, such as greater labour flexibility and the adoption of innovative payment systems.

However, as regards employment trends, the literature generated an open debate in terms of levels of labour required. Parker and Hartley (1991) suggested that most firms reduced employment, while Johnson (2001) claimed that privatization did not necessarily require massive public-sector lay-offs, and (albeit much earlier) Bishop and Kay (1989) actually suggested the possibility of employment increases after privatization. In contrast, Joshi (2000) in a study of restructuring in South Asia (i.e. Bangladesh, India, Nepal, Pakistan and Sri Lanka) looked at the social consequences of such reform and called for adequate measures for workers' protection and participation in order to raise public awareness and reduce workers' resistance to privatization.

It can be argued that there is always a need to raise public awareness on issues relevant to the impact of privatization on the workforce. One suggestion in this respect is to mandate employee-ownership of a certain percentage share in the privatized enterprise, alongside establishing compensation funds and retraining opportunities. On the political right, Johnson's (2001) evidence from the US suggests that privatization does not necessarily require massive public-sector lay-offs and indicates that public employees can benefit in the long term from private-sector management. Elsewhere, Kikeri (1998, 1999) examining the effects of privatization on labour and the mechanisms for governments to minimize the political and social costs of labour restructuring in privatization, points out that workers often recognize that reforms of inefficient public enterprises are inevitable, but lack information on what is likely to happen to them, She suggests that this lack of involvement can serve to exacerbate fears and resistance. According to Kikeri, efforts should be made to raise public awareness of the costs, benefits, timing and methods of privatization, in order to build a social safety net and develop regulatory arrangements for welfare. Both Chu and Gupta (1998) and Gupta *et al.* (1999) have examined impacts and experiences in relation to the social safety nets developed in connection with privatization. And Li (1996) notes that unemployment is the most difficult 'hard core' issue to resolve when a planned economy is transformed into a market one, such as in Central and Eastern European countries, Li indicating that the spectre of large-scale unemployment can seriously affect both political stability and the selection of reform approaches and methods.

Finally, Cook and Kirkpatrick (1998) also discuss how the transition of public enterprises (privatization) generates consequences in relation to employment and the labour market. These consequences can involve, variously, social protection benefits (particularly pensions), job security, wages and work conditions. Drawing on evidence from ten developing countries (in sub-Saharan Africa, Asia and Latin America), Cook and Kirkpatrick suggest that while few generalizations can be made as to the impacts of privatization on employment and social protection:

> it is often assumed that employment will fall when privatization occurs, since the new owners will be unwilling to maintain the overmanning and surplus labour associated with the public ownership of the enterprise. The loss of employment will obviously have an immediate adverse impact of labour's social protection status.
>
> (1998: 262–263)

## Conclusion

Over the past three decades, public enterprises have confronted widespread development problems such as multiple and often conflicting objectives, over-extended government intervention and poor economic efficiency. The situation has drawn considerable attention from academic researchers and policy-makers. For the improvement of efficiency, the main themes of the literature, theoretically and empirically, concern ownership change (mainly privatization), the creation of competition, and management and institutional reform. Overall, debates remain on-going between the advocates of competition, ownership change and management reform theories.

We have noted how a variety of policy solutions has been suggested, among which privatization has been a paradigm widely implemented in different economies. Indeed, privatization has been an international phenomenon for three decades, dealing mainly with a change of ownership from public to private. Our review of the literature has described how writers such as Boardman and Vining (1992) and Shirley (1983, 1997, 1999), plus various reports from the World Bank, stress that to effect transition successfully, issues of ownership are of greater import than those related to competing paradigms of competition creation and management reform.

We have suggested, however, that when it comes to the evaluation of economic success, the ownership-solution paradigm is accompanied by a range of constraints and prerequisites, notably concerning the realization of competitive markets and capitalist institutions. Sachs *et al.* (2000b) warn that although issues of ownership are indeed significant, privatization alone is an insufficient condition for success, since the role of institutions in processes of transition is crucial. They also remind us that privatization alone is not applicable to developing and transitional economies. Writers such as Cook and Kirkpatrick (1995, 1997, 1998), Carlin *et al.* (2001) and Yarrow (1999) suggest that the route to successful competition is made via, for example, the removal of entry and exit limits, deregulation and new regulation.

It is also argued that ownership change through mass privatization does not apply to all countries, with this being the case in those transitional economies where privatization prerequisites do not necessarily hold. The management-solution group suggests that public-enterprise reform should avoid sweeping privatization, as evidence shows that in very competitive markets private companies often fail due to poor management controls. Therefore, the building of institutional networks is central to successful transformation, as is the development of sound internal firm management. Writing from this perspective also draws attention to the possible long-term dysfunctional consequences of 'sweeping' privatization, such as market-chaos and social instability.

In sum, whereas the literature on public-enterprise reform acknowledges that 'ownership matters' (World Bank 1995; Shirley 1999; Shirley and Walsh 2000) it also acknowledges that ownership is not the only important factor in influencing economic performance and efficiency (Sachs *et al.* 2000a and b; Tsui and Lau 2002). Competition and market environment, and institutional and administrative systems, are also important factors (Carlin *et al.* 2001; Cook 2001; Nolan 2003; Hassard *et al.* 2005). The literature suggests a call for comprehensive analytical studies from an integrated perspective of economy, institutions and management. In addition, the transformation process of public enterprises generates extensive and far-reaching effects on labour, the employment relationship and social security in particular

(Kikeri 1998; Hassard *et al.* 1999a and b, 2004, 2006). In order to minimize the adverse affects of the transition of public enterprises, writers have claimed that it is crucial to raise public awareness of the costs, benefits, timing and methods of such transition through wide participation. Furthermore, the literature also suggests that adequate social security has an important role to play in the transition process of public enterprises.

# 2 Perspectives on China's reform path

## Introduction

The literature on transitional economies has examined transformation mechanisms from a range of theoretical and political perspectives. By and large, these perspectives have polarized around two main policies – radical privatization and gradual reform. The former is concerned primarily with the change of ownership from public to private hands: the latter, the introduction of competition and the improvement of managerial and institutional capability. We can discern in this literature differences between the more Messianic voice of earlier writing on economic transformation (e.g. Kornai 1990; Sachs and Woo 1994) and the increasingly reflective or measured tone of later theory and evidence (e.g. Kolodko 1999; Carlin *et al.* 2001; Sachs *et al.* 2000a and b; Estrin 2002; Nolan 2003; Bhaumik and Estrin 2005). We can also note striking differences in the policies and practices described in works which examine economic transformation in, on the one hand, ECE countries (notably Russia) (see Buck *et al.* 1999; Estrin and Wright 1999; Brown and Earle 2001; Estrin *et al.* 2001; Bevan *et al.* 2001; Angelucci *et al.* 2002) and on the other, those of the People's Republic of China (see Naughton 1994, 1995a; Rawski 1994; Nolan 1995a, 2001, 2003; Walder 1996; Kato and Long 2004; Hassard *et al.* 2004, 2006). This chapter examines such theories, perspectives and evidence, but centrally in relation to debates over China's reform path and whether it is to be characterized as radical or gradual.

## China's reform path: gradual or radical?

A large body of literature acknowledges that Chinese economic reform has taken a gradual path. It is argued that the main features of such a path reflect an emphasis on the economically incremental, experimental and evolutionary, or a situation where there is no rapid leap to free prices, cutting of state subsidies, trade liberalization or sweeping privatization of state enterprises (Zhang 1992; Macmillan and Naughton 1992a; Fan 1996; Walder 1996; Steinfeld 1998; Guthrie 1999; Nolan 2001, 2003). Such characteristics present themselves in marked contrast to those of the 'big bang' path, signified by immediate and massive privatization of public enterprises, and through the rapid release of price controls, state subsidies and restrictions on foreign competition and investment (Walder 1996).

As Naughton (1995a) indicates, the gradualist path allows a transition economy to grow out of a planned economy by the steady introduction of competition and market mechanisms. It slowly alters the mechanisms of the old planning system throughout an economy, while attempting to avoid significant social hardship stemming from rapid privatization. Fan (1996) notes similarly that China's gradual and incremental path to reform reflects a collateral approach in which a new system is established while allowing the old to continue. Eventually the old system is compelled to reform, with a relatively smooth transition of the economy being the result. Thus the basic method used in China's incremental approach to reform has been the 'dual-track' approach, where the overriding philosophy is that nobody should be made worse-off by the process. Instead, as economic reform evolves, most citizens are to benefit from it, and thus should in turn support it, even though many may not support every single reform measure.

The gradual path, however, has had its critics. Fan (1996) and Wu (1996), for example, suggested that a gradualist approach could be accompanied by 'corruption' (especially 'rent-seeking'), 'contradictions and costs of the long-term coexistence of old and new systems', 'excessive government intervention' and 'disparity and inequality of income distribution'. In addition, criticisms have come from those who see China's path as actually an integration and combination of gradual and radical (i.e. partial/limited and full-scale) reforms. Li (1996), for example, argues that any single term such as 'gradualism' is too simplistic and incomplete to describe the wide and complex reforms in China. Sachs and Woo (1994) argue further that China's reform has taken an ostensibly 'radical' path. They suggest that in the rural sector, for example, reform through the Household Contract Responsibility System (see later) was a kind of 'big bang' reform, with in any case the creation of the non-state sector moving China's economy inexorably toward generic privatization. Wu (1996), like Li (1996), also warns that the concept of 'gradualism' cannot fully describe China's complex reform process, and that, besides, a gradualist strategy did not best serve China's transition due to its associated weaknesses (noted above). Wu champions the integration of a general advancement in economic reform with radical breakthroughs in key economic areas. In so doing Wu essentially advocates a form of 'dual-track' approach through the integration of gradual and radical reform measures.

The major body of literature on China's transformation from a planned to a market economy, however, reflects a basic consensus that a gradualist approach to reform, under way for almost three decades, has produced effective and sustainable change. It is also argued that such gradualist economic policy needs to be integrated with more comprehensive welfare measures in order to minimize the social costs of reform (as discussed in later chapters). As China moves progressively towards a form of private ownership economy, it should be recalled that since the late 1970s it has been possible to obtain sustained improvements in economic performance based on a form of mainly public ownership of assets and without shock-therapy privatization.

## Transition in China and other planned economies

Although China and other transitional economies have historically displayed economic convergence (as economic systems operating under central planning) their reform for the common goal of improved economic efficiency has displayed marked and explicit divergence. As Cook and Nixson (1995) noted, in other previously centrally planned economies, such as those of Eastern Europe, political change generally preceded economic change. China, however, has progressively and intensively undertaken economic reforms since 1978, but with comparatively little political change. As such, China's reform programme has been successful without necessarily following what might be termed the dominant orthodoxy in transition theory (see Byrd 1991a and b; Macmillan and Naughton 1992; Naughton 1995a; Nolan 1995a; Walder 1996; Stiglitz 1999; Qian 2000; Xu 2000).

For more than a decade following the inception of reform under the 'open door' philosophy of the late 1970s, the principles for transforming China's state enterprises became embodied in the gradualist industrial policy of the CRS. This period saw the initial phases of state-enterprise organizational experimentation develop within a reform environment whereby state ownership remained dominant. As we discuss later, the CRS principles mainly concerned the expansion of management autonomy and the retention of profits (Child 1994; OECF 1998; Hassard *et al.* 1999a).

During the early to mid-1990s CRS reforms gave way to those embodied in a more adventurous economic policy, that of the MES. Here, property rights were required to be clarified, management skill was to be improved and partial privatization officially permitted. China's SOE transformation policy has subsequently followed the principles of the MES, which consist of four key elements: 'clarification of property rights', 'clear definition of rights and responsibilities', 'separation between government and enterprise management', and the adoption of 'scientific management'. The MES principles represent the trajectory for ownership restructuring and management reform until the projected culmination of this reform period in 2010. The MES has embraced reform which focuses primarily on new enterprise-management mechanisms, technical transformation and improvement, and the reorganization and restructuring of property rights and assets. However, due to political sensitivity, the MES has still not fully resolved the traditionally 'forbidden areas' of reform policy, namely those of surplus workers and senior management appointments.

In contrast, the ECE transitional economies have emphasized deregulation and privatization as the primary mechanisms of reform. Under the 'shock therapy' approach, public enterprises were encouraged to undertake schemes of rapid and mass privatization. These ranged from self-privatization in Hungary and Poland, to mass privatization programmes in the former Czechoslovakia, and Russia's voucher scheme and direct sales (Sachs 1993; Cook and Nixson 1995; Nolan 1995a; Ellman and Kontorovich 1998; Buck *et al.* 1999; Estrin and Wright 1999; Bennett *et al.* 2001; Angelucci *et al.* 2002).

Sachs and Woo (1994) attributed the difference between the transition experiences of the ECE and FSU states and those of China to different 'initial conditions'. Their view was that shock therapy transition would help ECE and FSU states rapidly to realize more robust economies, and that, in contrast, China would face the political trap of property rights, as it avoided the privatization of SOEs. This view has, however, been challenged by empirical evidence from comparative studies of transitional economies (Bhaumik and Estrin 2005).

Carlin *et al.* (2001), for example, suggest that the nature of competition in the product market has important effects on firm performance and that there is no statistically significant relation between privatization and performance. They suggest that state-owned firms and privatized firms that had formerly been owned by the state show no significant differences in sales or productivity growth. This is supported by Estrin's (2002) evidence from a comparative study of ECE countries. Estrin asserts that transition countries possess very different initial conditions and have employed a variety of policies with respect to privatization, price and trade liberalization and competition. Estrin's message is that privatization alone is not enough – effective corporate governance and hard budget constraints are also necessary conditions for enterprise transformation. Transition policies should thus be regarded as complements to, not substitutes for, enterprise restructuring.

Similarly, Sachs *et al.* (2000a), citing evidence from 24 transitional economies, warn that the reform process is a transformation of not only markets but also of government, and that the objectives of government are important determinants of privatization gains. Sachs *et al.* (2000b) argue that post-privatization experience has not always suggested improved economic performance. The immediate economic effectiveness and social acceptability of privatization depends on the existence of capitalist institutional underpinning. Where such underpinning is absent, even if the government is philosophically committed to effecting and enforcing reform, it is better to delay privatization until the right conditions are in place. Sachs *et al.* (2000b) conclude that privatization involving a change of title alone is not enough to generate improvements in economic performance, for privatization policies must be tailored to the (cluster-specific) level of the complementary reforms in place. In turn, complementary institutional reform does not guarantee improved efficiency unless a minimum level of privatization has already been attained. The idea of 'one size (privatization) fits all' policy does not apply to transition economies. This view is backed up by Kolodko's (1999) study of 'ten years of post-socialist transition', arguing it is naive to assume that a market economy can be introduced *tout fait* by 'shock therapy'. A market economy requires adequate market-supporting institutions and appropriate enterprise behaviour, which can be introduced only gradually because this requires new organizations, new laws and new behavioural patterns in various economic entities.

In the case of China, McNally and Lee (1998) and Shieh (1999) cast criticisms over adopting too close a government–enterprise relationship. It can be argued that radical political change preceding economic reform does not necessarily make for smooth transition, for such reform in the ECE and FSU countries was generally viewed as a failure. Taking the Russian example, the removal of the Party from economic management appeared to have been the single most important blow to the economy. The Party's withdrawal from the economy caused an institutional vacuum which resulted in serious disorganization and loss of economic control (Ellman and Kontorovich 1998). Cook and Nixson (1995) confirm that if the corresponding government authority has not been provided, there is a danger of institutions being erected but which operate in a vacuum, as witnessed in a number of transitional economies.

## Transformation mechanisms in the Chinese case

Within the broad literature on transition economies there are various ways of describing the reform process, such as partial to comprehensive, or gradualist to shock therapy (see Cook and Nixson 1995a; Jeffries 2001). In contrast to the radical style of reform, which is often characterized by political change preceding economic change, China chose gradual reform by focusing on economic reform but with substantial continuity in its political system. As Nixson (1995) notes, very few other transition economies have taken this or a similar path, the most notable perhaps being Vietnam.

It is acknowledged that Chinese-style economic reform has resulted in sustained growth for more than a quarter of a century. As such, China's reform progress has aroused considerable attention as a paradigm model of economic gradualism (Nolan 1995; Jeffries 2001). Arguments remain however about the preferred mechanisms for China's economic transformation, these generally reflecting the policy positions discussed previously. Also varying are the backgrounds of the main researchers in this field, who similarly mirror three main academic groupings. The first reflects the views of often critically oriented Western economists conducting research into centrally planned and transitional economies. Among those who would fit this description are, for example, Barry Naughton, Peter Nolan and Thomas Rawski. A second type is composed of economists working in China who have been exposed to the Western economic and management literature and who draw upon such theory in their professional work. Included in this group would be economists who have studied in American and British universities, for example, Lin Yifu, a competition-solution researcher who was formerly a doctoral student at

Chicago University, and Zhang Weiying, an ownership-solution researcher who previously studied for a doctorate at Oxford University. A third group is comprised of policy specialists who have worked in China's centrally planned system and experienced transition directly by participating in the design and implementation of policy and reform schemes. Examples of such professional policy makers would be Wu Jinglian and Li Yining.

Similar to the arguments on global transformation mechanisms discussed in Chapter 1, research on Chinese public enterprise reform by and large reflects the three primary theoretical orientations of ownership-solution, competition-solution, and management-solution. There is similarly a large and contested literature associated with these positions (see Li 1986; Fan 1994; Nolan 1995, 2001, 2003; Child 1994, 1996; Naughton 1995a; Parker and Pan 1996; World Bank 1997a; Leong 1997; Lin 1997; Lardy 1998; Cao *et al.* 1999; Nolan and Wang 1999; Hassard *et al.* 1999a and b, 2002, 2005; Wu 1999; Zhang, Weiying 1999; Xu 2000; Nolan and Yeung 2001). Over the years, the ownership-solution emphasis can be witnessed, for example, in the work of Li (1986, 1987), World Bank (1995, 1996, 1997a) and Zhang, Weiying (1997, 1999), all of whom advocate that China's SOE reform should focus on problems of property rights and state ownership change, for (they argue) reform without clarified property rights (e.g. the CRS) is reform that can neither promote efficient resource allocation nor avoid government intervention. In contrast, the competition-solution group (e.g. Lin *et al.* 1994, 1998, 2001; Lin 1997; Thoburn 1997) consider that in the Chinese context the introduction of competition and the realization of a fully competitive external environment is more important than a change in ownership, while the management-solution group (e.g. Shirk 1993; Wu 1993, 1999; Cheng 2000; Wei 2001) argue that state ownership of SOEs does not necessarily have to shift into private ownership, although in some cases ownership adjustment may be helpful, with priority here being given to management improvement and the creation of effective institutions.

## Ownership-solution group on China

Commonly held views among this group of economists – among whose high-profile Chinese representatives are Li Yining and Zhang Weiying – are that unclear definition of SOE property rights is, perhaps, the major source of the SOEs' inefficiency. They argue further that bureaucratic asset management systems serve only to weaken the monitoring capability of the state as the representative of the owner, the people. On the basis of these assertions they argue that the state, as the owner representative of the SOEs, has failed to supervise management in the state enterprises effectively. As a result, insufficient monitoring has allowed managers to pursue their own private interests at the expense of profit for the enterprise.

In order to solve the efficiency problem, privatization or property rights adjustment is suggested, for example, in papers by the World Bank (1997a),

Li (1986, 1987) and Zhang, Weiying (1997, 1999). Basically these writers argue that as the SOEs belong to 'the people', the state acts as owner-representative on their behalf. As owner-representative, however, the state cannot supervise management in the SOE sufficiently because of the high costs of monitoring under an imperfect market system. Thus, under state ownership the owner finds it impossible to compel the enterprise manager to work towards the maximization of the owner's interests. Managers of SOEs are therefore able to operate their enterprises largely according to their own interests without due monitoring by the owner. It is argued that enterprise management without owner supervision inevitably gives rise to inefficiency.

Given this scenario, Li (1986, 1987) advocated the establishment of a 'state shareholding system' as a major mechanism for transforming Chinese SOEs. Here, state assets are turned into state shares, and state asset operating companies are set up to enforce the functions of the state shareholders. Zhang, Weiying (1999), however, questions the state shareholding advocates on the basis that their proposals are problematic in three crucial respects – the 'mechanisms for managerial appointments', the 'value-adding of state assets', and the 'separation of government and enterprise operations'. Instead, Zhang, Weiying (1999) suggests changing state assets into creditor rights in order to clarify property rights more realistically and thus separate government and enterprise operations. To clarify property rights in corporate governance and establish effective incentive and control mechanisms, Zhang, Chengyao (2000) argues that genuine privatization is the only way forward for China's SOEs, supporting this argument by describing a number of cases of companies that have gone through such ownership restructuring in the late 1990s (see also the China Reform and Development Report – Expert Group 1999).

Similarly, Wu (in *Economic Daily* (*Jingji Ribao*) 12 February 1998: 5; 1999), in respect of China's MES policy on SOEs of 'grasping the large and releasing the small' (see later), warns that the Chinese authorities, in the drive to create internationally competitive state enterprises, should not be attempting to 'weld sampans together to form an aircraft carrier'. He discusses the problematic nature of subjecting state enterprises into 'forced marriages' or 'high-speed fattening', where entire industries are merged into a few large firms or one or two big enterprise groups. Such artificial restructuring, he argues, flies in the face of the need to clarify ownership and property rights in the drive to achieve genuine state-enterprise efficiency.

## Competition-solution group on China

In contrast, Lin (1997) and Lin *et al.* (1998) assert that the real causes of the SOEs' problems do not lie in the ambiguous definition of ownership but in the lack of a fully competitive external environment. They argue that the separation of, and conflict between, owners and managers has existed ever since the appearance of modern corporations and that ownership structure is not the pivotal issue in the SOE efficiency problem. The introduction of the shareholding system would not improve the SOEs' efficiency without the existence of a fair and competitive market.

Similarly Thoburn (1997) and Nolan and Wang (1999) suggest that privatization is not a necessary requirement for the improvement of enterprise performance in Chinese SOE reform, while according to Lin (1997) changing the SOEs' ownership to private ownership is neither a sufficient nor a necessary condition for an enterprise to be efficient. These writers assert that the most essential condition for reforming the SOEs is to eliminate their policy-determined burdens in order to foster competition. In so doing the vicious cycle from such policy-determined burdens to information asymmetry to soft budget constraints can be stopped. SOEs can thereafter be put into competition with private firms on a level playing field and, after the stripping of policy-induced burdens, determine whether or not to change ownership. Lin (1997) cites the cases of ownership change in the UK, Korea, India and some Latin American countries to justify this view, maintaining that in perfectly competitive markets there would be little difference between the performance of public and private firms. This is supported by Lin *et al.* (1998) who assert that if competition is sufficient to equalize public and private performance, then there is little need to consider the nature of ownership. In other words, privatization or ownership change does not necessarily solve the problem of soft budget constraints. The competition-solution group points out that in many transition cases the nature of soft budget constraints was no better than it was before privatization. And Nolan and Wang (1999) argue similarly that, from the experience of Hungary, Poland and Russia, there is no clear and straightforward way to privatize large SOEs. They stress further that the experience of large SOE reform has seen 'the main goals of reform become autonomy and competition rather than privatization' (Nolan and Wang 1999: 180).

In all, this group claims that, in the improvement of SOE performance, creating a competitive and functional market environment is more important than simply shifting the ownership from state to private hands.

## Management-solution group on China

In contrast again, highlighting the limitations of the ownership-solution approach in the Chinese context, the management-solution group stresses the importance of institutional change at the state macro-management level and management reform at the enterprise level. Wu *et al.* (1993) and Wu (1999) argue that in China a market system can be established on the basis of a pluralized property system with the presence of dominant public ownership. With appropriate management, they argue that this can evolve into a situation in which there exist a competitive market system, firms which are responsible for their own profits and losses and, importantly, market-suitable macro-management and government regulations.

A growing body of research has examined the emergence of China's new economic institutions, such as Guthrie (1999), Oi and Walder (1999), Qian (1999), Nolan (2001, 2003) and Tsui and Lau (2002). From the view of economic analysis, this literature on market-supporting institutions stresses the role of the legal structure, property rights, enterprise system, labour issues and state law/governance, and advocates the general improvement of state macro-management. In terms of the institutional foundations of China's market transition, Qian (1999) has discussed the role of four key factors – regional decentralization of government; encouragement of the entry and expansion of non-state firms (local government and private firms); financial dualism in government revenue and the lending side of the financial system; and market liberalization through the dual-track approach (where the 'plan track' and 'market track' coexist until the plan track is phased out subsequently: see later). Qian (1999) notes that each of these pillars of institutional change has contributed to China's transformation success, notably in that such institutional changes have released the potential for incentives, hard budget constraints and competition.

In the transition to the market, however, it is noted that institutions are frequently required to be built from scratch, rather than simply imitated from those characteristic of the West. In the process, some transitional institutions may, in fact, be more applicable to, and effective for, the transition situation (Qian 1999). Yang (1998) has warned of the incompatibility between certain Western-style market-supporting institutions and China's own institutional requirements. Among the examples offered are the incompatibility between the Corporation Law and the communist constitutional rules (Yang 1998) and that between state monopoly in the telecommunications sector and the Anti-Unfair Competition Law (Mueller 1998). Such literature emphasizes that successful economic development needs not only markets, but also market-supporting institutions, including constitutional order and the rule of law, which protect individual rights and provide effective checks and balances of government power.

### Enterprise–state relations

With regard to enterprise–state relations, Ma (1997) discusses what he sees as a particularly problematic legacy of the planned economy – excessive government intervention. As SOEs became both political and economic entities they came to hold dissonant sets of objectives and responsibilities. Zhang (2000) similarly, in a series of SOE reform case studies, offers examples of the adverse affects of government intervention. He emphasizes the contradictory nature of the SOEs' social and economic objectives and highlights how this has generally stifled their development in terms of efficiency and productivity.

It must be remembered, however, that whereas in a basic sense SOE reform in China is the separation of government and enterprise operations, in a deeper sense it is the separation of *ownership* (i.e. state as owner-representative) and operations. In this light, researchers have discussed what has been a particularly thorny problem for SOE reform – extensive administrative interventions in SOE *internal* affairs (Shirk 1993; Lan 1999; Wu 1999; Zhang 2000; Brodsgaard 2002). Notable has been interference in personnel decisions and, crucially, the process of making senior executive and other management appointments. According to a study by Liu and Gao (1999) of 762 listed enterprises in 1998, it was estimated that over 90 per cent of such formerly state-owned shareholding companies had the same person as Board director and general manager.

Researchers such as Shirk (1993), Ma (1997), Wu (1999), Zhang (2000), Brodsgaard (2002) and Morris *et al.* (2002) point to a number of problematic consequences emerging from the process of transforming state enterprises into truly economic entities. First, SOE managers do not have a free rein to manage the enterprise primarily by reference to the market and market institutions, but have to consider also the political and social preferences of their 'senior supervisors'. Second, government interference involves wage-setting characterized by nationally unified grades and managerial appointments that reflect scant regard for the 'rule of law'. And third, SOEs' major investment decisions need the approval of higher authorities (with, according to an OECF (1998) report, three-quarters of state enterprises not possessing the right to make decisions on large investments or the disposal of assets: see later chapters on these issues).

Elsewhere, Xu's (2000) empirical study of 500 Chinese SOEs, champions competition, control rights and managerial and internal incentives, while Cheng's (2000) research into the 'measures suggested for enterprise' argues the case for 'professional management'. Wei (2001) has also argued that adopting professional management systems should be regarded as a 'frontier issue' for state enterprises, and that economists who emphasize property rights and corporate governance have underplayed the importance of management institutions in the firm. Wei also argues that deploying the theory of the separation of ownership and control to explain the problems of the state firm is both 'outdated and misleading', for recent theory suggests that corporate governance concerns defining the relationship between monetary capital and human resource capital rather than the relationship between owner and manager. In particular, it concerns how to establish mechanisms for improving incentives and the control of human capital. Somewhat similar sentiments are expressed in Zhang and Zhong's (2000) 36 case studies of corporate governance in modern Chinese state-enterprise management.

Lin (1997) argues similarly that because information asymmetry finds SOEs in an advantaged bargaining position with the state for subsidies (even when SOEs make losses) a crucial task of state-enterprise reform policy is to realize more effective macro- and micro-management structures. Nolan and Wang (1999) echo the point, arguing that as ownership reform went deeper in the larger SOEs, they evolved progressively from state-administered plants towards ones characterized by pluralized institutional ownership and de facto management control.

From the corporate governance perspective, He (1999) compares three different models – the private shareholder-oriented model, the manager-oriented model and the legal-person, shareholder-oriented model, and concludes that, in the Chinese case, institutional legal-person, shareholder-oriented corporate governance should be fostered and used to replace the previous version of manager-oriented administrative intervention. As for the external conditions for establishing effective corporate governance, historically missing in the SOEs' environment are a developed stock market, a robust banking system and an institutionally strong legal framework.

Zheng and Wang (2000) and reports by the OECF (1998) and the China Enterprise Federation and China's Entrepreneurs' Survey System (CEF and CESS) (2001) offer detailed evidence on the various management problems SOEs have faced, especially with regard to insufficient autonomy and inadequate incentives. The CEF and CESS (2001) survey (of 1,075 SOEs) found that nearly 75 per cent of SOE managers were appointed by government, and only 20 per cent by SOE Boards of Directors. As regards incentives, the CESS (2000) survey revealed that pay incentives for SOE managers were far inferior to those of their peers working under other types of ownership system. Both surveys conclude that lack of executive autonomy and inadequate incentives for SOE managers represent major problems for the effective reform of SOEs. Shirk (1993), Qian (1999) and Song (2000) suggest further that macro-management reform is required similarly at the state level, this to include the reformation of institutional structures, redevelopment of administrative operations, and the transformation of government functions, in ways that align more appropriately with the overall goals of economic reform and enterprise restructuring.

## Labour and employment

In Chapter 1 we suggested that there has been relatively little research examining the impact of China's SOE reform on labour and employment. Yet, it is evident that China's SOE transition has resulted in dramatic downsizing (see later chapters). A large number of surplus workers have been, and are to be, made redundant, despite the lack of an effective social safety net. Researchers working in this area (e.g. Zhu and Dowling 1994, 2000; Zhu 1995; Warner 1995a and b, 1996a–f, 1997a and b; Freund 1998; Sheehan 1998; Hassard *et al.* 1999a and b, 2002, 2005; Wu 1999; Adams 2000; Ding *et al.* 2000; Benson *et al.* 2000; Solinger 2001, 2002, 2003, 2005; Blecher 2002; Cai 2002, 2006) suggest that economic transition, including enterprise transformation, not only generates a range of impacts on labour and employment, but also that labour, in turn, has generated a range of effects on the transition process. On the one hand, the transformation of SOEs replaces lifetime employment with contract employment (Ding *et al.* 2000), consequently changing the nature, content and form of the traditional employment-related welfare system. On the other, it places enormous pressure on social stability due to the extensive redundancy programmes introduced for the purpose of reducing the high proportion of SOE surplus labour (Warner 1996a and b; Wu 1999; Ding *et al.* 2000; Zhu and Dowling 2000; Blecher 2002; Solinger 2002, 2005). The impact of unemployment resulting from SOE reform has come to the centre of the political stage as it has generated much forceful resistance to economic transition (Ding *et al.* 2000; Zhao 2001; Hassard *et al.* 2002; Cai 2002; Solinger 2002, 2005). Indeed, due to fears of such resistance and instability, in the early to mid-1990s the fundamental transformation of SOEs was consistently deferred, with state enterprises serving to cushion social upheaval until the second half of the decade (Wu 1999). The process of SOE transformation, however, inevitably impacts on issues such as labour mobility, redundancy and welfare. It is claimed that state-enterprise transformation is generating such heavy impacts on SOE workers that the twin issues of surplus labour and social security now represent the 'hard core' of Chinese economic transition. Much more will be said on these issues in later chapters.

## Conclusion

The literature on China's SOE transformation describes how China has avoided sweeping privatization and resorted instead to the gradual evolution of reform through the creation of competition and management capability. China employs its own framework for economic reform, one that is qualitatively different from conventional transition theory. Where reform policy initiatives have concerned issues of ownership divestment, rather than these being confronted during the initial stages of transition, they only began to be realized during the second half of the 1990s. In contrast, management reforms at the macro and enterprise levels and the introduction of competition played important roles in the transition process before the 1990s. This was reflected notably in encouraging the growth of the non-state sector in order to place increasing competitive pressure on the state sector (Lin *et al.* 1998; Qian 1999). As regards the impact of China's economic reforms on labour and employment, the literature notes that transformation brings in significant changes to employment relationships and the related welfare structure. It also stresses that surplus labour is now *the* 'hard core' issue of state-enterprise transformation.

# 3 Economic transformation

## Context and content

## Introduction

This chapter describes the Chinese economic reform process in terms of key aspects related to the transformation of public enterprises from 1978 to the beginning of the present century. The aim is to provide a background to contemporary fieldwork-based studies of the transformation of SOEs in later chapters. In terms of structure, first we present a basic overview of the nature and development of the Chinese economic reform programme; second, we describe the transition process, phase by phase, including a general review of key features and instruments of reform; and third, we examine the role of specific economic measures, notably in terms of pricing, financial control, fiscal and government transformation.

## Review of the economic reform process

From 'liberation' in the late 1940s to the economic reforms initiated in the late 1970s, China's economy operated under a 'socialist planned model', one largely following the Marxian model and framework of the FSU. Economic management and control was carried out by means of administrative commands that were communicated from the central bureaucracy to individual enterprises. Since state ownership was favoured over other forms of ownership, resource allocation was determined by national plans, with decision-power being highly concentrated in state administrative departments (Nolan and Dong 1990; Naughton 1995a; Leong 1997; Qian 2000). The primary forms of distribution were characterized by egalitarianism, with motivation being politically driven and relying primarily on non-material or moral encouragement (Warner 1995a and b). In economic organization, government administration was directly involved in the management and operation of enterprises, which were underwritten by the state and fulfilled various tasks assigned by it. Responsibility for profits and losses resided outside of the executive domain of enterprises, there being virtually no market or private sector to speak of in an economy characterized by low levels of efficiency (Chen 1995; Pyle 1997). By the time of Mao Zedong's death in 1976, and after an epoch characterized by a series of controversial economic experiments and social movements, including the Great Leap Forward and the Cultural Revolution, China's total factor productivity was extremely low. When Deng Xiaoping came to power in 1978, the foremost task facing him and the country was to rescue an economy close to collapse.

Under such circumstances, economic reform was initiated from late 1978 to activate the economy and improve efficiency. Initially with state ownership largely intact, a series of experiments into deregulation and autonomy were introduced. To realize a shift from a planned to a market economy, the strategic approach was of gradual, evolutionary and incremental change. The result has been a reform process viewed by many leading commentators as phenomenally successful, notably in terms of economic growth (Stiglitz 1993, 1999; Nolan 1995a, 2001, 2003; Guthrie 1999). China's average growth of real GDP per capita was 8 per cent annually between 1978 and 1999 (World Bank 2000), with 'the number of people living in absolute poverty . . . [being] . . . substantially reduced from over 250 million to about 50 million in two decades' (Qian 1999: 1).

China's economic reform began with the agricultural sector in rural areas from late 1978. Not until 1984 did the focus of reform shift to urban areas with the reform of the large industrial SOEs. The reform of the agricultural sector was mainly characterized by de-communization or decollectivization, with the Household Contract Responsibility System (HCRS) being the key mechanism to trigger reform and inspire the enthusiasm of farmers. Under the HCRS, land was still collectively or state-owned, but contracted out to individual households for use. Although the peasant class did not possess land property rights, it was empowered to work land in order to maximize profits. Based on the 'dual-track' approach (see below), significant and continual price reform largely invigorated the agricultural sector.

As we will see, subsequent phases have witnessed significant reform of fiscal and financial systems. We shall also see how one of the most difficult areas of Chinese economic reform has been that of the large industrial SOEs, notably in that their management and operations were so deeply rooted in the planned system. Although we will outline the main phases by which SOEs have been reformed, we note also that, in the beginning, reform was not based on such a determined and coherent blueprint, but, rather, was ad hoc, incremental and experimental, under the mantra of 'crossing the river by feeling for the stones'. As reform went deeper, however, theoretical principles of economics, politics and other disciplines were employed readily as the basis for guiding practice. In so doing, a major ethos of reform has been that of the 'dual-track' (Fan 1996; Lau *et al.* 2000), where the old system is allowed to continue for some time without fundamental change, while a new system is created for the purpose of eventually replacing the old one. Through the Chinese economic reform process, there is no rapid leap to free prices, or sweeping liberalization or mass privatization. Instead, gradual dual-track mechanisms have led the way. Price reform was a typical example, with the dual-track price system being employed until the early 1990s. Under this system, the enterprise could not only sell products within a certain quota at a state-planned price, but also sell those above the quota at a market price, which was potentially higher than the state price. Another example is in currency convertibility. Until 1994 there was no unified currency exchange rate; instead, two different exchange rates (the national official rate and the market rate) coexisted officially (see Zhang 1992; Wang and Wong 1998). Similarly, for large SOEs there was no significant reduction of state subsidies until relatively recently. No mass privatization was implemented either, apart from attempts to privatize small and medium-sized SOEs. As we discuss later, large SOEs, which used to play such a dominant part in the Chinese economy, are still being reformed predominantly under continuing state ownership.

The reform process, therefore, is characterized by gradual marketization, decentralization and ownership diversification. It has received support where people's living standards have been seen to increase and the Chinese economy prosper by international standards (World Bank 1996, 2000; Qian 2000; Nolan 2001). Table 3.1 illustrates the significant economic growth in terms of GDP during the two decades following the commencement of reform.

As we shall see, however, the economic reform process has not always been a smooth or painless one. In particular, the restructuring of large SOEs has been both the centrepiece of, and major headache for, the reform process. Radical downsizing has caused millions of workers to be laid-off from state enterprises annually since 1997, this accounting for approximately one third of total SOE employees. It has been argued that this sector remains a significant challenge and obstacle to further economic development (Blecher 2002; Cai 2002; Solinger 2003, 2005). From the mid-1990s, challenges have emerged from the apparently deepening contradictions of the reforms. Dramatic job reductions and deteriorating financial performance characterize many public enterprises, this serving to threaten macroeconomic and social stability and add pressure to the goal of sustainable economic growth.

*Table 3.1* China's GDP growth (1978–1999) (billion yuan; growth rate = %)

| Year | GDP | GDP growth rate | Year | GDP | GDP growth rate |
|------|------|------|------|------|------|
| 1978 | 362.41 | 11.7 | 1989 | 1690.92 | 4.1 |
| 1979 | 403.82 | 7.6 | 1990 | 1854.79 | 3.8 |
| 1980 | 451.78 | 7.8 | 1991 | 2161.78 | 9.2 |
| 1981 | 486.24 | 5.2 | 1992 | 2663.81 | 14.2 |
| 1982 | 529.47 | 9.1 | 1993 | 3463.44 | 13.5 |
| 1983 | 593.45 | 10.9 | 1994 | 4675.94 | 12.6 |
| 1984 | 717.10 | 15.2 | 1995 | 5847.81 | 10.5 |
| 1985 | 896.44 | 13.5 | 1996 | 6788.46 | 9.6 |
| 1986 | 1020.22 | 8.8 | 1997 | 7446.26 | 8.8 |
| 1987 | 1196.25 | 11.6 | 1998 | 7834.52 | 7.8 |
| 1988 | 1482.83 | 11.3 | 1999 | 8191.09 | 7.1 |

Sources: SSB (1998: 55 and 57, 2000: 23, 55 and 256); Institute for Industrial Economy of the Chinese Academy for Social Science (2000: 35)

## Key economic reforms: periods and phases

Since 1978 economic reforms have experienced two broad periods, each containing two main phases. The first period, from 1978–1992, refers to reform under continuing state ownership, mainly implemented through the CRS and thus through increased delegation, expansion of autonomy and profit retention (Chen, D. 1995; Hassard and Sheehan 1997; You 1998). The second period, from 1993 to the present, refers to reform embracing a market system, with state ownership diversification and private ownership legalized, and being implemented mainly through corporatization, shareholding and establishment of the MES (International Monetary Fund (IMF) 1993; Naughton 1995a; Qian 2000; Hassard *et al.* 2004). Despite the differences in policies and practices during these two reform periods, there has been a general political philosophy for guiding the process of lifting large loss-making SOEs out of difficulties; that is 'Zhuada Fangxiao' or 'grasping the large while releasing the small'.

### *First reform period: 1978–1992*

#### *Phase one (1978–1984)*

The first phase of reform covered the period from 1978 to 1984; that is, from the Third Plenum of the 11th Central Committee of the Chinese Communist Party (CCP) in December 1978 to the Third Plenum of the CCP's 12th Central Committee in October 1984. Reform mainly centred on the expansion of enterprise and peasants' autonomy and profit retention. This initial phase focused on the agricultural sector in rural areas, and was triggered in December 1978 by 20 peasants representing 20 households in Xiaogang Village of Fenyang County in Anhui Province spontaneously putting their fingerprints on a 'contract' to divide the then commune's land among the households. Under such a contract, they promised to fulfil the procurement quota of grain to the state, but meanwhile obtained almost all control rights over production, except for land ownership. This practice soon spread to other parts of the province and in late 1980 the HCRS was officially endorsed. By the end of 1982, 80 per cent of households across the country had adopted it, and by 1984 almost all rural households had done so (Qian 2000). Academic analysts publicized the success of the system, with Macmillan *et al.* (1989), for example, estimating that total factor productivity (TFP) in agriculture had increased 32 per cent between 1978 and 1984. Another related factor, however, was that a large amount of surplus labour began to be generated for the emerging urban industries and TVEs. The introduction of the HRCS thus dismantled the 20-year people's commune system, where every 50 or so households was a basic unit for production and distribution. This reform was viewed as the first successful reform phase in China and laid the foundations for reforms of other areas of the economy.

With regard to the state industrial sector, initial changes similarly concerned expanding the levels of autonomy and introducing profit retention for discretionary use. Such processes were witnessed initially on an experimental basis within six Sichuan state industrial enterprises in late 1978, this being extended to a total of 84 Sichuan SOEs early the following year. In July 1979, central government issued five documents promoting the Sichuan experience nationwide, but again on a strictly 'experimental' basis. By 1980, about 60 per cent of SOEs (in terms of output value) had joined the experiments and begun to exercise some limited form of autonomy (Qian 2000). In April 1981, an official document for implementing the 'Economic Responsibility System' was issued so as to introduce the system more extensively into urban industrial SOEs. However, by 1984, reform of the industrial sector had still not attained the kinds of successes demonstrated in the agricultural sector. Indeed, it was widely recognized that the reform of the state-owned industrial enterprises had seriously lagged behind. As such, the reform process moved on to a further phase, one representing a much sharper focus on the problems of urban industrial enterprises.

*Phase two (1985–1992)*

The second phase, from 1985 to 1992, saw significant reforms being promoted in urban industrial sectors, albeit that these were far more complicated and their reform much more difficult than those of rural agriculture. Encouraged by the success of agricultural reform, urban industrial enterprises undertook a similar series of price, fiscal and financial reforms. During this period dual-track market liberalization and the CRS were to be the main themes of reform.

A typical dual-track approach was seen in price reform. In 1985, the dual system of 'planned track price' and 'market track price' for industrial goods was formally put in place. Under the dual-track price system, the planned prices were initially maintained but then gradually 'relaxed' during the early 1990s. At the same time, goods produced above the planned quota were allowed to be sold at market prices.

From early 1987, the CRS was actively promoted and rapidly spread among state enterprises. Under this system, contracts based on negotiation between enterprises and relevant levels of government or government departments were established, generally for a minimum of three years. Wu (1999) notes that by the end of 1987, 78 per cent of SOEs had implemented some CRS reforms, while Parker and Pan (1996) found that by 1992 CRS reforms were being undertaken by 95 per cent of SOEs.

The CRS represented the core of SOE reform until weaknesses with the system became increasingly apparent in the early 1990s (see Chapter 5). In July 1992 the 'Regulations on Transforming the Management Mechanism of State-owned Industrial Enterprises' was issued in order to make the CRS more robust, especially regarding levels of managerial autonomy. This regulation granted enterprise managers greater 'control rights'; these covering, for example, issues of foreign trade, production, labour and wages. Despite the implementation of these control rights, however, administrative interventions from government continued to characterize state-enterprise operations and interactions.

Within this reform phase, however, there was a general retrenchment period from 1988–1992, as the economy became overheated. While such reforms were adopted to spur demand and production, a concomitant economic product was rapidly rising inflation. As by early 1988 the annual inflation rate had reached double-digit levels, a rectification programme was launched to cool the economy. The retrenchment measures succeeded in stabilizing prices, but led to a sharp economic slowdown. An increasing number of SOEs began to make significant losses and inter-enterprise arrears continually increased. Because of a range of weakness and limitations associated with the CRS, the system was deemed incompatible with the new economic environment and likely to hamper further economic reform (see Hassard *et al.* 1999b). Concerned with lack of progress on SOE reform, and centrally a perceived need to transform the operational mechanism, the concept of the 'socialist market' economy was legislated for at the 14th CCP Congress in September 1992. For the first time the establishment of a market economy was endorsed as China's reform goal, such an important ideological breakthrough marking the start of a new reform stage.

### Second reform period: 1993–present

*Phase one (1993–1997)*

In wake of legislation to promote a socialist market economy in 1992, a wide range of strategic and operational measures have been undertaken to deepen the base of economic reform. The key notion of reform is 'corporatization' and the establishment of an MES whose projected completion date is 2010. The landmark document was the 'Decision on Issues Concerning the Establishment of a Socialist Market Economic Structure' adopted by the Third Plenum of the 14th CCP Central Committee in November 1993. This decision marked four major advances in the reform strategy: creating a 'rule-based system', establishing 'market-supporting institutions', the 'clarification of property rights' and 'ownership restructuring'. This decision advocated a coherent programme and appropriate sequencing of reforms, under the mantra of 'combining (reform) package with breakthrough' (see Wu 1999).

Since the mid-1990s, reform efforts have been increasingly directed towards the consummation of a market-supporting external environment. Associated measures include the adoption of a unified foreign exchange rate and tax rates, redefinition of fiscal relations between local and central government, realization of a centralized monetary system, and the establishment of a social welfare safety net. For SOE reform, the MES was established as a guiding framework in terms of property rights, ownership divestiture,

separation of government and enterprise operations, and the professionaliza-
tion of internal management. It also signalled, for the first time, that the public
ownership of SOEs could be diversified through various forms of ownership
change, including privatization.

However, this phase saw a serious deterioration in the performance of
SOEs. By the end of 1995, a study of 302,000 SOEs (accounting for over
99 per cent of all SOEs) revealed that their total state assets amounted to
7,278 billion yuan, with total debts of 5,176 billion yuan, that is, a debt–asset
ratio of 71 per cent (*People's Daily*, 6 May 1996: 2; Gao and Yang 1999).
Moreover, of the 7,278 billion yuan worth of assets, 2,059 billion represented
land occupied by the SOEs. If this portion of the assets was discounted, then
the real state assets of China's SOEs amounted to only 5,192 billion yuan,
approximately the same as the total debts (Gao and Yang 1999).

Gao and Yang (1999) also noted that of the 302,000 SOEs investigated,
255,000 (or 84 per cent) were actually 'small' SOEs, employing 23.47 million
workers, and accounting for approximately 30 per cent of the total employees
in the SOE sector. Gao and Yang (1999) calculated the characteristics of
such small SOEs, defined as 'local' employers. Table 3.2 shows that while in
1995 small SOEs accounted for well over 90 per cent of the total number of
local SOEs, in terms of assets, debts and employees they only accounted for
around 30 per cent or so in the local state-owned economy. Gao and Yang
found that most of these small SOEs ran into losses and suggested that it was
such enterprises that hindered the development of the local economy; for by
1997 the SOE sector as a whole was, for the first time, reporting losses. Under
such circumstances, in September 1997, at the 15th CCP Congress, a new
SOE reform policy was announced: the aforementioned 'grasping the large
(SOEs) and releasing the small'. This breakthrough in reform allowed small
and medium-sized SOEs to diversify their ownership structures and, in
particular, go to the private sector.

*Phase two (1998–present)*

Since 1998 the reform process has been characterized above all else by
attempts to 'lift large loss-making SOEs out of difficulties', this phase seeing
a heavy emphasis on ownership divestment and the consummation of the
market environment. In pursuit of perfecting the MES, government policies
have continued to reflect the slogan of 'grasping the large, releasing the small',
within a period that has also seen significant reform to the Chinese banking

*Table 3.2* The share of small SOEs in the local Chinese economy (1995) (%)

| SOEs | Employees | Total assets | Total debts |
|------|-----------|--------------|-------------|
| 94.8 | 36.86 | 28.1 | 29.4 |

Source: Gao and Yang (1999)

system. The official government policy for establishing a programme for lifting large loss-making SOEs out of difficulty initially saw efforts made to rescue 4,230 loss-making SOEs within three years starting from 1998. In these enterprises, measures for tackling bad debts were implemented through debt-equity swaps beginning in 1999, this witnessing experiments with the shrinking of state-holding shares in SOEs and, thus, for the first time, a limited number of shares becoming tradeable. As such, a form of ownership that was predominantly public has since become increasingly diversified, with small and medium-sized SOEs in particular being encouraged to diversify through various economic mechanisms (see later). In the process, there has been an emphasis on the market becoming the primary mechanism for the allocation of resources. The portion of private ownership has increased rapidly while a large number of state enterprises have been allowed to go into the private sector. At the same time, reform measures have been taken to transform government functions so as to make them more compatible with a market system. The reform measures established in 1998, for example, saw the number of industrial ministries drastically reduced, many also being transformed into 'bureaux' or 'industrial associations'. However, as significant industrial restructuring, notably downsizing, has come to the centre of the reform stage, serious social and economic issues have been encountered.

## Strategic instruments of reform

A range of economic mechanisms have been employed in the process of China's economic transition and transformation. We will outline what are, perhaps, the three major mechanisms seen as essential to achieving overall economic reform – marketization and ownership diversification; decentralization; and the introduction of competition (Lau 1998, Qian 2000).

### Marketization and ownership diversification

The process of marketization is carried out mainly through the introduction of market forces/mechanisms into almost every aspect of economic activity. In China, the market was initially a supplement to the state plan but gradually has supplanted it. Prices that used to be singular and fixed by central plans have given way to market-determined prices. Now the prices of all consumer goods and more than 95 per cent of producer goods are subject to the market. In concert, labour 'markets' have also been transformed, as the state relinquishes its former responsibility for allocating jobs to people. Workers who previously enjoyed an 'iron-rice bowl' no longer have such a guaranteed job for life, as instead they increasingly face the possibility of redundancy.

The impact of ownership diversification has mainly been felt in small and medium-sized SOEs. Large-scale privatization began in 1995, with 1997 seeing further implementation of ownership change under the 'grasping the large, releasing the small' policy. One initial implication of 'grasping the large' was to keep a sub-set of around 1,000 of the largest and most strategically important enterprises state-owned (see later), but with the vast majority of small and medium-sized SOEs being allowed to go to the private sector. By the end of 1996, up to 70 per cent of small SOEs had been privatized in pioneering provinces such as Shandong, Sichnan and Guangdong, and about half were privatized in many other provinces (You 1998; Qian 2000; Hassard *et al.* 2004). By 2010, it has been estimated that the share of the state economy in GDP terms should decrease to around 25 per cent. Of the total industrial output value, the state industrial sector will amount to around 20 per cent. The main forms of ownership change include direct sale, shareholding for liability companies, stock market listing, holding companies, merger, bankruptcy, and joint-venture, with, in recent years, privatization being used principally for small SOEs. The change of ownership structure for the first two decades of reform can be seen in Table 3.3, which indicates the evolution of ownership divestment through the reform process, with the proportion of the state-owned economy continually declining.

### *Decentralization*

As noted, decision-making power in the pre-reform era was highly concentrated at central government levels. In particular, state investment and the allocation of raw materials were accomplished through the material supply system, the heart of central planning. Under economic reform, state control over investment has steadily eroded along with a radical reduction in the scope of mandatory planning. Much economic decision-making power is now delegated to the provincial and local government levels. In the late 1990s, Wang and Wong (1998: 48) offered a vivid example of this trajectory when they described how 'foreign direct investment projects of less than US$30 million can be directly approved by the provincial authorities'. Such decentralization has involved revenue sharing between central and local government in order to encourage local government to take greater control and initiative in developing the local economy. With regard to decentralization at the state enterprise level, the trajectory has been for greater autonomy to be granted in order to make enterprise managers more sensitive to key

*Table 3.3* Share of state-owned and non-state-owned economy in China (1978–1997) (%)

| | GDP | | | Employment | | | Investment | | | Industrial Output Value | | |
|---|---|---|---|---|---|---|---|---|---|---|---|---|
| Year | 1978 | 1992 | 1997 | 1978 | 1992 | 1997 | 1978 | 1992 | 1997 | 1978 | 1992 | 1997 |
| State | n/a | 44.3 | 35.8 | 78.3 | 63.2 | 54.7 | 100 | 68 | 52.5 | 77.6 | 48.1 | 25.5 |
| Non-state | n/a | 55.7 | 64.2 | 21.7 | 36.8 | 45.4 | 0 | 32 | 47.5 | 22.4 | 50 | 74.5 |

Source: SSB (various years) (also see Gao and Yang 1999: 259–260)

business needs related to profit and efficiency. Within state enterprises, managers have been granted more and more autonomy in decisions regarding product pricing, production operations, investment and labour management (such as compensation, promotion and recruitment) (Hassard *et al.* 1999b, 2004).

## The introduction of competition

Competition was actively encouraged in the Chinese economy after 1978. This was mainly embodied in the promotion of the secondary economy and private enterprises. The rationale was that legalizing the secondary economy in order to let it grow outside of the planning system was politically more expedient than deregulating the state economy itself (see Shirk 1993; Wang and Wong 1998; Qian 1999). In the main, competition was fostered through the growth of the non-state sector and opening it up to international competition, which we will discuss in more detail shortly.

## Reform outside the existing state system

Whereas in 1979 over 70 per cent of gross fixed investments were directed to the state-owned sector, by 1996 this had declined to around 50 per cent. The size of the state sector has shrunk as its proportion of the gross value of production has reduced, from nearly 80 per cent in 1978 to less than 30 per cent currently. The non-state sector has far outstripped the growth of the state sector, with the rapid acceleration of the former being largely attributed to the expansion of the TVEs. As Qian (1999: 11) described, 'between 1978 and 1993 the share of non-state enterprise increased from 22 percent to 57 percent, which happened without any privatization of the SOEs'. Similarly Wang and Wong (1998: 49) noted how 'as of 1994, TVEs accounted for almost half of the aggregate industrial output and almost two-thirds of the aggregate industrial employment of China'.

Intense competition from the non-state sector largely forced the state sector to find new methods of survival. As noted, in late 1997 the government began the more radical policy of 'Zhuada Fangxiao', with the result that the majority of previously small state enterprises were allowed to go to the private sector. The private sector thus grew from almost nil in 1979 into the largest sector in terms of retail sales (Wang and Wong 1998). As the Institute for Industrial Economy of the Chinese Academy for Social Science (IIECASS 2000: 382) confirmed:

> From 1989 to 1997, the number of private firms increased from 90,581 to 960,726 at an annual growth of 34.3%; the number of employees increased from 1.64 million to 13.49 million at an annual growth of 30.1%; the output value increased from 9.7 billion yuan to 392.3 billion yuan at an annual growth of 58.8%.

This report goes on to suggest that, by the end of 1998, 'the number of private firms was 1.2 million with total employees numbering 17 million. The output value of these private firms was 585.3 billion yuan and their sales turnover was 532.3 billion yuan' (IIECASS 2000: 437). The rapid growth of the non-state sector has thus increasingly contributed to the development of overall industrial growth (as Table 3.4 indicates), intensifying the level of competition with the state sector and representing an important impetus for building a market economy.

*Opening up to the outside world*

From the beginning of the reform movement, the Chinese government decided to 'open up' to the outside world, notably for the procurement of finance, investment and expertise. This policy has not only provided foreign capital, technology and management, but also effected intensive competition, especially international competition. To implement the opening up policy, the concept of special economic zones (SEZs) was suggested in 1979, these being established initially on an experimental basis in coastal regions during the early 1980s, then on a more national basis thereafter. The first SEZs were founded in the southern coastal region during 1980, these being at Shenzhen, Zhuhai and Shantou in Guangdong Province, and Xiamen in Fujian Province. In 1984 the process was expanded to 14 cities and 12 economic development zones in northern and middle inland regions, while the following year 51 cities and counties in the Pearl River Delta, Yangzi River Delta and Minnan Delta were set up as coastal economic development zones. The major SEZs of Hainan province and Shanghai Pudong were set up in 1988 and 1990 respectively, while in 1992 a further six cities along the Yangzi River and 13 border cities in Jilin province and the capital cities of all provinces and autonomous regions were established as open development zones or cities.

To promote foreign trade and attract investment, SEZs operated under special economic policies and provisions, such as lower tax and bank interest rates. In the 1990s, many cities which did not qualify as either SEZs or 'open cities' nevertheless established 'development zones' to enjoy tax benefits,

*Table 3.4* Contribution of the state and non-state sectors to industrial growth (1986–1996) (%)

|  | 1986 | 1990 | 1991 | 1992 | 1993 | 1994 | 1995 | 1996 |
|---|---|---|---|---|---|---|---|---|
| State sector | 35.05 | 22.90 | 31.76 | 26.47 | 10.11 | 11.39 | 13.99 | 10.95 |
| Non-state sector | 64.95 | 77.10 | 68.24 | 73.53 | 89.01 | 88.61 | 86.01 | 89.05 |

Source: (adapted from) IIECASS (2000: 383)

increased autonomy and attract domestic and foreign investment. By the end of 1998, 62,500 companies in 39 industries had been created by either foreign investors or those from Taiwan, Hong Kong and Macao. In 1998, the industrial output value of these companies was 1,775 billion yuan, accounting for 15 per cent of the total national industrial output value (IIECASS 2000: 88). Accompanying this was an enormous flow of foreign direct investment (FDI) into China. In the 1990s China received tens of billions of dollars of FDI per year, with the opening-up policy rapidly promoting foreign trade. Tables 3.5 and 3.6 show the amount of utilized foreign capital and FDI from the mid-1980s to the late 1990s, with the average annual growth rate of actually utilized foreign capital during the 1990s being around 20 per cent.

The implication from Tables 3.5 and 3.6 therefore is that 'opening-up' saw China receive considerable foreign capital which served to develop the economy enormously. Although levels of actually utilized foreign capital fluctuated along with the national economy, the influx of FDI into China remained comparatively stable throughout the 1990s.

Other benefits arising from the opening-up policy are seen in Table 3.7. Between 1978 and 1998, total import and export trade increased more than 15-fold, of which export trade grew nearly 20-fold. During the first 20 years of reform, 330,000 contracts were signed with overseas investors, with actual foreign capital utilized through these contracts and agreements amounting to US$407 billion (IIECASS 2000: 86).

Reform initiatives in line with the opening-up policy continued through-out the 1990s and into the 2000s. Notable toward the end of the 1990s was the launch in October 1999 of China's 'Western Development' campaign, which drew attention to the investment needs of some of the most under-developed regions of the country. The 'Western region' includes 11 provinces, autonomous regions and municipalities under the direct administration of central government, namely Shanxi, Qinghai, Sichuan, Yunnan, Guizhou, Ningxia, Xinjiang, Inner Mongolia, Gansu, Tibet and Chongqing. It covers 5.4 million square kilometres, or 57 per cent of the country's land, and has a population of approximately 300 million people, or 25 per cent of the total population. More than half of the country's identified natural resources are in the region. Since 2000 Beijing has empowered the Western region to attract foreign investment through granting the kinds of preferential economic policies and provisions that have long applied to coastal areas. And crucially in November 1999, a bilateral agreement was reached with the US on China's

*Table 3.5* Amount of foreign capital actually utilized (1985–1999) (US$ billion)

| Year | 1985 | 1990 | 1995 | 1998 | 1999 |
|------|------|------|------|------|------|
| Amount | 4.65 | 10.29 | 103.21 | 63.20 | 52.01 |

Source: (adapted from) IIECASS (2000)

*Table 3.6* Utilized foreign direct investment in China (1987–1998) (US$ billion)

| 1987–1992 (average) | 1993 | 1994 | 1995 | 1996 | 1997 | 1998 | 1999 |
|---|---|---|---|---|---|---|---|
| 4.65 | 27.5 | 33.8 | 38.0 | 42.3 | 45.2 | 45.6 | 40.4 |

Source: (adapted from) Jeffries (2001: 221)

*Table 3.7* China's foreign trade and foreign currency reserves (1978–1998) (US$ billion)

| Year | Total import and export | Total export | Total import | Foreign exchange reserves |
|---|---|---|---|---|
| 1978 | 20.64 | 9.75 | 10.89 | 0.84 |
| 1980 | 38.14 | 18.12 | 20.02 | –1.3 |
| 1985 | 69.6 | 27.35 | 42.25 | 2.64 |
| 1990 | 115.44 | 62.09 | 53.35 | 11.09 |
| 1994 | 236.62 | 121.01 | 115.61 | 51.62 |
| 1995 | 280.86 | 148.78 | 132.08 | 73.6 |
| 1996 | 289.88 | 151.05 | 138.83 | 105.03 |
| 1997 | 325.16 | 182.79 | 142.37 | 139.89 |
| 1998 | 323.93 | 183.76 | 140.17 | 144.96 |

Source: (adapted from) SSB (1999) and IIECASS (2000)

proposed access to the World Trade Organisation (WTO), this paving the way for subsequent accession on 11 December 2001, this finally cementing China's extensive and intensive involvement in the world economy.

## Further key reforms issues

We now examine further areas of reform relating to prices, finance/banking, taxation, investment and government transformation. These are explored in terms of their relation to SOE transformation and provide further background to fieldwork studies of SOE reform described in later chapters.

### *Price reform and the dual-track approach*

Economic experience prior to 1978 had suggested that pricing fixed (partially or wholly) by the state promoted inefficient factors of production and suboptimal use of resources. Underpricing, for example, resulted in a serious shortage of supply in both agriculture and industry, while in the service sector (in transport, housing, education and medical care) it failed to stimulate development. As a precondition for rationalizing resource allocation, price reform therefore became a key aspect of the economic reform process.

We can identify two main stages of price reform. The first was from 1978 to 1984, during which time the government used the method generally to 'stimulate the market'. State pricing departments raised the prices of commodities for which demand exceeded supply and vice versa, this promoting a trend towards more balanced planned prices for some commodities. The second stage began in 1985 with the implementation of the aforementioned dual-track pricing system. At this stage, market forces were allowed to intervene in the price formation of the means of production. The dual-track pricing system allowed the market to determine the prices of above state quota production, so that commodities of the same type could be sold at two different prices, a state price for planned output and a market price for above quota production. Within the quotas, sales and purchases were meant to be administratively directed at controlled 'low' prices. Beyond the quotas, inputs and outputs of the goods were allowed to be traded freely at higher prices. Examples are described in Table 3.8.

The most notable feature of the examples listed in Table 3.8 is the significant gap between state and second-track prices, a factor that served ultimately to move the price system from central planning towards a market orientation. However, it also drew criticism in that the process brought with it a set of unanticipated by-products, such as the manipulation of quotas, corruption and inequitable competition for resources. This system was therefore abolished in 1993, but within an economic process whereby price reform increasingly moved away from a state plan and towards being market-determined. This saw the share of the 'state mandatory' price (fixed price) continuously decline, with 'state guided' prices (floating prices) being used as a cushion to the realization of 'market prices' (free prices). In 1994 the State Planning

*Table 3.8* Examples of state and second-track prices (yuan per ton)

|  | State price | Second track price | Ratio of second-track to state price |
|---|---|---|---|
| *Milled rice (retail)* |  |  |  |
| Beijing | 400 | 2,000 | 5.0 |
| Guangzhou | 600 | 1,400 | 2.3 |
| *Producer goods* |  |  |  |
| Wire rod | 610 | 1,680 | 2.8 |
| Thin steel plate | 870 | 4,602 | 5.3 |
| Medium steel plate | 570 | 1,804 | 3.2 |
| Pig iron | 293 | 752 | 2.6 |
| Aluminium | 4,000 | 16.077 | 4.0 |
| Cement | 90 | 193 | 2.1 |
| Caustic soda | 640 | 2,986 | 4.7 |

Note: prices for rice refer to November 1989. Data for producer goods refer to December 1988, plus average prices posted in 24 provincial markets.
Source: (adapted from) Fan and Nolan (1994: 27)

Commission announced that only 4 per cent of national production would now be subject to mandatory plans (see Tables 3.9–3.11).

Other writers, notably Parker and Pan (1996) and Lardy (1994) have also discussed the general phasing-out of the state plan price. Based on their research, Table 3.12 illustrates that, prior to reform, the prices of 97 per cent of retail commodities, 94 per cent of agricultural products and all capital goods were determined by state planning. By 1993, however, as a result of pricing reform, only 5 per cent of retail commodities, 10 per cent of agricultural products and 15 per cent of capital goods, were subject to state pricing. Whereas at the beginning of the 1990s, Sun and Sun described how 'in price management, local authorities and enterprises have been given some pricing power, resulting in the replacement of the state monopoly in pricing with a

*Table 3.9* Phasing out the plan price: agricultural products (% of output value)

|  | *1978* | *1985* | *1989* | *1993* |
|---|---|---|---|---|
| Plan price | 94.4 | 37.0 | 35.5 | 10.4 |
| Guide price | 0.0 | 23.0 | 24.3 | 2.1 |
| Market price | 5.6 | 40.0 | 40.4 | 87.5 |

*Table 3.10* Phasing out the plan price: industrial goods (% of output value)

|  | *1978* | *1985* | *1989* | *1993* |
|---|---|---|---|---|
| Plan price | 100.0 | 64.0 | 60.0 | 13.8 |
| Guide price | 0.0 | 23.0 | n/a | 5.1 |
| Market price | 0.0 | 13.0 | 40.0 | 81.1 |

*Table 3.11* Phasing out the plan price: total retail sales (% of sales)

|  | *1978* | *1985* | *1989* | *1993* |
|---|---|---|---|---|
| Plan price | 97.0 | 47.0 | 31.3 | 4.8 |
| Guide price | 0.0 | 19.0 | 23.2 | 1.4 |
| Market price | 3.0 | 34.0 | 45.5 | 93.8 |

Source: (adapted from) Wang and Wong (1998: 66–67)

*Table 3.12* Share of the planned price (%)

| *Year* | *Retail commodities* | *Agricultural products* | *Capital goods* |
|---|---|---|---|
| 1978 | 97 | 94 | 100 |
| 1993 | 5 | 10 | 15 |

Source: (adapted from) Lardy (1994: 11); Parker and Pan (1996: 109)

system of pricing by the state, the enterprise and the market. This has created conditions for revitalizing enterprises and enlivening the market' (1990: 63), today the prices of the vast majority of goods are subject to market forces.

### Financial reform

Prior to 1979 China employed a single banking system that operated in concert with the central administrative structure. The People's Bank of China (PBC) was the only bank that issued currency and made working capital loans. Before 1983, the banking system served a very limited purpose in the economy, as a highly centralized planning system operated mainly through collecting revenue from state enterprises and allocating investment through budgetary grants. The PBC provided the credit needed by enterprises to implement plans for producing physical output and monitored the cash used to cover labour costs. Investments in fixed assets in SOEs were all direct transfers or grants from the government budget.

In line with economic decentralization and market-oriented reform, the banking system has subsequently been compelled to change in order to meet the requirements of a more robust financial environment. In 1983, in a significant reform, direct grants were replaced with interest-bearing loans to agriculture, construction, and production enterprises in an attempt to solve the 'soft-budget' problem. Consequently, the banking system became the primary channel through which investments were financed and the central authority exercised macroeconomic control. At the same time, the importance of budgetary expenditure in economic adjustment declined rapidly as efficient resource allocation became more closely linked to the performance of the banking sector. In the process the PBC began to act on behalf of the State Council to execute monetary control and financial administration. In particular, it took responsibility for: drawing up and implementing monetary and interest rate policies; directing and supervising banks, non-bank financial institutions and insurance companies; and examining and approving the establishment, merger and dissolution of financial institutions and insurance companies.

During the period of economic transition, banks have not tended to engage in trust, insurance or securities businesses, or invest in trust or investment companies, while securities and insurance institutions have not been involved in banking or trust business. Similarly, commercial banking has been separated from investment banking. Non-bank financial institutions, however, have begun to operate and compete with state banks for savings and loans, while foreign banks have recently been allowed to operate in China. Overall the central government has moved towards the establishment of a Western style monetary management system with indirect measures playing the key roles. Reform measures have worked toward the gradual elimination of various forms of state administrative control, including credit planning, interest rate management, and restrictions over cross-bank competition.

During the 1990s the banking system saw a wide variety of specialized banks become major channels of enterprise finance under the transition process. Under the PBC (the central bank), the major specialized banks and non-bank institutions have included, for example, the Agricultural Bank of China; Bank of China; People's Construction Bank of China; Industrial and Commercial Bank of China; The Bank of Communications; Long-term Development and Credit Bank; Import-Export Bank; Agricultural Development Bank; Rural Credit Cooperatives; Urban Credit Cooperatives; and other small regional banks. This restructuring of the banking sector was based on the belief that a decentralized system would operate more efficiently. Each of these financial institutions, especially the major commercial banks, was to serve a designated sector in the economy. Such an approach would prevent undue competition among the banking institutions and require prospective customers – peasants, industrial enterprises, and trade or foreign-invested companies – to deal with a single institution. Each of the specialized commercial banks would pursue its own targets, operate in its assigned business area and observe the regulations set by central government and the central bank (especially the priorities and criteria set out for making loans).

Such reforms prompted the Chinese banking sector to expand from working capital provision into fixed asset investment credit. With the promotion of financial markets and their associated instruments (e.g. commercial bills, bonds, stocks, shares) China began to develop allied institutions such as inter-bank, bond and stock markets. In 1990 the Shanghai Stock Exchange was established, with Shenzen being founded the year after. By October 1998, there were, respectively, 430 and 405 companies listed on these exchanges (Zhang and Zhong 2000). In 1995 China's first private shareholding bank, Minsheng Bank, was approved by the State Council and the PBC. The specific purpose of this bank was to lend to small businesses in both the collective and private sectors. By the end of 1997, there were:

> 3,500 urban credit cooperatives, 48,586 independent accounting rural credit cooperatives, 60,996 non-independent accounting branches of credit cooperatives, 244 trust and investment companies, 90 bond companies, 72 financial corporations of group companies, 3 foreign financial corporations, 4 sino-joint financial corporations and 6 Chinese offices of foreign financial corporations.
>
> (Wu 1999: 272–273)

Since the mid-1990s the government has initiated a series of liberalization programmes in an attempt to shift towards a system of indirect monetary control and efficient financial supervision. An important document with respect to such banking reform was the 'Decision on the Reform of the Financial System' passed in December 1993. This was ostensibly a blueprint for the establishment of a modern commercial banking system. The reform measures were to include the complete elimination of the credit plan, the relaxation of control over the scope of bank business and interest rates, separation of commercial from policy lending, and the use of indirect monetary control (Lardy 1998; Wu 1999).

Further reform measures followed in the second half of the 1990s. In 1995, the Commercial Bank Law, a milestone in banking regulation, was enacted, which provided greater autonomy to banks and required the maintenance of an 8 per cent capital adequacy ratio. In 1996, the government implemented money supply control methods, reduced deposit interest rates, and planned the phasing-out of the quota system for credit and loans. In November 1997 at the 'National Financial Work' conference, decisions were taken to establish market-supporting financial institutions and regulating/monitoring systems within approximately three years. In 1998, banking reforms included reform- ing the PBC itself (namely, downsizing and restructuring) and making the central bank the only institution supervising and controlling all other financial institutions as well as regulating monetary policies. The Securities Law was stipulated in December 1998 and came into effect in July 1999, constituting another landmark for financial supervision. Also in the late 1990s several high-profile banks and investment companies closed or went bankrupt, including the Hainan Development Bank and the Guangdong International Trust Investment Company (GITIC). GITIC was the first bankruptcy of a financial institution in Communist China's almost 50-year history. These failures represented a strong signal that the government was determined to discipline state financial institutions.

Indeed, in 1999 four asset management corporations (AMCs) were estab- lished in order to speed up bank restructuring and the enforcement of debt-equity swaps with SOEs and state banks. By July 2000, AMCs had purchased over RMB1 trillion (US$133 billion) of non-performing loans (NPLs), accounting for about 60 per cent of the total NPLs in the system. The AMCs funded this initially with capital injected by the Ministry of Finance, with central bank credit and bonds being issued with a government guarantee. Some of the SOEs' bad debts were swapped into equity of their sub-companies (see later), and the AMCs therefore became the owners of these companies. The objective was that through their new ownership rights, the AMCs would be able to restructure some of these loss-making SOEs and thus halt the state banks' practice of 'pouring household savings into the SOE black hole' (Chi 2000). All these reforms were expected to contribute significantly to a more efficient allocation of financial resources and the supervision of financial business.

During the period of economic reform, however, the financial sector has often displayed relatively low levels of efficiency, especially in relation to the distribution of loan funds. While profitable enterprises have often faced fund shortages, loss-making enterprises have expected to receive significant credit support. Liberalization of the banking system has not automatically ensured the stability of the financial system, which is crucial to the stability of the economic environment overall.

The relaxation of banking control in China, in fact, created serious macroeconomic problems in 1992–1993, when many banks and their affiliated non-bank financial institutions poured resources into imprudent activities, notably speculations in the real estate and stock markets (Ma 1997; Lardy 1998). The increasing share of NPLs in banks' total outstanding loans, and the increasing share of household deposits in their total liabilities, created pressure for banks to consider the quality of their assets and the liquidity risks involved. With virtually all banks in China during the 1990s being state-owned, it was suggested that 'a high degree of state ownership is not only associated with poor lending decisions but also frequently is accompanied by overstaffing, overdevelopment of branch networks, and other practices that contribute to relatively high operating costs' (Lardy 1998: 16–17). The lack of legal infrastructure and incentives suggested that the AMCs alone would not be able to solve the problems of the banking sector. Lardy (1998: 181) cautioned that 'recapitalizing the banks will be a waste of fiscal resources if the enterprise sector is not simultaneously subject to hard budget constraints'.

It can be argued similarly that the creation of specialized banks led to the formation of a series of bank monopolies, and that the increase in the magnitude of the banking sector proved to be no substitute for its greater liberalization, which would foster competition among banks, reduce the costs of intermediation, and facilitate a more efficient allocation of credit. Indeed, the government's involvement during the 1990s was still perhaps too great, especially in areas such as credit planning, interest control, and the restriction of non-state-owned bank activities.

Because of their state-owned and virtually monopolistic form, during the reform period banks have tended to be slow in improving their facilities and services. This is perhaps not too surprising given that banks have been able to count on the 'automatic' deposits of enterprises to which low interest rates are paid. As enterprises had little say in choosing their banking provider, deposits did not flow elsewhere, even though banking services may have been poor. It must be remembered that banks have frequently been in a position of fund supplier and thus responsible for the survival of the enterprises holding accounts with them. The enterprises, in turn, have depended on their banks, for when an enterprise runs into trouble, or makes significant losses, the choices are that its bank supports it, it accumulates debts, or it collapses. Since banks have not taken ultimate responsibility for their loans, the dangers of bad loans have, therefore, often been largely ignored. This is one crucial reason why bad debts, especially the 'triangular' debts of the state enterprises, have mounted.

Frequently SOEs, as major borrowers of the state banks, have acted as if there was no need to repay bank loans, given that SOEs and the banks were both state-owned. Commentators have noted how SOEs have often been loathe to repay loans even if they could, in the expectation that the bank would eventually write-off the debt. Another reason is that during the transition period SOEs have had to house some portion of surplus labour and provide social welfare as a cushion of social stability. According to Lardy (1998: 118), 'enforcing hard budget constraints on state enterprises makes little sense if they are not first relieved of the burden of providing a broad range of social services'. In 1993, 1994, 1995 and 1998 the government reported write-offs of 3.6 billion, 1.7 billion, 1.6 billion and 4.0 billion yuan respectively for bad and non-performing debts of key enterprises and key industries (Lardy 1998).

Clearly, as China liberalizes its banking sector by commercializing state banks and introducing more competition among banks, it must establish robust financial regulations to prevent instability in the financial sector. As commentators have suggested, a system of prudent and protective regulations is required to ensure the future stability of the banking system.

## Fiscal reform

Fiscal reform has been one of China's most important reform areas. In the reform era the traditional revenue remittance system has been largely replaced by a tax system which, in many respects, resembles a generic Western model. This has *inter alia* allowed enterprises to compete on a more equal footing, reduced the scope of government involvement in the productive sector, and decentralized the fiscal management system by granting localities greater flexibility in collecting revenues and making expenditure decisions.

### Reform of central–local government fiscal relations

Before 1980, China's fiscal system was characterized by centralized revenue collection and fiscal transfers; that is, all taxes and profits were remitted to the central government and then transferred back to the provinces according to expenditure needs approved by the centre. Since the early 1980s, however, central-provincial fiscal relations have undergone three major reform phases. In 1980, the highly centralized system was changed into a revenue-sharing system in which the central and provincial governments began to 'eat in separate kitchens'. There were three basic types of revenue under this reformed fiscal system: 'central-fixed revenues' (or revenues/taxes that accrue to the centre); 'local-fixed revenues' (or revenues/taxes that accrue to the localities); and 'shared revenues' (or revenues/taxes shared between the centre and the localities). During the period 1980–1984, about 80 per cent of the shared revenues were remitted to the central government with the remainder being retained by local governments. Almost all revenues, except for a few minor central-fixed revenues, were collected by the local finance bureaux, but with the bases and rates of all taxes, whether shared or fixed, being determined by central government.

Although some localities became more enthusiastic about collecting revenues during the 1980–1984 period, an undesirable by-product of the uniform sharing formula was the creation of surpluses in wealthy provinces and deficits in poor ones. In 1985, the State Council redesigned the revenue-sharing arrangements by varying schedules according to localities' budget balances in the previous years. The central government allowed financially weak regions to retain more revenue, while maintaining a tight grip on regions that were the most important sources of central revenue, including Shanghai, Beijing, Tianjin, Liaoning, Jiangsu and Zhejiang. Revenues from these regions generally grew more slowly than the national average, since the high share of remittance dampened local enthusiasm for expanding the tax base.

This situation was largely mitigated in 1988 by the State Council's development of a new set of central-provincial revenue sharing methods, which included special conditions for such provinces. The 1988 Fiscal Contract Responsibility System (FCRS) increased the general revenue share retained by the localities, but particularly so for those that were major contributors to central government revenue. These contracts, however, were not strictly adhered to and were revised repeatedly for some regions. In 1991, when the FCRS was due to expire, the central government was unable to negotiate a satisfactory replacement. As a result the system was extended until the end of 1993, with limited modifications on revenue-sharing ratios and quotas.

Since 1978, both total government revenue as a percentage of GNP and the share of central government revenue in total government revenue have declined rapidly. From 1978 to 1993, the ratio of total government revenue to GNP declined from about 32 to 14 per cent, with central government's share, after revenue-sharing, declining from 51 to 37 per cent. Since the late 1980s, central government has been increasingly concerned with the potential political and economic consequences of its weakening fiscal power, and has repeatedly expressed its intention to increase both the government revenue/ GNP ratio and the ratio of central government revenue to total government revenue. Although this proposal was written into the 8th Five Year Plan (1991–1995), the decline of these two ratios continued between 1990 and 1993. In an attempt to raise the two ratios, as well as to strengthen central government's ability to deploy tax and expenditure policy instruments, the central government decided in late 1993 to replace the FCRS with the 'tax assignment system'.

After the 1993 tax assignment reform, the central-fixed taxes were mainly to include: customs duties; a value added tax (VAT); income tax on centrally owned state enterprises; turnover taxes (on railways, banks and insurance companies); and income taxes from financial institutions set up by the headquarters of the PBC. In contrast, taxes collected by local governments (i.e. the local-fixed taxes) were mainly to include business tax (except for turnover taxes of banks, railways and insurance companies), income tax of locally owned state enterprises, and personal income tax. The shared taxes were mainly to include VAT, securities trading tax and natural resources tax. The plan was to divide VAT revenue 75 per cent to central government and 25 per cent to local government, with securities trading tax to be collected only in Shanghai and Shenzhen in the form of a stamp duty that would be divided 50:50 between central and local coffers, and with the large proportion of the natural resources tax to be held by local governments in the short term.

One of the major differences between the new and old systems was that, instead of letting the localities collect virtually all taxes, the central government was to set up its own agency, the National Tax Service, to gather both the central-fixed taxes and shared taxes. The Local Tax Service would collect only the local-fixed taxes. It was stated as an objective of this reform that the centre would gradually control over 60 per cent of total revenue, of which about 40 per cent would relate to central government expenditure, with the remaining 20 per cent being allocated to local governments through central government grants.

While the 1993 tax assignment system reforms introduced more trans- parency and stability to the revenue-sharing system, in the years that followed many elements of the old system remained. The centre had agreed for such reform to be carried out in a gradual, progressive fashion in order to appease those provinces whose local governments strongly opposed the changes. As a result, the revenue-sharing formula under the new system was designed so that a province would retain no less revenue than it did in 1993. The retained revenue of a province in 1993 would be used as the basis for calculating the amount of shared revenues returned from the central government to the local governments after 1994. The centre would thus increase its share of total government revenue only from the increase in shared revenues, mainly from VAT. To win the support of local governments, the centre also promised to allow the tax exemptions approved by provincial governments to continue and not to shift new expenditure responsibilities to the localities.

*Enterprise taxation before 1994*

Prior to 1978, fiscal policy played a very limited role in macroeconomic management. Its main function was to allocate budgetary resources to sectors and enterprises in order to fulfil the state-set production plan. SOEs remitted almost all their profits to the government and received investment support from the government through the budgetary channel. As the government raised revenue through profit remittances from SOEs, there were no personal or enterprise income taxes and thus no significant tax policies.

In 1979, the government introduced the profit retention system, under which SOEs were allowed to retain a portion of their profits. The chief objective of this reform was to provide incentives for enterprises to increase profits. However, the system was not standardized, as each SOE had to negotiate its revenue retention rate with its supervisory government agency (normally the industrial bureau). Moreover, the government frequently revised retention rates according to the actual profits of the SOEs, thereby penalizing those of high performance. In 1983–1984, the profit retention system was replaced by a system in which all SOEs paid standard income taxes according to the tax law. At the same time, the depreciation funds of SOEs were separated from the government budget and placed under enterprise control.

The uniform enterprise income tax system introduced in 1983–1984 was criticized, however, for creating an unequal distribution of retained profits across enterprises. Complaints were heard from SOEs with a large number of retirees, those receiving little capital investment from the state, and those subject to government price controls. As such, in 1988 the SOE income tax system was replaced by the CRS, under which SOEs remitted a certain amount or percentage of their profits to the government based on individually negotiated contracts. Many scholars correctly pointed out that the CRS closely resembled the profit retention system applied during 1970–1984, in the sense that the profit-sharing schemes under both regimes were based on ad hoc, one-to-one negotiations.

In addition to profit remittance under the CRS, SOEs were also subject to 'income adjustment tax', special levies on profits, and a number of turnover taxes. The income adjustment tax was designed to reduce the gap in per capita after-tax profits across enterprises by correcting the profit differentials created by initial conditions and government policies (e.g. initial state investment in the firm, location and degree of price control). By design, the rate of the adjustment tax negotiated between each SOE and the government was highly discretionary and differentiated. The state enterprises therefore bargained energetically with their line ministries to obtain favourable terms on this tax (see Chapter 5).

Another major problem of the enterprise tax system before 1994 was that different types of enterprises were taxed at different rates. For example, profits of large and medium SOEs were taxed at the notional rate of 55 per cent; collectively owned enterprises were taxed according to a progressive rate structure; and foreign invested companies were taxed at 33 per cent, except in SEZs and coastal open cities. In addition, there were numerous conditions under which an enterprise could be exempted from taxation or enjoy reduced tax rates.

*The 1994 tax reform*

There were three major problems with the tax system before 1994. First, it failed to provide incentives for enterprises to increase their tax bases (together with several other factors discussed later in this chapter, this led to a decline in the revenue/GNP ratio from about 35 per cent in 1978 to 13 per cent in 1993). Second, tax burdens were distributed unequally across enterprises based on the form of ownership. And third, there were as many as 37 separate taxes, many of which overlapped and sometimes contradicted each other.

To address these problems, the government launched a major tax reform in 1994. As noted, this reform introduced a clear distinction between national and local taxes and established a national tax bureau and local tax bureau, with each responsible for its own tax collection. This tax reform made it very difficult for local governments to reduce national taxes as they did in the past (see Qian 2000; Ma 1997). The main changes introduced in the 1994 tax reform can be summarized as follows:

1   *Turnover taxes.* The previous system of turnover taxes included VAT, product tax and business tax. The 1994 reform substantially broadened the coverage of VAT, which now applied to all manufacturing, wholesale and retail enterprises, regardless of whether they were domestic, foreign-owned or joint-venture. For most products the VAT rate became 17 per cent, a rate higher than those applied before, and was collected on the basis of the product's origin, unlike the consumption-based VAT applied in many Western countries. VAT became the single largest source of government revenue, accounting for 42 per cent of total government revenue in 1994. A business tax of 3 to 5 per cent was applied to services other than retail and wholesale businesses (such as entertainment, food, insurance, financial and transport services) and to real estate sales. The 1994 reform also included a consumption tax, which applied to a small number of consumer goods (such as alcohol and tobacco). When the new tax system was introduced, the product tax and the industry and commerce tax assessed on foreign-invested enterprises were abolished.

2   *Enterprise income tax.* The tax reform cut income tax rates for large and medium-sized SOEs from 55 per cent to a uniform 33 per cent. This rate now applied to all types of enterprises regardless of ownership. The proportional 33 per cent included a 30 per cent national tax and a 3 per cent local surcharge. The latter was designed to be applied flexibly by the localities. At the same time, the income adjustment tax and mandatory contributions to various funds formerly levied on SOEs (including 'the state energy and transportation construction fund' and 'the state budget adjustment fund') were abolished.

3   *Personal income tax.* The 'personal income adjustment tax' which applied to individuals, and the 'tax on private businesses in urban and rural areas' which applied to privately owned businesses, were replaced in 1994 with 'personal income tax'. A uniform personal income tax was now applied to Chinese workers, with deductions allowable for foreigners. A progressive rate from 5 to 45 per cent was applied to income from wages and salaries, and one from 5 to 35 per cent to income from the business activities of private manufacturers and merchants and to subcontracting and rental income. A 20 per cent flat rate was applied to income from publications, remuneration for services, patents and copyrights, interest and dividends, rental and transfer of assets, and other sources.

## Investment reform

In China the term 'investment' refers specifically to investment in fixed assets made by direct financial allocation. Prior to reform, there existed a weak investment system which was directly administered and planned by government. Under this system, the direct financial allocation by the state did not have to be repaid. Over 70 per cent of fixed investments flowed into the state sector, predominantly the SOEs. Through reform, China has abandoned such heavy reliance on budgetary financing of investment. Investment, particularly in the state sector, is now financed primarily through banks; that is, after the 'bank loans for budgetary grants' (*Bo Gai Dai*) and 'investment for loans' (*Dai Gai Tou*) reforms. By the end of the last century, such investment in the state sector had declined to around 50 per cent; the investment structure by ownership (1979–1999) is described in Table 3.13.

Several steps were taken to reform the nature of the investment system. State budget investment changed to the form of credit rather than direct allocation. The major proportion of capital for enterprise fixed assets came from loans and the state stopped the funding of working capital. Subsidies directed at the public enterprises were substantial, and many of them were used to rescue loss-making state enterprises in the 1990s. In 1994, the subsidies absorbed by the SOEs amounted to 1.5 per cent of GDP, with the effect that such imbalance crowded-out investment in the non-state enterprises. At the industrial and enterprise levels, it can be argued that irrational investment still exists. While reinforcement of local autonomy since the 1990s has encouraged many regions to make active investments in order to survive, many investments have been seemingly excessive or even duplicated. Considering the situation in, for example, the bicycle, motorcycle, VCD player and beer brewing industries, where small enterprise networks are often extremely confused, there has been a history of irrational investment by local SOEs, in particular, paying little attention to economies of scale.

Problems have also arisen from the fact that the partially reformed financial system still largely functions through state-owned banks and institutions, with the latter frequently displaying an inability to allocate capital efficiently. Another shortcoming of the system is that, under state ownership, it involves

*Table 3.13* Investment structure in fixed assets by ownership (1979–1999) (%)

|                  | 1979 | 1985 | 1990 | 1995 | 1996 | 1999 |
|------------------|------|------|------|------|------|------|
| State-owned      | 72   | 66.1 | 65.6 | 54.4 | 52.5 | 53.4 |
| Collective-owned | n/a  | 12.9 | 11.9 | 16.4 | 15.9 | 14.5 |
| Individual       |      | 21.0 | 22.5 | 12.8 | 14.0 | 14.1 |
| Joint-owned      |      |      |      | 0.6  | 0.6  | n/a  |
| Shareholding     |      |      |      | 4.3  | 4.5  | n/a  |
| Others           |      |      |      | 11.5 | 12.5 | 18.0 |

Source: (adapted from) SSB (1997: 32; 2000: 168)

*Table 3.14* Allocation of investment by ownership in fixed assets (1980–1996) (%)

| Year | State | Foreign-funded | Shareholding | Collective | Individual |
|------|-------|----------------|--------------|------------|------------|
| 1980 | 82 | – | – | 5 | 13 |
| 1981 | 69 | – | – | 12 | 19 |
| 1982 | 69 | – | – | 14 | 17 |
| 1983 | 67 | – | – | 11 | 23 |
| 1984 | 65 | – | – | 13 | 22 |
| 1985 | 66 | – | – | 13 | 21 |
| 1986 | 66 | – | – | 13 | 22 |
| 1987 | 63 | – | – | 15 | 22 |
| 1988 | 61 | – | – | 16 | 23 |
| 1989 | 61 | – | – | 14 | 25 |
| 1990 | 66 | – | – | 12 | 22 |
| 1991 | 66 | – | – | 13 | 21 |
| 1992 | 67 | – | – | 17 | 16 |
| 1993 | 61 | 6 | 2 | 18 | 12 |
| 1994 | 57 | 10 | 3 | 18 | 12 |
| 1995 | 54 | 11 | 4 | 16 | 13 |
| 1996 | 53 | 12 | 5 | 16 | 14 |

Source: Lardy (1998: 29)

the build-up of enormous liability to households, the source of the savings that the banks have channelled to SOEs. Besides, the policy of setting high growth rates by both central and local governments has, to a large extent, caused investment fever and led to a spate of duplicate investments. Such overinvestment almost certainly raises production costs for many firms and worsens the situation of resource allocation as well as industrial structure. (Table 3.14 illustrates the allocation of investment by ownership between 1980 and 1996, with the future investment trend being notable from 1992 onwards.)

## Government transformation

Although the transformation of government administrative structures generally accompanies economic transition, in the Chinese case the basic bureaucratic system, established in the planning era, has remained intact, despite several rounds of reform being proposed. Major reforms of government administrative structures were suggested in 1982, 1988, 1993 and 1998, the common feature being institutional reorganization. However, the context of such transformation has seen the activities of state interest groups, whose primary purpose is to supervise the development of public enterprises, often serve to frustrate the separation of government and enterprise operations (see later chapters). In contrast to the directions of official policy, their activities are frequently seen as incompatible with the objectives and requirements of market-driven reform.

## The 1982 reform

In 1982, the first organizational reform of the government administrative apparatus was launched to 'reduce redundant staff' and 'employ younger cadres'. In so doing, the number of ministries and departmental committees subordinate to the State Council was to be cut from 100 to 60. Official statistics for 38 ministries and committees showed that the number of ministers/vice ministers, directors/deputy directors of departments decreased by 67 per cent and the average age of the staff was lowered from 64 to 58 years old. However, the reform was mainly centred around the abolition or merging of organizations, while other aspects of the administrative system, especially the functions of government departments, were not transformed according to the needs of market-oriented economic reform. Indeed, by 1988, the number of departments under the direct control of the State Council (previously reduced from 100 to 60) had actually increased to 72 (Gao and Yang 1999).

## The 1988 reform

Conscious of the need for more considered government transformation, in 1988 the 7th National People's Congress adopted a second organizational reform proposal, one designed to restructure the ministries and commissions of the State Council in line with the objectives of gradual economic restructuring. Heeding lessons from the previous reform phase, the task of transforming government functions was set out more realistically. During this round, the number of units subordinate to the State Council was to be reduced from 72 to 68, with such reform not being carried out hastily, but based on a series of local government experiments across China. In the process approximately 50 per cent of departments had their functions expanded, while the remaining 50 per cent were streamlined. The process did not simply merge organizations or reduce staff, for the objective was to change the administrative functions of the Party and to redefine the relationship between government departments.

## The 1993 reform

The 1993 wave of government reform was aimed at reappraising the role of the state in society. This round was to be more radical, the objective being to produce a more streamlined and efficient administrative system. In the process, the number of ministries, commissions and immediate subordinate organs under the State Council was to be reduced from 68 to 50. In addition, the number of non-permanent bodies of the State Council was to be cut from 85 to 29. In concert, the departmental bodies of various ministries and commissions under the State Council were cut (by 8 per cent) and a large number of civil servants made redundant. Governments at provincial level reduced their departments to less than 20, resulting in a workforce discount of approximately 30 per cent, while the city governments of Beijing, Tianjin and Shanghai cut their departments to less than 30, with a resulting headcount reduction of 34 per cent (Jiang 1997). Governments at both provincial and city levels thus had far fewer departments, with a significant proportion of staff working at various levels being made redundant.

In the wake of the 1993 government reform, the 'three fixes formula' (*'ding zhineng, ding jigou, ding bianzhi'*) was established; that is, the fixing of functional structure, internal organization/institutions, and headcount. Most departments in charge of economic administration were restructured or merged, but no longer as government administrative bodies. The functions of key economic organs, such as the State Planning Commission, the State Economic and Trade Commission, the Ministry of Finance and the People's Bank, were redefined, specialized and professionalized. Such reform strengthened the state's ability to utilize macro-regulatory leverages such as prices, taxation, finance and fiscal administration. Streamlined relationships, slimmer administration and improved work procedures, thus helped to promote increased government efficiency. Importantly, this reform was carried out in line with the transformation of enterprise mechanisms and the development of the market system. It marked a step change in the transformation of government functions.

However, despite the above reforms, the transformation of government was far from compatible with the developmental needs and promotion of markets. Too many economic departments performed specialized government functions rather than those associated with truly economic institutions and entities. As such, further reform was required to improve government functions relating to macro-regulation and supervision, indirect administration, and the general departure from micro-management.

*The 1998 reform*

The 15th CCP Congress in September 1997 made strong signals for the continuing reform of government institutions. Subsequently, in March 1998 'The Scheme for Reforming the State Council' was approved at the 9th National People's Congress. The principles of this reform were to transform government functions according to the requirements of the socialist market economy. This would see the separation of government and enterprise activities, restructuring of government organization by reinforcing macroeconomic regulation and control, strengthening of the legal system and social services, and readjustment and reduction of specialized economic departments.

Under this reform, the number of ministries and commissions subordinate to the State Council, except for the General Office, would be trimmed from 40 to 29, and the 33,000 staff working at these ministries and departments reduced by approximately 50 per cent. This task was to be accomplished by the end of 1998 (Gao and Yang 1999). By following the 'three fixes formula' organizations could be merged, removed, down-graded or even established.

Some major ministries (including those of coal, textiles, chemicals, metallurgy, domestic trade, industrial machinery and light industry) were down-graded into bureaux subordinate to the State Economic and Trade Commission (whose main responsibility was now industrial regulation, not direct enterprise management) while those newly established numbered among them the Information Industry Ministry and the Labour and Social Security Ministry (Gao and Yang 1999).

Similar reform was undertaken at local government level. From province to city and county levels, the reduction rate in terms of numbers of organizations and headcount was approximately 50 per cent, with the total number of civil servants being reduced to around 4 million (Qian 2000). Unlike previous reforms, where redundant civil servants were frequently moved from one government department to another, this time all redundant staff were required to be 'removed completely from an organization of the ministry', thus 'clearing out their offices and removing their names from the payroll' (Gao and Yang 1999). This administrative reform was the largest and most radical since the founding of the People's Republic of China in 1949. Through such reform, the relationship between central and local government was qualitatively redefined. Central government would be responsible for policy-making, macro-regulation and control, while local government would focus on policy implementation and the provision of social services.

In terms of the relationship between government and enterprise, this would be redefined in the following ways: the government would own the creditor's equity according to its capital inputs in the enterprises, assign special auditors for the enterprises to monitor capital operations and profits/losses, and be in charge of the appraisal and appointment of major leaders/managers of the enterprises. Enterprises, on the other hand, would operate in a largely autonomous fashion (in line with laws and government rules), be responsible for profits and losses, and pay taxes according to tax regulations. Enterprises would thus be responsible for maintaining the value of, and adding value to, state-owned assets, and not impairing the creditor's equity.

## Conclusion

Since China embarked on the reform of its economic system in 1978, a number of significant reforms have been introduced to change the ways in which the traditional central-planning economy operates, these being aimed ultimately at the establishment of a 'socialist market' economy. Over the last quarter of a century the reform process has led to dramatic improvements in economic efficiency. The adopted style of 'gradual' rather than 'shock therapy' reform has generally been viewed as successful by international standards. Overall the reforms have displayed the following characteristics.

First, the approach to reform, as a whole, was gradual, evolutionary and incremental. New reform policies tended to be adopted initially on an experimental 'trial-and-error' basis, with measures being piloted in one or more selected sectors or areas. If a measure or policy was deemed practicable then it was disseminated on a larger or even nationwide scale, sector by sector or region by region (often from coastal to inland). Such economic reform was first initiated in the agricultural sector, with the HCRS being at the heart of the process. Based on the successful experience of the agricultural sector, the reform process then moved to the industrial sector in urban areas. Like in agriculture, the CRS for enterprises became widely implemented in Chinese industry. A key feature of this phase of reform was the 'dual-track pricing system', a gradualist method adopted in the transition to a market-based economy.

Second, direct and mass privatization of public enterprises has not played a significant role in China's economic reform. Rather, management contracting, corporatization, shareholding and gradual ownership diversification have marked the transformation process. A distinctive feature of China's reform process has been its retention of public ownership as an ideological philosophy. Because radical reform of the state sector was perceived to be politically sensitive, a strategy of reforming out of the established system was adopted to offset any potential for political and social instability. However, the subsequent 'releasing' of small SOEs generated a wider spirit of privatization, albeit one subject to various political constraints.

Third, the introduction of competition has been achieved largely by encouraging the non-state sector (collective and private elements) and the 'partial' opening of SOEs to external competition. The recipient of enormous support under the reform process, the non-state sector has served to boost the market economy. As such, TVEs, collective-owned enterprises (COEs) and foreign or foreign joint-venture enterprises have all proliferated rapidly during the process. The non-state sector has become a major contributor to economic growth and also provided intense competition to the state sector. During the early–mid-1990s, the growth rate of TVE and COE TFP was two to three times that of state enterprises. Since then the share of the non-state sector in the total gross value of industrial output has increased further. Moreover, the process of 'opening-up' to international competition has seen China become one of the most successful nations for attracting FDI. This has promoted the adoption of advanced technology and international management practices and institutions.

In sum it can be argued that the basic components of the Chinese reform process since 1978 have consisted of: (i) devolving greater levels of authority to local governments and state enterprises; (ii) deploying instruments for revenue sharing, profit retention and tax-for-profit to increase efficiency; and (iii) promoting marketization through introducing market forces philosophies and mechanisms for deregulation. Originating in the agricultural sector, the reform process spread to the industrial sector and urban areas, and currently emphasizes the comprehensive restructuring of China's economy. However, the transformation road from central planning to a market economy has not always been a smooth one. Many problems remain unresolved and new challenges emerge as the process enters advanced stages of transition. The transformation of public enterprises, in particular, represents one of the thorniest problems for the state, notably in terms of how to deal with the many social issues related to making large numbers of state-enterprise workers redundant.

# 4 Reforming China's state enterprises

## Introduction

We have noted that from the establishment of the People's Republic of China in 1949 China basically adopted a Soviet style of socialism. As such China's SOEs subsequently reflected the Soviet model of industrial organization. By the end of the 1950s, private firms had been largely eliminated in favour of SOEs and collectives, with, in the decades that followed, public ownership being the prevalent form of the economy. Prior to economic reform, it was the government that set plans and targets for SOE production, allocated resources, appointed managers and arranged investment. In other words, SOEs were owned, run and funded by the government; they were not responsible for either profits or losses. By reference to published statistical data, this chapter explores the nature, development and reform of China's SOEs and, in particular, analyses their: size and structure; economic and social roles; industrial performance; management systems; and impact on labour. In so doing we examine some of the generic economic reform themes identified in Chapter 3 but with specific reference to the restructuring of urban industrial state enterprises.

## SOE size and structure

By the end of 1995 China had 305,000 SOEs (excluding 24,000 financial enterprises) of which 87,900 were 'independent accounting industrial SOEs'. Of these 87,900 enterprises, which accounted for 62 per cent of the total assets of industrial enterprises, 15,700 were 'large and medium-sized' industrial SOEs, while 72,200 were classified as 'small' in terms of the State Statistical Bureau of China (SSB) 1995 standard (see Gao and Yang 1999; also Liu and Gao 1999; Wu 1999).

At this time, the total assets of the 305,000 SOEs was only 7,472 billion yuan (equivalent to US$900+ billion) of which non production assets (e.g. houses, schools and hospitals) accounted for around 20 per cent. The published statistical data suggest that state assets were widely scattered among state enterprises (Wu 1999). According to Liu and Gao (1999: 67) the total debts of SOEs amounted to 5,176 billion yuan (equivalent to US$600+ billion), with the average ratio of debts to assets being 69.27 per cent.

Of the total population of industrial SOEs, large enterprises accounted for 5 per cent, medium-sized enterprises for 13 per cent, and small enterprises for 82 per cent (Liu and Gao 1999). Reports by both the SSB (1996: see Gao and Yang 1999) and OECF (1998) indicated that most of the state industrial enterprises were in mining and manufacturing industries. According to the SSB (1996) report, the number of mining and manufacturing SOEs was 69,500, of which the number of medium-sized to large SOEs was 14,800. The report indicates that the total assets of these enterprises were about US$600 billion. The SSB (1996, 2000) reports also suggested that, under the reform process, the total number of state-owned industrial enterprises continually decreased through the 1990s. As Table 4.1 indicates, between 1991 and 1999 the number of industrial SOEs decreased by 40 per cent or so, from 104,700 in 1991 to 61,300 in 1999.

According to the SSB (1995) report, industries of which the state owned 100 per cent of the assets included post, airline, railway and defence; those of which the state owned 90 per cent or above included petroleum (95 per cent), electricity (91 per cent) and coal (90 per cent); and industries with over 75 per cent state asset ownership included metallurgy, finance, gas and water industries (see Table 4.2; Liu and Gao 1999: 101).

In terms of the share of taxes submitted to the state, the large state-owned industries (e.g. railway, post, airline, iron and steel, automobile, petroleum, finance) traditionally accounted for approximately 85 per cent of total SOE taxes (Liu and Gao 1999). With regard to value-added, in 1992 the state-owned proportion in 32 of the 39 major industries accounted for more than 50 per cent. However, just five years later, this percentage had declined significantly, to below 50 per cent for the majority of industries. The notable exception here was that the state-owned proportion was still dominant (i.e. over 50 per cent) in 11 of the most basic monopolistic industries (e.g. water, coal, gas, etc.). Table 4.3 shows this decline of the state-owned proportion of value-added in the main industries in 1997, indicating the relative decline

*Table 4.1* The total number of industrial SOEs (1991–1999)

| Year | Total number |
|------|------------|
| 1991 | 104,700 |
| 1992 | 103,300 |
| 1993 | 104,700 |
| 1994 | 102,200 |
| 1995 | 118,000 |
| 1996 | 127,600 |
| 1997 | 110,000 |
| 1998 | 64,700 |
| 1999 | 61,300 |

Note: Data after 1995 refer to SOEs and also those where the state holds a controlling share.
Source: SSB (1996: 401; 2000: 407)

*Table 4.2* Percentage of state ownership in industries (%)

| Percentage | 100 | 90–95 | >75 |
|---|---|---|---|
| Industries | Post | Petroleum | Metallurgy |
| | Airline | Electricity | Finance |
| | Railway | Coal | Gas |
| | Defence | | Water |

Source: SSB (1995)

*Table 4.3* State-owned proportion of value-added in industries (1997) (%)

| Industry | Percentage | Industry | Percentage |
|---|---|---|---|
| Petroleum extraction | 96.13 | Tobacco | 97.87 |
| Timber logging and transport | 95.28 | Water | 85.65 |
| Petroleum processing | 81.59 | Coal | 78.34 |
| Smelting of ferrous metals | 75.10 | Electric power | 73.87 |
| Smelting of non-ferrous metals | 54.86 | Gas | 63.80 |
| Non-ferrous metals mining and dressing | 51.65 | Transport equipment | 44.56 |
| | | Ordinary machinery | 33.78 |
| Medical and pharmaceutical | 36.57 | Textile | 30.48 |
| Rubber products | 29.25 | Electronic and telecommunications equipment | 23.15 |
| Papermaking and paper products | 25.88 | | |
| Chemical fibre | 19.95 | Electric equipment and machinery | 18.47 |

Source: Gao and Yang (1999: 249–250; adapted from SSB 1993–1998)

of state ownership in these industries due to market-oriented reform. By 1999 the share of state ownership had further declined.

In 1996, of the number of 'large' industrial enterprises in China, SOEs accounted for 70.09 per cent of the total, this representing 69.89 per cent of output value, 75.98 per cent of asset value, and 85.45 per cent of total employment. Indeed, until the late 1990s, the investment rate in the state-owned economy was still high, accounting for over 50 per cent of total investment within what amounted to an extremely wide range of industries and sectors (Liu and Gao 1999).

Still the structure of the SOEs was such that, in terms of fixed assets, there were too many small enterprises, and thus a lack of scale economies, even after years of effort towards building large group companies. For example, in 1996, the assets of a large individual SOE were, on average, only 0.692 billion yuan (about US$0.08 billion) (Liu and Gao 1999). There was thus a long way to go towards the goal of achieving significant economies of scale, with this being most obvious in industries such as automotive, machinery and steel.

Almost a decade later, in terms of their share of employment and fixed assets, China's SOEs continue to represent a significant sector of the economy. The general goal of the state, however, remains that of converting large and medium SOEs into shareholding corporations whilst enlivening small SOEs through acquisitions, mergers, leasing and sales. Small SOEs, in particular, have been allowed to go to the private sector in a variety of forms. As such, the most visible change in the profile of the industrial structure in the last decade has been the diversification of forms of ownership, with policies of 'corporatization of the large' and 'releasing of the small' signalling a sharp reduction in the number of SOEs.

## Importance of the SOEs

Traditionally the importance of SOEs in the Chinese economy has resided in their status as a significant provider of government fiscal revenue, employment and social services. The SOEs as a whole dominated industrial production, and China's economy, for almost half a century. At the turn of the century, industrial SOEs still accounted for around one third of national production, more than half of total assets, and over half of total investment (their share of total investment actually rose from 61 per cent to 70 per cent between 1989 and 1994, but declined significantly thereafter). Moreover, during the 1990s SOEs absorbed over half (over two-thirds in the 1980s) of urban employment and provided about 70 per cent of government fiscal income. Although the SOEs' share of gross industrial output value has declined throughout the reform period, and notably so during the early 2000s, it still accounted for more than a quarter in 1999 (see Table 4.4).

### Role in employment

With regard to employment, between 1978 and 1991 the number of workers officially registered within the state-owned sector actually increased, by about

*Table 4.4*  Share of state ownership of industries in gross industrial output value (1978–1999) (%)

| Year | State-owned |
|------|-------------|
| 1978 | 77.6 |
| 1985 | 64.9 |
| 1990 | 54.6 |
| 1991 | 56.2 |
| 1992 | 51.5 |
| 1993 | 47.0 |
| 1994 | 37.3 |
| 1995 | 34.0 |
| 1996 | 28.5 |
| 1997 | 25.5 |
| 1998 | 28.2 |
| 1999 | 28.2 |

Source: SSB (1998: 433, 2000: 407)

*Table 4.5* Employment contribution of the state-owned sector (1978–1999) (million yuan)

| Year | Urban employees | Total employees in state-owned units | Employees in SOEs | Year | Urban employees | Total employees in state-owned units | Employees in SOEs |
|------|-----------------|--------------------------------------|-------------------|------|-----------------|--------------------------------------|-------------------|
| 1978 | 95.14 | 74.51 | n/a | 1994 | 184.13 | 108.90 | 43.69 |
| 1980 | 105.25 | 80.19 | n/a | 1995 | 190.93 | 109.55 | 43.97 |
| 1985 | 128.08 | 89.90 | 38.15 | 1996 | 198.15 | 109.49 | 42.78 |
| 1990 | 147.30 | 103.46 | 43.64 | 1997 | 202.07 | 107.66 | 40.40 |
| 1991 | 152.68 | 106.64 | 44.72 | 1998 | 206.78 | 88.09 | 27.21 |
| 1992 | 156.30 | 108.89 | 45.21 | 1999 | 210.14 | 83.36 | 24.12 |
| 1993 | 175.89 | 109.20 | 44.98 | | | | |

Source: SSB (1994: 84 and 374; 1996: 87; 1998: 127 and 432; 2000: 408)

a third, to around 107 million (see Table 4.5, and Parker and Pan 1996). Between 1991 and 1997, this figure remained relatively stable, but thereafter decreased, to 88 million in 1998 and 83 million in 1999. Of all workers in the state-owned sector, the SOEs absorbed around 40 million or so until 1997, when the employment figure became reduced markedly, to around 27 million in 1998 and 24 million in 1999 (SSB 1998, 2000). Until the late 1990s, the share of industrial employment of the SOEs was even higher than their share of fixed capital, at around 65 per cent. However, the percentage of the urban working population employed in the state-owned sector, which amounted to around 63 per cent in 1992, was reduced to around 55 per cent by the end of 1996 (OECF 1998: 31), mainly due to employment adjustment in the SOE sector. By the end of 2000 more than 20 million workers had been laid-off from the SOE sector since the mid-1990s, of which more than 10 million were having difficulties finding new jobs.

Although the official, registered urban unemployment rate of the mid–late 1990s was only around 3–4 per cent, when 'hidden' unemployment (surplus workers and internal lay-offs in the SOEs) is included, this figure goes well into double digits. As Liu and Gao (1999) suggested, by the end of 1997 the actual urban unemployment rate was around 19 per cent. Such large-scale unemployment has brought with it enormous threats to social stability, which have intensified the dilemma of SOE reform in the early 2000s (see later) and also constituted a reason why significant measures to reform the large urban SOEs have been delayed time and time again.

### Provision of social welfare for workers

Traditionally one of the primary roles of SOEs has been the provision of basic social security, which has also served as a mechanism for ensuring social stability. Workers in SOEs have normally benefited from the provision of major welfare services such as housing, children's education and health care, or cradle-to-grave welfare as it is commonly known. An OECF research paper of the late 1990s (OECF 1998) suggested that the average amount of social security per SOE was 3 per cent of sales revenue.

In the case of housing, for example, until the late 1990s (before dramatic housing reform was undertaken) SOEs were responsible for offering housing to employees free or with substantially subsidized rent, this accounting for 5 per cent or so of employee wages. At this time about 20 per cent of SOE assets were non-production fixed assets, the majority being houses for employees (Liu and Gao 1999). SOEs have also customarily established and run schools and hospitals, and provided virtually free health care and education for employees and their children. In the late 1990s, the costs of employee health care alone accounted for more than 15 per cent of the total amount of wages paid to SOE employees (Liu and Gao 1999). As employees also relied on the state enterprise for their pensions, each SOE was characteristically a mini-welfare state.

Although in theory SOEs are being relieved of the burden of providing such extensive social service provision, in practice this is a slow process and is being achieved in a very piecemeal manner. SOEs are still required to shoulder a significant portion of social welfare, as a transitional 'cushion', this being likely to continue into the foreseeable future until a robust social safety net is set in place.

## SOE reform measures

As mentioned, prior to the commencement of reform in 1978 SOEs were fully owned, funded and run by the government. The state enterprise did not have any significant decision-making power over production, investment or distribution. Enterprises submitted all their profits to the government and took little or no responsibility for losses. The main aim of SOE reform, therefore, has been to release state enterprises from central planning administration in order to make them adaptable to the market economy. Although a number of measures have been undertaken to enhance state-enterprise efficiency and competitive capacity, there has been no coherent strategic blueprint for such measures. SOE reform as a whole has been undertaken on a trial-and-error basis, from incremental, enterprise-oriented reform of the 1980s to the emphasis on reforming the institutional environment from the 1990s (IMF 1993; Liu and Gao 1999; Zhang, Weiying 1999; Hassard *et al.* 2004).

### *Initial SOE reform and the responsibility system*

As noted, the origins of SOE reform in China are to be found in a programme of expanded enterprise autonomy introduced into six SOE factories in Sichuan Province in October 1978 (see Chapter 3). The philosophy for this experiment was that, after meeting official state expectations, these SOEs would have a certain amount of decision flexibility in terms of their production plans, product marketing, worker employment and technological innovation. In particular, they would share profits according to specified 'state plan' and 'above-plan' retention rates. By the beginning of 1979, the number of SOEs in Sichuan Province involved in this experiment had expanded to 84, with from 1980, the Sichuan provincial government also experimenting with the adoption of (for some SOEs) a unified profit retention rate and change from profit remittances to company taxes (see Huang 1999).

On the basis of the initial results from Sichuan, in 1979 the central government devised a similar experiment for enterprises throughout China, and especially in Beijing, Tianjin and Shanghai, announcing a new 'responsibility system' for profits and losses. The core of this was to allow SOEs to retain a share of profits, enjoy accelerated depreciation and sell above-plan output. In these early phases, SOEs undertaking such reforms were allowed to retain 3 per cent of their profits, this representing a major breakthrough from the pre-reform relationship between state enterprises and government. The number of SOEs adopting this responsibility system rose to 6,600 by June 1980, and to about 42,000 by early 1981. By 1983, almost all SOEs had adopted this 'economic responsibility system' (Huang 1999). In sum, the core components of early SOE reform were the granting of greater autonomy to enterprises and allowing profit-sharing between SOEs and government.

### *Tax for profit and contract responsibility*

In the second phase of reform (1983–1986), the focus was on the adjustment and regulation of rights, responsibilities and benefits between enterprises and government. The major reforms during this period were experiments with tax-for-profit measures, the promotion of the 'repayable loan' system (to replace 'free grants'), and the nationwide implementation of the CRS.

In the reform of the financial distribution system, the profits and taxes that the enterprise should submit to the state were combined into one item, and the enterprise submitted a percentage sum to the state and retained the remainder. In 1983, only 50 per cent of enterprise profits were combined with taxes, the other 50 per cent being submitted completely as state fiscal income. In 1984, this was changed to 100 per cent of profits being combined with taxes. The main purpose of this was to replace the previous co-existence of tax and profit remittance with a simple taxation system, one whereby SOEs could pay taxes by following state regulations. In the process, the policy of 'two fees and four taxes' was levied on SOEs, this promoting, on the one hand, annual fees for 'fixed assets' and 'working capital financed from budgetary grants', and on the other, a 50 per cent 'income tax', plus 'real estate tax, vehicle tax and adjustment tax' (Huang 1999). As Wu (1999) has argued, however, from the state's perspective the strategic implementation of such tax-for-profits reforms regularly fell 'well short of expectations'.

In order to reduce the pressure on state fiscal investment in SOEs, while strengthening control over the SOEs, investment in enterprise fixed assets was changed from state fiscal grants into loans from the state bank. At the end of 1984, it was decided that all state investment would be on a 'repayable' rather than 'free grant' basis, allocated through the state banking system. However, at a time when the central plan still controlled the major proportion of SOEs' activities, state enterprises could hardly exercise much autonomy, with state intervention being the normative mechanism for resolving conflicts between the state plan and SOE objectives. The reform of 'bank loans for budgetary grants' largely failed because state banks could not effectively force unprofitable SOEs to repay the loans.

By the end of 1986, efforts were being directed at exploring various forms of enterprise-oriented reforms, these including the evaluation of shareholding systems. However, due to the absence of basic economic conditions and institutions, and the nature of China's legal environment of the time, the more readily acceptable CRS was confirmed as the reform process that would provide SOE managers with greater levels of autonomy (Wu 1999).

### Experimenting with the CRS

As the preferred method for reforming SOEs, the CRS not only emphasized the rights, responsibilities and incentives of state enterprises, but also held the advantage of maintaining state ownership. The nationwide implementation of the CRS was thus to bring clarification not only of the responsibilities and authority of enterprises, but also of their supervisory bureaux. The main aims were to reduce government intervention in the operation of SOEs and to make the enterprise financially independent, thereby focusing on profit rather than on plan fulfilment (Fan 1994). The CRS was also considered a relatively stable system, given that contracts were to be signed for periods of 3–5 years, with the possibility thereafter of extension to a second or third similar term. So the CRS was to be widely introduced into the state sector, with shareholding systems only being allowed on an experimental basis in a limited number of SOEs.

The most widely used form of CRS was the Contract Management Responsibility System (CMRS) (see Chapter 5). This system comprised three main elements: (i) the 'Contract Management System'; (ii) the 'Manager Responsibility System'; and (iii) the 'Internal Contract System' (Pyle 1997). Important among these was the Contract Management System, which represented a formal contract between the enterprise and the state. This also had three main components: (i) a profit-sharing scheme; (ii) projects for upgrading the enterprise's technology and management; and (iii) a scheme for determining wages and bonuses that were contingent upon the enterprise's performance (Pyle 1997: 96).

By the end of 1987, 78 per cent of SOEs had implemented the CRS (Wu 1999) and were thus operating under a philosophy of separating property rights and control rights, the 'contract' concerning profits and taxes that the enterprise submitted to the state. By 1992, the number of SOEs operating under the CRS had expanded to 95 per cent, this including nearly all large and medium-sized SOEs (Parker and Pan 1996). Thereafter, the CRS remained at the core of the SOE reforms until, increasingly, weaknesses with the system were identified in the early–mid-1990s, weaknesses that began to hamper further reform (Hassard and Sheehan 1997, see also Chapter 5).

Ultimately, the operation of the CRS in the urban industrial sector was not deemed as successful as it had been in the agricultural sector, as it generally fell below expectations in terms of separating government and enterprise activities. An unexpected by-product of the system was an apparent stress on short-termism of SOE performance, which, it was believed, led to rising prices and general disorder in the economy. Contrary to government expectations, the CRS also failed to yield substantial increases in SOE profitability, as instead the government revenue/GNP ratio continued to decline.

In sum, the common feature of these initial phases of SOE transition was that state ownership remained largely unchanged. Reforms were based on the theory of the separation of property rights and operating rights, with a focus on the readjustment of the income redistribution relationship between enterprises and government. During this transition stage, the contract system was at the heart of reform measures.

### Problems with the CRS

Why did the contract system have to be phased out and replaced by new measures (mainly the MES) by the early 1990s? To answer this, it is necessary to look in greater detail at the main features of the contract system and their associated problems.

A key feature of the contract system was the definition and clarification of the role of the enterprise/factory manager's 'responsibility system'. As outlined in the 'State-owned Enterprise Law' (issued in 1988), under the CRS, the enterprise/factory manager 'exerts official power and receives legal protection', is the 'legal representative of the enterprise' and takes 'full responsibility for the construction of the physical and mental civilization of the enterprise'. Under this law, the *enterprise* manager was authorized to carry out the functions shown in Box 4.1.

In contrast, the *factory* manager's autonomies were more pragmatic, centring on the right to occupy and use properties whose management was entrusted by the state. The 1988 Enterprise Law granted the factory manager 13 such autonomies (OECF 1998: 123), as Box 4.2 describes.

The rights outlined above, however, were never fully granted to enterprises and this limitation of provision made the implementation of such 'autonomies' difficult if not impossible. Whereas the CRS did go some way towards 'releasing the energies' of the SOEs, as a system it was increasingly associated with structural weaknesses, these presaging its ultimate phasing-out during the early–mid-1990s.

---

*Box 4.1* 'Enterprise manager's autonomies' (under the 1988
  Enterprise Law)

1   Decide on the plans of the enterprise or apply for plan approval
    based on the relevant regulations of the state.
2   Decide on the establishment of the administrative organization of
    the enterprise.
3   Propose appointment and dismissal of managers at the deputy
    factory manager level to the supervisory authorities of government.
4   Appoint or dismiss medium-level management.
5   Submit important proposals on provisions relating to wage revision,
    distribution of bonuses, employee welfare, etc. And request
    discussion and decision at the employees' congress.
6   Reward and punish employees based on the law, and propose
    rewards and punishments for deputy factory managers to the
    supervisory department.

                                                    Source: OECF (1998: 123)

---

Weaknesses with the CRS were manifested in many respects. A first
emerged from the fact that there were significant disparities in terms and
conditions between enterprises implementing the system. In particular, as a
result of the process of bilateral negotiation of contracts for individual
enterprises with state authorities, there were no definite regulations regarding
the rate of profit quotas, which could range from 5 to 20 per cent.

Second, there was a general failure to resolve the problem of property rights.
Under the CRS, property rights between the state and the enterprises were
ambiguous, which resulted in unclear distribution and control relations (Lee
1996). Indeed, the CRS failed to alter significantly the behaviour of either
state organs or enterprises in respect of property rights. Under the CRS the
'negotiation' – which was an integral part of setting state-enterprise contract
profit quotas – tended to institutionalize older state habits of direct interference
in the running of SOEs. Thus, the need for a real separation of management
and ownership constituted a reason for abandoning the CRS and adopting
new models of enterprise reform.

Third, we have noted that an unanticipated by-product of the CRS was a
stress on short-termism in SOE performance. As a CRS contract normally
ran for only three to five years, there was a tendency for managers to
concentrate primarily on the basic quantitative targets set out in the contract,
and, in turn, to neglect, for example, fixed-asset maintenance, technology
upgrading/investment and the enterprise's long-term development strategy
and needs (Zhang 1992; Hassard *et al.* 1999a). Whereas on the one hand,
short-term behaviour was manifested in offering workers wage increases and

---

*Box 4.2* 'Factory manager's autonomies' (under the 1988 Enterprise Law)

1 Independently determines the production of the products and services.
2 Has the right to request adjustment of directive plans when necessary supplies and sales of products are not secured, and has the right to accept and refuse production outside the directive plans.
3 Independently chooses suppliers and purchases input goods.
4 Independently determines the prices of products and services.
5 Independently markets the products of the enterprise concerned.
6 Negotiates with foreign enterprises, observing the provisions of the State Council, concludes contracts, reserves and uses a prescribed percentage of foreign currency income.
7 Controls and uses reserved funds according to the provisions of the State Council.
8 Leases or transfers fixed assets for consideration based on the provisions of the State Council. In this case, the manager is required to use the profits for the renovation of facilities or technological innovation.
9 Determines the form of wages and the distribution method of bonuses as according to the condition of the enterprise concerned.
10 Employs and dismisses workers in conformity with the laws and the provisions of the State Council.
11 Determines the establishment and the number of staff of the organization.
12 Has the right to refuse any requisitioning of personnel, goods, funds, etc. by another organization.
13 Has the right to have associated management with other enterprises or business units, investment in other enterprises or business units, and hold the stock of other enterprises in conformity with the laws and the provisions of the State Council, and the right to issue bonds based on the provisions of the state council.

Source: OECF (1998: 124)

---

bonuses for meeting immediate contract performance goals, on the other, there was a general failure to provide incentives for the long-term effective management and control of enterprises. Short-term inducements could thus operate at the expense of the enterprise's development needs (Shirk 1993; Gao and Yang 1999; Liu and Gao 1999; Wu 1999).

Fourth, in practice the CRS was characterized by limited levels of enterprise responsibility. Whereas enterprises were to a large extent responsible for their own profits, the state remained responsible for their losses. At the end of the century, more than half of all SOEs were loss-making, with over 80 per cent of small and medium-sized SOEs having made considerable losses throughout the 1990s. The CRS was unable to stem the practice of loss-making SOEs receiving substantial state subsidies, this representing a considerable drain on limited financial resources. While SOEs were not responsible for their losses, under the CRS many SOE managers were granted considerable amounts of executive discretion under the Director Responsibility System, such autonomy without responsibility representing a major contradiction of the system (Hassard *et al.* 1999a).

Fifth, poor management performance, limited improvement in management quality, and managers' stripping of state assets were all features of the CRS. This lack of professionalism among enterprise managers was often reflected in declining profits/increased losses, low rates of productivity, and high ratios of debts to assets. In 1994, 11 per cent of all the SOEs had liabilities that exceeded their assets (OECF 1998) and in 1995 this figure rose to 16 per cent, with the average ratio of debt to assets (of all but financial SOEs) being 69 per cent (Liu and Gao 1999).

Although under the CRS, contracts stipulated that the level of profit remittance to the government should be guaranteed, in reality when an SOE made losses the government would re-negotiate the amount of revenue remittance, increase subsidies, or offer special credits (Lardy 1998; Wu 1999). Under such soft-budget constraints, with loans provided by state-owned banks with little motivation to monitor enterprises, SOEs lacked sufficient incentives to improve their financial performance. Instead, bargaining with the government for a lower remittance quota or a low-interest loan often proved more effective (and easier) for raising an enterprise's profit than striving to improve productivity.

### The socialist market, modern enterprises and ownership divestment

The policy of establishing the 'socialist market' economy was passed at the 14th CCP National Congress in 1992. Subsequently, the 'Decision on Issues Concerning the Establishment of a Socialist Market Economy' was adopted by the Third Plenum of the 14th CCP Congress in November 1993. Legislation for a market economy signalled a breakthrough in political ideology, one that impacted heavily on the reform process. The core component of reform at this phase was the establishment of an MES with 'autonomy and monitoring' being the two key elements of reform. Monitoring became a renewed emphasis in SOE reform when it was held that enterprises would continue to neglect their economic responsibilities without sufficient accountability (Zhang, Weiying 1999). In the process, SOE reform began to move from the adjustment of distribution relationships and authority reallocation between government and enterprise towards the greater clarification of property rights and ownership.

The MES was promoted on an experimental basis nationwide from the end of 1994 (see Chapter 6 for details of the initial MES and kindred GCS experimental programmes). The original state definition focused on four main issues: (i) specification of property rights; (ii) delineation of responsibilities and levels of authority; (iii) separation of the functions of government and enterprise; and (iv) promotion of scientific management. At its core the MES was a system in which the state, in theory, was largely prohibited from direct intervention in enterprise management. State enterprises, in turn, would become legally responsible for their management, profits and losses, tax payments, asset maintenance and the like.

The main organizational form of the MES movement was to be a share-holding system. For SOEs to be turned into shareholding companies, this would see not only the state exercising rights over enterprise assets, but also shareholders, including other state or non-state entities and potentially individuals. The main advantages of the shareholding system were deemed to be: (i) separating government ownership from enterprise management; (ii) mobilizing and rationalizing the allocation of financial resources; and (iii) providing greater financial and decision-making autonomy to enterprises so that they could respond to changing market conditions (IMF 1993).

By the end of 1997, 2,562 large and medium-sized industrial SOEs were in the process of adopting MES measures, this representing around 150 million workers/staff and total assets of almost 4,000 billion yuan. According to the state statistical report, of these enterprises 1,943 had by this time completed MES transformation, of which 612 were transformed into 'shareholding limited companies', 768 into 'limited liability companies', and 563 into 'companies with the state as the sole shareholder' (Enterprise Reform Division of China State Economic and Trade Commission (ERDCSETC) 1999: 26).

### Deepening ownership divestment

From the mid-1990s, the SOE sector experienced a significant decline in performance. According to statistics from China's Finance Ministry, in 1998 the SOE sector for the first time made a net loss, of 7.8 billion yuan. Statistics suggest that by June 1998, almost 50 per cent of the state-owned industrial enterprises had made losses, this figure rising to over 55 per cent in the case of the large and medium-sized industrial SOEs (Gao and Yang 1999).

Given a marked increase in the number of loss-making SOEs at a time when the state was promoting the view that public enterprises could realize their potential in a mixed ownership economy, reform measures became directed at more fundamental and strategic issues of restructuring. Such reform included widening and deepening SOE ownership diversification through the further development of the MES, and specifically effecting the state policies of 'grasping the large (SOEs), releasing the small' and the three-year programme of 'lifting large loss-making SOEs out of difficulty' (Hassard *et al.* 2005). To this end, the SCS and shareholding generally were to be promoted through fundamental industrial restructuring founded on the reorganization of state assets.

The measure of 'grasping the large, releasing the small' was officially proposed in 1997 and put into action nationally from 1998, being implemented in line with industrial restructuring and state asset reorganization. Under this policy, only about 1,000 of the largest SOEs, holding around 70 per cent of SOE fixed assets and generating about 80 per cent of profits and taxes, were to be retained under government control and thus to benefit from a high level of state protection. These enterprises were predominantly in sectors considered to be of 'strategic importance', including electricity generation, automobiles, electronics, iron and steel, machinery, chemicals, construction materials, transport, aerospace and pharmaceuticals (Nolan 2001; Hassard *et al.* 2002). Historically, these sectors have tended to be characterized by strong economies of scale and scope; they were also identified as those most crucial to the growth and defence of a modern, industrial and technically advanced society. In contrast, the small and medium-sized SOEs would be allowed to divest from strict public ownership, including going to the private sector.

Accompanying such industrial restructuring and state asset reorganization, in 1998 a breakthrough was achieved in the separation of government administration from enterprise operation, when the State Council component departments (excluding the General Office of the State Council) were cut from 40 to 29 (Gao and Yang 1999: 217) (see Chapter 3). Thus, many industrial bureaux were either abolished or changed into professional industrial agencies (rather than administrative bodies), which correspondingly reduced the degree of intervention of bureaux with commercial interests. The trend was for industrial ministries and bureaux to be reorganized into hybrid economic entities. In relation to enterprises, some of these organizations performed coordinating and supervisory roles similar to those of the head offices of multi-divisional firms or conglomerates. They also performed regulatory functions, covering all enterprises in the industry regardless of their ownership status. For example, many of the industrial bureaux were transformed into holding companies for the enterprises previously under their supervision.

In essence, under the 9th Five Year Plan (1996–2000) the reform of 'grasping the large' SOEs saw central government select 1,000 SOEs to form the core of the MES that was to be realized by 2010. Most large SOEs were transformed into shareholding companies while, as noted, small SOEs were given scope to move to the private sector through a wide range of forms. Those that had lost the market demand for their products or services, or simply made net losses, were ordered to close, file for bankruptcy or merge as appropriate. In other words, ownership diversity became the main strategic approach to developing small enterprises.

One of the main aims of 'grasping the large' was to establish three to five firms in the world's largest 500 enterprises by the year 2000 (see Smyth 2000).

In order to achieve this, extra funds were to be channelled by government into a select number of large enterprises. In November 1997, six SOEs were selected to receive special government support – the Shanghai Baoshan Steel Works, the Haier Electrical Appliances Group, the Sichuan Chongqing Electrical Appliances Group, the Shanghai Jiangnan Shipbuilding Corporation, the Beida Fangzheng Group and the Huabei Pharmaceutical Corporation. In 1998 each of these enterprises was promised at least 20 million yuan for technical renovation (Smyth 2000).

Another aim was to develop a number of enterprise groups in strategic sectors. A wave of conglomeration and enterprise mergers thus began to sweep across the main industries. The immediate result was the formation of 'national corporations' that were expected to be the driving force of industrial modernization. A total of 512 large enterprises at national and subnational levels were first targeted, these being accompanied by the emergence of a multi-tiered organizational network of state asset management bureaux, operating companies and supervisory committees.

So, to reverse the loss-making trend of SOEs, in 1998 central government proposed the three-year programme for 'lifting loss-making SOEs out of difficulty'. This scheme was intended to reverse the fortunes of at least 3,000 loss-making SOEs, while at the same time strengthening the capability of the 1,000 'large group' SOEs. The main measures of the three-year programme reflected strong state 'regulation', 'guidance' and 'strategic reorganization' of assets'. The aim was to nurture the market competitiveness of large 'cross-section', 'cross-region' and 'cross-ownership' enterprises (Liu and Gao 1999). State inputs were reflected in infrastructure construction, provision of debt-to-equity options, and support in the general fight against corruption.

By the end of 1999, of the 6,599 large and medium-sized SOEs identified in 1997 as making serious losses, 3,211 (49 per cent) were reported as either having turned losses into profits or else eliminated deficits (*China Daily*, 30 September 2000). According to the same report, by September 2000 the percentage of these SOEs that had managed to turn a profit had increased to 55 per cent. Furthermore, the statistics of China's Finance Ministry suggested that, in 1999 and 2000, the SOEs as a whole made profits of 114.58 billion and 283.38 billion yuan, respectively, with the State Economic and Trade Commission (SETC) statistics denoting that, by early 2001 'at least 65 per cent of China's large and medium-sized SOEs have reversed their money-losing trends' (*China Daily*, 6 March 2001).

## Mechanisms of SOE transformation

Before we turn to case examples of SOE reform in subsequent chapters, we now offer details of the major underlying mechanisms of the transformation process in terms of the analytical framework established in earlier chapters – namely *competition, ownership change* and *management reform*.

### Competition and competitive markets

In the early phases of the reform process, notions of competition and competitive markets were mainly embodied in the promotion of the secondary economy and private enterprise. This is because the legalization of the secondary economy (and letting it grow outside the planning system) was considered politically more expedient than deregulating the state economy as a whole (Shirk 1993). The non-state sector, in being nurtured by government and given preferential treatment – through, for example, low tax rates and fewer restrictions on salaries – subsequently gained considerable competitive advantage over the state sector. The rapid development of the non-state sector (including TVEs, joint-ventures, private firms, etc.) considerably raised the level of competitive pressure on the state sector, and notably the SOEs. Over time, the non-state sector successfully percolated, from public ownership, resources such as labour, finance and production materials.

Although some industries faced only modest competition from non-state companies until the mid–late 1990s (e.g. electric power, coal and petroleum), in many others state-owned firms receded rapidly (e.g. textiles, electronics, computers). Also whereas under the planned economy, costs of raw material inputs (including petrochemical products, grains, cotton, electricity, transportation and coal etc.) were kept low for political reasons, they subsequently rose substantially due to price liberalization. As infrastructure reforms failed to keep pace with rising costs, this worsened the profitability of many SOEs that lacked strength in competition with either more efficient SOEs or enterprises of other ownership systems.

However, in the face of increasing competitive pressure on state enterprises, many SOE managers (as well as state industrial bureaucrats) gradually became advocates of market freedoms. SOE managers began to put pressure on government to extend to them some of the freedoms afforded to non-state sector enterprises. If such reforms were extended, SOEs would be able to compete with firms of other types of ownership for labour, materials and financial resources. Thus, competition would be created not only among state and non-state firms, but also among local governments and regions. During the 1990s, demands were made from both inside and outside the SOEs for forms of ownership change that would realize more fundamental enterprise transformation. With the emergence of a market-supporting environment (albeit one lacking institutional maturity) ownership change had become a legitimate item on the reform agenda.

### Ownership change

As noted, state sector ownership reform emerged in earnest during the mid-1990s, under the guidance of the MES, with the shareholding system becoming the main instrument. Restructuring under the shareholding system initially took four main forms – stock companies, exclusively state-funded companies, state holding companies and asset reorganization. By the end of

1996, all 100 SOEs in an initial State Commission for Economic Restructuring experiment had completed their various processes of 'corporatization'. In addition, 2,343 SOEs were selected by various local authorities for the MES experiment. In all, the experiment involved 10.04 million employees and 1,940 billion yuan of assets. According to Liu and Gao (1999: 264) by the first half of 1997, 540 (23 per cent) of these enterprises had been transformed into shareholding limited companies; 540 (23 per cent) had been changed to limited liability companies; and 909 (39 per cent) had changed into wholly state-owned companies; with the remainder having yet to complete their transformation.

A larger number of transformation systems were used for the ownership divestment of small SOEs (see Table 4.6). According to figures for 1996, of the restructuring systems on offer, the largest percentage (35 per cent) of small SOEs adopted the experimental 'shareholding cooperative system' (Liu and Gao 1999). By the end of 1999, there were more than 400,000 shareholding firms, of which shareholding limited companies amounted to around 6,000 (ERDCSETC 1999: 1). The variety of forms of small SOE transformations and the usage rate of each form are indicated in Table 4.6.

Since the mid-1990s, therefore, the reorganization of property rights has become the centrepiece of SOE reform with the shareholding system the main vehicle of transformation. By the end of 1997, 745 enterprises had been listed on domestic and overseas stock markets and their gross market value accounted for 23 per cent of GDP. In March 1998 the number of listed enterprises had risen to 762, while by end-October 1998, the figure was 878 (Zhang and Zhong 2000). As we discuss later, however, in the reform process shares held by the state within such limited companies have often accounted for 50 per cent or more, with these public shares (i.e. state and legal person shares) not being allowed to circulate in the stock market.

## Management reform

We have suggested that progress with the transformation of large SOEs was

*Table 4.6* Forms of small SOE transformations and their usage rate (1996) (%)

| | |
|---|---|
| Reorganized for enterprise group | 1.69 |
| Merger | 5.47 |
| Corporatization | 7.8 |
| Shareholding cooperative system | 35.13 |
| Contracting and leasing | 15.7 |
| Operation under principal | 15.24 |
| Sale or let | 11.02 |
| Joint-venture | 3.42 |
| Bankruptcy | 1.03 |
| Others | 3.81 |

Source: Liu and Gao (1999: 268)

hampered by the lack of a mature institutional environment. Reform at the macro level necessarily includes institution building involving the restructuring of state industrial bureaux and component departments under the State Council. In Box 4.3 we outline key dates and activities in the construction of such market-supporting institutions during the period of heightened reform from the mid-1980s to the late 1990s.

Management reform at the enterprise level has been regarded as crucial to the development of appropriate incentive and property rights systems. Giving state enterprises greater autonomy within a market economy has long been considered the key to optimizing incentive schemes. It is argued that unless enterprises attain relatively full autonomy, the necessary incentives for achieving improved levels of competitiveness and capability will remain elusive. To achieve this, it is suggested that state enterprises must exercise greater discretion in terms of personnel and investment rights. The solution is thus a management one, with state-enterprise structures being reformed based on the principal of the separation of government and enterprise, this being accompanied generally by the establishment of a State Asset Management Committee (see Gao and Yang 1999).

According to a survey of SOEs by the OECF published in the late 1990s (OECF 1998), SOE management costs grew dramatically from the mid-1980s to mid-1990s. Here 'management costs' are defined as wages plus other costs generated in relation to the management and organization of production, such as:

> welfare expenses, depreciation costs, union costs, social and amusement expenses, real estate taxes, tax on the use of automobiles and ships, tax

---

*Box 4.3* Key market-supporting institutions (1986–1999)

| | |
|---|---|
| 1986 | Bankruptcy Law |
| 1988 | Enterprise Law |
| 1992 | 'Socialist market economy' established |
| 1992 | Law on the Administration of Tax Collection |
| 1993 | Anti-unfair Competition Law |
| 1994 | MES experiment |
| 1994 | Corporation Law; Labour Law |
| 1995 | Budget Law |
| 1995 | Commercial Bank Law; Central Bank Law |
| 1998 | Securities Law |
| 1998 | Restructuring of government ministries/commissions |
| 1999 | Private ownership incorporated into Chinese Constitution |

Sources: www.qis.net/chinalaw;
www.law-bridge.net/e-laws.html

*Table 4.7* SOE profits and real wages (1985–1996)

| Year | SOE net profits (billion yuan) | Profit-capital rate (%) | SOE/collective (1985 = 100) | |
|------|------|------|------|------|
| | | | Real wage | Labour productivity |
| 1985 | 70.6 | 17.7 | 100.0 | 100.0 |
| 1986 | 63.5 | 14.0 | 103.2 | 89.2 |
| 1987 | 72.6 | 13.8 | 102.1 | 79.5 |
| 1988 | 81.0 | 13.4 | 103.6 | 68.2 |
| 1989 | 56.3 | 8.0 | 105.3 | 62.9 |
| 1990 | 3.9 | 0.5 | 108.3 | 58.9 |
| 1991 | 3.5 | 0.4 | 105.9 | 53.6 |
| 1992 | 16.6 | 1.5 | 108.7 | 44.1 |
| 1993 | 36.5 | 2.7 | 108.6 | 32.3 |
| 1994 | 34.6 | 2.2 | 117.8 | 26.0 |
| 1995 | 12.5 | 0.7 | 114.0 | 23.3 |
| 1996 | −30.9 | −1.5 | 120.7 | 19.8 |

Source: SSB (1996, 1997)

on the use of land, stamp duty, technology transfer costs, depreciation expenses for intangible assets, training expenses for employees, labour insurance premiums, unemployment insurance premiums, research and development costs, bad debt loss, etc.

> (OECF 1998: 62, based on the definition of the
> Chinese Industrial Enterprise Accounting System
> (Fiscal Department) December, 1992)

Over-spending on direct and indirect wages increases management costs, with increases in management costs themselves being a major factor in the profit suppression of an industry. As Table 4.7 illustrates, between 1985 and 1996 the net profits made by the SOEs declined dramatically. Moreover, while the relative wage bills of SOEs to collective enterprises increased by 21 per cent during this period, their relative labour productivity declined by almost 80 per cent.

The OECF (1998) study suggested that three factors lay at the heart of the increasing management costs in SOEs – that enterprises were 'not yet properly separated from government', lacked 'insider control' (i.e. professional management expertise), and suffered from 'undue managerial manipulations' (a reference to rapid wage increases and high employee social welfare costs). The OECF survey also indicated that, in the short term, the shareholding system did not contribute significantly to reducing management costs or effecting the separation of government and enterprise.

## SOE management systems

Under the post-1978 experiments in state-enterprise reform, two major systems of management have been experienced in the majority of SOEs – the 'factory system', based on principles of the contract responsibility approach, and the 'corporate system', with the shareholding system as its main ownership form.

In general, the factory system has included elements of the manager responsibility system, contract system and leasing system. Under this approach, enterprise management was founded on principles laid down in the State-owned Enterprise Law (1988) and the Autonomous Management Rights Regulations (1992). Guidelines for the 'proper stewardship' of enterprise state assets under the factory system were established in the Regulations Governing the Supervision and Management of State-owned Enterprises' Property (1994).

In contrast (as we discuss in more detail later) the evolving corporate system, whether in the form of the state-owned limited liability company, the limited liability shareholding company, or the wholly state-owned company, has modelled its basic forms of enterprise control on Western corporate systems of management, this being subject ultimately to the Company Law (1993). Since the mid-1990s the corporate model has been progressively promoted and become increasingly popular as SOEs have shifted towards the adoption of shareholding systems.

The OECF (1998) investigation illustrated the total distribution of the major SOE management systems at the end of 1995 (see Table 4.8). The survey noted that the percentage of enterprises under the corporate system had grown from just 0.1 per cent in 1991 to around 6–7 per cent in 1995, and that thereafter the trend was accelerating rapidly, with state-owned limited liability companies seeing the largest increase.

A variety of problems and challenges had emerged in relation to the initial factory management system as well as for the transition from the factory system to the corporate system. To appreciate the nature of these problems we will consider some of the regulatory and legislative forms upon which modern Chinese SOE management systems are based. In particular we will examine the landmark '14 autonomies' established for SOEs under the 1992 Autonomous Management Right Regulations, which were promulgated as a more concrete form of the Enterprise Law (see Box 4.4).

*Table 4.8* Distribution of SOE management systems (December 1995)

| Type of enterprises | Number of enterprises (overall percentage %) | Percentage of total state capital occupied (%) |
| --- | --- | --- |
| Factory system enterprises | 247,000 (81.8) | 85.2 |
| Corporate system enterprises | 20,004 (6.62) | 9.62 |
| Shareholding, joint-venture and partnership | 2,000 (0.6) | 0.9 |
| Domestic allied management enterprises | 3,000 (1.0) | 1.4 |

Source: OECF (1998: 120)

*Box 4.4* 'SOEs autonomies' (under the 1992 Autonomous
Management Right Regulations)

The right to decide on:

1  production;
2  price of products and services;
3  independent sale of products;
4  selection of suppliers;
5  foreign reserve funds;
6  investment;
7  use of reserve funds;
8  disposal of assets;
9  joint operation and mergers with other units;
10  hiring and firing of employees;
11  personnel management;
12  distribution of wages and bonuses;
13  organization of internal division;
14  the right to refuse requisition.

Source: OECF (1998: 124)

It can be argued that among the 14 autonomies, the rights to decide on the disposal of assets and on matters related to personnel management were among the most difficult to operate in practice. The core problem was the extent to which the state, as an owner of the SOEs' 'property', should reserve control over such issues. The debate was protracted, given the degree of ambiguity in the relationship between management autonomy and the property ownership of the state. A contradiction was identified whereby an apparent 'abuse of management autonomy' by enterprises coexisted with an apparent 'lack of management autonomy' (OECF 1998). In order to clarify state property ownership, the Regulations Governing the Supervision and Management of State-owned Enterprise's Property were proposed in 1994. These 'Supervision Regulations', as they became known, promoted the concept of the 'corporate property rights' of enterprises. In an attempt to clear up confusion over the issue, the regulations stipulated that 'enterprises have corporate property rights and independently control property where the management is entrusted by the State based on the law. The government and supervising organizations should not directly control the corporate property of the enterprises' (OECF 1989: 129).

However, despite this attempt at clarification, the concept of 'corporate property rights' remained a confusing one in terms of the management autonomy of SOEs. Under the Chinese Enterprise Law, the term 'management right' is defined as the right to 'occupy, use and dispose' of property, based on law whereby management is 'entrusted' with the enterprise by the state. This provides that the government retains the right to: 'decide on the directive plan', 'examine and approve investments', and the 'partial use of the enterprises' property'. Clearly there remain ambiguities in the definition of 'management rights', since the term, in reality, applies only to 'administrative' management rights, for there is no accompanying change in the relations of property. The Enterprise Law, the 'Autonomous Management Right Regulations' and the 'Supervision Regulations' failed to resolve the problems of SOE management, for new ones emerged in the process of their implementation. Autonomy was not granted easily while property rights lacked substance. This led to the absence of the 'real' owner of state assets and the emergence of the problem of 'insider control', notably due to poor enterprise monitoring. As the enterprises' property rights remained limited, a role for government intervention remained. As a result, the tendency was for SOE management to neglect asset value protection and the overall development of the enterprise, and instead to focus on securing short-term profitability and greater employee income (OECF 1998).

## Financial, fiscal and technical status

To turn to the financial status of SOEs, Table 4.9 offers figures for industrial SOE performance based on their annual total profits and losses from 1978–2000. In terms of their annual losses, these rose markedly from 4.2 billion yuan in 1978 to 34.9 billion yuan in 1990 and 87.1 billion yuan in 1997 (SSB 1997). In terms of total profits, whereas before 1990 the industrial SOEs turned profits on a regular basis, from 1990 to 1995, their relative profitability became more erratic. In terms of the profile of combined profits and losses, we note that during the 1990s SOEs experienced deteriorating financial performance, with by 1996 and 1997 about 50 per cent of SOEs being loss-making and the state sector as a whole being in deficit.

Indeed, during the 1990s, SOEs ran into considerable debt, with much of this being accumulated bad debts. In 1994 the average ratio of debts to assets for all industrial SOEs was a massive 67.9 per cent (see Table 4.10). By scale of enterprise, the ratio of debts to assets of small and medium-sized SOEs was much higher than that of large SOEs – more than ten percentage points according to the SSB. By the end of 1995, the ratio of debts to assets of the large state-owned industrial and commercial enterprises had increased to an average of 65.9 per cent, but with the ratio being over 80 per cent for half of these enterprises (Wu 1999). Among the 16,000 largest SOEs, about 5,900 (37 per cent) were now significantly loss-making (Liu and Gao 1999).

Interestingly, according to statistics for around 120,000 state enterprises in 1994, the average ratio of debts to assets of (85,023) 'traditional' enterprises was only 2.2 percentage points higher than that of the (38,912) 'new' enterprises, suggesting that the debt issue was essentially a phenomenon

*Table 4.9* Profits and losses of state-owned industrial enterprises (1978–2000)
(billion yuan)

| Year | Losses | Profits | Year | Losses | Profits |
|------|--------|---------|------|--------|---------|
| 1978 | 4.20 | 50.88 | 1989 | 18.02 | 74.30 |
| 1979 | 3.64 | 56.28 | 1990 | 34.88 | 38.81 |
| 1980 | 3.43 | 58.54 | 1991 | 36.70 | 40.22 |
| 1981 | 4.60 | 57.97 | 1992 | 36.93 | 53.50 |
| 1982 | 4.76 | 59.77 | 1993 | 45.26 | 81.73 |
| 1983 | 3.21 | 64.09 | 1994 | 48.26 | 82.90 |
| 1984 | 2.66 | 70.62 | 1995 | 63.96 | 66.56 |
| 1985 | 3.24 | 73.82 | 1996 | 79.07 | 41.26 |
| 1986 | 5.45 | 69.00 | 1997 | 87.10 | 42.78 |
| 1987 | 6.10 | 78.70 | 1998 | n/a | 52.5 |
| 1988 | 8.19 | 89.19 | 1999 | n/a | 99.8 |
|  |  |  | 2000 | n/a | 239.2 |

Sources: Liu and Gao (1999); SSB (1998, 2000); IIECASS (2000)

*Table 4.10* Debts/assets of all SOEs by scale (1994) (billion yuan)

| Enterprise scale | Total assets | Total debts | Ratio of debts to assets |
|------------------|--------------|-------------|--------------------------|
| Large | 2,361.142 | 1,498.026 | 63.4 |
| Medium-sized | 779.318 | 589.759 | 75.7 |
| Small | 704.212 | 522.604 | 74.5 |
| In total | 3,844.67 | 2,610.386 | 67.9 |

Source: SSB (1995) (cited in Liu and Gao 1999: 80)

related to the economic system rather than the industry (Liu and Gao 1999). Figures provided by Lardy (1998) illustrate how on an annual basis the debt/asset ratio increased sharply between 1990 and 1995, in total by over 30 per cent during this period (see Table 4.11).

At the end of the 1990s, the debt–asset ratio of the SOEs was still extremely high. According to statistics by the SSB (2000) for 1999, while the total assets of all SOEs (including enterprises with a controlling shareholding by the state) were 8,047 billion yuan and their circulating assets were 3,104 billion yuan, the total liquid debts were 3,183 billion yuan. In the main, these debts were now loans borrowed from the state-owned banks.

The SOE sector has long been a major contributor to Chinese government revenue. From 1985 to 1998, industrial SOEs submitted income taxes of 908 billion yuan. In 1998 alone, the industrial SOEs submitted sales taxes and VAT amounting to 99 billion yuan (IIECASS 2000).

Table 4.12 shows the degree to which government revenue relies on tax revenue. From 1985 to 1999, the total income taxes from SOEs (as against the total government tax revenue) declined from over 29 per cent to less than 6 per cent. This trend became particularly marked in the 1990s, being linked

*Table 4.11* Debt–asset ratio of all SOEs (1990–1995)

| Year | Debt–asset ratio (%) |
| --- | --- |
| 1990 | 58 |
| 1991 | 61 |
| 1992 | 62 |
| 1993 | 72 |
| 1994 | 75 |
| 1995 | 85 |

Source: Adapted from Lardy (1998: 41)

*Table 4.12* Contribution of SOEs to government revenue (billion yuan)

| Year | Total government revenue | Total government tax revenue | Total subsidies to loss-making SOEs | Contribution of SOEs income tax | SOE income tax in total tax revenue (%) |
| --- | --- | --- | --- | --- | --- |
| 1978 | 113.23 | 51.93 | | | |
| 1980 | 115.99 | 57.17 | | | |
| 1985 | 220.48 | 204.08 | 50.7 | 59.58 | 29.19 |
| 1990 | 293.17 | 282.19 | 57.9 | 60.41 | 21.41 |
| 1991 | 314.95 | 299.02 | 51.0 | 62.76 | 20.99 |
| 1992 | 348.34 | 329.69 | 44.5 | 62.48 | 18.95 |
| 1993 | 434.90 | 425.53 | 41.1 | 58.29 | 13.70 |
| 1994 | 521.81 | 512.69 | 36.6 | 60.98 | 11.89 |
| 1995 | 624.22 | 603.80 | 32.8 | 75.94 | 12.58 |
| 1996 | 740.80 | 690.98 | 33.7 | 82.23 | 11.90 |
| 1997 | 865.11 | 823.40 | 36.8 | 79.44 | 9.65 |
| 1998 | 987.60 | 926.28 | 33.3 | 74.39 | 8.03 |
| 1999 | 1,144.41 | 1,068.26 | 29.0 | 63.90 | 5.98 |

Source: SSB (2000: 256–258; 1998: 272 and 273)

to the deteriorating performance of the SOE sector as a whole. Meanwhile subsidies started to be given to loss-making SOEs, which in 1985 accounted for about 25 per cent of total government tax revenue. Such subsidies continued to flow into the SOEs throughout the 1990s, although by 1999 the subsidies for loss-making SOEs accounted for only 3 per cent of total government tax revenue. Indeed, both income taxes submitted and the subsidies absorbed by the SOEs dropped 23 percentage points between 1985 and 1999.

In addition, in 1997 an IMF report suggested that SOE technology was significantly outmoded. The report claimed that equipment was often deficient, due to insufficient capital for renovation and maintenance, and often abused, as a result of the prevailing emphasis on short-termism in performance (IMF 1997). Not only did these features lead to low quality of enterprise assets but also placed severe constraints on the development of new products and the enhancement of product quality.

Similarly, a state investigation of industrial capability in the mid-1990s (reported in Liu and Gao 1999) suggested an average gap of 20–30 years in terms of technology level between China's domestic SOEs and kindred international enterprises. The investigation noted further that only around 10–15 per cent of state-enterprise technology was of a level comparable to that with which international enterprises were operating ten years or so previously. This investigation highlighted the extremely low levels of product quality from state enterprises and how outmoded technology not only increases product costs but also those associated with environmental pollution.

## Enterprise transformation and labour

As we discuss in subsequent chapters, the reform process has generated significant implications for labour-management systems within SOEs. On the labour side, there has been a general shift from lifetime employment and cradle-to-grave welfare to contractual employment and enterprise-individual contributory welfare. The specific impacts on labour can be seen in wage and bonus incentives, job reduction programmes and employee welfare schemes. Through the reform process, incentives have been diverted from the previous 'egalitarian' model to a more 'flexible' one (Cooke 2005). In addition, there are now few guarantees of job security, with levels of job reduction in some industries being dramatic since the mid–late 1990s, this resulting in millions of SOE workers being laid-off.

### *Changing incentives*

Wage reform has been a key component of China's SOE restructuring. Under the transition process the pre-reform national wage system was rejected and, instead, a firm-determined, individually differentiated and merit-based system increasingly employed. Before the 1985 wage reform, the basic industrial system was the traditional 'eight-grade' system, which was highly centralized and tightly controlled by the state. In 1985 a new 'fifteen-grade' system replaced the eight-grade. When SOEs were subsequently allowed to devise their own wage forms, this state-sponsored structure was henceforth only to be treated as a 'reference system' (You 1998). The important change was that wage structures were to become progressively open-ended, with the fixed base part being supplemented by a 'floating' element. Indeed, the main objective of such wage reform was to enlarge progressively the floating part and reduce the fixed part. In order to break the 'iron wage' system, many SOEs decided to float a certain proportion of the fixed base wage (You 1998). Ultimately the forms of wage system most commonly practised became: (i) base salary + floating efficiency salary + bonuses (where the base salary is sometimes partially or even entirely floated); and (ii) base salary + post (skills) awards + premiums for service length + efficiency pay (often known as the '*Gang-ji*' (or 'post skill') wage system as the post or role skills are the main indicators of wage differentiation). (Other forms of wage system employed were the basic 'price-rate' wage system – employed in industries where individual production could be calculated easily – and the 'job-driven' wage system – used where jobs required specific forms of technical expertise.)

As such, also restored under the reform process were wage bonus systems. In 1984 the State Council announced reforms that would allow SOEs more direct control over remuneration. As a result, not only was the ceiling for bonuses subsequently removed, but SOEs were also allowed to decide their own forms of bonus distribution. One effect, however, was that for many large SOEs the growth of bonus payments became difficult to control, with You (1998: 114) noting for example that 'according to an official survey in Hunan in 1985, bonus payments constituted more than 30 per cent of total wages in all industrial sectors' (You 1998: 114). The state's desire to control such growth led to the creation of the 'bonus tax', designed to bring bonus payments in line with state macro-regulation. Despite this, however, the growth rate of bonuses has constantly exceeded the limits set by the state.

By the early 1990s, therefore, the state had realized that wage control through administrative means (albeit more indirect than before) could no longer achieve the goal of 'macro wage balance'. Similarly, at the micro level, normative bureaucratic controls over wage structures were seen as increasingly ineffective; as for example, a manager's salary being limited to no more than four times that of an ordinary worker (Zhang 2000). New methods of wage regulation were thus developed, and increasingly market-based wage determinants were taken into account. From the early 1990s a new distribution model for the state sector gradually emerged and became official policy in 1995, namely '*Gongzi Zhidaoxian*' or the state 'wage guidance line'. Heralded as China's future industrial wage mechanism, the model would 'stipulate both minimum and maximum wage levels for work units in the light of the national economic situation', but with the important proviso that 'under this guidance, the state firms formulate their own wage grades' (You 1998: 117). The wage guidance line was to be determined by the principle that:

> the increase of the wage aggregate of a given firm should be kept below the increase of its profitability (based on tax remittance/profit retention ratio), and the real and average income of workers should be kept below the growth rate of their productivity (based on the increase of the net output value).
>
> (You 1998: 117)

In prompting decentralization of wage decision power, this reform was seen as further progress towards the marketization of the state sector. While, on the one hand, the 1994 Labour Law (under whose auspices such wage policies were realized) set out a number of additional basic workers' rights and social insurance conditions, on the other, it strengthened the ability of SOEs to legitimize redundancy and shed surplus labour (Warner 1996a and b, 1997a and b; Lee and Warner 2006).

### Surplus workers

We have noted how under the pre-1978 Mao-era employment policy, China's SOEs were not simply economic units but were also major welfare and livelihood providers. Due to the pursuit of full employment at the expense of economic efficiency, overstaffing became a common problem for all China's state enterprises. From the beginning of the 1980s to the early 1990s, this sector absorbed nearly two-thirds of the Chinese urban labour force. As SOE transformation gathered pace throughout the 1990s, the adverse effects of carrying a large percentage of surplus workers became increasingly apparent. The Enterprise Reform Division of the China State Economic and Trade Commission (1999) calculated that if the total surplus of SOE workers was calculated at 30 per cent, the expenditure on each surplus worker would be about 4,000 yuan annually. As such, the total expenditure for all SOE surplus workers would amount to approximately 96 billion yuan (equivalent to US$11.5 billion) annually, with this estimated cost actually being greater than the annual total profits for SOEs during the 1990s.

As surplus labour was considered the most serious obstacle both to improving SOE performance and furthering economic reform, significant SOE downsizing was undertaken from the mid-1990s (see Table 4.13). A common slogan of the period was 'the older and larger the SOE, the more surplus workers it houses'. Some of the largest and oldest SOEs, notably those that had existed for around half a century, were estimated to employ in the region of 50 per cent of surplus workers. In terms of demography, the emerging profile was that the more SOEs a region or city had, the more likely it was to be hit by large-scale redundancy, and thus to inherit high levels of unemployment, notably long-term unemployment. The three north-eastern provinces of China were paradigm examples, with the city of Shenyang being particularly hard hit in this respect. In sum, radical job reduction programmes began in the mid-1990s and remain in progress a decade later.

In order to control overstaffing, while avoiding social unrest resulting from redundancies, many SOEs adopted extremely gradual transitional measures (see later chapters). A common practice has been to lay off surplus workers but treat them as 'internal retirees' who receive a basic level of pay plus associated welfare benefits. These workers are provided with training

*Table 4.13* Number of laid-off workers (1996–2000) (million people)

| Year | 1996 | 1997 | 1998 | 1999 | 2000 |
|------|------|------|------|------|------|
| SOE laid-off workers | 7.2 | 7.87 | 6.1 | 6.5 | 6.57 |

Source: www.stats.gov.cn/tjgb/ndtjgb

and help with re-employment, but without being directly registered as 'unemployed' in the community. From September 1997 a system of 'minimum living allowances' for those laid-off was set up by local governments, and by August 1998, 486 cities (i.e. over 70 per cent of major cities) all over China had established such allowances (Wu 1999). By the end of 2000 the minimum living allowance system, based on funds shared by government and related enterprises, had been established in all cities and towns in China (SSB 2000).

### Employee welfare

In order to lighten the social burden on state enterprises and transform them into genuine economic entities, reform measures have been, and are being, taken to shift enterprise-based employee welfare to community-based social security systems. Economic reform has extensively changed the situation of cradle-to-grave welfare under which the SOEs used to be solely responsible for their employees' welfare, including life-long employment, housing, medical expenses, pension, and even children's schooling. The major breakthrough in this respect took place in March 1998, during the 9th National People's Congress, when the Chinese government set out reform measures on housing and medical care, which were both extremely important components of the SOE employee welfare system. As the OECF (1998) investigation indicated, the average amount of social security costs (including housing and medical care) per SOE was 3 per cent of sales revenue. The 1998 reform of housing represented a genuinely dramatic breakthrough in that its 'marketization' of housing distribution meant that:

> From the first of July 1998, the Chinese government abandoned its current scheme of governmental departments and state-owned enterprises offering apartments to employees with free or substantially subsidised rent, and introduced a new scheme that allowed individuals to buy residential housing and own property.
>
> (*China Newsletter* 1999: 19)

Similarly, with regard to medical welfare, the *Beijing Review* of 29 March–4 April 1999 revealed that significant reform of the medical insurance system was to be undertaken. Such reform saw employees required ultimately to contribute to their health care, pensions and education. Thus, SOEs were able to begin shedding their considerable social welfare burdens and, in so doing, focus their attentions more fully on issues of productivity and performance.

However, several years on, with welfare reforms still not fully established and a robust social security net not completely in place, SOEs continue to fund elements of the social security burden. When the burden of paying basic living expenses for millions of laid-off workers is added, SOEs currently have to shoulder extremely heavy social responsibilities and transitional costs. Frequently state enterprises bear responsibility for the costs of employee welfare in relation to unemployment, medical care and pensions.

## Conclusion

Although the share of the state-owned sector continues to decline, it remains significant in China's economy. SOEs continue to provide much-needed revenue to government and contribute significantly to urban employment. The reform of large SOEs, therefore, remains at the heart of China's economic reform programme. Widely regarded as the most difficult area of reform, it has been characterized by a complicated and uneven experimental process. Initially seeing an enterprise responsibility system adopted, mainly through implementation of a contracting system in the 1980s, subsequent experimentation has focused on 'corporatization' and the establishment of the MES from the mid-1990s onwards.

In the process of transformation, SOEs have been confronted with difficulties arising from deteriorating profitability and increasing debts, which demand further reform of ownership and governance. Reforms in the 1990s turned on the establishment of the 'modern enterprise' and its aim to overcome the problems of the factory system. The government took steps to convert a great majority of large and medium-sized SOEs into corporations, which were expected to adapt to market conditions with clarified property rights and strong internal management. In so doing, shareholding was perceived to be the most effective way to deepen the reform of SOEs, with, in recent years, the SCS in particular being implemented widely in small and medium-sized enterprises.

However, several problems have emerged in the process of corporatizing the SOEs. One of the most enduring has been the definition of state-owned property rights. The current reform of SOEs aims to clarify property rights further as well as resolve problems relating to the optimization of enterprise governance structures and the professional management of human resources. Although competition has been continually fostered since the beginning of the reform period – through, for example, the encouragement of TVEs, COEs and the introduction of international competition – this essentially relates to competition from outside the state sector rather than within. It can be argued that China's SOEs still need to be exposed more readily to market-based competition on a sectoral basis.

Finally, the reform process has generated far-reaching impacts on labour, notably in terms of employment and welfare. On the one hand, millions of workers have been laid-off from SOEs since the mid–late 1990s as the state sector shrinks under the reform process. On the other hand, there remains the lack of a robust social safety net for unemployed workers. As we argue in the chapters that follow, given these circumstances, state enterprises will continue to play a major role in employee welfare provision for the foreseeable future.

# Part II

# Reform programmes, surplus workers and labour unrest

# 5 Rise and fall of the Contract Responsibility System

## Introduction

We have discussed how debates on economic restructuring in China have revolved primarily around the adoption of market mechanisms in a gradual transition from the centrally planned economy that existed in China up until 1978. In this chapter we examine one important aspect of these debates, that relating to the discontinuation of the CRS which governed relations between the enterprise and the state in China from the early 1980s until 1994–1995. This analysis is derived mainly from textual materials (official reports, journals, newspapers, etc.) and qualitative, interview-based, field research conducted by members of the research team in the mid-1990s at Beijing's Capital Iron and Steel Corporation (Shougang), since this was the flagship of the CRS experiment and exemplifies some of the system's problems, which came to be perceived by the state to outweigh its benefits. Although Shougang is an untypical enterprise in important respects – mainly due to its special status in China (see below) – its experience with the CRS and its problematic transition from this system make it an important case study in the debate on state-enterprise reform in China.

## The Shougang Corporation

We begin with an overview of the Shougang Corporation's operations during the 1980s and 1990s. During our period of field research (1994–1997) the Shougang Iron and Steel Works (founded 1919) in Shijingshan, west Beijing, employed on its 84 square kilometre site around 150,000 of the Corporation's total workforce of well over 200,000. At the time, the Shougang Corporation was emerging as a major industrial enterprise on the world stage. The company literature of the mid-1990s noted that since the late 1980s Shougang had been empowered to 'engage directly in import and export business', 'set up plants and run joint-ventures abroad', and 'conduct labour services'. In addition it had been encouraged to 'do business in the fields of finance and foreign trade'. The Corporation's ambition was to become a 'transnational enterprise', following a decision made in late 1992 to accelerate the expansion of its activities abroad.

By the mid-1990s, Shougang, already China's fourth largest industrial enterprise and third largest steel producer, had signalled its ambitions in the international market place. For example, through its wholly owned subsidiary Shougang Holdings (Hong Kong) Ltd it acquired a series of listed Hong Kong companies, and in the process forged some powerful alliances, including a partnership with billionaire Li Ka-shing in a steel company (Shougang Concord International Enterprises). The company's Hong Kong investments also facilitated additional capital-raising in the local market. Other notable overseas investments included taking control of the Mesta Engineering Company of the US in 1988, and purchasing the Hierro iron-ore mine in Peru for US$180 million in 1992. Within China, the company had diversified into shipping, construction, computers and tourism.

Shougang was only able to reform its business practices and develop its business interests in this way because from the early 1980s, state controls over the company's activities were relaxed considerably. In 1979 the decision was taken to develop the CRS experiment as part of China's economic reform programme, and Shougang, as one of China's largest and best-known state enterprises, was selected as the flagship of the programme. Before the CRS was introduced, Shougang was state-owned and state-managed; net incomes had to be handed over to the state, and funds for investment had to be examined, approved and distributed by the state. In 1978, the President of Shougang could only approve expenditure of up to 800 yuan. The task was one of reforming a large state-owned corporation through integrating government administration with enterprise management, and creating a sense of 'enterprise' on the part of workers in the process.

It should be noted that Shougang was not chosen to pioneer the CRS solely because of its size and significance in the regional and national economy. Rather, the unusual scope granted to it to diversify into businesses other than steel (such as its licence to run its own bank) was attributed by many of Shougang's competitors in China, as well as by outside observers, to the superior political connections of the Chairman and head of the Corporation, Zhou Guanwu, who was in charge from 1954 until the spring of 1995. In particular, Zhou's close relationship with Deng Xiaoping, under whom he served during the civil war of the late 1940s, is seen as the key to his almost unparalleled freedom to pursue business opportunities at home and abroad. It was also noted at the time that several of Shougang's high-profile international acquisitions followed hard upon Deng Xiaoping's highly publicized visit to Shougang in May 1992 (*Far Eastern Economic Review*, 23 March 1995: 46–47). The changing fortunes of the Shougang Corporation and the rise and fall of the CRS more generally were, therefore, bound up with issues of elite factional rivalry within the CCP and the post-Deng succession struggle which was on-going more or less openly for a number of years. Without digressing too far into obscure kremlinology, this political context has to be borne in mind when considering even apparently neutral aspects of the SOE reform programme of the time. Where an enterprise had been as closely associated with a top Party leader for as long as Shougang had with Deng Xiaoping, the influence of intra-elite rivalries becomes highly relevant.

Developing upon themes established in Chapter 4, we now offer an expanded account of the problems with the CRS as they became apparent during the years in which it operated, problems which eventually led to the discontinuation of the system. We then look at the specific experience of Shougang under the CRS, the roots of the Corporation's troubles during this period, and how Shougang fared in its attempts to make the transition from the CRS to subsequent phases of reform.

## The CRS

The CRS operated at two main levels: enterprise-level contracting with the state (the state contract system), and internal contracting within the enterprises' businesses (the internal contract system). Although the phasing-out of the CRS was on-going from *circa* 1994–1995, many enterprises, including Shougang, opted to retain the internal contract system, usually termed the 'economic responsibility system'. In the steel industry, the CRS was introduced during the course of the 6th Five-Year Plan, 1980–1985, and was eventually adopted by 85 per cent of enterprises within the industry. It was modified several times during its existence in the light of enterprises' experiences in applying it. The main variations were a mid-1980s shift from profit remittance to taxation of profits (which proved unpopular with enterprises since it generally required them to turn over more money to the state and retain less for investment and development) and the subsequent return to the system of contracted profit remittance.

### *The state contract system*

Under the CRS, two types of state-enterprise contract existed. An enterprise would contract either to turn over a fixed percentage of its profits each year to the state during the course of the contract, or turn over a certain amount out of profits which would be increased annually at a fixed rate. Shougang's CRS contract was of the latter type.

In 1980 when the term of its contract began, it agreed to pay the state a sum based on 1978 profit figures, with this to rise at an annual rate of 7.2 per cent for the term of the contract, 14 years. Most state-enterprise contracts, it should be noted, ran for a much shorter period than Shougang's 14-year term, typically for three years, or at most five. This is another respect in which the Corporation was treated as a special case.

Where a fixed percentage of profit was turned over to the state by an enterprise, this could vary between 5–20 per cent. In both types of state-enterprise contract, surplus profits were then at the disposal of the enterprise for purposes of investment, acquisitions, restructuring etc. The concept was akin to the Western notion of the corporation as 'legal person'. The CRS thereby promised to replace the policy whereby only government agencies could represent state enterprises.

### The internal contract system

While the state contract system operated at the government-institutional level, at the organizational level was the internal contract system, which operated as a form of target-setting cascade. To quote former Shougang President, Luo Bingsheng (now Executive Deputy President of the China Iron and Steel Association):

> First we broke down the profits Shougang contracted to the government and our operating goals into various targets of profit, quantity, cost, quality, consumption etc., which were contracted by second-level companies to Shougang, then those targets were decomposed level by level through factories and mines, workshops, teams and groups to each post and individual.
>
> (Luo 1993: 14)

This cascade of targets thus encompassed operational requirements, levels of material consumption, the maintenance of facilities and conformance to regulations. As Luo outlined:

> By so doing, a contracting network of 'from top to bottom, from centre to margin' was formed in the whole company, which had every staff member and worker know his/her definite contract task . . . The internal contract system has created an initiative of all staff members and workers.
>
> (Luo 1993: 15)

Internal contracting at Shougang, as in other large corporations, was both vertical, as described above by Luo, and horizontal, that is between Shougang's component sub-companies.

A more nebulous aspect of the internal contract system at Shougang was the attempt to develop an 'enterprise culture' under the 'Essence of the People' philosophy. This policy was based on six main principles – 'value of innovation'; 'enterprise spirit'; 'excellent work style'; 'business morals'; 'responsibility of ownership'; and 'consideration to national interests, enterprise interests, and individual interests'. The latter principle repeats the familiar mantra of the whole industrial reform programme in China – the state, the enterprise and the individual will all benefit from increased enterprise autonomy. In fact, as we shall see below, Shougang was to stand accused of seeking to benefit only itself and its workers under the CRS, thereby flouting central reform policies and guidelines.

## Effects of the CRS

At an international seminar hosted by the Corporation in October 1993 to discuss the effects of the CRS ('The International Seminar on Shougang Contract System', attended by the first author along with delegates from Hong Kong, Russia and the US) Shougang's senior executives suggested that the system had been extremely successful at the company. Luo Bingsheng and his colleagues described how transnational and transbusiness diversification had contributed to the very high annual growth in profits of about 20 per cent during the period of CRS reform. Shougang was seen to have benefited from increased autonomy in investment and management, and also from improved staff commitment.

As many delegates were aware, however, the Shougang CRS seminar had been arranged as a last ditch effort to save what was already a condemned system of state-enterprise reform (note: the seminar was held only weeks prior to the Third Plenum of the 14th CCP Congress in November 1993, which ratified the 1992 policy to establish a 'socialist market' economy). A number of issues had been identified while the CRS was in force that were regarded as sufficiently serious to warrant the withdrawal out of the system and the development of new models to tackle the 'deep problems' of state-enterprise reform (Hassard and Sheehan 1997).

The following discussion of these problems refers to the generality of Chinese steel makers which operated the CRS during the 1980s and early 1990s, as well as to the specific case of the Shougang Corporation.

### *Disparities between enterprises*

As noted, one of the main problems with the CRS had been the disparities that had arisen between enterprises as a result of the process of bilateral negotiation of contracts between individual SOEs and state authorities. There were no definite regulations regarding the level at which profit quotas were set; as mentioned, a range of 5–20 per cent existed. The precise terms of the state-enterprise contract varied according to such factors as: the nature of the enterprise; the industrial sector and geographical area to which it belonged; the extent to which it was burdened with obsolete equipment; the pre-CRS levels of investment; and so on. In the case of Shougang, it was allowed very generous contract terms because of its need to invest in improved technology. As well as retaining the lion's share of its profits during the 14-year course of its contract, the Corporation also benefited from artificially low depreciation rates enshrined in the terms and conditions. This flexibility was built into the CRS from the start, because it was intended as a transitional stage in state enterprises' development and because across-the-board regulations on SOE contracts would have resulted in many enterprises failing to reach their targets. State enterprises, and particularly the largest of them in important industries such as iron and steel, were not to be set up to fail under the CRS; bankruptcy was not an option at this stage. This meant, of course, that the CRS ultimately would not promote more efficient allocation of scarce resources, despite this being an important aim of the reform programme as a whole.

It is generally accepted that the CRS did have benefits for many enterprises in terms of increased autonomy and improved management; for example, retained profits in CRS enterprises increased four-fold between 1986 and 1993. But the lack of a standard contract or of transparent, definite regulations governing profit remittance eventually resulted in management and state dissatisfaction with the system. Re-negotiation of contracts and disputes over profit quotas became common, especially where one enterprise found out that a comparable one had negotiated a better deal. Since the process of quota-setting relied so much on bilateral negotiation, politically well-connected enterprises were able to use their connections to their advantage. This seems to have been the case at Shougang, since the terms of its contract were unusually favourable to the enterprise rather than the state. The profit turned over to the state by Shougang was based on 1978 figures; that is, before the Chinese economic reforms had really begun in industry. Furthermore, although Shougang's actual profits increased at an annual rate of 20 per cent during the 1980s and early 1990s, its remittance to the state only increased at 7.2 per cent per year. Thus, the Corporation was one of the few which 'got rich first', as Deng Xiaoping had urged. The state authorities did, of course, receive more money from Shougang than they had done before the CRS was introduced, but they did not benefit to the same extent as the Corporation itself, thus violating the fundamental principle of reform benefiting state, enterprise and individual alike.

### Short-termism

Short-termism has been widely noted as a direct effect of the CRS, particularly in the many enterprises where a three-year contract was the norm. Although in some respects the CRS is viewed as having improved management performance in the enterprises involved, there was also a clear tendency for managers to concentrate on the quantitative productivity targets laid down in the contract to the neglect, for example, of fixed-asset maintenance, investment and technological improvement. As the pursuit of short-term profit came to the fore, some enterprises did seem to be achieving prodigiously under the CRS, but reported profit rates were often misleading since there was no longer-term development strategy behind them. Such short-termism seems to have been a direct result of the system of above-quota profit retention and thus as inherent to the CRS itself. Additionally, depreciation costs were not always included in contracts, or if they were (as with Shougang) the rate might be set artificially low.

Despite its efforts in the direction of vertical integration (such as its overseas purchases in Peru and the US), and despite the unusually long term of its contract with the state, Shougang was not immune from the problem of short-termism. Although technological development did take place during the term of its contract in Shougang's core steel-making business, the Corporation is also reported to have relied upon importing second-hand equipment to introduce new lines of production that would bring quick returns to boost short-term profitability. Problems of short-termism were, indeed, identified and discussed within Shougang while the CRS was still in operation ('Shougang Reforms' Editorial Committee 1992), but evidently not resolved.

Overall the general neglect of technological innovation (except where this would result in a quick increase in production volume and increased profit) and prioritizing of quantity over quality were particularly disappointing outcomes of the CRS, since the industrial reforms had been specifically aimed at improving enterprises' performance in these two areas, which had traditionally been weak spots of the state sector in China.

### Impact on the tax system and government revenue-raising

As noted in our earlier descriptions of the CRS, there was a change in the system from the mid-1980s as profit remittance by enterprises was replaced by taxation of profits, followed by a reversion to the original scheme of fixed-rate profit remittance as a result of enterprise objections to having to hand over more to the state under the taxation scheme (Liu 1987). This caused confusion in the tax system, with the situation being complicated further by the fact that some CRS enterprises had negotiated special fixed rates of VAT and other taxes as part of their contracts with the state, thus placing limits on state revenue. Fiscal and enterprise reforms were intended to disentangle profit and tax and ensure that not only all SOEs, but enterprises of all types, including collectives and joint-ventures, were subject to the same tax rates, with no special deals for favoured institutions. The 1992 CCP decision to implement the 'socialist market economy' was reflected in the emphasis on competition between enterprises of all ownership types on an equal basis, including the establishment of a level playing-field as far as taxation was concerned. This not only removed discrepancies in the tax treatment of state and other enterprises in China, but also finally ended the special arrangements from which certain SOEs had benefited under the CRS.

### Levels of enterprise and managerial autonomy

Although enterprises were, to a large extent, responsible for their own profits under the CRS, the state remained responsible for losses (Liu 1987). Since around half of all SOEs in China were regularly loss-making (and many had made losses for years), this represented a considerable drain on limited resources. This lack of responsibility for losses within CRS enterprises cast doubt over the claimed success of the system; and in any case, given the continued losses in many of the SOEs involved, it clearly did not succeed in all of them. The other side of the equation was that the CRS was unable to prevent continued government interference in the running of SOEs. This remained a major problem in the industry of China generally, and a removal or reduction of government interference became one of the primary aims of the subsequent MES reform programme (see Chapter 6).

To some extent, then, the CRS seems to have brought the state the worst of both worlds. At a time when the state remained responsible for SOE losses, SOE managers operating the CRS reportedly failed to come to terms with the increased decision-making powers it had bestowed. In a few cases autonomy was perceived to have gone too far, with certain top managers seemingly able to do whatever they wanted, including engaging in forms of business from which competitors were excluded. Again, Shougang is often mentioned as a prime example of this, and no doubt the Corporation's top political connections were a factor in its favourable treatment. But in other, less exceptional cases, too, the problem of 'autonomy without responsibility' was frequently mentioned as a problematic feature of CRS reform experiments. Thus, as part of subsequent reform measures (and notably those under the MES) managers were explicitly reminded of their responsibilities to the state as well as to their staff.

Although during the 15 years of its existence some managerial improvement had been observed in enterprises practising the CRS, in general, serious problems remained. Financial and cost management were singled out as areas of particular weakness. It was regularly claimed that CRS managers focused on the financial terms of their contract with the state to the neglect of other areas of SOE business. Furthermore, it became a criticism of some SOE managers that they were only concerned with telling the higher levels of the industrial bureaucracy what these officials wanted to hear regardless of what was actually happening within their enterprises. Comments along these lines were commonly made by academic analysts of management in the steel industry, by workers and even by SOE managers themselves. Doubts were continually expressed regarding how far such management behaviour could, or would, change in Chinese SOEs as the reform era progressed.

### Failure to resolve the problem of property rights

Under the CRS, 'ambiguous property rights between the state and the enterprises resulted in ambiguous distributional and control relations' (Lee 1996: 109). The main problems were those of insufficiently clear regulations on income and control rights over retained profits, and the considerable amount of bargaining, rule-bending, and collusion between state and enterprise authorities that went on in practice. Once China embarked on the course of economic reform, and specifically reform of SOEs, it was necessary to consider how to separate management from ownership, and the CRS was originally intended as a new institutional arrangement that would facilitate this separation (Chen, F. 1995). But making the terms of the state-enterprise contract legally enforceable failed to alter significantly the behaviour of either state organs or enterprises in respect of questions of property rights. As such, the need for a real separation of management and ownership became commonly cited as a reason for abandoning the CRS and adopting new models of enterprise reform. The 'negotiation', which was an integral part of setting state-enterprise contract profit quotas under the CRS, also tended to institutionalize older (pre-reform) state habits of direct interference in, or control over, the running of SOEs (Lee 1996).

One important manifestation of this problem was the question of management's disposal of state assets. This was permitted under the CRS provided that the funds so acquired were applied to technological improvement. In practice, however, as discussed above, technological improvement was extremely limited, with technical and maintenance departments among the biggest losers in terms of influence within the enterprise (Chen, F. 1995). It is now believed that the decentralization of authority that took place during the CRS allowed considerable abuse of state assets for quick profit, and under subsequent systems of enterprise reform, managers' responsibilities included an obligation at least to maintain the value of state assets, if not to increase them.

### The social welfare burden on large enterprises

Clearly, the continued social welfare burden was a problem of the external institutional environment rather than a flaw of the CRS itself, but it was still something that was not provided for under that system, and which had to be dealt with if the autonomy of large SOEs was to mean anything in practice. Enterprises implementing the CRS continued to be responsible for providing a wide variety of social and other services to employees and their dependants, and this necessarily had a significant impact on their profitability and autonomy over personnel matters. Under subsequent models of reform, responsibility for employees' social welfare was, in many cases, though not all, beginning to be transferred from enterprises to local government. As was stressed by several of our informants in the Chinese steel industry, enterprises could not create a socialist market economy on their own; the government had to play its part as well with the creation of a robust social-security system.

## Fate of a CRS flagship

Arguments such as the above were raised by Chinese economic analysts as early as the mid-1980s (see Lee 1996). As a result, by the early 1990s the debate over the future of Chinese state-enterprise reform had basically been won by those who were critical of the CRS in practice. In the case of Shougang, however, there appeared two powerful arguments in favour of continuing with the CRS – Shougang's much-vaunted business successes, and the personal backing which this CRS flagship still enjoyed from China's paramount leader.

Both of these arguments soon evaporated. Shougang's success under the CRS had always been attributed by its rivals to the special terms of its particular deal with state authorities rather than to the superiority of its reform blueprint. Apart from its unusually long contract (14 years), these special terms included its low depreciation rates, its permission to exclude bonuses from normal wage costs, and its freedom to make overseas acquisitions and gain for some of its companies a Hong Kong stock exchange listing. Given that even with all these advantages Shougang still fell prey to many of the common defects of the CRS, the critical argument appears a persuasive one.

In addition, Deng Xiaoping's advanced age and failing health sharply reduced his influence over the direction of enterprise reform; it seems also to have weakened significantly his ability to protect what was known throughout China as his favourite SOE from its critics and rivals. After the decision was taken to bring the CRS experiment to an end, the problems with this particular reform system came to be seen as the very least of Shougang's difficulties. From early 1995, the Corporation experienced accusations of high-level corruption and of seriously polluting the capital, had its freedom to run non-steel businesses curtailed, and was compelled to sell 80 per cent of its 100 per cent stake in its own Huaxia Bank because of unspecified 'organizational difficulties' (*Far Eastern Economic Review*, 7 December 1995: 83).

Of particular critical notoriety was that Zhou Beifang, the son of Zhou Guanwu and Chairman of the Corporation's Hong Kong subsidiary, Shougang Concord International Enterprises, was arrested on corruption charges in mid-February 1995; his father retired from his post at the head of the Corporation immediately afterwards (*Far Eastern Economic Review*, 2 February 1995: 16; 23 March 1995: 46–47). The Shougang case was not directly connected to the bigger Beijing corruption scandal which had resulted in the resignation of Chen Xitong, head of the Beijing Party apparatus, and the suicide of Beijing Vice-Mayor Wang Baosen, (*Far Eastern Economic Review*, 13 June 1996: 29), but both of these corruption investigations were clearly being used as political weapons in the struggle to succeed the ailing Deng Xiaoping and to define his legacy.

The pollution accusations could be interpreted as a sign that, rather than simply returning to the normal status of a large SOE in need of reform, Shougang was actually being victimized by critics who were looking for ammunition against the Corporation beyond the deficiencies of its CRS programme. These accusations were made in mid-1996 when the company was visited by an inspection team from the National People's Congress (China's parliament) and accused of being responsible for half of Beijing's sulphur dioxide emissions and two-thirds of its carbon monoxide emissions (*Far Eastern Economic Review*, 27 June 1996: 30). This serious pollution of the capital was said to date back to the late 1970s. Even if these figures were accurate (for they appear to be suspiciously round numbers, but on the other hand Shougang's main plant, located not far out in the city's western suburbs, was an enormous one, which lacked modern, environmentally friendly technology to deal with its emissions), it seems somewhat surprising that no one raised this huge pollution problem at any point during the preceding 20 years. A possible conclusion is that, without its powerful protectors in high places, Shougang was now considered fair game by critics who would have had to hold their peace in the past.

To appreciate the extent of the difficulties in which Shougang found itself, it is necessary to be aware of how far this particular enterprise had to fall from its position of almost unparalleled privilege. Shougang was not just another state-owned steel maker; it was not even just another very large state-owned steel maker employing around a quarter of a million people who would be likely to cause the state serious problems were they ever to find themselves out of pocket or out of a job in significant numbers. The unusual political significance that accrues to things that happen at Shougang can be illustrated with reference to two incidents involving the Corporation's workers. First, there was the matter of the participation of Shougang workers in the independent unions formed during the 1989 Democracy Movement in Beijing (and in more than a dozen other cities as well). The participation of workers from Shougang was well documented; these workers were seen and spoken to, and their banners photographed, by reliable eye-witnesses to the demonstrations (Han 1990; Lu Ping 1990; *South China Morning Post*, 9 March 1990: 12). Yet, even before the crackdown on the Movement had really begun, the official trade unions, the Shougang Corporation itself, and the local and national Party authorities went to enormous lengths to try to prove that no genuine employees of the Corporation were involved and that work attendance and production were at normal levels (*China Daily*, 19 May 1989: 1; Foreign Broadcast Information Service Daily Report – China, 13 June 1989: 30).

In part this display of concern was simply a reflection of the Chinese authorities' general anxiety about any serious unrest involving workers, and in particular about any attempts by workers to organize themselves. The large-scale involvement in 1989 of workers from large and relatively successful SOEs such as Shougang was also a new phenomenon. In the past, workers' protests had tended to involve the relatively disadvantaged in China's industrial hierarchy, such as temporary and contract workers, apprentices etc. But the focus on Shougang and the lengths to which the authorities went, protesting perhaps too much that everything was normal in the western suburbs, demonstrated the particular importance attached to Deng's 'pet state enterprise' (*Far Eastern Economic Review*, 11 March 1993: 25). Despite the relatively high wages and bonuses received by most Shougang employees in the heyday of the CRS, occasional mutterings of workforce discontent were still heard (*Far Eastern Economic Review*, 18 November 1993: 64). Similarly, when retired women workers from the Corporation demonstrated outside the central leadership compound in Beijing over disputed pension entitlements, it made front-page news (*South China Morning Post*, 17 February 1993) not just because a public demonstration at such a sensitive political site was still a rarity in China, but also because of Shougang's status as a model of enterprise reform enjoying Deng's close personal support.

As the flagship of the CRS programme and the recipient of great publicity in this role, Shougang might well have expected to experience some sort of backlash once the system had become discredited, becoming as much of a focal point for criticism of the CRS as it had once been for its praise. As noted, when still in charge of the corporation, Zhou Guanwu had attempted to mount a last-ditch campaign to defend the CRS and Shougang immediately before the Party plenum which took the decision to abandon the (external) CRS in late 1993, demonstrating his concern about possible repercussions for Shougang if the programme it had pioneered were to be completely discredited (*Far Eastern Economic Review*, 23 December 1993: 9). However, there was reportedly some support even within Shougang itself for ending the CRS. Managers' attitudes tended to be determined by whether or not they could easily meet the targets that were set for them under the CRS, and by the early 1990s those managers who were feeling under pressure from tough targets did favour abandoning the CRS.

Yet, if it was true that Shougang's success owed more to the political connections of its top leadership than to the CRS, it could also be argued that the Corporation should have been able to ride out the criticism of a particular phase of the reforms and go on to take its place among the enterprises piloting the next reform programme, bolstered by its well-known links to Deng Xiaoping and others. Indeed, even after the official abandonment of the CRS, the Corporation's President, Luo Bingsheng, announced that Shougang still had ambitions to be the world's largest steel producer by the turn of the century, and was hoping to 'list in New York' at some point (*Far Eastern Economic Review*, 9 June 1994: 73). But this optimism evaporated the following year. Shougang was not, in fact, originally included among the enterprises piloting either of the subsequent main SOE reform programmes launched – the MES and the GCS – although it was later included in the latter sample group of companies.

Given that the decision to abandon the CRS was well founded in the light of the experiences of so many enterprises implementing it, and that this decision had already been taken in the late autumn of 1993, more than a year before Shougang ran into serious difficulties, it seems that the Corporation's woes were more bound up with the Deng succession struggle than they were with any continuing need to attack proponents of improving and refining, rather than abandoning, the CRS. The Shougang Corporation's sudden fall from grace during this period seems not to have been brought about by its high-profile association with a discredited reform programme. The converse line of reasoning, that the Corporation's other difficulties, detailed above, were used to further discredit the CRS programme, is not really convincing either since the argument about the defects of this system had basically been won before 1995. Rather, it seems to be the case that those who live by their political connections, die by them also. Shougang's fortunes changed dramatically in the period immediately following the publication of the three-volume celebration of the Corporation's reforms, including contributions from both Chinese and foreign observers, in 1992 ('Shougang Reforms' Editorial Committee 1992). If Shougang is viewed more broadly as a representative of Deng's whole enterprise reform strategy, then attacks on the Corporation during the mid-1990s make more sense than if the already-defunct CRS programme were the target of the criticism.

That Shougang's difficulties were closely linked to the political transition taking place in China was confirmed in February 1996, when the *China Reform Daily* newspaper, the organ of the State Commission for Economic Restructuring, launched an open attack on the Corporation's management and direction under Zhou Guanwu. The new leadership of the Corporation was praised for having 'shifted their emphasis from being unique and defiant towards the state's macro-level control and adjustment (policy) to toeing the line of the party's central committee ... This has enabled Shougang to intensify its reform drive' (*China Reform Daily*, 14 February: 1). In a direct swipe at Zhou Guanwu himself, the article also noted that 'Management at Shougang has changed from a patriarchal dictatorship to a democratic and scientific decision-making system which respects opinions of experts and the workers' (ibid.). More generally, the report blamed not only Shougang itself but Deng Xiaoping's rapid reform strategy, for the problems of economic overheating which had been brought under control by a three-year austerity programme overseen by then Vice-Premier Zhu Rongji (*Hong Kong Standard*, 17 February 1996: 5; Foreign Broadcast Information Service Daily Report – China, 21 February 1996: 16–17). Cautious growth targets set by the Party centre in 1992 were disregarded after Deng Xiaoping's famous remark that 'slow economic growth is not socialism' gave the green light to the more developed coastal provinces to push ahead regardless. His visit to Shougang the same year, which sparked off a new round of international acquisitions for the Corporation, was seen in the same light. Both Shougang's conduct and Deng's broader reform strategy, in turn, became disavowed by the so-called 'third generation' of top Chinese leaders.

With the CRS abandoned by its flagship and throughout the industrial hierarchy, there was clearly a need for some sort of new reform blueprint, preferably one that could tackle some of the outstanding problems in enterprise structure and management which the CRS had either failed to resolve or had not addressed at all.

## Conclusion

Shougang's original exclusion from the 'national group' of MES/GCS pilot enterprises may have been as much for political as economic reasons, for the State Economic Restructuring Commission, the institution behind the *China Reform Daily*, which attacked Shougang's record under Zhou Guanwu, had a hand in selecting the national pilot enterprises. But clearly the transition was likely to be a difficult one, as Shougang lost much of the special treatment that contributed to its success under the CRS and had to find ways of maintaining its profitability in a changed economic environment. With the CRS no more, the Corporation would have to pay tax at the same rate as every other enterprise, its depreciation rates being revised upwards, and its bonuses a part of its regular wage costs, rather than coming straight out of retained profit. All these changes necessitated a marked improvement in the Corporation's finances to cope with the downward pressure on its profitability.

Staff and workers at Shougang benefited from its high level of retained profits during the term of its CRS contract in the form of bonus increases some 40–60 per cent higher than increases in basic salary during the same period. Since bonuses generally form such a significant proportion of state workers' monthly pay (typically around 15 per cent), any marked reduction in levels of bonus would have an appreciable impact on workers' budgets and morale. Workers' bonuses were suspended for a while during the spring of 1995 when accusations of high-level corruption at the Corporation first became public and Zhou Guanwu retired (*Far Eastern Economic Review*, 23 March 1995: 46). Given the changed circumstances under which Shougang found itself operating, bonuses could not return to their previous high levels, and this engendered workforce dissatisfaction with management.

Despite its much-vaunted levels of profit under the CRS, the Shougang Corporation also had a serious debt problem by 1993, the penultimate year of its CRS contract. The many competitive advantages enshrined in its contract with the state, the focus of much resentment elsewhere in the industry, could not protect it entirely from the general problems of Chinese industry and, like others, it was trapped in a web of triangular debt between SOEs, as well as being affected by falling demand for steel from the domestic construction industry. In late 1993 the Corporation was granted an emergency state loan of 400 million yuan to deal with this situation (*Far Eastern Economic Review*, 18 November 1993: 63). Given the size of the Corporation, like other comparable Chinese steel makers it continued to receive state subsidies in one form or another and was not threatened with bankruptcy, in keeping with the new official policy slogan of 'grasping the large, releasing the small'. So although its era of enjoying special treatment had ended, it still belonged to a class of enterprises that the state was not yet prepared to abandon completely to the mercies of the market.

# 6 Modern enterprises, group companies and surplus labour

*With Xiao Yuxin*

## Introduction

This chapter examines, on the one hand, state-enterprise experimental reforms developed under the Modern Enterprise and Group Company systems, and, on the other, the effects of the successive rounds of workforce downsizing that have accompanied them. In so doing we develop a line of analysis in concert with both the 'old' (DiMaggio and Powell 1991) and 'new' (Nee 1998) paradigms of institutional theory in sociology and organization theory, in that we explore the ways in which institutions serve to constrain or encourage organizational action, using an empirical case study to examine particular processes and outcomes.

In analysing relations between enterprises, communities and the state, we adopt a variant of the 'political-institutional' perspective in organization theory, thereby accepting the views of writers who claim this offers a robust framework for the empirical analysis of state-enterprise relations in socialist economies. Nee and Stark (1989) and Chen, D. (1995), for example, suggest this perspective offers a clear orienting framework for analysing the transition towards corporatization and a market economy. Child (1994), White and Liu (2001) and Nolan (2001) have argued further that Chinese enterprise management reflects politics in ways that are specific to the People's Republic of China, and that the specificity grows closer the more the enterprise is tied by ownership and control to the state institutional structure. Such processes are apparent in the non-marketized part of the state sector, which remains largely incorporated into the state administrative apparatus, despite central government attempts to delegate the management of reform and encourage local initiatives.

In developing this analysis, however, we do not offer unqualified support for a variant of institutionalism that suggests consistency and uniformity in the reform process. This would paint an overly rational picture of institutional relations and practices which, in the present case, are frequently disparate and disorderly. Instead, given the often chaotic nature of the reform process, we develop a political-institutional approach that reflects how the management of SOEs is both influenced by, and in turn influences, the network of relations established between the enterprise, the community, local government and the state. In so doing, we attempt to identify how such political-institutional forces influence enterprise and sectoral behaviour, while at the same time acknowledging significant variations in the experience of reform.

In what follows, then, we present results from a second textual- and fieldwork-based study of enterprise reform in China's SOEs and extrapolate from the findings to speculate on some of the consequences arising from such large-scale organizational restructuring. In so doing we analyse, initially, generic structures and processes of enterprise reform, in terms of institutional-organizational relations and directions of change, and subsequently the effects of SOE restructuring in terms of particular organizational outcomes, especially those stemming from rounds of corporate downsizing.

## The MES and GCS experiments

Begun in 1994 and 1992 respectively, the MES and GCS experimental reform programmes were designed to achieve the 'corporatization' of China's SOEs which, in the pre-reform era, were social and political as much as economic entities. These experimental programmes were piloted by the state in large and medium-sized state enterprises, including a number of large steel corporations. Initially 56 large state enterprises piloted the GCS with the aim of developing a parent holding company and a large group of subsidiaries that would have a high degree of management autonomy from the parent and be capable of competing in world markets through reorganizing their resources, assets and structure. In addition, 100 other enterprises were involved in a basic MES restructuring experiment. In fact, though, the 56 GCS pilots were also undertaking MES-style reforms internally, so that in effect there were 156 national MES pilot enterprises in late 1994 (Hassard and Sheehan 1997). In addition to these, other firms, including one in our sample (see below), were subsequently selected as pilot enterprises by their provincial governments. Indeed, as it became judged to be an effective strategy for reform, MES-type restructuring became adopted by companies that were not officially included in any pilot project, this pattern being familiar from previous rounds of reform in China, where experimental blueprints tended to become general in industry by the time they were formally adopted as official policy, the CRS being a case in point (Chen, D. 1995; Hassard and Sheehan 1997; see Chapter 4 for further details).

The MES reform programme as originally defined consisted of three main elements: reform, reconstruction and restructuring (*gaige, gaizao, gaizu*). As discussed previously, the main elements of the programme were: the clarification of property rights; clearer definition of rights and responsibilities; the separation of government and management functions; and the development of 'scientific' enterprise management. In practical terms, the realization of the programme's aims involved the adoption of new enterprise-management mechanisms, technical transformation and improvement, and the reorganization of property rights and assets. The MES/GCS experiments were intended to introduce to China's SOEs modern management mechanisms and elements of the Western corporate system, which for many in China were seen as factors that had enabled Western companies to fend off government interference more successfully than their Chinese counterparts.

A final aspect of the programme was to be the removal, or at least the substantial reduction, of the social welfare burden on state enterprises, which was seen as a major obstacle to future SOE profitability and international competitiveness. As we have discussed, large SOEs in China have traditionally been 'societies in miniature' (*xiao shehui*) responsible for the cradle-to-grave welfare of all employees and their dependants. In theory, this significant social welfare burden was to be transferred primarily to local government, although, as we discuss below, in practice this has frequently proved difficult to negotiate and effect.

## Researching MES/GCS reforms

Our analysis is based predominantly on evidence from two main sources: (i) visits to state-owned steel companies undertaking MES/GCS reforms; and (ii) textual materials on the philosophies, practices and effects of SOE restructuring. Following pilot visits to a number of corporations during 1995 and 1996, field data were collected by the team on a regular, mostly yearly, basis from 1997–2005. In the main our information is derived from series of semi-structured interviews, although in addition we have collected statistical and observational data during our field visits. In our 'main sample', eight steel SOEs carrying out MES/GCS restructuring have been regularly consulted, most on a recurrent, two-year cycle basis.

In terms of size of workforce, our MES/GCS companies range from one of the largest steel manufacturers in China, with a payroll of over 200,000 workers, to a relatively small producer employing around 17,000. Our eight case companies are located in separate cities in north, east, central, south-east and south-west China. In addition, visits have been made to several sub-companies of our eight corporations and also to SOEs operating in other sectors of the Chinese economy. This information also informs our analysis.

In the majority of our fieldwork visits, we were allowed to observe operational processes and conduct interviews with senior executives, group level managers and engineers. Interview information was collected in the main by way of hand-written notes, although on a few occasions permission was granted for sessions to be tape-recorded. In addition to our company visits, we also collected interview data from representatives of universities and ministries with professional and/or research experience of MES/GCS reforms. In the main, our interview sessions were conducted on a group basis, with typically 3–5 people being consulted at a time. Interview sessions could last a whole morning or afternoon.

One fairly novel aspect of the research process was that in addition to the 'formal' interview programme, one member of the research team (a former member of faculty, and graduate, of the iron and steel university in Beijing, with close contacts at each company) arranged a personal 'familiarization' visit at each plant approximately a fortnight to one month in advance. The objectives of these visits were three-fold: (i) to finalize the formal interview programme; (ii) to collect additional information that would inform the interview sessions; and (iii) (and importantly) to collect 'sensitive' data on productivity, performance and manpower levels, etc. that might not be revealed comfortably in a formal interview situation.

## Reluctant reformers: MES and GCS restructuring in practice

Traditionally all state enterprises in China, even relatively small ones, aimed for total vertical integration. Since the early 1990s, however, in the interests of specialization, efficiency, product diversification, and clarification of company functions, the steel-making SOEs in our sample have been engaged in a process of industrial fragmentation, mainly separating off component parts that are involved in their core line of production (i.e. iron and steel) from others which may be engaged in completely unrelated lines of business, working towards the model of a parent holding company with a range of more or less autonomous subsidiary companies. The core iron and steel subsidiaries maintain a fairly close relationship with the parent company, although still enjoying some degree of management autonomy, while the other sub-companies, including social-service companies, have a much higher degree of autonomy from the parent. The formation of sub-companies is seen to offer a number of advantages – to spread responsibility for results throughout the group; to provide increased opportunities for gaining access to capital (especially overseas); and to absorb surplus labour from the core iron and steel businesses. Also dividend income from sub-companies (or profit quotas) can be used by the parent company to help cover enterprise social welfare costs where these have not, as yet, been transferred to local government.

The concept is for all sub-companies eventually to be formed into shareholding or limited-liability companies that will be responsible for their own profits and losses. Such companies will be able to attract outside investment, borrow from banks and enter into joint-ventures with foreign companies in their own right. This ability to attract much-needed outside investment is a primary reason for their formation. Shares in those shareholding and limited-liability companies that are listed on the stock market can be bought by anyone, including individuals, while shares in those not yet listed can only be bought by institutional investors; such 'public-oriented legal persons' (Lee 1996) might be state-owned banks or insurance companies, other SOEs or state trade unions. In many instances 'triangular' debt owed to government bureaux, state-run banks and suppliers has been converted into shares to aid corporations so indebted as to be virtually insolvent in Western terms. Under MES/GCS reform, creditors have generally accepted these arrangements, as there seemed little likelihood of recovering money unless some sort of debt write-off was undertaken to enable the corporation to continue in business. Under current provisions, core iron- and steelmaking sub-companies generally remain funded by the parent company, and the parent company mostly retains a controlling stake of at least 51 per cent in its sub-companies. However, we have found examples of parent-company stakes of less than 51 per cent, while individual shareholdings can total as much as 20 per cent.

Sub-companies are responsible for their own profits and losses, although the latter responsibility is sometimes phased in over a period of several years, with a sliding subsidy from the parent company, to offset losses, which is gradually reduced to nothing. The parent company is only responsible for the money it has invested in the sub-company, although as mentioned above some sub-companies remain funded exclusively by the group corporation. In principle sub-companies can decide on their own staffing levels and appoint their own managers without the approval of the parent company. In practice, however, they are expected to consult with the parent company over any large reductions in their workforce and in the appointment of the top one or two managerial posts. Sub-companies are allowed to recruit new staff from outside the group, but clearly there is also pressure on them to take up the slack where redundant workers in other parts of the group are in need of new posts. More will be said about surplus labour as an effect of MES/GCS reform later.

The degree of control that sub-companies have over their production targets varies depending on whether the group company is their main customer or whether they sell most of their product outside the group. In general, they are free to look for markets anywhere, but where they provide a key input to group steel production (e.g. an iron-ore mining sub-company) the group's orders must be met before production can be sold outside to the highest bidder. Similarly, inputs can in theory be bought in from any competitive supplier, but in practice many of our case company informants suggest it is common for sub-companies to choose to work mainly within existing group relationships whether seeking markets or materials. Parent companies still have considerable influence over most sub-companies whatever the regulations on corporate structure and governance might say on paper. The parent company must be informed of all sub-company investment decisions and must give permission for any investment above a certain amount. At one steel corporation for which we have figures, the investment ceiling for sub-companies is RMB30 million.

As noted, China has won praise for the gradual, pragmatic reform path it has followed since 1978, particularly in comparison with the 'shock therapy' strategy of countries within Eastern Europe and the FSU (Child 1994; Nolan 1995a, 2001, 2003; Guthrie 1999; Buck *et al.* 2000; Tsui and Lau 2002). But, successful though it appears to have been to date, for the largest SOEs, still to be resolved effectively are enduring and politically sensitive issues of employment restructuring, enterprise ownership and the SOEs' relationships with central and local government. The very nature of the large SOE in pre-1978 China made it likely that any radical restructuring would inextricably be bound up with wide-ranging reforms such as the abolition of subsidized housing and the effort to set up an urban welfare state run by local government and jointly funded by the state, employers and employees. Furthermore, recent stages of reform have witnessed large SOEs also being exposed to fluctuations in international markets to a much greater extent than they were ten years ago, despite the fact that in the case of steel, most Chinese production still goes to satisfy domestic demand.

The early years of the MES/GCS reform programme saw SOEs affected by a period of significant economic difficulty in the region. Around 1997–1998, after the onset of the Asian financial crisis, some of our steel corporations found themselves competing for domestic business with Japanese and Russian firms, as these sought new markets to replace those lost in Southeast Asia, and at the same time having to find new export markets of their own. The resulting price competition reduced profit margins which were often not generous to begin with.

In recent years, the conflicting demands placed upon large SOEs by central and local governments continue to hamper the achievement of certain reform goals. For example, the largest and most technologically advanced steelmaking SOEs have seen profits soar during the recent boom in demand for steel and consequent rise in prices. But strong demand in recent years has also led to a proliferation of new, small mills, often set up under local-government auspices, that have strained supplies of raw materials and transport capacity and so driven up costs. In addition, as smaller state-owned steel plants come under government pressure to close down or merge with larger rivals as part of the current 'consolidation' of the industry, large SOEs once again have to absorb additional surplus labour, wage and pension responsibilities.

Besides unexpected external factors, domestic conflicts of interest between the local and central state and institutional problems of ideology and politics continue to hinder progress in state-enterprise reform. Change has generally gone furthest in those areas that are purely internal to the corporation, although even here the influence of existing institutional power structures remains strong in many respects. Superficially, at least, MES/GCS enterprises in China do now more closely resemble typical Western corporate structures. Our steel corporations now generally have a Board of Directors chosen by shareholders who select the general manager. But for large, state-owned steel makers, in most cases the main or sole shareholder is still the state, which means that in practice candidates for the Board are recommended and appointed by the government, i.e. the CCP, just as top enterprise managers always were before the MES/GCS reforms. It was admitted in two of our corporations that, to date, changes in corporate structure were still more 'form than substance', with the ideal of shareholder control essentially falling prey to continued government interference (see Chapter 9). The reportedly high level of government interference in the appointment of Boards of Directors has thus far negated one of the main purposes of the MES/GCS programme, the separation of government and management functions. As a further example of the conflicting pulls of local and central government interests in large SOEs, the top management of most of the remaining large state-owned companies are appointed by the central State Enterprise Supervisory Committee (SESC) and undergo up to a year of training in the Central Party University in Beijing after their appointment. For these managers, the performance-related pay arrangements under which they are obliged, for example, to safeguard and increase the value of the assets under their control are set out in a contract with the SESC, and not with the company itself.

Problems have also arisen during the period of reform with attempts to alter the distribution of institutional power within the state enterprise. Before the reforms, such power mainly rested with the so-called 'old three committees', the Party branch, management and the official trade union (with the latter very much under the thumb of the other two, except within a very narrowly drawn welfare remit). Under MES/GCS reforms they were to be replaced by the 'new three committees': the Board of Directors, the Board of Supervisors, and the Shareholders' Congress. If carried out as intended, such reform would have directly attacked the vested interests of many in the old structure, notably the Party and the official trade union, thus generating resistance. Under the MES and GCS programmes, the Board of Directors ought to be the highest level of decision-making, but this was always the role of the Party in the past, and the Party has proved reluctant to relinquish its power. Many enterprises, including some of our steel companies, have fudged the issue by appointing the branch Party chairman as vice-chairman of the Board of Directors as well, so that the same person could give orders wearing either 'hat'. It should be noted that in various Chinese institutions, there is a long history of Party-member vice-chairmen exercising considerably greater de facto power than non-Party chairmen, so cases where the Party chairman has not been given the top position on the Board do not necessarily represent a concession of real power within the company. Pre-existing managers were often transformed into a new 'Board of Directors' by a stroke of the pen, with Party and union organizations finding a place on the Board of Supervisors. The Party disciplinary secretary might typically chair the Board of Supervisors, while the chairman of the trade union would serve as vice-chairman or some such prominent position. Over the last decade this disposition has frequently allowed power to remain in essentially the same hands within an enterprise but under different titles. The question of how to break up the old vested interests in state-owned industry has been described to us as a 'forbidden area' of reform, since it touches on the question of the role of the CCP in a mixed economy and the 'proper' limits of its political-institutional power.

Far from operating on a level playing-field, therefore, SOEs in China are still subject to varying treatment from central and local authorities according to their particular status and history, as well as being affected by regional policy variations (Solinger 1996; Goodman 1997; Putterman and Dong 2000; Hassard *et al.* 2004). The crucial role of local government can be seen in the very selection of SOEs as reform pilots in the mid-1990s. One corporation in our sample was co-opted as a national GCS pilot against its own preferences, and several were compelled by local government to absorb into the group smaller, loss-making companies that would otherwise have gone bankrupt, throwing their employees out of work. Another policy was for the finances of autonomous sub-companies to be treated separately from those of the parent, so that only limited financial help would be forthcoming from the parent if the sub-companies continued to make losses. Little benefit was to be gained from this shifting around of unprofitable enterprises by anyone except local government, which divested itself of the responsibility for small enterprises' losses and had wage payments guaranteed by the large group corporation. In this respect it should be noted that late- or non-payment of wages has been a major cause of labour unrest in China since the 1990s. Local government has also tended, for obvious reasons, to favour enterprises under its control over those placed under the authority of a central government department or bureau, leading the latter to complain that they need more 'government interference', not less, as long as they are not competing on equal terms in a well-established and properly regulated market economy.

So do the results of the present reform phase, as it approaches its appointed end in 2010, constitute a degree of privatization of the remaining large and/or strategically significant SOEs in China? The answer from SOE managers would be a definite 'yes'. Managers in our sample firms have been prepared to discuss quite openly the extent to which their subsidiary companies, welfare services, company housing, etc. have been or will be privatized. However, they also compare their position adversely with that of managers in joint-ventures, foreign-owned and private enterprises, resenting their general lack of control over the disposal of the assets they have built up. Although the degree of frustration expressed is considerable in terms of the constraints (from both central and local government) under which they still have to operate, managers seem to expect their views to be reflected in shifts in policy and an easing of those constraints in the near future. This is reflected in the somewhat easier passage to stock market listing which some of our case-study companies are now experiencing. Into the late 1990s, several companies reported having to play tactical cat-and-mouse games with regulators over the names of the sub-companies being listed, in order to downplay the extent to which some of China's largest steel makers were now permanently up for sale. Smaller sub-companies, especially in interior provinces, still indicate that permission for stock market listings is sometimes given or withheld for reasons that have more to do with the state of company–government relations than the business case being made. Large and high-profile companies in the industry, however, have generally overcome their earlier difficulties with trying to slip major assets past the regulators.

Another straw in the wind for the steel industry was seen during the March 2005 National People's Congress, in which the industry was conspicuously missing from the list of those considered strategically significant and needing to remain in state ownership for the foreseeable future. Steel was included in the original list at the September 1997 15th CCP Congress at which former Party General Secretary Jiang Zemin announced that only about 500 of China's largest and/or most strategically significant SOEs would thereafter be kept in the state sector, with the rest left to the vagaries of the market. The 2005 omission is far from a positive statement of the imminent privatization of the steel industry, but it is unlikely to have been accidental. Despite the continuing reluctance of the top Party leadership to use the term 'privatization' as freely as many top managers in SOEs do, it would be hard for them to deny the nature of what is happening in many companies on the ground. But whereas acceptance of high-profile stock market listings in the steel industry no longer seems problematic, the debate about methods and forms of privatization is still somewhat constricted with regard to large SOEs. For example, regulations issued in April 2005 by the Ministry of Finance and the State-owned Assets Supervision and Administration Commission ruled out the possibility of management buy-outs (MBOs) in large SOEs (those with fixed assets of more than RMB50 million) (*South China Morning Post*, 15 April 2005). MBOs of some of the SOEs cut adrift by the state after September 1997 were often at knock-down prices, which created popular discontent and labour unrest fuelled by suspicions of corruption in the pricing and transfer of assets built up over many years by now-redundant workers. Examples were so widespread that MBOs in general gained a bad name in China. The government clearly does not wish a still-controversial means of handling former state assets to be applied where very much larger asset values, and the feelings of very much larger workforces, are at stake.

Overall, SOE managers are not going ahead on their own initiative with further reform; they are not pushing the boundaries of what is permitted by central-government policy and ideological constraints. Compared with the freer experimentation of the early 1980s under former leader Deng Xiaoping's 'Nike Doctrine' (named for his advice to local officials not to ask permission for their reform experiments if they knew the answer would be negative, but to 'just do it' and tell the authorities later if it worked), SOE managers today seem not to feel that unilateral action is the right course to adopt. This strengthens our feeling that they expect concessions to their views in central government policy within the next few years, concessions that might finally put them on a par with managers in other sectors of the Chinese economy. This is a process that has been considerably delayed by conflicts of interest between local and national government and SOEs, as well as by continuing ideological reluctance to see the 'commanding heights' of the industrial economy sold off, but which, it seems, cannot be put off indefinitely.

## Enterprise reform and surplus labour

It was anticipated at the beginning of the reform era in the early 1980s that the state enterprise's transition from a 'society in miniature' (*xiao shehui*), providing extensive social and economic benefits to its members, to a purely economic entity would reduce the control that enterprise authorities had previously been able to exercise over a dependent workforce, increasing the likelihood of collective resistance and unrest developing (Perry 1997; Lu and Perry 1997; Gu 1999; Goldman and MacFarquhar 1999; Naughton 1999; Solinger 1999). In fact, the extent to which the state-sector workforce was kept docile and politically passive under the iron rice-bowl system (see Walder 1986, on this issue) has been somewhat exaggerated (Perry 1994; Sheehan 1998; Hassard *et al.* 2004), but it is true to say that the loss of non-wage benefits and employment security under 'market socialism' has made this group much more restive, particularly during the last 15 years of reform.

Since 1997, unrest caused by plant closures and redundancies has become a prominent feature of industrial life in China, particularly, though not exclusively, in the 'third front' regions of the south-west and the heavy-industrial rust-belt of the north-east. Discontented workers have also proved adept at using the proletarian rhetoric of the Maoist period to press for social justice in the new economic environment, phrasing their demands in class terms that the authorities find uncomfortable to deal with. The problem faced by enterprise authorities since the late 1990s is, therefore, one of how to reconcile workers with a strong sense of class status and entitlement to the fact of large-scale job losses, so that necessary workforce reductions can be carried out without provoking significant collective resistance or protest. In this respect, our research has revealed the construction of a range of institutional strategies for minimizing the potential for workforce unrest. In particular, we have identified several ways of redefining the employment relationship so as to reduce workforce numbers without having to resort to compulsion, contrasting this with the way in which the process has been handled in other, primarily smaller enterprises, where it has, to date, more frequently generated overt opposition and resistance.

Although precise definitions of state-sector 'surplus labour' vary, the term generally reflects 'the difference between actual and desired levels of employment' (Kuehl and Sziraczki 1995: 72) or, more specifically, the number of workers over and above what the enterprise requires to operate at its maximum profit capacity, at its maximum production capacity, or at its standard level of production and capacity utilization. In May 1997 the State Commission for Economic Restructuring (SCER) predicted that 15–20 million surplus workers in the state sector would lose their jobs by the year 2000, an estimate that turned out to be conservative. The SCER also estimated the total number of surplus workers in SOEs at 54 million, or close to half of the total workforce (*South China Morning Post*, 7 May 1997). The proportion of surplus labour in SOE workforces, of course, varies across enterprises and is affected by factors such as enterprise size, industrial sector and geographical location (Hussain and Zhuang 1997). Our pilot interviews (1995–1997) revealed that steel sector SOEs planned to reduce their core workforces by between 15 and 50 per cent during the period of the 9th Five-Year Plan (1996–2000). Interviews during 1998–2000, however, indicated that lay-off targets in many of our case-study enterprises were unlikely to be met before the revised deadline of December 2003. Reasons for this slippage in the schedule included SOEs resisting lay-offs due to the economic downturn that began in the autumn of 1998 and a continuing reluctance on the part of SOE management and official trade unions to impose compulsory redundancies on employees who had not found alternative work or training (more will be said about this later). Moreover, as unrest became more widespread from 1997, it slowed down parts of the general reform process. Even housing reform, a relatively popular and unproblematic part of the divestment of SOEs' welfare responsibilities, was temporarily held up by the frequency and severity of labour unrest in 1997–1998, which made local and national government reluctant to force the pace of redundancies for fear of provoking further discontent. But despite recurrent extensions to deadlines for workforce reductions in some SOE sectors, the general programme of lay-offs involving unprecedented numbers of the industrial labour-force has continued, and the problem of how to deal with such a high proportion of surplus labour is one that still largely falls to SOEs themselves to solve; the role of other institutions, such as local government and employment services, will be touched upon later.

## Defining the worker

The definition of a worker in the People's Republic of China has always been an inclusive one, with trade union membership, for example, available to both manual and non-manual workers whose wages represented their sole or main source of livelihood, and specifically including workers with no fixed employment. Yet this apparent inclusiveness concealed considerable differentiation in the treatment of workers, and this had both economic and political purposes (O'Leary 1998; Solinger 1999; Baum and Shevchenko 1999; Whyte 1999; Tsui and Lau 2002; Hassard *et al.* 2004). The state and enterprise institutions always distinguished between permanent, temporary and contract workers, between unionized and non-unionized labour, and sometimes between male and female workers or between older, more established employees and new, young entrants to the workforce, in an attempt to limit the proportion of the industrial workforce that was entitled to the most extensive welfare benefits and which enjoyed virtually unassailable security of employment for life (White 1989). These conditions are often assumed to have been typical for Chinese workers in general, but in fact the true 'iron rice-bowl' was only ever available to a minority of permanently employed, unionized state-sector workers at the biggest and most prosperous urban enterprises. As well as the obvious cost savings achieved in limiting the size of this privileged group, the distinction made between the core of the industrial workforce and its more marginal members was also a useful one whenever authorities had to deal with outbreaks of protest from workers, as they could maintain that those involved were, by virtue of their second-class employment status as temporary or contract workers, apprentices, etc., not 'real' proletarians, thus maintaining the illusion of across-the-board working-class support for the CCP.

In line with this practice of differentiating between categories of worker to control entitlement, data from our MES/GCS research have shown that enterprises needing to make cuts in their workforce have done so initially by getting rid of non-core or marginal employees, and then by persuading other, permanently employed workers to transfer to less secure forms of employment relationship within the work unit. This time-consuming and gradual process has frequently depended for its success on a prior period of education and propaganda to convince work-unit members that it is essential for large numbers of them to leave the unit for the sake of its viability. Our informants suggest that it has also depended on the ability of local authorities to step in with basic social security provision for former SOE workers who have lost their access to a wide range of welfare benefits along with their jobs. The notion appears to be that protest and resistance to job losses can be greatly reduced if the effects on the core workforce, the group with the strongest sense of entitlement to security, are minimized by leaving as many of them as possible in post, and by making the process of leaving the unit as gradual and voluntary as possible for those affected. It has been suggested to us that large state enterprises could afford this approach, but smaller or loss-making SOEs could not, and instead tended to treat their entire workforce as equally and instantly expendable. Consequently, workers' protests against job losses since the late 1990s have most often occurred among employees of this type of enterprise. The question remains, however, as to whether the methods employed by the larger enterprises can continue to avert widespread unrest given the substantial numbers involved. It also remains to be seen whether the assumption will be borne out in practice that members of the workforce redefined as marginal will tolerate the severing of their relationship with the work unit without significant protest. Quite early in the process, our respondents in some areas of China were already suggesting that the ability of sub-companies to employ surplus workers transferred out of core production lines was reaching saturation point.

## Workforce reductions in large SOEs

Much management literature on the Chinese economy suggests that in recent years enterprises have been given more autonomy over the recruitment and retention of employees, and that the flexibility allowed to individuals in moving between jobs has also increased (Gu 1999; Solinger 1999; Putterman and Dong 2000; White and Liu 2001; Meyer 2002; Hassard *et al.* 2004).

Evidence from our research, however, suggests that the state sector in China is still far from realizing a genuine labour market as a result of MES/GCS reforms. Enterprise managers in the largest SOEs are acutely aware of the government's reliance on them, rather than on any other institutions, to avoid the social disruption associated with large-scale redundancies and rising urban unemployment at a time when the development of a non-enterprise welfare safety-net is still in process. Accepting that it is not possible at present for the 'society in miniature' of the state enterprise to shift its burden of excess employees completely onto society, large SOEs have had to find other ways of relocating surplus members of their workforce. Our research indicates that this is particularly true in 'third-front' inland locations such as Sichuan, Yunnan, and even Hubei, while workforce reductions in coastal locations such as Shanghai and Guangzhou have proven easier due to the greater availability of alternative employment opportunities.

One marginal group in the workforce that presents itself as an obvious target for downsizing is employees on fixed-term contracts. Contract employment was introduced in China in 1986, but as a politically unpopular measure likely to meet with stiff resistance if applied to permanent workers already in post, on its introduction it was only applied to new entrants to the workforce, and the actual proportion of workers employed on fixed-term contracts consistently fell short of targets, remaining below 20 per cent of the total in SOEs in the early–mid-1990s (Warner 1995a and b; Sheehan 1998). Our investigations suggest that although in theory contract employment is now universal in all SOEs throughout China (since 1995), in many cases employers are often very reluctant to terminate contracts just to get rid of surplus labour, rather than for unsatisfactory performance. We have found that some large SOEs in our sample have replaced contract workers at the end of their contracted period of employment with otherwise redundant permanent workers from within the group. But given the limited proportion of such contract employees in the workforce as a whole in some enterprises, this is not a viable method in itself of making the large cuts in core employment that many large SOEs still aim to complete.

Our interviews suggest further that given their reluctance to force permanently employed workers out of the unit altogether, many large SOEs have instead sought to develop internal labour markets, with workers being shifted out of over-manned core production units and into new sub-companies set up solely for the purpose of absorbing surplus labour (see Chapters 8 and 9). Many large, state-owned corporations now typically contain within them sub-companies running such businesses as shops, hotels, restaurants and travel agencies, as well as social-service companies and companies engaged in any kind of manufacturing or service provision where profits can be made, with the products and services of these companies having no connection at all with the core business of the parent company itself. Considerable numbers of workers have been involved in these shifts. In one of the large state-owned steel companies we have studied, the number of employees transferred out of core iron- and steel-producing units into sub-companies now exceeds the number remaining in iron and steel production by 40 per cent. Our interviews indicate therefore that, in theory, sub-companies have autonomy over their own levels of employment and recruitment of new staff from outside the group, but in practice there has been strong pressure on them to take up surplus labour from within the group rather than recruit from outside.

During the period of MES/GCS reforms, some of our large SOEs set up labour pools for surplus employees where they could undergo re-training for vacant posts elsewhere within the group. Such workers may remain in the group labour pool for up to two years, but ultimately their employment could be terminated by the enterprise if no suitable post was found for them within that time. Alternatively, they could retain their employment status within the enterprise once the two-year period in the labour pool had passed, but instead of continuing to receive their basic salary they were only paid the monthly amount calculated by the local government as the minimum necessary to cover basic living expenses. This is an example of the proliferation of different forms of employment status within the enterprise through which unambiguous dismissal of surplus workers has been avoided. Here also we have observed a tendency to extend the deadlines originally laid down for the final severing of the employment relationship, often in response to downturns in the economy or to local labour unrest.

In our sample MES/GCS enterprises a range of employment forms has been developed, which includes not only permanent waged employment, retraining and redeployment within the company, voluntary severance, and early retirement, but also stages in between. For example, a practice for dealing with surplus workers at one of our larger plants is 'retirement within the company', in which such workers remain in post with no annual increases in pay. Alternatively, surplus workers may remain in post without pay but retaining their status as an employee of the unit. This retention of a formal link with the work unit has security benefits for the workers concerned, allowing them, for example, to take advantage of schemes to sell-off enterprise housing to workers at below-market prices, while obtaining work elsewhere or becoming self-employed. The alternative to retaining such a link is *liang bu zhao*, or (loosely translated) 'don't call us and we won't call you', meaning that the worker will not look for any further help from the unit, and the unit has no further call on its former employee. The various forms of employment status now in existence in the state sector help to account for the discrepancy between China's official urban unemployment rate (which stands at around 4.5 per cent) and the much higher figures routinely given by academic analysts and even the official trade unions in China, which include the large numbers of workers who have retained some sort of formal relationship, paid or unpaid, with their work unit but are not actually going to work. Estimates for the proportion out-of-work based on this definition range from 8 per cent to more than 20 per cent, with some of the highest rates in areas such as the north-east that have concentrations of large and loss-making SOEs.

Besides creating vacancies elsewhere within the enterprise for surplus workers and restricting entry from outside the group, large SOEs are also attempting to increase the number of workers exiting from the group. One method of doing this, common to all our case-study enterprises, is to encourage and facilitate early retirement. In some cases employees taking advantage of early-retirement schemes can receive a lump-sum investment from the group company in order to help them start up their own business. To make voluntary severance for workers of any age more attractive to those wishing to change jobs or go into business on their own, the requirement for these employees to pay back the costs of their training if they leave the corporation has been removed at certain of our case companies. Inevitably, companies have found that it is not necessarily the right employees, from the enterprise's point of view, who volunteer for this sort of scheme, and some have introduced various incentives to ensure the retention of key technical personnel in particular.

Although the above measures are aimed at increasing the number of surplus workers leaving the enterprise altogether, to date many large SOEs have been reluctant to force out surplus employees who do not wish to go (see Chapters 8 and 9). Despite the 'headline numbers' laid-off from our case-study companies eventually meeting the targets set, probing in interviews revealed that much surplus labour was still hidden within the group, in the sense that the group company was still ultimately responsible for paying the wages or pensions of workers nominally employed elsewhere. A significant proportion of surplus labour has merely been moved around within large SOEs, rather than being forced out altogether, although some of our companies have resorted to making compulsory redundancies. It should, perhaps, be mentioned that managers' unwillingness to terminate the employment of any worker who does not have an alternative destination is not just based on the fear of causing unrest, important though that is. It also results from the strong sense of responsibility towards employees that is particularly evident among the older generation of managers, now often approaching retirement age, and who have not completely abandoned the values and attitudes of the pre-reform era in this respect. Our research suggests that such an attitude can also be detected in some younger managers, particularly in western or interior provinces, although it is much less prevalent. The experience of one large, state-owned steel maker that has attempted to cut the Gordian knot of continued financial responsibility for workers who are technically no longer its employees has not been an encouragement to any of the others to try it. In 2003, workers from Anshan (now Anben, from August 2005) Iron and Steel rejected the one-off severance payment they were offered as it was lower than similar payments made by other local SOEs and less than the company could afford based on its published accounts (Anshan was listed on the Shanghai Stock Exchange), and took their street protests on the issue all the way to Beijing (*China Labour Bulletin* 2003, *passim*).

Although the role of government institutions in determining SOEs' levels of employment has been reduced during the economic reform period (Hay *et al.*. 1994; Rawski 1995; Lu and Child 1996; Lee 1999; Tsui and Lau 2002), our research suggests that local governments and labour bureaux still have influence or authority in some respects. Some managers in our MES/GCS companies continue to complain of government interference in areas where they have autonomy on paper. Large SOEs are still sometimes compelled to employ workers (often those laid-off by other enterprises) whom they do not need or want. Moreover, a number of the SOEs in our study have been forced into mergers with loss-making SOEs primarily in order to safeguard jobs in such struggling firms. Some enterprises seem better able than others to fend off unwanted impositions of this kind by local government, either because of variations in policy between different cities or regions, or because of the particular circumstances of the enterprise concerned and its past relationship with local authorities. Our informants also suggest that during the last decade the Labour Law has shifted some of the responsibility for helping the unemployed to find work onto local government institutions rather than leaving enterprises to bear the whole burden. Also the national government in 1997 introduced a period of one to three years' compulsory training for all new entrants to the labour force, a measure also intended to ease employment pressures.

The caution exhibited to date by management in large SOEs when dealing with workforce reductions is understandable. Labour unrest fuelled by discontent over job losses, always recognized as a possible consequence of reform, has long since become a fact of life in Chinese industry and society. Although core, permanently employed state-sector workers were traditionally regarded as the working elite and thus the least restive segment of the Chinese working class under CCP rule, by the 1990s this had changed. State workers were in the vanguard of the 1989 Democracy Movement as a newly aggrieved group suffering significant relative deprivation under the reforms, and angry in particular about high levels of official corruption and inflation (Walder and Gong 1993; Sheehan 1998). Given the social and political risks involved in drastically reducing workforce numbers in very large SOEs, enterprise managers have made great efforts, as our respondents noted, to 'make the channel before the water comes'; in other words, to have schemes for re-employing or otherwise dealing with surplus workers in place well before they are needed by large numbers. Managers in our MES/GCS companies have put considerable effort into preparing the workforce in advance of radical restructuring, notably through seeking to justify the job reductions on economic grounds and persuading workers to accept them.

Managers stress the new opportunities available to some workers in the reform environment, and this is not just propaganda: the chance to change jobs, and in particular to set up in business independently, is genuinely welcomed by some state employees. Our interviews reveal that success stories of former SOE workers making their fortunes are widely publicized in an attempt to overcome workers' fears of losing the security of permanent state employment, with some success. Again, managers stress the importance of beginning the process of persuasion well in advance of announcing major job losses. It is plain to all involved, however, that not everyone who leaves state employment does better elsewhere. Our research suggests that a key task of management is to convince employees that some will have to leave the enterprise if any are to prosper, as in the 'market socialist' environment enterprises cannot carry high levels of surplus labour while attempting to restructure themselves to compete in national and world markets. This approach seems to have been relatively successful to date in our sample companies, if not in whipping up real enthusiasm for downsizing among state employees, then at least in engendering a mood of resigned acceptance of the end of the 'iron rice-bowl'. In addition to quantitative changes in the labour force (fewer jobs) and qualitative changes (different jobs, changing status of employment etc.), there has also been evidence from our field visits of the gradual introduction of many Western-style human-resource management practices, such as pay related to performance and work intensification.

## Downsizing SOE management

Our investigations suggest that the relative insulation of management and Party officials from the insecurity of employment has been a particular affront to aggrieved workers' sense of fairness, with the question being raised publicly in the state-controlled *Workers' Daily* as to why SOE senior managers seem rarely to be left without jobs, only the workers. However, it is not only members of the rank-and-file workforce who are surplus to requirements in SOEs, for many state enterprises are seeking to reduce management numbers and streamline their administration. Nevertheless, informants have suggested to us that this has proved even more difficult than getting rid of production workers, and is an area where enterprises do not have complete autonomy. As mentioned above, the Party retains a say over senior SOE managers' appointments above a certain level, as well as influence over the many senior managers who are Party members. Our research indicates that the longstanding 'iron arm-chair' of cadres has proved more durable than workers' 'iron rice-bowls', there often being a tendency to move under-performing managers sideways rather than down.

Increasingly under MES/GCS reforms, however, managers have been employed on (usually three-year) contracts that can be terminated if they do not meet certain performance criteria. Given the unintended consequences of the CRS (see Chapter 5; Chen, D. 1995; Hassard and Sheehan 1997), the targets specified in managers' contracts under MES/GCs have not been limited to ensuring certain levels of profit. MES/GCS contracts have also included an obligation to increase, or at least maintain, the value of state assets. Our research confirms that systems of audit and appraisal, both internal and external, have been developed to check that assets are not being run down or disposed of improperly, as has happened in the past.

Nevertheless, although managers *can* have their contracts terminated at the end of the three-year period, this does not mean that they necessarily *will*. In our fieldwork, top managers at the group level still speak of the difficulty of dealing with the vested interests of enterprise cadres. Efforts to convince some surplus managers of the benefits of self-employment, backed with start-up funds in some cases, are continuing, and as with production workers, the importance of widespread advance consultation to maximize acceptance of the changes is emphasized. At one of our case-study enterprises, management-level posts were to be reduced by 25 per cent through a process that saw all managers reapply for their jobs. In this case, top management and those employees who would be working under them listened to the candidates' presentations and expressed their preferences in a vote. In the event, every effort was made to accommodate the unlucky 25 per cent through early retirement, the creation of alternative posts in sub-companies, and facilitating self-employment; the company allowed plenty of time for the process, and in the end only one in ten of the surplus managers actually left the company. It is noteworthy that this occurred in one of our smallest case-study SOEs, where fewer managers had their status buttressed by Party membership and where an unusual degree of both upward and downward mobility between management and shop-floor posts was evident.

The restructuring of large SOEs under MES/GCS, however, has provided scope for reducing managerial numbers as sub-companies have gained increasing autonomy over many aspects of their operations, enabling the parent-company administration to be streamlined. One of the larger state steel companies in our sample increased efficiency and achieved a 30 per cent reduction in staff numbers at the corporation level through reorganization of functional departments. Other enterprises have progressed towards their goal of simplified administration resulting in staff reductions of around the same level. In some enterprises, administrative departments with duplicated or overlapping functions have been merged and reorganized. For example, one steel corporation in eastern China merged four departments previously responsible for separate aspects of construction projects into one entity. Separate HRM departments and training centres for production workers and managers have also been successfully combined. In some of our companies, management centralization has been adopted to achieve staff reductions, as finance and other departments have been abolished at the sub-company level and their responsibilities taken over by delegated personnel from the parent company's administrative departments. This can only be done in sub-companies engaged in the group's core production area; however, for others, it would cause an unacceptable reduction in managerial autonomy.

As noted earlier, SOEs ought to enjoy greater flexibility in managerial appointments and dismissals under MES/GCS. Under these reforms a Board of Directors chosen by shareholders is designated as the highest level of decision-making, but as we have stressed this was always the role of the Party in the past and it is still proving reluctant to give up its power. As government continues to be the main or sole shareholder in many large SOEs, it still carries as much weight in management appointments at the highest levels as it did in the past.

## Future directions of SOE reform

As to the future, recent official pronouncements suggest that China is planning to accelerate the convergence and re-distribution of its state-owned assets. For example, Li Rongrong, minister in charge of the State-owned Assets Supervision and Administration Commission (SASAC), announced in September 2005 that SASAC is to design measures to promote the redistribution of state-owned assets and the regrouping of state-owned firms, with such measures taking effect from 2006 (*Xinhuanet* 2005a). Li, who is ostensibly the chief commissioner of China's central SOEs, suggested that such regrouping will be on the basis of 'market principles' and overseen by the SOEs' own Boards of Directors, which signals a step change in managerial autonomy. Since its establishment in 2002, the main task of the SASAC has been to foster around 80 to 100 globally competitive corporations. Thus far it has succeeded in reducing the number of centrally administered SOEs from 196 in 2002 to 169 (as of September 2005), mainly through mergers and acquisitions. During the process of converging of state-owned assets, the toughest obstacle the SASAC faces is again removing redundant workers from loss-making SOEs, and central government has recently offered financial help to such SOEs for them to lay off workers or else claim bankruptcy (*Xinhuanet* 2005a).

Another relatively recent development is that, in a circular published in February 2005, the State Administration of Taxation announced that large SOEs adopting debt-to-equity swaps would receive new tax breaks to boost their financial strength (*China Economic Net* 2005). This policy appears to be oriented at stimulating SOE performance through relieving the burden of heavy NPLs. According to the circular, the new package of tax breaks mainly includes the exemption of VAT and consumption tax for SOEs. The tax breaks would operate as a kind of capital support by the government to intensify SOE reforms. China established four AMCs – Huarong, Cinda, Orient and Great Wall – in 1999 to tackle the rising NPLs of the country's four major banks – the Industrial and Commercial Bank of China, Bank of China, the Agricultural Bank of China and China Construction Bank. From that time, the four AMCs conducted debt-to-equity swaps involving more than 400 billion yuan (US$48.3 billion) of debt (*China Economic Net* 2005). Such debt-to-equity swaps were aimed at helping debt-ridden large SOEs overcome their huge financial burdens. The debts were transferred into equities which the AMCs controlled in the enterprises, with a new holding company being set up according to the contract of the debt-to-equity swap. Since April 2000, participating SOEs have stopped paying interest on loans to banks, which is reportedly equivalent to an annual sum of 24 billion yuan (US$2.9 billion) (*China Economic Net* 2005).

Finally, officials in north-east China's Liaoning Province have recently announced that international investors will in future be able to take 'full control' of large SOEs currently under the province's control (*Xinhuanet* 2005b). A statement by Liaoning Province's Vice-Governor Li Wancai suggested the only exceptions would be SOEs under central government control and coal mines. Liaoning is one of the last bastions of the planned economy in China, where SOEs still dominate. Thus far international co-operation in this province has been restricted to small and medium-sized SOEs and private companies. Under the guidance of 'Document No. 36', Liaoning will promote initially around 200 enterprises for international cooperation, predominantly in petrochemicals, pharmaceuticals and general manufacturing (*Xinhuanet* 2005b). This policy, promoted in Liaoning via central government under the 'Office for Revitalizing the Old Industrial Base in Northeast China under the State Council', is designed to help the industries in the Northeast 'rust-belt' attract more investment. To revive the region, the central government has thus provided preferential policies for foreign companies that invest. In brief, Document No. 36 appears designed to encourage large-scale SOE reform by loosening the twin bonds of debt and redundancy.

## Conclusion

This chapter has examined the experience of MES/GCS reforms in the Chinese steel industry since the mid-1990s through a perspective that emphasizes the institutional roles of enterprises, communities and organs of the state. This perspective has offered a lens for interpreting and explaining the relative inertia experienced in the state-owned steel industry during the last decade in attempts to manage enterprise restructuring and economic reform.

Our analysis suggests that the MES/GCS reform process in general has been hampered by a number of political-institutional factors, in particular the political imperatives of the Chinese government and the fact that property rights have remained relatively weak and moves towards clarification tentative. Of the various effects of the reform process, the 'surplus labour' problem is the most serious; that is, the need to reduce core workforces without dramatically increasing unemployment and thus causing political and social instability. In this respect the SOEs in our sample have often found it difficult to do much more than reform internally while waiting for change in the policy environment that will enable them to take more radical steps. The relative lack of reform progress in certain SOEs can thus be viewed as a rational attempt to respond to conflicting signals from institutions that frequently have different interests in the enterprise.

The analysis in the second half of the chapter has focused on this core issue of the redundancy or redeployment of surplus SOE production workers and managers and how this is fraught with practical and political difficulties. Our view is that further progress will continue to depend on great care being exercised to avoid unacceptable costs in terms of social and political upheaval. As noted, China has won praise in the past for its gradualist approach to such sensitive areas of reform, in contrast to the countries of Eastern Europe and the FSU. But urban unemployment is already at higher levels than during previous phases of reform, and the numbers involved in the latest phase of restructuring have been unprecedented. The next few years will present a great challenge all the way up the hierarchy from enterprise management to central government. If the warning signs of protest by laid-off workers continue to be heeded, China can still succeed in its gradual restructuring of employment away from the state sector bequeathed to it by the FSU. But the ruling party has to deal with a state-sector workforce that has developed a strong sense of its own class identity and rights, and which is increasingly prepared to defend these rights.

We have noted also how under MES/GCS-style reforms the state enterprise has largely shifted away from the old Chinese form of a 'society in miniature', catering for a range of its employees' social and economic needs, to that of an ordinary market employer with much more limited responsibilities to its workers. The likely response to this from workers is the adoption of the usual weapons of labour-capital confrontation familiar from other countries and other eras in China, such as strikes and the organization of independent trade unions. Workers are now increasingly prepared to use such weapons in defence of their own concepts of fairness and social justice, exhibiting a continuing attachment to the egalitarian values which, in the past, were assumed to have been foisted on them by previous leftist Chinese regimes, but which now appear to have had a basis in many workers' genuine social preferences and values. Despite the divisions deliberately fostered between different sections of the workforce, in an era when only a limited number of core, permanent SOE workers can count on remaining in their jobs, workers show less inclination to express resentment at the privileged few among them who remain secure. Instead, they frequently direct their anger higher up, to the decision-makers who seem to be immune from the insecurity that they are enforcing on others, and whose incompetence or even corruption workers ever more frequently blame for the plight of loss-making enterprises. The case for independent trade unions, or at least for representative organizations that are a great deal more responsive to members' interests than China's present state-controlled unions, is becoming unanswerable in this new era of industrial relations in the state sector. Past experience suggests that attempts by the official unions to take a more independent role themselves as an intermediary between employees and an increasingly confident new managerial elite are likely to founder on the Party's insistence on its own overriding control of labour organizations. As a result discontented workers are likely to find few effective means open to them for resolving disputes short of taking to the streets.

Managers and local government alike are very aware of the potential dangers of an alienated urban working class, and there have been signs of concerted attempts to protect what was always a key constituency for the Party by reserving certain new jobs or self-employment permits, or even entire lines of work, for unemployed former SOE workers. In cities such as Beijing and Shanghai, for example, certain occupations have been reserved for permanent city residents rather than rural migrants in an attempt to vacate tens of thousands of posts for laid-off urbanites. This type of programme, however, conflicts with the socialist market ethos, which dictates that the established working class must now compete with migrants from the countryside for the available work. There is thus conflict among institutional policy-makers about how far the old state-sector workforce can, or should, be protected from the rigours of the market.

The old system of 'organized dependency' (Walder 1986) in the largest state enterprises was designed to control workers by enmeshing them in a network of 'clientelist' relationships with the work-unit leadership, on whom they depended not just for their wages but also for housing and extensive educational, medical and other social services for themselves and their families. But this was not successful all the time: dependency could breed defiance as well as docility (Perry and Li 1997; Sheehan 2000; Morris *et al.* 2001). In the era of market reform this type of comprehensive welfare package, only ever available to a minority, is being abolished, and what now emerges as perhaps an unexpected legacy of the pre-reform era is a state-sector workforce which, despite its divisions, has certain class values in common and which it is increasingly prepared to defend against the inroads of the market. Clearly the situation for workers left within the SOEs greatly differs from those laid-off. While we would agree that there is a culture of insecurity within SOEs' workforces, that there is work intensification within the labour process, that there is greater managerial prerogative, and that there is increased welfare commodification, there remains considerable variation between enterprises and Party patronage is far from over. While the painstaking efforts of government and employers to prepare workers for the 'reality' of reform and engender a culture that accepts work insecurity have had some effect, the authorities are not yet out of the woods with regard to the emergence of collective resistance to reforms that have eroded workers' most cherished benefit, their security of employment.

We note, finally, that as labour protest becomes increasingly commonplace in China's cities (see next chapter), the customary central-government policy of buying-off those groups that cause the most disruption, by providing extra funds to pay overdue wages, pensions and redundancy benefits in the most restive industrial regions such as the north-east, becomes increasingly problematic. Setting the precedent of only meeting the demands of those involved in the most severe outbreaks of unrest risks providing workers with the perfect excuse for disorder, as was the case in the troubled mid-1950s when workers justified their resort to strikes, demonstrations and violent confrontations with managers with the logic that such managers 'bullied the good, but feared the bad' (Sheehan 1998: 74). Each year of SOE downsizing leaves more workers stranded in the ranks of the long-term unemployed and often facing real poverty and hardship for the first time in their lives, and many of them are far from reconciled to their fate. They tend to lose out in the competition for scarce employment opportunities to other groups: to migrants from the countryside, who are sometimes preferred by employers because they are regarded as more malleable and less likely to stand up for their rights; to new young entrants to the urban workforce, who tend to have a much higher level of education than the middle-aged cohort, often targeted for downsizing, which missed out on much of its formal schooling because of the Cultural Revolution; and even to ex-service personnel being returned to civilian life as China's armed forces modernize. It could be argued that all that is averting a major crisis in urban China is the fact that unrest is still largely localized and sporadic in nature, and that attempts to organize independent trade unions have so far only been successful for a short time and on a small scale. However, unrest in the regions hardest hit by reform-related downsizing, such as the south-west and the north-east, may yet reach a critical mass and overwhelm the methods of preventing commotion on which enterprise managers and different levels of government are presently relying to contain the anger of a workforce that increasingly regards itself as the main, indeed the only, victim of China's vaunted economic reforms.

# 7 State capitalism, labour unrest and worker representation

## Introduction

This chapter develops an analysis of how workers in China's SOEs have responded to the changing nature of those enterprises during the reform period since 1978. In particular we examine the causes of the rising incidence of labour unrest among SOE employees from the second half of the 1990s onwards, as drastic restructuring of the state sector began to take place and unemployment reached its highest levels in China for decades. Protests over lay-offs, bankruptcies and unpaid pensions and wages reached the stage where parts of the present reform programme became threatened with delay as local and national governments sought to contain workers' resentment. Yet, as will be seen below, sometimes these efforts to mollify workers succeeded only in further stoking their anger at what they perceived to be patronizing and token concessions that did not address their most important concerns.

We also examine the tensions in China between state capitalism and state corporatism in terms of the ruling CCP's relationship with urban industrial workers. We explain how the CCP has responded to labour pressure for better industrial and political representation since the late 1980s. The Chinese government has shown particular concern over attempts to form independent labour organizations in this period, seeking instead to contain an increasingly restive working class, now subject to a high level of employment insecurity, within the framework of state-controlled unionism. Thus the CCP's relaxation of centralized control over a more open, 'mixed' economy has not been matched in the area of labour representation by a greater tolerance of autonomous organization, leading to intensifying conflict with labour particularly in economically disadvantaged areas of the country.

## Whither SOE workers?

As noted in earlier chapters, SOE workers have conventionally been viewed as a privileged group within Chinese society, an elite section of the workforce amply compensated for its still relatively low wage levels by the benefits of the 'iron rice-bowl' system of lifelong job security and enterprise provision of social welfare. Lack of labour mobility and dependency on the enterprise for such things as subsidized housing, medical care, children's schooling, etc., in turn, have been identified as the reasons for SOE workers' relative political docility and loyalty to the ruling CCP, at least up until the end of the 1980s. We have noted how 'organized dependency' (Walder 1986), whereby workers were enmeshed in a network of individual patron–client relationships in the workplace, has been seen as a successful means of preventing disgruntled workers from resorting to any form of organized, collective resistance in most circumstances. This view clearly has some basis in fact, as the largest, best-resourced and most prestigious SOEs were, until the second half of the 1980s, the least likely to experience major unrest among their workforces.

We have argued, however, that the benefits of the 'iron rice-bowl' were always deliberately limited to a minority of the industrial workforce as a whole (Sheehan 1998; Hassard *et al.* 2006; see also White 1989), with often much less generous benefits on offer in the far more numerous small and medium-sized SOEs, which therefore could not necessarily count on such docility from their workers. The general view that the Chinese industrial workforce has been notable for its passivity and the ease with which it could be controlled has, in any case, been challenged by other accounts which stress the relative frequency of unrest among Chinese workers. Such studies have noted the involvement of SOE workers in periodic protest movements, which have questioned the legitimacy of the Party that claims to rule in their name (Davis 1988; Chan 1993; Perry 1994; Perry and Li 1997; Sheehan 1998; Hassard *et al.* 2004). Even with reference to the pre-reform period, the depiction of SOE employees as a favoured elite unwilling to bite the hand which fed it was somewhat one-sided, and since 1978 the steady undermining of the 'iron rice-bowl' as reform progressed has further reduced the effectiveness of what was never a completely reliable method of containing workers' grievances and assertions of collective interests.

The recent outbreaks of unrest, therefore, are not simply the reaction of a previously privileged group to the loss of its exclusive benefits. Rather than campaigning to reinstate the enterprise-based paternalism of the past, many SOE workers now explicitly reject it. Such workers are instead organizing independently to press demands for the legal rights, which they feel are due to them now that they have found themselves in an insecure, quasi-capitalist employment relationship in their enterprise. These legal rights include the right to adequate welfare and pensions and the right to organize their own trade unions.

## Reform and workers in the 1989 Democracy Movement

Before analysing the situation of workers in the most recent phase of SOE reform, we turn first to an examination of workers' responses when the CCP government first expressed its intention to end the 'iron rice-bowl' in the late 1970s and early 1980s. Given the early success of the agricultural reforms in boosting rural incomes, workers had expectations of substantial material benefits from the urban reforms, expectations that were deliberately encouraged by the authorities (Yang 1989). Workers also anticipated a marked improvement in enterprise management, the incompetence of which they saw as being at least as important a factor in low industrial productivity as their own much-criticized job security and egalitarianism (White 1987a and b; Sheehan 1998). Yet, alongside these positive expectations, the fear of a return to the pre-1949 era of high levels of job insecurity and unemployment also became evident at an early stage.

However, workers' misgivings about reform were much more than simple opposition to a change in the nature of the Chinese enterprise which would rob them of their material privileges. Workers have not, in fact, at any stage been opposed to reform as such; they of all people have been very well aware of the many problems within state-owned industry in China and of the need for significant change to improve efficiency and raise productivity. Rather than seeking to preserve the old system for its own sake, they have opposed corruption and perceived unfairness in the conduct of the reforms and increased inequality and economic hardship for workers' households as a result of reform. They have also consistently objected to the assertion that the blame for the poor performance of state-sector industry should be laid at their door. Throughout the reform period the government has stressed the old, egalitarian 'eating from one big pot' mentality of the 'iron rice-bowl' employee as the main or even the sole cause of China's low labour productivity (Howard 1991; Sheehan 1998). But while the state-controlled press presented the excessive job and wage security of the 'iron rice-bowl' as a distortion of socialism, SOE workers themselves persisted in viewing it as, perhaps, the only unequivocal achievement of the pre-reform era, and certainly the feature of that era which had most value to them.

By the end of the 1980s job insecurity had emerged as workers' main worry in the new economic environment (Walder 1989; Wilson 1990; Warner 1995a and b). Despite the very slow implementation of measures such as the introduction of contract labour, a 'job security panic' (Walder 1991: 478) arose, not just among the minority actually affected by the introduction of fixed-term contracts, but across virtually the whole of the state-sector workforce. This new perception of insecurity, together with concerns that stagnating wages were being overtaken by high urban inflation, in large part accounts for the willingness of so many workers to support and participate in the student-initiated Democracy Movement of spring 1989. But another factor that must be taken into account is the extent to which workers felt their social and political status to have fallen as a result of the reforms. Measures such as the introduction of the Factory Director Responsibility System (FDRS) (Chevrier 1990; Child 1994) and the general emphasis on increasing the power of top managers at the expense of workers, the workers' congress, the official trade unions, and even the enterprise Party branch, severely eroded any sense workers had previously had of being 'masters of the enterprise' in any real sense. The danger that the FDRS would undermine the (in any case inadequate) machinery of democratic management in Chinese enterprises had been recognized at the time the system was introduced, but nothing was done to prevent this outcome, and by 1989 the labour-movement press was comparing highly centralized management under the FDRS to the Soviet-inspired 'one-man management' of the early 1950s (*Workers' Daily*, 27 June 1989).

The contracting-out of enterprises to managers for fixed periods also contributed to workers' perceptions of themselves not as employees of the state with the political status that went with that, but simply as hired hands, wage-labourers with no stake in the enterprise beyond 'working for the factory director', whom they had come to perceive as, in effect, the 'owner' of the enterprise (Wang and Wen 1992: 265). Where contracting-out decisions involving their own enterprise were announced to workers on the evening news without any prior consultation, this could only increase their sense that they were being treated as part of the fixed assets of the establishment which management could dispose of as it pleased. To workers it seemed that there had been a final breach in the social contract which had offered them security of employment, a minimum standard of living and a limited say in management in exchange for tolerating low pay and not organizing independent unions. This breach of an implicit industrial and political bargain left workers in a much more unambiguously antagonistic relationship vis-à-vis management and state authorities. Their increasingly frequent response to this shift in the months leading up to the 1989 Democracy Movement was the use of the strike weapon and self-organization (although these types of action were by no means as rare before the late 1980s as is often supposed), and the Movement itself saw the widespread formation of autonomous workers' organizations explicitly intended to play a political role beyond the enterprise as well as defending workers' interests within it. SOE workers, including some from several of the largest and most prestigious enterprises in the country, took a particularly prominent part in the Movement in 1989, although the CCP has consistently sought to down-play or deny this (Hassard and Sheehan 1997; Sheehan 1998).

## Workers and enterprise reform in the 1990s

So already in the Democracy Movement of 1989, SOE workers had manifested 'a growing desire . . . to be treated as full citizens' (Walder and Gong 1993: 28–29), declaring that 'we are not prison labourers who happen to live in society, but legal citizens of the republic' (Mok and Harrison 1990: 118). They also showed clear signs of perceiving themselves to be in much the same position vis-à-vis state-enterprise management as employees in privately owned establishments which, in turn, they saw as giving them the right to form completely independent organizations through which to defend their collective interests against those of SOE management. These trends only intensified as the 1990s progressed, and particularly so since the long-anticipated announcement came in September 1997 at the 15th CCP Congress that henceforth only about 500 of the largest and most strategically significant SOEs would be kept in long-term state ownership, with the rest allowed to close, merge or go bankrupt as the market dictated. The unprecedented large-scale lay-offs from SOEs that have since taken place have only reinforced the view of many SOE workers that they have become the main losers in the reform process to date. The level of job insecurity that brought workers onto the streets during the late 1980s and in the 1989 Democracy Movement paled into insignificance when compared to the plans of many large SOEs to shed up to 50 per cent of their workforces (Kuehl and Sziraczki 1995; Hassard and Sheehan 1997). The high incidence of unrest among former and current SOE employees should not, therefore, come as any surprise, and nor should the fact that protests are frequently accompanied by calls for independent unions.

### Responses to SOE downsizing in the late 1990s

We have outlined previously how managers in the state sector have been charged by the government with the responsibility of avoiding widespread unrest among workers through the careful preparation and conduct of lay-offs, and this is a responsibility that the top management of the largest SOEs generally take very seriously. They also in most cases have benefited from a level of resources that enabled them to 'make the channel before the water comes', in other words, to prepare or facilitate acceptable alternative destinations for redundant workers before the latter were actually forced out of the SOE workforce. As we have described, in the mid–late 1990s many large SOEs established internal labour markets to provide retraining and redeployment for surplus workers, and also set up a range of service-industry sub-companies to absorb redundant labour, as well as offering incentives for early retirement or voluntary severance in the form of start-up funding for small businesses (Sheehan *et al.* 1998; Hassard *et al.* 2006). However, these SOEs also set themselves deadlines by which very large reductions in the workforce were to be achieved (and Premier Zhu Rongji's insistence on a 2000 deadline for 'turning round' all SOEs was constantly repeated in the press), so that even here it would not be possible to avoid compulsory redundancies for much longer. The largest SOEs were by no means immune from unrest over job losses, unpaid wages and pensions and the like in any case, and large-scale compulsory lay-offs were only to be expected to add to the discontent.

The situation was already much more serious, though, for small and medium-sized SOEs, many of which had long been running at a loss. Since the mid-1990s levels of unrest, sometimes involving violence, have been highest among the downsized workers of these companies. The smaller and less prosperous SOEs have lacked the resources to cushion the blow of redundancy for workers, as well as often not being able to afford the necessary employer's stake, which would enable their workers to participate in pilot social-insurance and pension projects, for example. They were more likely to be declared bankrupt or taken over by more successful firms at very short notice, often with no consultation with the workforce whatsoever, leading some workers to speak of East European-style 'shock treatment' as they were thrown out of work without warning to find they had only limited access to welfare provision to keep them from poverty (*China Labour Bulletin* 1998f). The lack of consultation or even information about these vital decisions seemed to be an important factor prompting workers to take their protests to the streets around the plant or to surround local government offices in an attempt to force the authorities to talk to them. It has probably not helped the situation that the usual mechanisms for consultation within the enterprise, the workers' congress and the trade union, never particularly effective even in the pre-reform era, have been thoroughly undermined by the reforms' tendency to stress managerial prerogative above all else. In many cases managers who have grown accustomed to exercising unchallenged authority do not merely neglect consultation with workers, but are actively hostile towards it. It is very noticeable, too, that areas that pushed ahead fastest with programmes of small and medium-sized SOE bankruptcies, such as Sichuan Province in the south-west, experienced particularly frequent and widespread protests by the workers affected. Thus the post-15th CCP Congress policy of freely allowing SOE bankruptcy, merger and takeover, in many respects was a recipe for increased labour unrest nationwide.

### *'Rights, not charity'*

Even where SOE workers accepted the need for restructuring involving lay-offs, there was no acceptance that it should be carried out regardless of the impoverishment of workers who could not rely on regular receipt of benefits, pensions or emergency cost-of-living allowances from the local government. To demonstrate the extent of the economic hardship caused by the lay-off policy, figures from the SSB indicated that 39 per cent of urban households experienced a drop in income during 1997, mainly because of the impact of lay-offs and unemployment, and to the 15 million laid-off in 1997, a further 11 million were predicted to be added by the end of 1998 (*China Labour Bulletin* 1998c). Around 53 per cent of urban households below the official poverty line contained a member who had either been made redundant or who, although technically still employed, was not actually working and thus was only receiving a fraction of normal wages. In the mid-1990s even those still employed and working normally could go unpaid for months at a time (Sheehan 1998). It is important to remember, therefore, that workers were not simply complaining that a very comfortable economic position had got a bit less comfortable; real hardship had been caused by the scale of the lay-offs, and notably so since the beginning of 1997. It is also true to say, though, that former SOE workers did feel keenly the loss of their previous social and political status, especially where the 'loyal pioneers of building socialism' in the old heavy-industrial heartland had been reduced to hawking goods on the city streets, the sort of work previously the preserve of poor migrants from the interior provinces (Schueller 1997: 105). But besides this loss of face, the 'new poor' (*South China Morning Post,* 11 April 1997) of laid-off SOE workers had genuine worries about finding money for family medical bills, children's schooling, and even putting food on the table, and for many this was the first time in their lives that they had experienced this level of insecurity (Wang, X. 1993).

Discontent and unrest in the last years of the 1990s reached such a level that an official response to head off outright rebellion had to be made. Official statements well into 1997 continued to emphasize the unfortunate necessity of throwing large numbers out of work, urging those affected to change their ideas about their entitlement to employment and the type of job they could expect (*South China Morning Post,* 19 September, 16 December 1997). But since then, much more stress has been laid on making proper provision for unemployed workers in terms of benefits and retraining opportunities, and on offering emergency assistance to households who cannot make ends meet.

However, some of the efforts of managers, the official trade unions and local government representatives to express sympathy and offer practical help to impoverished workers have only provoked further anger among the recipients of these gestures. During the late 1990s the presentation to workers of food parcels and cast-off clothing by the official All-China Federation of Trade Unions (ACFTU) was characterized as

> a nauseating and clumsy combination of propaganda and alms-giving, increasingly resented by workers who feel that they deserve more than charity. The answer to unemployment is real training for real jobs, not charity from government ministers seeking photo opportunities in fleeting and stage-managed visits to the homes of the poor.
>
> (*China Labour Bulletin* 1998a: 1)

Besides televised aid visits to workers' homes, other charitable gestures included pre-winter collections for needy workers with, for example, collection points for warm clothing, food and cash donations being set up outside a number of public buildings in Beijing in 1997, including outside the Ministry (now the Bureau) of the Metallurgical Industry (*South China Morning Post,* 21 October 1997).

Visits to workers' homes to offer aid to the needy have a long history in China, going back to the 1950s, but were even then viewed with suspicion by workers who saw them as little more than a public-relations gesture that did not solve the underlying problems they faced (Sheehan 1998). They are even less well regarded by many workers now, as the Democracy Movement theme of the need for enforceable legal rights, rather than paternalistic benefits that can be bestowed or withheld at the whim of the authorities, has returned to prominence in the last few years. Again casting themselves as the main victims of reform, SOE workers point to the sweeping changes that have been made in China for over a quarter of a century and increasingly express the view that measures such as the establishment of a non-enterprise-based welfare system and other legal protections for workers could, and should, have been possible as part of this wholesale restructuring of Chinese society and the economy. They reject the argument that there is no money to fund such projects, insisting that it is, rather, a question of the government's priorities.

It is certainly noticeable that during the reform era the passing of laws that do offer some degree of protection for workers' interests, such as the Labour Law and the Enterprise Law, has lagged far behind the establishment of a centralized, disciplinarian and uncommunicative management style on the shop floor. While it is mostly the foreign-invested manufacturing operations around the SEZs that have become notorious for their harsh, almost militarized style of management and abuse of workers' rights, SOE management has also been influenced to a certain extent in the same direction, with the work system featuring quota increases and speed-up, longer working hours, new controls over labour attendance, and the use of monetary sanctions and penalties to control labour. This has been a steady trend for years in pioneer areas of urban reform such as the south-east, so that the passing of the Labour Law in July 1994, asserting for the first time in law that workers were the true masters of the enterprise, could have little effect against such a well-established trend of power being concentrated in top management's hands while workers felt themselves to have been reduced to the status of hired labour. In their demand for legal rights rather than paternalist gestures, restive workers are mirroring developments in oppositional political movements in China, and the legal line of argument is one that could prove extremely difficult for the government to deal with given its own rhetoric on the importance to successful reform of the rule of law.

## *The impact of corruption*

With reference to the 1989 Democracy Movement, Walder (1989: 34) noted that corruption and inflation then 'had the effect of politicizing workers' dissatisfaction' with the impact of economic reform. Many years on, the issues of corruption and unemployment are playing a similar role. Corruption is generally acknowledged to be widespread in China, with the government itself running high-profile national campaigns against graft and taking pains to publicize cases where officials have been caught and convicted of corruption offences. It is impossible to know how much corruption is occurring in the present phase of state-enterprise restructuring, but there is certainly considerable scope for it, as companies are merged, taken over or declared bankrupt in increasing numbers and assets disposed of at very short notice with minimal public debate or information about the process. What is most striking, though, is that corruption is now almost universally suspected by workers in decisions about the fate of their enterprises. Here again the almost total lack of advance warning, let alone consultation, with the workforce before such decisions are announced only adds to suspicions that the decision-makers have something to hide. Corruption is also frequently suspected where factories are still in operation and goods are leaving the warehouse, but workers are told there is no money for wages, as in the following case from Hunan province in the late 1990s:

> At our factory, we went to the union because we haven't been paid for two months . . . The answer we got from the union guy was: 'Even the union funds haven't been paid, go and see the manager.' So we went to the boss and he said: 'The factory doesn't have any money at the moment. As soon as we have the cash, we will definitely pay the wages.' . . . These answers don't add up. We are still clocking on every day, production is going on as normal, and the warehouse certainly isn't crammed full with unsold goods. So how come there is no money?
>
> (*China Labour Bulletin* 1998e: 1)

In the economic climate of the present reform period, it is commonly speculated that goods leaving an SOE's warehouse are being dumped on the market at prices that earn the enterprise little or no profit. SOEs in the building materials, metallurgical, machinery, textiles and petrochemicals industries, among others, have been warned about such dumping by the government. It is also quite possible that in this and many other cases, any money that is coming in to the enterprise is needed to cover outstanding loans or other liabilities and cannot be spared even for basic wages. But although workers accept indebtedness as a common reason for the closure of SOEs or the failure to pay wages, they tend to blame the extent of the debt itself on previous mismanagement and corruption at the top, still seeing management misconduct or incompetence as the root of the problem. While only a few documented cases of this type have been given prominence in the state-controlled media, there is a much more general and widespread tendency among the state-sector workforce to see corruption and mismanagement as the main and most plausible explanations when the closure of an enterprise is announced or when wages go unpaid, and this only enhances the animosity already evident between managers and workers.

The CCP government's own statements about the dangers of corruption in the process of state-enterprise restructuring add credence to workers' suspicions. Decisions about the closure or merger of SOEs and the establishment of the share-holding system in SOEs have both been identified as areas where particular care must be taken to guard against corruption. As noted, under the MES measures have been adopted to prevent the improper disposal by managers of SOE assets, something that was a major problem under the CRS. We have also noted how under the MES and GCS reform programmes, managers were explicitly charged with increasing, or at least maintaining, the value of state assets as part of their contracts of employment. But during 1997, for example, corrupt disposal of assets was highlighted as the major factor in the bankruptcy of a textile factory in Shanxi, where 5,400 workers had gone unpaid for more than a year (*South China Morning Post*, 26 September 1997). Workers' own statements now frequently refer to managers having enriched themselves through the illicit disposal of state assets, often while their own wages were being paid irregularly or not at all, and then leaving the SOE to its fate and moving on unscathed to another post, seeing this as a universal pattern. Again, official warnings and measures taken to guard against this type of action tend to be taken by workers as confirmation of the scale of the problem. The asset-disposal form of corruption acts as a politicizing factor in workers' discontent in a specific way, helping to reinforce the impression among many workers that SOE managers are, in effect, the 'owners' of the enterprise, or at least can behave as if they are. Thus an element of class-based animosity enters into workers' attitudes to enterprise restructuring, adding to the politicizing effect of the whole issue of official corruption.

## Labour representation under state capitalism

We turn finally to tensions between 'state capitalism' and 'state corporatism' in the relationship between the CCP and urban industrial workers, and examine how the CCP has responded to labour pressure for better industrial and political representation since the late 1980s. The Chinese government has shown particular concern over attempts to form independent labour organizations in this period, seeking instead to contain an increasingly restive working class, now subject to a high level of employment insecurity, within the framework of state-controlled unionism. Thus, the CCP's relaxation of centralized control over a more open, 'mixed' economy has not been matched in the area of labour representation by a greater tolerance of autonomous organization, leading to intensifying conflict with labour, particularly in economically disadvantaged areas of the country.

In framing such analysis we are concerned with the third of the perspectives identified by Pollard (2003) in his paper on state capitalism and demo-cratization in the Philippines – the libertarian Marxian perspective. As set out in his paper, the three main premises of this perspective are: that the means of social production is held privately from the working classes and those who depend on them for survival; that there is no empirical evidence that these people control the organizations controlling the ruling Communist Party; and that the top Party leadership gets its wealth and power like a more ruthless and collective capitalist class extracting surplus value produced by the labour power of the politically impotent working classes. This is a perspective on the relationship between the CCP government and workers in the People's Republic of China which had begun to be articulated by workers themselves at points of crisis in that relationship as early as the 1950s. During the Cultural

Revolution (1966–1976), the idea of the CCP as a new, exploitative ruling class extracting surplus value from the working classes and passing on its privileges to its descendants became a common one among the more radical participants in the movement, and it was an idea that many of them carried over into the first stirrings of China's democracy movement in the late 1970s and early 1980s. The inspiration of Poland's Solidarity movement only gave extra impetus to an existing mood among activists that Chinese labour, if it ever could have regarded the CCP and the Party's subordinate institutions as representing its own interests, now was in obvious need of independent organizations to defend those interests, within the workplace and in society. The official trade unions, those affiliated to the ACFTU, had proved to be wholly inadequate defenders of labour's interests at any point where those interests came into conflict with those of the state. In a state-corporatist model, the official unions have been the only organization in China permitted to represent workers' collective interests and grievances to state authorities. The unions' 'transmission belt' function between labour and the state is supposed to work in both directions, but historically in the PRC it has mainly operated in a top-down way, as a means of imposing state preferences onto workers.

During the 1990s the Chinese state was faced with a number of conflicting priorities regarding the relationships between itself, labour and the official trade unions. In the aftermath of the 1989 protests, the official unions were punished for the support they had offered to the Movement, publicly in the form of a financial contribution, but by some accounts also more significantly in backing a proposed general strike in mid-May 1989 (Wang, S. 1993). A number of leading figures in the ACFTU were purged, and the official unions at all levels were encouraged to lead the condemnation of the 'illegal' independent labour organizations formed during the Movement. Yet, the official unions still had an important role to play as a 'transmission belt' between labour and the state, and this role grew in importance as the state increasingly withdrew from direct involvement in management at the enterprise level (Zhang, Weiying 1997). We have described how this separation of government and management functions was a key aim of the MES reform programme. As we have noted, the other key feature of SOE reform since 1997 has been a programme of unprecedented large-scale SOE lay-offs, and here too, the assistance of the official unions and the workers' congress has been important in the preparatory work carried out within enterprises to engender minimal acceptance, if not enthusiasm, among the workforce of the necessity of shedding labour for the sake of the company's future.

Since China's accession to the WTO, it has also become more important for China's official unions to be recognized internationally as legitimate representatives of the interests of Chinese labour. This seemed to be one of the main motives behind the October 2001 revision of the Trade Union Law. The revised Law contained provisions that potentially offered workers in China more control over their unions and more scope to use the union's legal rights to defend their own interests, though much of this was still undermined by the overarching insistence on the ACFTU's political subordination to the CCP and its key responsibility for economic development rather than for representing the interests of labour (*China Labour Bulletin* 2001). It appears to have been sufficient to win back the ACFTU's position on the governing body of the International Labour Organization (ILO), which the official unions had lost in 1989 because of their acquiescence in the suppression of the 1989 protests (Chen 2002). These developments were also possibly a response to pressure from within China's official unions for greater autonomy to defend members' interests in an era of general intensification of the labour process, a punitive style of management and the ever-present threat of unemployment. Indeed, some within the ACFTU appear to recognize that this is the only way the official unions will ever be able to undercut the growing appeal of independent unions in China.

We have noted, however, that the overriding priority of the CCP government since the late 1990s has been the maintenance of social stability; that is, the avoidance of widespread and serious unrest such as might threaten the government's hold on power. We can comment on how this basic concern has affected the implementation of other policy priorities if we look again at how the programme of lay-offs in large SOEs has progressed since 1997. Initially the government's statements on the issue stressed that the short-term pain of the process for those who lost their jobs was a price that had to be paid for the longer-term viability of the companies concerned, particularly as once China had joined the WTO those companies would soon be subject to the full rigours of international competition. A change in attitude was perceptible by early 1998, however, as far more attention was given to aiding laid-off workers and their families financially and to expressing sympathy for their predicament. As noted, many SOEs revised their plans to complete lay-offs by the end of December 2000, allowing themselves another three years to finish the process. One reason for this apparent change of heart was the effects of the 1997 regional financial crisis, which put many SOEs in economic difficulties as they faced increased competition from countries that had devalued their currencies. But as we have argued previously, the main reason was the upsurge in labour unrest, strikes and protests which the redundancy programme had sparked off. The incidents that gained the most press attention (and it has to be assumed that many incidents go entirely unreported, given the restrictions under which Chinese and overseas journalists operate within China) most often involved the workforces of smaller SOEs, those who had been left to sink or swim on their own after September 1997, and which had either failed to pay workers for months at a time, or had closed down or been sold off very abruptly in a way that suggested corrupt dealings to the workers who had lost their jobs. But, as we have argued, larger SOEs, including some of the best known in China, were certainly not immune from unrest, and they also responded to increased government pressure to maintain stability by adopting an even more cautious and gradualist approach to lay-offs, hence the three-year extension of their original deadlines for shedding surplus labour.

This, then, became the dilemma for the Chinese state: it wished to withdraw from enterprise management almost completely and leave managers in charge of most decisions, and it wished to transform its remaining SOEs into internationally competitive corporations that would function solely as economic entities, not as providers of welfare benefits and full employment as a social good, which was the role of SOEs in the Mao era. But the effects of reform are, perhaps, convincing more and more workers of the necessity of having an independent union organization under their democratic control which can defend their interests against the impositions of an increasingly assertive new managerial elite. While the state refuses to follow the logic of the diversification of Chinese society in the reform period and permit any labour organization with a significant degree of autonomy from government, the stage is set for increasingly sharp and frequent confrontations between the state and labour.

The extent to which the state really has withdrawn from management in China's remaining SOEs varies from enterprise to enterprise. In general terms, autonomy has been most fully realized in areas where reform has progressed the furthest, typically the eastern seaboard and areas such as Shanghai and Guangdong Province, while in the interior a real shift in authority in SOEs is still more potential than actual. But, as noted, the area where state interference is most often reported is in questions of employment and the divesting of surplus labour. We have noted also how a number of large SOEs which pioneered the MES reform programme have been compelled by local authorities to take over loss-making enterprises, not in order to reform them and return them to profit, but primarily in order to guarantee the wages and pension payments owed to those companies' employees. This directly contradicts the general line of MES reform, which is to reduce as far as possible the social and historical obstacles to large SOEs' international competitiveness, namely a high proportion of surplus labour and the obligation to act as a welfare state in miniature for employees. This has occurred even in areas where, in general, the aims of reform in freeing management to manage without state interference have to a large extent been achieved.

SOE management, despite the setting of apparently firm and final deadlines by which large-scale lay-offs must be completed, is also fudging the issue of redundancies, partly as a result of government pressure to avoid provoking protests, and also because of a persistent thread in managers' attitudes of paternalist concern for workers' fate once laid-off and a Mao-era distaste for disposing of surplus labour as if it were just another asset of the enterprise. We have described how MES/GCS restructuring involving the proliferation of sub-companies has enabled large SOEs to transfer large numbers of workers to autonomous sub-companies, many of which have been set up mainly, or solely, for the purpose of absorbing surplus labour. Once this has been done, the parent company is able to report a 'headline' reduction in its workforce which appears to show that the targets for getting rid of surplus labour are being met, although in fact it will still, in the last resort, be responsible for meeting the wages of the workers transferred into a sub-company, and therefore has not freed itself from the surplus-labour burden which is deemed to be a major obstacle to SOE profitability, productivity improvements and international competitiveness.

The Chinese state remains wary of provoking social unrest through pushing ahead too radically with key reforms affecting labour. Moreover, it remains reluctant to abandon its state-corporatist approach to the representation of interests in a rapidly diversifying society and permit truly autonomous representation of the interests of groups such as labour. It has been observed that the CCP has taken a cautious approach in dealing with actual instances of unrest, attempting to avoid bloodshed in confrontations between the security forces and protesting workers as far as possible. But the state's perception that independent labour organizations are an intolerable threat to its prerogatives can be seen in its treatment of the leaders of such protests (such as the Liaoyang Four: see *China Labour Bulletin* 2002–2003, *passim*), where it has resorted to accusations of terrorist tactics as well as long prison sentences in order to discredit and contain those who have attempted to set up independent organizations, even acting against them outside China's own borders on occasion. This situation also leaves large SOEs unable to carry through the reforms that are supposed to enable them to compete on the world stage now that WTO membership requires them to do so, and to date there are no signs that the new leadership of the CCP is any better equipped to resolve this dilemma of reform than were the previous generation of leaders under Jiang Zemin. Labour's predicament in China after more than 25 years of reform will continue to generate protest and attempts at independent organization, and measured repression is unlikely to represent a viable solution in the longer term.

## Conclusion

The scale and conduct of the present round of SOE workforce reductions has brought about an increased incidence of unrest, strikes and other protests among the workers affected. From the mid-1990s onwards, protests became so common in some areas of China that a Politburo Standing Committee member was reported to have returned from a tour of the provinces complaining that he had frequently been unable to use the main entrance to local government buildings because of 'the almost daily occurrences of jobless workers and destitute pensioners laying siege to the headquarters of provincial and municipal administrations' (*China Labour Bulletin* 1998b: 1). In recent years the CCP leadership has taken the trend of frequent labour unrest very seriously, recently rating it the third most worrying threat to stability in China after the activities of separatists in the Muslim north-west of the country and the Tibetan independence movement, with the formation of independent workers' organizations cited as a particular cause for concern. Although in some cases concerned managers at large SOEs extended their deadlines for achieving workforce reductions, so as not to aggravate the situation further, small and medium-sized SOEs tended to press ahead regardless.

The use of service sub-companies to absorb unemployed SOE workers has been successful up to a point, but many of these companies have also been reported to be losing money themselves, and there are concerns about market saturation. Thus this major method of dealing with potentially restive surplus labour is looking fallible as a sustainable solution to the problem. Neither is the diversion of redundant SOE workers into self-employment without difficulties: it is striking how often in recent reported instances of unrest, including many where violent clashes with police are alleged to have occurred, taxi and pedicab drivers have been involved, many of whom are former SOE employees. Some municipal governments developed a policy of reserving a certain proportion of the restricted number of taxi licences for laid-off SOE workers, but street protests have occurred where attempts have been made to tighten up licensing procedures or to increase the fees payable by drivers to the local authorities. The SOE background of these drivers seems a plausible explanation for their very frequent resort to street protests. Already among the obvious losers in the reform process, they do not take kindly to any further official action that makes it more difficult for them to earn a living.

It is all the more troubling for the CCP government that SOE workers' protests in the late 1990s and early 2000s were increasingly both politicized and organized. The belief that independent unions are the only means by which workers' interests can be protected in the new, insecure environment brought about by reform is now more widely held among workers than at any time since 1949. In addition to efforts to form autonomous organizations or to propagate the idea of doing so, a number of workers have also attempted to stand as candidates in local people's congress elections on a platform of workers' rights and/or proper, legally guaranteed provision for laid-off workers. These local elections have repeatedly served as a focal point for unrest and pressure for political reform in China during the post-Mao period, perhaps most notably in the autumn of 1980, when many worker-activists involved in the Democracy Wall Movement stood, or attempted to stand, for election as a way of publicizing their views and highlighting the gulf between the citizens' rights laid down in the Chinese constitution and local authorities' actual response to any challenge from outside the Party establishment. This type of legal or constitutional challenge to the CCP government is much more difficult for the authorities to deal with than a disruptive street protest, which can be categorized as selfish and misguided trouble-making. It also poses the threat of a link between restive workers and other oppositional political movements in China which are increasingly resorting to the same legalistic tactics.

As well as calls for, and attempts to organize, independent unions, there have also been moves by workers towards the formation of independent watchdog organizations to monitor and combat official corruption, and sometimes the same activists have been involved in both independent union-organizing and anti-corruption groups. Official corruption is routinely spoken of wherever SOEs are failing to pay wages or being closed down, and workers' allegations about the privileged, secure and luxurious lifestyles of corrupt managers and officials bear a striking resemblance to similar accusations made by worker-activists during the 1978–1981 Democracy Wall Movement and the 1989 Democracy Movement. The politicizing role of corruption-related grievances even extends to the inadequate provision of welfare for laid-off workers, with the official warnings issued against the misappropriation of funds intended for the unemployed giving credence to protesting workers' suspicions that money intended for them is being improperly diverted. Again, precedents can be found for this type of suspected corruption as a trigger for labour protest, going back to the 1950s. Most incidents of protest and self-organization by workers can still be described as local, sporadic and short-lived, albeit increasingly common. The police have tended to move swiftly against anyone involved in what might develop into an illegal organization, and since independent trade unions are never allowed to register with the local authorities (such registration being a requirement of all organizations in China), they are all de facto illegal. But the corruption issue and the emergence of class-based animosity towards the managerial 'owners' of SOEs give an important and explicitly political dimension to the general discontent evident among present and former SOE employees. As more join the ranks of the unemployed, it is very likely that the activists who are pushing the cause of independent unions most strongly will find a large and ready audience for their views, creating the potential for another serious crisis in the CCP government's troubled relationship with the industrial workforce.

# Part III

# Contemporary studies of enterprise restructuring

# 8    Restructuring Wuhan Iron and Steel

## Introduction

In this chapter and the one that follows we offer detailed assessments of economic reform at two of the eight large, state-owned steel enterprises whose operations we have studied since the mid-1990s. In so doing, we focus not only on generic processes of enterprise restructuring, but also, and importantly, on the financial and accounting implications of such reform. In particular, our analysis highlights trends in the profitability and performance of these enterprises for the period 2000–2005. Whereas in the present chapter we analyse such issues in respect of the Wuhan Iron and Steel Company, in the next we do so for the Tangshan Iron and Steel Company.

## Restructuring Wugang

The Wuhan Iron and Steel Group Company (informally known as Wugang) is located on the south bank of the Yangzi River in the east part of Wuhan, Hubei province, in central China. In 1952 it became the first large iron and steel complex to be set up after the founding of the People's Republic of China. From the very beginning Wugang represented one of the very large state enterprises that constituted the 'commanding heights' of China's pre-reform planned economy. In terms of its overall community headcount, at its peak in the early 1990s Wugang's population exceeded 300,000. By the end of 2003, after a quarter of a century of economic reform, it still retained over 110,000 workers on its direct payroll. Like other large Chinese SOEs, in addition to steelmaking businesses, the structure of Wugang has incorporated, for example, schools and universities, clinics and hospitals, a police force, a fire brigade and farms (*Wugang Yearbook* 2003). As such, relative to other SOEs that provided cradle-to-grave social welfare benefits for their employees and employees' dependants, Wugang has long been a very large 'society in miniature'.

Indeed, in 1991, Wugang was officially categorized by central government as one of China's 'extra large' state enterprises, being consistently ranked throughout the 1990s as one of the nation's top ten firms by assets. In terms of production, Wugang currently produces over 10 million tons of iron and steel annually (Chinasteel.com, 18 December 2005) and is the third largest steel maker by production in China, behind Shanghai Baosteel and Liaoning Anben Steel (formed from the Anshan and Benxi merger, August 2005). Among the world's steel makers, Wugang is ranked twenty-first in terms of crude steel production (International Iron & Steel Institute 2005), whereas technology-wise it is ranked second in China. Importantly, Wugang has over 30 per cent of the Chinese silicon steel market, a high-end downstream product required for automobile manufacture.

What makes Wugang interesting in terms of economic reform is not only its extremely large size but also the fact that since its founding it has been regarded by both planners and reformers alike as a strategic plant within a strategic industry. Since 'liberation' in the late 1940s, it has been deemed a 'socialist model enterprise' and as such has been visited by several state leaders (in the 1950s, Mao Zedong visited Wugang, followed by Deng Xiaoping in the 1970s, and by Jiang Zemin in late 1980s and 1990s). Being a socialist model enterprise implies that Wugang has consistently demonstrated high levels of commitment and compliance to the policies of the CCP. In so doing, its development represents a clear reflection of CCP industrial strategy.

In 1999 the CCP listed Wugang as one of China's 39 'backbone' SOEs, and currently it is one of the nation's remaining (*c.*170) 'centrally administered' state enterprises. Over the last ten years, it has been part of the so-called 'national team' of strategically important enterprises that the central government has groomed to become 'globally competitive'. In the five-year plan for the steel industry issued in 2001, Wugang was positioned to become the leading steel maker in central China; the four other major regional steel makers identified were Baogang in the east (Shanghai), Angang (now Anben) in the north-east (Liaoning), Shougang in the north (Beijing, but probably soon to be relocated to a nearby city, Tangshan, see Chapter 9), and Panzhihua in the west (Sichuan). As Wugang is placed on the government's priority list of state enterprises, the challenges it confronts are also those shared by the other 'national team' members. Wugang's reform process thus reflects the problems and issues that challenge China's large strategic SOEs as they strive to become world players in their industries.

In this chapter, therefore, we offer a detailed case analysis of Wugang in order to depict how the economic reform process in China has affected the management and operations of a 'national team' enterprise. In so doing we begin with a brief analysis of Wugang's 'corporatization' process based on public/company documents and interviews with senior managers during 2004–2005. This is followed by a detailed examination of Wugang's relative level of corporate profitability based on the available financial and account-ing information. Finally, based on interview and textual data, we assess the company's achievements in relation to solving inherent problems arising from the economic reform process, especially those of over-manning, the reduction of the social welfare burden, and the separation of ownership from management.

## The corporatization process

### *Underlying principles*

While there is no official definition of 'restructuring' in the context of SOE reform, one that can perhaps be considered close to official is that provided by two members of China's Academy of Social Sciences, who defined it as the process in which a state firm, through corporatization (*gufenfa*), 're-organizes and restructures its fixed assets, business units and human resources to meet the requirements of becoming a modern enterprise according to Company Law and other government and party directives' (Yu and Luo 2005: 2). Although Wugang was a pioneer in experimenting with 'modern enterprise' restructuring, starting its (GCS) reform process in 1992, it was not until mid-2004, when all core steel manufacturing assets were injected in its already listed subsidiary, Wuhan Steel Processing Company Limited (WSPC), that it completed its major restructuring mission. In that 12-year period, Wugang closely followed Beijing's directive on becoming an MES, and thus the need to achieve: the clarification of property rights; clearer definition of rights and responsibilities; the separation of government and management functions; and the development of 'scientific' enterprise management.

As noted previously, the first two parts of the directive aim to resolve problems arising from the jumbling of assets within an SOE. As assets in a pre-reform SOE belonged to 'the people' (as represented by different government agencies) there was little pressure on administrators to define and separate the property and personnel of different business units, social units and administrative units, since they all came under the same umbrella, the state enterprise. In an organization with no clearly defined boundaries between units, it became difficult to assess a unit's performance and apply other efficiency measures. The necessity of clarifying property rights as well as corporate rights and responsibilities thus became evident when the state began to allow SOEs to raise funds by listing parts of their assets overseas or domestically. As such, 'who owns what?' and 'who produced what?' naturally became questions that investors and analysts wanted answering (Walter and Howie 2003).

These first two parts of the MES formula, therefore, formed the basic guidelines when Wugang restructured its core and non-core business, and other social welfare *danwei*. Wugang tried to define clearly which subsidiaries owned what, while at the same time attempting to separate the liabilities and rights of individual business and non-business units. Such tasks, however, proved to be both difficult and lengthy. In deciding which units were to be separated from the parent company and become subsidiaries,

Wugang followed three main principles: first, what was pared-off should itself form an independent whole; second, its product must have market value and be competitive; and third, in the first years after separation, to ensure the welfare of employees, the holding company would continue to provide a subsidy to the newly formed subsidiary (although this would decrease over time and eventually cease altogether).

### Restructuring from 1992

Wugang claimed to be the first large SOE to attempt to separate its core- from non-core business (*Wugang Yearbook* 2001). In December 1992, the same year that Deng Xiaoping visited the south, Wugang put its service business and some of its non-steel operations (including property development, property management, food processing, kitchen equipment manufacturing, travel business and two hospitals) under a new company, the Wugang Enterprise Development Company. In addition, it placed six mines and four other units that provided supportive mining services under a new mining company, Wugang Mining Industry Company. These two companies had their own separate legal status. And in 1994, Wugang put all its utilities-related business – including water supply, electricity generation, oxygen generation, gas supply and heat supply – under a new company, the Wugang Power Factory. Apart from such initiatives, however, little further progress was made until 1997.

In 1997, following the stimulus provided at the 15th CCP Congress, Wugang accelerated the implementation of its restructuring plan. By the year end, 20 subsidiaries were restructured into limited liability companies and became independent legal business units wholly owned by Wugang. In 1998, the Wuhan Steel Processing Company Limited (WSPC), a shareholding limited company was established and subsequently in 1999 listed on the Shanghai Stock Exchange. WSPC's assets consisted of two profitable upstream steel producers – a cold rolling mill and a silicon steel factory. As of early 2003, Wugang as a group company had 29 limited liability companies as subsidiaries. In principle, these subsidiaries were to have independent legal status, full managerial autonomy and be financially independent. Among the 29 'subsidiaries' (all steel or steel-related businesses) 21 were wholly owned, with Wugang maintaining the controlling stake in the remaining eight. According to our informants, by early 2003 only a few of Wugang's 29 independent subsidiaries were loss-making, the rest by this time having become profitable and thus no longer in receipt of any further subsidy from the parent.

In addition, Wugang encompassed ten directly supervised social service units that included hospitals and clinics, schools and tertiary educational institutions and a security organization. It also controlled four branch companies that involved non-steel businesses – a beverage company, a food processing company, a travel agency and a utilities company. As of end-2003,

Wugang also had three self-financed collectives and two directly supervised businesses in transportation and facilities maintenance. All of the above-mentioned subsidiaries, branch companies and social service *danwei* in Wugang's organizational chart were placed directly under top management and so considered as *erji gongsi*, literally 'second-tier companies'. There were 56 other business units managed and/or owned by the second-tier companies.

Not long after the turn of the century, therefore, Wugang was able to claim it had more or less completed the formation of a GCS, consisting of a parent holding company and two tiers of subsidiaries, and based upon the principles of the MES (*Wugang Yearbooks* 2002, 2003, 2004; all include detailed organizational charts).

### Stock exchange listing

The listing of WSPC in 1998 marked a milestone in Wugang's corporatization programme. The initial public offering (IPO) of WSPC provided RMB1.35 billion (US\$162 million), this representing a relatively small fund for technological improvement. Senior managers at Wugang have informed us that the company, like other SOEs, has frequently experienced severe shortages of development funds. Chinese state managers had learnt the benefits of equity financing well before Deng Xiaoping's official endorsement of the securities markets in 1992 (Walter and Howie 2003). By 1986, over 6,000 enterprises had raised funds by selling shares. In 1990, the State Council announced restrictions on the shareholding experiment allowing only state firms to be listed and outlawing other small, over-the-counter markets that had been burgeoning during the 1980s. The State Council also outlawed several small stock exchanges and only allowed stock trading to take place on the Shanghai and Shenzhen stock exchanges. The main reason for restricting listing to state firms and two exchanges was to exercise tight control as to who could be listed and where. The Tiananmen protests in 1989 sent a warning to Beijing that public interests at large had suffered from the reform process and tighter control on the reform experiments, especially the stock markets, was necessary. What also prompted increased state control was that before 1999 there had been no unified securities law governing listing issues and protecting investors, only the rules set by the individual exchanges. Until 1998 when the first private enterprise listing took place, the Chinese securities markets were basically operated for the benefit of state firms (Zhang 2004). While not all corporatized SOEs were listed, listings were endorsed in the MES programme as a means to meet the financing needs of state-enterprises (Zhang 2004). Some commentators have even suggested that the driving force behind the shareholding experiment was state-enterprise managers' thirst for funds (Walter and Howie 2003). Currently, about two-thirds of the total capitalization in Chinese stock markets is still in the form of state shares (*Hongkong Standard*, 5 February 2005).

## Partial listing versus overall listing

In terms of the amount of listed assets, there are two forms of listed SOEs on the market. In the first ten years or so, the common way was to carve out and list the principal productive assets of an SOE. This form of listing is termed partial listing (*fencha shangshi*). The reasons for the popularity of partial listing in the 1990s were two-fold. First, not all assets in an SOE could meet the listing requirements of the exchanges. And second, the state set a quota limiting the size of a state firm's assets that could be listed. This restriction was made because of the state's worry that China's relatively young stock markets did not have the capacity to absorb big IPOs. If there were too many big listings, the markets might be flooded with supply and stock prices might drop, which would discourage investors and impede the growth of the domestic stock markets (Walter and Howie 2003). In 2003, the policy on listing appeared to have changed, for the Bank of China, the China Construction Bank and the Commercial Bank of China were given permission to list the majority of their core business assets – that is, for an 'overall listing' (*zhengti shangshi*).

Wugang is one of many state firms that did not list all its productive assets at its primary listing. As said, in 1999 it only listed two of its steel making factories. In mid-2004, however, Wugang sold seven other steel making factories to the listed subsidiary, WSPC, for 9 billion yuan (about US$1.1 billion). WSPC financed the acquisition by issuing 2 billion new shares (*South China Morning Post*, 15 June 2004). Of these shares, 1.2 billion were actually sold back to the parent, with the rest to the public and other institutional investors. After the acquisition, WSPC was renamed as Wuhan Iron and Steel Company Limited (WISCO), which reflects that the listed firm is a fully integrated steel producer. Wugang's shareholding in WISCO was reduced subsequently to 76 per cent from the original stake of 85 per cent. To quote the WISCO 2004 annual report, Wugang has now 'completed the process of overall listing of its core business' (*zhuye zhengti shangshi*). WISCO's progressive acquisition of its parent's core productive assets thus signalled that ultimately all of Wugang's steel assets would be acquired by WISCO and become part of the listed company (*Interfax*, 31 May 2004). Since 2003, this gradual asset-injection strategy has been a popular method for large SOEs to corporatize their productive assets, allowing the state to reduce its shareholding incrementally. (A high-profile example of a large SOE that gradually sold its productive assets to its listed subsidiary is the Hong Kong and New York listed China Telecom (*South China Morning Post*, 20 May 2004).)

### Problems of partial listing

The recent experiences of WISCO may serve as an exemplar for resolving some of the problems that have been associated with partial listing. Partially listed SOEs have been accused of violating the MES directives of clear property rights and the clarity of rights and responsibilities between the parent and the listed subsidiary. Being the majority shareholder, a parent company has power over the subsidiary in appointing senior managers and making key decisions. This poses a moral hazard for the parent by creating an opportunity to transfer funds generated from the listed company to itself, thus encroaching upon the interests of minority shareholders (Yu and Luo 2005). Substantial connected transactions between the listed subsidiaries and other companies within the group have been common practice (Deng 2004). In the case of Wugang, 30 per cent of its total sales in 2004 of RMB7 billion (US$0.84 billion) were connected transactions between the listed company and the parent or other subsidiaries of the parent. In addition, the listed company also made purchases of 9 billion yuan from the parent's subsidiaries. This type of widespread connected transaction has caused investors and analysts alike to doubt the real profitability of the listed firm and has raised concern over whether business decisions are really aimed at maximizing profits of the listed company. To repeat, who owns what and how much are major questions associated with such processes, for minority shareholders often do not know exactly what they are purchasing. Nonetheless, the bottom line for shareholders in the listed SOEs is the stock price and the company's future profitability. In the next section, therefore, we analyse the financial status and, in particular, the levels of profitability of Wugang and its listed arm, WISCO/WSPC since 2000. In so doing, we first present separate accounts of the finances of Wugang and WISCO/WSPC and subsequently offer an integrated assessment of their financial standing.

## Financial analyses of Wugang and WSPC

Assessing the profitability of Wugang is not a straightforward task. Since not all of Wugang's assets are listed, it has no obligation to disclose all financial information to the public. Thus except for the financial information on Wugang's listed subsidiary, no complete financial statements of Wugang's other steel and non-steel business are available. In Wugang's Yearbooks, only limited information of the group's consolidated statement is provided together with a few data items related to its non-steel business. Moreover, there is no mention of how the steel and non-steel business units are defined for accounting purposes as well as notes to explain other accounting details. This lack of accounting information makes the interpretation and comparison of the ratios more difficult. Nevertheless, assuming the available financial information is prepared according to the national accounting standards promulgated in 1993, which are similar to international accounting practices, we have computed several key ratios for Wugang's steel business (see Table 8.1). For comparison, we have also computed equivalent sets of data for the world's largest listed steel makers and the largest listed steel makers in China. Complete lists of the world's largest listed steel makers and China's largest listed steel makers are given in Appendices 8.1 and 8.2 at the end of the

*Table 8.1* Comparison of financial performance – Wugang versus largest listed
Chinese steel firms and the largest steel firms globally

| Year | Wugang | Wuhan Steel Processing Co. Ltd (WSPC) | PRC composite | Global composite |
|---|---|---|---|---|
| *(A)  Profitability – net margin (%)* | | | | |
| 2003 | 6.70 | 8.36 | 13.14 | 0.37 |
| 2002 | 4.31 | 8.82 | 8.66 | −1.31 |
| 2001 | 3.45 | 11.11 | 6.46 | −2.57 |
| 2000 | 3.44 | 10.21 | 7.14 | 0.60 |
| *(B)  Profitability – return on equity (%)* | | | | |
| 2003 | 9.78 | 9.7 | 17.85 | 4.11 |
| 2002 | 4.16 | 11.64 | 11.82 | −1.22 |
| 2001 | 3.21 | 15.05 | 8.73 | −35.24 |
| 2000 | 3.01 | 15.53 | 6.46 | 3.8 |
| *(C)  Asset management – average collection period (days)* | | | | |
| 2003 | 7 | 53.35 | 44.08 | 57.18 |
| 2002 | 38 | 45.84 | 50.24 | 90.77 |
| 2001 | 52 | 50.29 | 53.73 | 42.46 |
| 2000 | 75 | 9.72 | 56.21 | 38.71 |

| Year | Wugang | Wuhan Steel Processing Co. Ltd (WSPC) | PRC steel industry index | Global composite |
|---|---|---|---|---|
| *(D)  Asset management – inventory turnover (times per year)* | | | | |
| 2003 | 6.14 | 14.98 | 12.00 | 4.5 |
| 2002 | 3.02 | 12.27 | 11.47 | 4.27 |
| 2001 | 2.97 | 11.06 | 10.41 | 3.98 |
| 2000 | 2.97 | 9.12 | 12.22 | 3.94 |
| *(E)  Asset management – fixed asset turnover (times per year)* | | | | |
| 2003 | 0.85 | 1.81 | 1.53 | 1.59 |
| 2002 | 0.63 | 2.2 | 1.22 | 0.92 |
| 2001 | 0.61 | 2.03 | 1.16 | 0.88 |
| 2000 | 0.61 | 2.54 | 1.45 | 0.87 |

| Year | Wugang | Wuhan Steel Processing Co. Ltd (WSPC) | PRC composite | Global composite |
|---|---|---|---|---|
| *(F)  Financing – total debt/total assets (%)* | | | | |
| 2003 | 56.21 | 23.84 | 43.17 | 78.28 |
| 2002 | 48.13 | 26.70 | 46.93 | 79.06 |
| 2001 | 48.05 | 30.03 | 45.5 | 69.67 |
| 2000 | 51.10 | 28.09 | 35.31 | 62.12 |
| *(G)  Financing – payout ratio (%)* | | | | |
| 2003 | n/a | 101.35 | 41.09 | 15.5 |
| 2002 | n/a | 17.54 | 60.67 | n/a |
| 2001 | n/a | 83.25 | 63.92 | 12.9 |
| 2000 | n/a | 82.8 | 63.31 | n/a |

chapter, with Appendix 8.3 presenting selected financial data and ratios for Wuhan Iron and Steel.

## Financial performance of Wugang and WSPC

### *Wugang versus WSPC*

The world's steel markets started to recover in late 2002. As such, 2003 proved to be an outstanding year for Wugang, as reflected in the substantial increase in its net margin and return on equity (ROE). Its net margin rose from around 3–4 per cent in 2002–2003 to 6.7 per cent in 2003, which was slightly lower than WSPC's 8.36 per cent. Wugang's ROE also grew to 9.78 per cent, double of that of 2002 but on par with that of WSPC. During less favourable years for the steel industry (e.g. 2000–2002), WSPC was by far a more profitable company than Wugang. Over that period, WSPC's net margins were consistently double that of the parent. Thus, it seems that the assets carved out of Wugang for the creation of WSPC were among the most productive.

Judged by asset management ratios, WSPC appears to be much better run than its parent. As a measure of efficiency, over the four-year period analysed, the inventory turnover of WSPC averaged about 12 times, whereas Wugang's only averaged about four times. Fixed asset turnover was also more than double the rate of Wugang's over this period; its fixed asset turnover was about 2.1 over the four years, whereas Wugang's was consistently lower, at 0.9. This implies that Wugang as a parent company employed significantly more fixed assets for each dollar of revenue it generated.

In terms of capital structure, WSPC incurred much less debt than Wugang. WSPC financed its assets with less than 30 per cent debt, whereas Wugang was half debt-financed.

### *Wugang versus global steel leaders*

SOEs generally do not present an image of high profitability and good management. However, Wugang partially proved that this was not always the case, when judged by industry standards. As an SOE, Wugang's profitability in the steel business is surprisingly good when compared with the world's largest steel makers. Between 2000 and 2002 the company remained profitable with both its net margin and ROE at 3–4 per cent levels, whereas the profitability of the world's largest producers swung from negative to marginally positive over the same period. In 2003, both Wugang and the largest world steel makers recovered but Wugang recorded much higher profitability. However, it is clear that Wugang did not utilize its assets as efficiently as its world counterparts. Except for accounts receivable, its asset management measures were below the benchmark for the world's largest producers. Wugang thus appeared to have invested too much in fixed assets relative to the need for such assets.

In relation to capital structure, it is also surprising that the debt ratio of Wugang is so much less than the world benchmark; that is, far different from the general impression of debt-ridden SOEs. Wugang's debt was around 50 per cent whereas the world leaders averaged over 70 per cent of debt financing. From the payout ratios, the world largest steel makers depended heavily on retained earnings (retaining over 85 per cent) for future investment whereas WSPC paid out the majority of earnings (80 per cent) to its shareholders. This is somewhat inconsistent with the rapid technological advancement it sought to achieve. Most likely, it reflects the wishes of the primary beneficiary – the largest shareholder, its parent, Wugang – which owned 85 per cent of WSPC during that period.

### What was the profitability of Wugang's non-steel units?

The (incomplete) consolidated statement of Wugang does not explicitly describe how well its non-steel units have operated. There was little information published except for the figures shown in Table 8.2.

The annual reports for 2001–2003 suggest that Wugang's non-steel business has been profitable since 2000, albeit with a thin margin. The figures in Table 8.2 also show that Wugang's non-steel business was quite large, with sales exceeding 40 per cent of its steel revenue.

## To what extent has Wugang reduced its redundancy problem?

### The problem nationwide

We have discussed elsewhere in this book the extent to which China's SOEs are over-manned. This is largely the result of the SOE's traditional role as an urban employment provider in the planned economy. In addition to meeting production needs, SOEs hired staff for the sake of helping local government to keep unemployment levels to a minimum (Xiao 1997). Hiring employees' dependants was also part of the 'settlement' role of SOEs. Besides, the life-long employment terms in the pre-reform period precluded the possibility of

*Table 8.2* Wugang's non-steel business – published financial data (million yuan)

| Years | 2002 | 2001 | 2000 |
|---|---|---|---|
| Sales | 9,466 (48%) | 7,473 (41%) | 7,050 (40%) |
| Pre-tax profit | 566 | 113 | 100 |
| Margin (= pre-tax profit/sales) (%) | 5.98 | 1.51 | 1.42 |

Note: Percentages in brackets indicate the ratios of sales of non-steel business relative to sales of steel business.
Source: *Wugang Yearbooks*, 2001–2003

state firms sacking unproductive employees. An egalitarian approach to compensation complicated the overstaffing problem by not providing incentives for employees to work effectively and efficiently. Thus, over the years state enterprises employed far more workers than they required for purposes of production (Sun 1997). Wugang's managers still apparently feel obliged to create employment for the dependents of employees. As one senior manager at Wugang's stated recently:

> Wugang is a big enterprise. If employees' dependants are employed, Wugang will have less worry. That is a stabilising factor. That is why we created jobs [for workers' dependants] to provide service to Wugang . . . If the qualifications and experience [of the candidates] are the same, the children of Wugang's employees are given priority to be hired.

While accurate statistics as to the extent of surplus labour in the state sector are not generally available, reports suggest that the surplus was about one-third to one-half of the total SOE workforce in the mid-1990s, or around 35–55 million employees (*South China Morning Post*, 7 May 1997; Lin *et al.* 2001; Solinger 2002). We have suggested previously that the extent of surplus labour varied in different industries and in different regions. In some heavy industrial regions in the north-eastern provinces, higher rates of over 50 per cent were reported, whereas lower rates were found among state firms along the east coast, where the non-state economy was more developed. In industries such as textiles, coal mining, metallurgy, petrochemicals and defence manufacturing, surplus labour was more prevalent. In general, surplus labour was more likely to be found among unskilled, middle-aged workers with lower than secondary school education (Zhang, Weiying 1997). We have noted how since 1997 the state has often encouraged the laying-off of surplus labour, with from the early 1990s some 60 million state enterprise employees being made redundant (Solinger 2005).

### *Wugang: transferring the surplus labour problem from core- to non-core business*

Like other large SOEs we have studied (see Chapter 6) Wugang did not apply massive lay-offs to alleviate its surplus labour problem. In fact, as one senior manager recently informed us, for many years lay-offs were 'hardly heard of' at Wugang. Instead, it applied two main strategies: first, the transfer of surplus labour from its core (i.e. steel-making) business units to other non-core subsidiaries, a process termed 're-channelling' (*fenliu*) in China; and second, it offered incentives for voluntary early retirement

The extent of surplus labour in Wugang can be assessed by applying an industry measure. In the steel sector, one estimate of how efficiently a firm deploys its employees is the output of crude steel per employee. In 2003, the average production of steel plants in the European Union and in North

America was slightly below 600 tons per employee, while Japanese efficiency was about 10 per cent higher at 650 tons per employee (International Iron & Steel Institute 2004). Wugang cited the world average as its benchmark when setting goals for reducing its workforce (*Wugang Yearbook* 2001; interviews with senior executives). As shown in Table 8.3, whereas in 1992 employee productivity at Wugang was extremely low (at 43 tons per employee), this has risen dramatically in recent years (to e.g. 560 tons per employee in 2003). In fact, the figures show that Wugang doubled its production in ten years while cutting its direct steel workforce by almost 87 per cent.

The above figures make Wugang look reasonably effective when compared with other world steel makers. But such figures only represent a small fraction of Wugang's total workforce. In 2002, Wugang had a total of 112,402 people on its register of staff and workers (*zaice*) but only 89,078 had actual positions (*zaigang*). The substantial difference between the *zaice* and *zaigang* numbers is unique in China's SOEs, reflecting the human resource measures adopted in the past as well as those new measures aimed at reducing over-manning. *Zaice* workers include not only those employees who have tangible work roles, but also retirees for whom state firms still need to provide social and pension benefits, plus others who are 'in transition'; that is, in the process of being relocated to other work units within the enterprise (see Chapter 6).

As we have noted previously, while admitting that SOEs have far too many surplus employees, large enterprise managers have, nevertheless, faced tremendous pressure to retain them. Being sacked by an enterprise is called *chuming* in Chinese, a term that literally means taking a worker's name off the company register. In an era when a comprehensive social (non-enterprise) safety net is still to be established, and when external labour markets are still emerging, sacking a state employee can be akin to taking away his or her citizenship. A worker who becomes 'off-the-register', especially in the older or interior industrial regions, may not receive housing or housing subsidy, family medical support, labour insurance or education and retirement entitlements.

In this context, to encourage employees to 'leave', state firms such as Wugang were allowed to apply two main measures. One was to offer a lump

*Table 8.3* Wugang's production of crude steel per employee

| Year | Total production of crude steel (million tons) | No. of direct steel workers | Production of crude steel per employee (ton/employee) |
|------|-----------------|----------------|----------------|
| 1992 | 4.78 | 112,470 | 43 |
| 2000 | 6.65 | 26,000 | 253 |
| 2001 | 7.09 | 14,850 | 477 |
| 2002 | 7.55 | 15,648* | 482 |
| 2003 | 8.40 | 15,000* | 560 |

Source: *Wugang Yearbooks* 1993, 2001–2004

sum to buy out an employee's tenure and any associated future benefits they were entitled to receive; the employee would then sever his or her connection with the state enterprise. The other was to continue to provide employees with some basic living allowances while encouraging them to find jobs outside the state firm, keeping their names on the company's register for a period of two to three years. Those who accepted this offer became '*zaice*-but-not-*zaigang*' employees, which also included those whose positions became redundant when their social service units were transferred to local government. (Further details on the restructuring of social service units are presented later.)

As of 2002, there were about 23,000 *zaice*-but-not-*zaigang* employees at Wugang, a number equivalent to about one-fifth of total number of (*zaice*) staff and workers, or one-quarter of those that actually had positions (*zaigang*). These workers were not required to attend work, but in general still received a basic monthly allowance, which was equivalent to one-half to three-fifths of their original wages, although in some cases workers kept their full salary as the allowance. Such workers were also permitted to keep their pension and other social benefits, while their allowance was linked to, and increased in line with, general salaries within the unit. Another major difference with *zaice* employees was that they did not receive the bonus payments afforded to *zaigang* employees.

### Settlement of surplus workers

Between 1993 and 2002, Wugang implemented seven restructuring programmes all of which involved a large-scale reduction of employees in its steel businesses. According to the 2003 annual report, Wugang's direct workforce for its steel businesses was officially reduced from 112,470 in 1992 to 14,850 in 2001, a reduction of almost 100,000 people (*Wugang Yearbook* 2003: 67–70).

A question that naturally arises from this apparently massive staff reduction is – where did those 100,000 people go? The answer is that while some left the firm and others turned into *zaice*-but-not-*zaigang* employees (by choice or by reaching retirement age) the majority of the reduction in direct steel workers resulted from transfers to other group subsidiaries.

In 1993, Wugang established a new arm, Xingda, to provide a wide range of services – including vehicle repair, security, food and beverages, trading and construction maintenance – with a large percentage of surplus workers being transferred to these newly established subsidiaries. As an example, the majority of the maintenance staff for one of Wugang's steel factories was transferred to a new subsidiary whose main role, as a sub-contractor, was to provide maintenance services for the same plant. As a dedicated company it was, in theory, allowed to sell its services outside Wugang, but Wugang remained its priority client. As one senior manager informed us, the transferred employees did not actually notice any difference after the transfer – they serviced the same machines and ostensibly did the same job.

Service companies by nature are labour intensive. Given the size of Wugang, it is itself is a major consumer of services. Thus, it is possible for some kinds of service businesses to survive simply by drawing customers from within the group. This type of internal transfer signals the existence of an internal labour market. At Wugang's steel units, internal transfers have seemingly gone a long way to solving the 'headline' surplus labour problem. As one senior manager commented, Wugang has, in effect, 'simply transferred the redundancy problem from its steel business to its non-steel subsidiaries' (see also Yu and Luo 2005). Table 8.4 shows the consequence of Wugang's employment strategy.

It can be seen from Table 8.4 that Wugang's non-steel business was assigned over 80 per cent of the group's employees but only generated 19 per cent of revenue. While this can be partly explained by the fact that steel business units are highly capital intensive and non-steel business service units are relatively labour intensive, it also implies that the surplus labour problem is higher in non-steel service units.

So did Wugang substantially reduce its surplus labour? Taking Wugang as a whole, the reduction over the last ten years or so appears relatively insignificant. It can be argued that overall the size of its (core/non-core) workforce has not changed that much from the figures for direct steel workers given in 1992. In the main, Wugang has re-categorized employees and moved the surplus steel workers to other group subsidiaries.

## Reduction of the social welfare burden

In 2003, China's SOEs operated about 11,000 primary and high schools and 6,100 hospitals. Overall they spent approximately RMB46 billion (US$5.5 billion) on various auxiliary services that in other economies would be the responsibility of society (*Xinhua News Agency*, 30 April 2004). As of the end of 2002, about 7 per cent of Wugang's staff and workers served in such social service units. It had 2,664 *zaice* workers in its primary and secondary schools,

*Table 8.4* Wugang's steel and non-steel business (as of end 2002)

|  | Steel business | Non-steel business and social units | Wugang total |
|---|---|---|---|
| *Zaigang* (on-the-job) employees | 15,648 (18%) | 73,430* (82%) | 89,078 (100%) |
| *Zaice* but not *zaigang* workers | 1,848* (8%) | 21,476* (92%) | 23,324* (100%) |
| Total workers on the register (*zaice*) | 17,496 (16%) | 94,906 (84%) | 112,402 (100%) |
| Revenue | RMB19,172 million (81%) | RMB9,466 million (19%) | RMB28,638 million (100%) |

Note: * Computed by the authors.
Source: *Wugang Yearbook* 2003

3,159 in its hospitals and 676 in its security force. Its kindergartens and pre-schools had another 971 *zaice* workers.

### Separation policy

From the beginning of 2003, Wugang started gradually to separate its social service units from the group company. Social service units were restructured and their resources reorganized into separate entities. Subsequently there were two routes available to follow. One was to transfer the social service units to the local government. This primarily applied to those units whose services were considered as the government's responsibility and where there were corresponding government units to take them over, such as the police force, schools and hospitals. The other route was that those units whose services had market value and could compete, would be helped to become 'marketized', and thus run like a private company that charged for its services at a market rate, for example, kindergartens.

Despite state directives that local governments should take up the majority of the SOEs' social welfare burden, such transition has not been straight-forward. The transfer process has involved considerable negotiation between enterprises and local governments. As a teacher at one of Wugang's post-secondary institutions suggested:

> What [social service] units to be transferred, what particular assets to take over, they [local government] have the right to choose. What the city government likes most are those units that have the fewest people but the most fixed assets . . . Also local government wants money from Wugang when taking over those social responsibilities. The final result [as to what to take over, how and when] depends on the negotiation between Wugang and the local government.

### Separation in practice – schools, hospitals and kindergartens

In terms of subsidizing the separated social service units, the general rule is that the holding company will continue to provide financial support for three to five years. In the first year, the subsidy is 100 per cent of the budget, then 80 per cent in the second year, and 60 per cent in the third year. Eventually, the subsidy is reduced to zero.

Wugang's schools, for example, were given a five-year transition period. However, an initial problem emerged in that the local (Qingshan district) government was reluctant to take on non-teaching and non-managerial staff over 45 years of age in the case of women and over 50 in the case of men. Workers who exceeded these age limits simply lost their jobs after the transfer. While some workers with additional skills were re-employed in other subsidiaries, those that were not so lucky had to *jujia xiuxi*, 'rest at home', thus becoming members of the '*zaice*-but-not-*zaigang*' workforce.

A further problem with this transfer saw disagreement over who would take up the leading posts. For example, while Wugang traditionally employed its own directors for its primary and secondary schools, there was also a single director of education for Qingshan district. As none of the directors wanted to lose power over the transfer, much political wrangling ensued, which apparently slowed the process. As a senior manager at Wugang diplomatically informed us, 'It is likely that Wugang's school directors will continue to keep their positions as directors along with the one from the government for a period of time.' Overall, the transfer of schools appears to be welcomed by Wugang's teachers, notably as government teachers locally have tended to receive higher wages. In contrast, unskilled workers attached to Wugang's schools have signalled their desire to remain with the state enterprise in the likelihood that they will receive a better compensation package.

In the transfer of hospitals, Wugang has experienced even greater difficulties. According to our informants there have been three major reasons for this. First, Wugang's hospital facilities were far poorer than those of the local government, making the take-over unappealing. Second, the best Wugang doctors had already pursued other opportunities and so there were few quality medical professionals left. And third, and importantly, the proportion of Wugang non-medical support workers was considered too high, with the result that the local government did not want to take over such a large proportion of surplus personnel. As senior managers at Wugang informed us, in situations such as this, where the levels of support workers looks unappealing, the state enterprise has found a way to speed up the negotiation process with the local government; that is, since local government is forbidden to raise tax levels and more funds are always welcome, the transfer process tends to become smoother and faster if Wugang agrees to offer additional, after-transfer funding.

In contrast, Wugang's kindergartens were relatively competitive and their services had a ready market. They were, therefore, prime targets to be marketized. For a while Wugang continued to subsidize their operations (in line with the subsidy formula outlined above) but eventually they became financially independent.

The direction of separating Wugang's social service units was, therefore, clear – either transfer them to local government or marketize them after restructuring into independent entities. As noted, the transition period for both methods lasts from three to five years with Wugang continuing to subsidize the operations of those units according to a sliding scale. Shifting the social welfare burden to local government, however, has not always been easy for Wugang and the process often reflects a power struggle among those whose vested interests are affected. For local government, it is willing to take over an element of social service provision if it appears to represent a good deal. As for workers, our interviews suggest that they are happy to cooperate if they either receive higher wages or are presented with an improved compensation package after transfer. In any event, those employees who become surplus to requirements as a result of the separation process are often left to Wugang to re-assign to other group subsidiaries.

### Workers' reactions to restructuring

Although elsewhere we discuss at length instances of increasing labour unrest resulting from state workers' dissatisfaction with, for example, job losses, severance pay, change of employment terms, and/or loss of welfare benefits (see Chapter 7, also Cheng 2004; Li 2004; Solinger 2005), our interviews with Wugang workers and managers suggested that the restructuring process has not, thus far, generated significant levels of grievance or resistance. We were told that the forms of industrial protest that have taken place elsewhere in China, notably in the rust-belt provinces of the north-east, such as large-scale demonstrations or collective appeals to action, have not been replicated at Wugang. As one worker informed us, '*Jiti shangfang* (a visit to management by a group of employees) did take place, but that because of their concern for the future employment for their children. There have been no major demonstrations.' This lack of significant protest perhaps reflects the fact that, overall, there have been relatively few direct lay-offs over the years at Wugang. Even though it is widely acknowledged inside the enterprise that the subsidiaries are over-manned, the management of Wugang seems reluctant to sack surplus workers. As one senior manager noted, 'Even if subsidiaries want to lay off workers, they have to get approval from the parent company. The laid-off employees will have no place to go if they are forced to leave. Lay-off is a serious matter.'

Relatively low levels of resistance may also reflect improvements in standards of living for a large percentage of the workforce during the reform years. In contrast to examples of cash-strapped SOEs where employees have been owed salary and/or deprived of welfare benefits, Wugang has seemingly managed to avoid a major downturn in living standards for the majority of its workforce. In 1998, for example, when enterprise housing reform commenced and state enterprises were allowed to sell their housing units to employees, Wugang started an aggressive project to develop a self-contained landscaped complex with 10,000 apartment units for its workers. When the project was completed in 2002, the units were apparently sold to employees at cost; that is, at about one-third to half of the market value. (Wugang also provided some long-service employees with additional discounts.) One result of this development was that the average area of living quarters for Wugang workers was over 13 square metres, compared to the national average of 9 square metres. For those employees who rented units, they were charged similarly at about one-third of the market rate, with the rental agreement continuing into retirement.

However, secondary data on industrial unrest suggest the picture at Wugang is not such a benign one. The *China Labour Bulletin* of 4 March 2003, for example, reported a protest by retired Wugang workers in which over 300 retirees railed against proposed changes to the enterprise's medical health care services; changes that would effectively terminate the low-cost medical coverage provided by the enterprise. It was reported also that the official trade unions of Wugang's factories pressurized their members not to participate in this protest. For whatever reason, this event was not mentioned by any of the workers or managers we interviewed in September of that year.

On the whole, the workers and managers we interviewed seemed to accept that changes to the enterprise were inevitable and felt the direction of reform was generally correct. Furthermore, they did not suggest they had suffered unduly during the period of reform, despite the fact that the 'iron rice-bowl' policy had ceased after the introduction of contract employment in the mid-1980s, or that from 2002 all Wugang employees were to be hired on a fixed-term contract basis. Our sample of workers and managers, however, may not have been fully representative of the population as a whole, especially given Wugang's involvement in choosing many of our interviewees.

### Continued government intervention in Wugang's operations

Although during the past decade the state has consistently emphasized the separation of politics and enterprise, notably in Beijing's proposals for achieving a 'modern enterprise system', both central and local government have regularly intervened in Wugang's operations. Wugang's status as one of the *c*.170 centrally supervised large SOEs that the state is grooming to be internationally competitive, appears to legitimize central government's intervention in the enterprise's major strategic decisions. This is reinforced by the fact that Wugang has been 'strategically positioned' by central government to be the leading steel maker in central China.

A notable example of such intervention was that, in 1999, Wugang was forced to merge with Pangda Steel of Hainan Island. As a senior executive at Wugang informed us, this merger would not have taken place if Wugang had a choice, for Hainan Pangda had a history of significant loss making and appeared to offer little in terms of competitive advantage to Wugang. Indeed, after the merger Hainan Pangda's loss-making trend continued at least to the end of 2002 (*Wugang Yearbook* 2001–2003).

It has recently been announced that Wugang has 'merged and acquired' the 'less profitable' Liuzhou Iron and Steel, a smaller steel enterprise in the southern province of Guangxi, the agreement being signed on 19 December 2005 in Nanning, Guangxi's capital city (cnhubei.com, 20 December 2005; *China Daily*, 21 December 2005). According to this agreement, Wugang will invest 6.506 billion yuan (US$802 million) to hold a 51 per cent stake, while Liuzhou Iron and Steel – in the form of a government holding – will buy a share of 6.25 billion yuan (US$740 million) representing the remaining 49 per cent, in a 'merger' that will see Wugang take control of all Liuzhou's mills and plants. This is virtually the first case of a trans-provincial merger and acquisition in China's steel industry. With Wugang's acquisition earlier in 2005 of Ezhou Steel, this cements the enterprise's position as the nation's third largest steel producer and reinforces the government's strategy for it to be a truly global player.

More prosaically, local government also continues to pressure Wugang to finance more of the province's social welfare development, contrary to the state's intention to remove the enterprise's social functions and foster it as a purely economic entity. According to senior managers we interviewed, given the current shortage of provincial welfare funds, local government still considers that Wugang has a range of social responsibilities. For instance, Wugang was asked to contribute to maintaining the roads in the city because some of its premises were along them. It was also asked to help fund many of the poorer townships in the province, given the enterprise's history of helping townships in, for example, the funding of education, building of factories, and replacing of old facilities. (Wugang also operates factories that are staffed by the disabled.) As noted by one Wugang senior manager: 'There are a lot of hidden taxes to Wugang.'

As Wugang retains an important role in the government's macro industrial strategy so, in turn, is its own corporate strategy very much influenced by the state. Also being a prominent enterprise in the district of Qingshan and the city of Wuhan, Wugang is expected to continue being financially involved in certain social services even though, in theory, state policy should allow it to rid itself of this burden.

## Conclusion

Overall Wugang seems to have benefited from the reform process in general and under the MES/GCS in particular. From the early 1990s, steel production facilities have been upgraded to among the best in China and crude steel production increased by 76 per cent from 1992 to 2003. Developments following on from the enterprise's recent acquisitions of Liuzhou Steel and Ezhou Steel will see capacity eventually increase from 10 to 20 million tons annually. Profitability in the last few years has been above the world average and the separation of non-steel business and social units is well under way. As such Wugang appears to be a 'model enterprise' for what the state wants a 'national team' SOE to do and how it should do it during the current reform era.

Despite this there remain worries over, for example, the way surplus labour is to be handled and the prospect of resistance resulting from those potentially to be laid-off and who consider their benefits to be infringed. Thus far Wugang seems to have met with only minor resistance from its workers despite the widespread organizational changes made in the restructuring process. Furthermore, from a reading of Wugang's annual reports one gets the impression that the company has successfully transferred surplus workers out of its steel business, making its steel units look lean. However, the majority of surplus labour has, in fact, been transferred to the non-steel businesses and thus remains in the group. It can be argued that the improvement in Wugang's steel business was obtained at the expense of its non-steel business, with the overstaffing problem remaining widespread in the non-steel units. The question remains of how long can Wugang maintain such shuffling around of its surplus labour? And linked to this is the question of how long can the company avoid significant and overt industrial unrest? Wugang has yet to resolve its surplus labour problem – if this is not settled satisfactorily in the years to come it will most likely serve to engender significant resistance from workers.

In addition, while official industrial policy suggests that Beijing wants SOEs to terminate their social welfare functions, Wugang's role as a 'little government' has remained throughout the 1990s and into the new century. In so doing it grasped the opportunity to provide the 'last dinner' in housing benefits to its employees by building a brand new 10,000-unit housing complex. As a result, housing benefits at Wugang are above the national standard. Given Wugang's profitability, it is able to provide relatively generous terms and conditions when settling with laid-off workers and changing the nature of employment contracts. And Wugang's management is not shy about discussing its paternalistic responsibilities towards its employees and their dependants. In the enterprise's own assessment of its achievements in the 1990s, substantial coverage in the Yearbooks is given to how well Wugang has improved the living quality of its employees and also the strategy it has adopted to effect the 'quiet settlement' of surplus workers and thus maintain social stability for the company. In the minds of Wugang's managers, providing adequate social welfare appears to remain a priority. As such, much of the enterprise's political role still dominates its strategic actions. When asked what the overall goal of the company was, a Wugang senior manager responded, 'To take up the *responsibility* of producing steel for the country' (emphasis added).

In sum, reform at Wugang has been constrained by its paternalistic responsibilities inherited from the old planned economy together with political concerns over maintaining social stability during economic transition. As a result, settlement of surplus workers continues to be a key issue of Wugang's reform efforts, especially in the current phase of reform aimed at separating-off its steel business from its non-core business units and social service units.

# Appendix 8.1: World's largest steel companies (2000–2003)

| Rank | Company | Output (million metric tons crude steel) | Location of headquarters |
|------|---------|------------------------------------------|--------------------------|
| **2003** | | | |
| 1st | Arcelor | 42.8 | Luxembourg |
| 2nd | LNM Group | 35.3 | Netherlands |
| 3rd | Nippon Steel | 31.3 | Japan |
| 4th | JFE | 30.2 | Japan |
| 5th | POSCO | 28.9 | Korea |
| **2002** | | | |
| 1st | Arcelor | 44 | Luxembourg |
| 2nd | LNM Group | 34.8 | Netherlands |
| 3rd | Nippon Steel | 29.8 | Japan |
| 4th | POSCO | 28.1 | Korea |
| 5th | Shanghai Baosteel | 19.5 | PRC |
| **2001** | | | |
| 1st | Arcelor | 43.2 | Luxembourg |
| 2nd | POSCO | 27.8 | Korea |
| 3rd | Nippon Steel | 26.2 | Japan |
| 4th | LNM Group | 19.2 | Netherlands |
| 5th | Shanghai Baosteel | 19.1 | PRC |
| **2000** | | | |
| 1st | POSCO | 26.5 | Korea |
| 2nd | Nippon Steel | 25.6 | Japan |
| 3rd | LNM Group | 17.2 | Netherlands |
| 4th | Thyssen Krupp | 16.1 | Germany |
| 5th | Riva group | 14.2 | Italy |

Source: International Iron & Steel Institute 2001–2004, *World Steel in Figures*. URL:http//www.worldsteel.org/

## Appendix 8.2: China's largest steel companies (2000–2003)

| Rank | Company | Output (million metric tons crude steel) |
|------|---------|------------------------------------------|
| **2003** | | |
| 1st | Shanghai Baosteel | 19.9 |
| 2nd | Anshan Steel | 10.2 |
| 3rd | Shougang | 8.4 |
| 4th | Wugang | 8.2 |
| 5th | Maanshan Steel | 6.1 |
| **2002** | | |
| 1st | Shanghai Baosteel | 19.5 |
| 2nd | Anshan Steel | 10.1 |
| 3rd | Shougang | 8.2 |
| 4th | Wugang | 7.6 |
| 5th | Maanshan Steel | 5.4 |
| **2001** | | |
| 1st | Shanghai Baosteel | 19.1 |
| 2nd | Anshan Steel | 8.8 |
| 3rd | Shougang | 8.2 |
| 4th | Wugang | 7.1 |
| 5th | Maanshan Steel | 4.8 |
| **2000** | | |
| 1st | Shanghai Baosteel | 10.9 |
| 2nd | Anshan Steel | 8.8 |
| 3rd | Shougang | 8.0 |
| 4th | Wugang | 6.7 |
| 5th | Maanshan Steel | 3.7 |

Source: International Iron & Steel Institute, 2001–2004,
*World Steel in Figures.* URL:http//www.worldsteel.org/

# Appendix 8.3: Selected financial data and ratios of Wuhan Iron and Steel Company Limited

| Data/Ratio | 2004 | 2003 | 2002 | 2001 | 2000 |
|---|---|---|---|---|---|
| Revenue | 24,148.16 | 6,806.86 | 6,758.14 | 6,326.62 | 6,925.28 |
| EBIT | 4,914.32 | 909.00 | 897.76 | 825.71 | 875.65 |
| *EBIT/Revenue** | *20.35%* | *13.35%* | *13.28%* | *13.05%* | *12.64%* |
| Net income | 3,203.58 | 569.26 | 595.90 | 703.14 | 706.89 |
| *Tax rate* | *32.15%* | *34%* | *33%* | *14.50%* | *15.68%* |
| *Net income/Revenue (net margin)* | 13.27% | 8.36% | 8.82% | 11.11% | 10.21% |
| Total assets | 30,404.85 | 7,708.11 | 6,982.05 | 6,676.00 | 6,331.30 |
| *Total asset turnover (times)* | *0.79* | *0.88* | *0.97* | *0.95* | *1.09* |
| Current assets | 11,064.37 | 3,759.36 | 3,721.88 | 3,398.38 | 3,488.68 |
| Fixed assets | 19,080.98 | 3,761.21 | 3,070.17 | 3,120.63 | 2,728.10 |
| *Fixed asset turnover (times)* | *1.27* | *1.81* | *2.20* | *2.03* | *2.54* |
| Cash and equivalent | 3,920.04 | 2,124.14 | 1,772.80 | 1,433.28 | 1,690.67 |
| Net bills, accounts and other receivables | 873.75 | 994.99 | 848.72 | 871.70 | 184.51 |
| *Average collection period (days)* | *13.21* | *53.35* | *45.84* | *50.29* | *9.72* |
| Inventory, net | 4,911.66 | 454.29 | 550.86 | 571.88 | 759.59 |
| *Inventory turnover (times)* | *4.92* | *14.98* | *12.27* | *11.06* | *9.12* |
| *Return on assets(ROA)* | *11.17%* | *7.92%* | *8.65%* | *10.58%* | *11.75%* |
| Current liabilities | 9,564.32 | 1,475.60 | 1,680.81 | 1,566.13 | 1,478.44 |
| *Current ratio* | *1.16* | *2.55* | *2.21* | *2.17* | *2.36* |
| *Accounts payables and advances as % of current liabilities* | *63.24%* | *87.74%* | *63.50%* | *53.40%* | *52.16%* |
| Accrued payables and welfare | 88.13 | 36.85 | 80.54 | 71.01 | 13.37 |
| *Total debt/total assets* | *42.75%* | *23.84%* | *26.70%* | *30.03%* | *28.09%* |
| *Equity multiplier (times)* | *1.75* | *1.31* | *1.36* | *1.43* | *1.39* |
| *ROE (return on equity)* | *18.40%* | *9.70%* | *11.64%* | *15.05%* | *15.53%* |
| NOPAT (net operating profit after tax) | 3,396.07 | 610.17 | 603.62 | 706.53 | 744.24 |
| Operating assets | 26,927.25 | 7,273.62 | 5,700.51 | 5,719.24 | 6,188.73 |
| *NOPAT/operating assets* | *12.61%* | *8.39%* | *10.59%* | *12.35%* | *12.03%* |
| Expenditure for fixed assets, intangible assets and other long term assets | 12,072.66 | 601.97 | 342.30 | 783.92 | n/a |
| EPS | 0.41 | 0.23 | 0.29 | 0.34 | 0.34 |
| Shares outstanding (millions) | 7,838.00 | 2,508.58 | 2,090.48 | 2,090.48 | 2,090.48 |
| % of shares owned by holding company | 75.81% | 84.69% | 84.69% | 84.69% | 84.69% |
| Total dividends | 1,959.50 | 576.97 | 104.52 | 585.33 | 585.33 |
| *Payout ratio* | *61.17%* | *101.35%* | *17.54%* | *83.25%* | *82.80%* |
| DPS (dividend per share) | 0.25 | 0.23 | 0.05 | 0.28 | 0.28 |

Notes:
* Figures in italics indicate ratios.
WISCO formerly WSPC until mid-2004.
Monetary amounts are expressed in millions of RMB.
2004 figures include new assets acquired within the year.
Source: *Annual Reports* 2000–2003, Wuhan Steel Processing Limited; *Annual Report* 2004, Wuhan Iron and Steel Co. Ltd

# 9 Restructuring Tangshan Iron and Steel

## Introduction

In this, the second of our detailed case studies of contemporary enterprise reform and restructuring, we examine the Tangshan Iron and Steel Group Company Limited, commonly known as Tanggang, another extremely large Chinese state-owned steel maker. Like other sizeable state enterprises, it is subject to the government's restructuring directives and remains a target of its corporatization plan. In terms of scale, Tanggang is currently not as large as Wugang, but has been one of the top ten steel makers in China since 1979. In 2003, it was ranked fifth by production of crude steel, after Shanghai Baosteel, Liaoning Anshan (now Anben), Wugang and Beijing Shougang. Worldwide it was ranked thirty-third in scale of operations (International Iron & Steel Institute 2004). In terms of employees, in 2003 Tanggang had 39,776 on its direct payroll plus 10,236 retirees (*China Steel Yearbook* 2004: 242). In line with the recent spate of 'consolidation policy' mergers among state-owned steel enterprises, in November 2005 Tanggang's acquisition of the smaller Hebei iron and steel concerns of Chengde Steel and Xuanhua Steel was formally approved by the provincial government, the merged enterprise to operate under the title of 'New Tanggang'. As we discuss later, however, of higher profile news-wise has been the recently proposed relocation of (west Beijing-based) Shougang to Tangshan by 2010, this signalling the future merger of two giant steel enterprises.

## Restructuring Tanggang

Tanggang is located in Hebei province, about 120 kilometres to the south-east of Beijing. It was established in 1943 by a Japanese private company supported by the then Japanese government of occupation. After the Japanese were defeated in 1945, Tanggang became an SOE in 1948. Presently, Tanggang is not under the direct administration of the state, but subject primarily to the supervision of the Hebei provincial SASAC. That is to say, in the eyes of the central government, Tanggang is not currently an enterprise on its 'priority list' for development, even though it remains one of the key (*zhongdian*) steel enterprises in China and also one of the 500 enterprises that the state decided to retain under long-term ownership.

The fact that (as things stand: see later) Tanggang is not placed under central administration is actually considered unjust by some of the Tanggang senior managers we interviewed. Although Tanggang is located in one of the nation's foremost areas of national resources for the production of iron and steel (i.e. iron ore and coal – Hebei province has the third largest reserves of iron ore in China), according to our interviewees it has never been afforded the resources and opportunities to expand to the size of other inland steel enterprises (see also TISCO *Annual Report* 1997). In particular, it has not been able to expand to the size of rival inland steel makers such as Maanshan Iron and Steel in Anhui and Shougang in Beijing, which do not have such close access to relevant natural resources, but which benefited from the 'third front' project that encouraged the building of heavy industry in inland regions in the pre-reform period, and also from the nation's 'strategic positioning' plan for state steel makers in recent years (*China Metallurgical News*, 27 June 2001). If the proposed merger with Shougang takes place, however, strategic relations between the new enterprise and the state may alter radically.

Being under provincial administration makes Tanggang an interesting comparison case to Wugang. As we discuss in later sections, relative to Wugang, Tanggang has been slower to separate its non-steel and social service units from its core steel business. Another feature that differentiates the restructuring processes of Tanggang and Wugang is the format that Tanggang adopted when listing its steel assets on the Shenzhen Stock Exchange. In contrast to Wugang, it applied the strategy of 'overall-listing'; that is, listing all or the great majority of its operational steel making assets at one time, rather than incrementally. Given the overall-listing of Tanggang's subsidiary, Tangshan Iron and Steel Company Limited (TISCO) in 1997, there are available public financial statements and company accounting information from which to analyse and assess its financial and related performance. It is also possible to make a before-and-after listing analysis using the pre-listing financial information made publicly available by the stock exchange. The overall-listing experience of TISCO, therefore, makes it easier to answer the question – 'is the restructured company more profitable?' Or to phrase it differently, 'have Tanggang's assets been better and more efficiently utilized by TISCO, an independent listed subsidiary that inherited Tanggang's steel-making assets?' Or again, to invoke a mantra of the SASAC, the government agency that has been assigned to represent the state since 2003 – 'has TISCO preserved and created value for the state, the majority shareholder?' (see *People's Daily* (RMRB), 2 June 2003; *China Daily*, 7 April 2003). In addition to answering these questions in relation to Tanggang, we also address kindred issues that are likely to affect the future viability of large state enterprises as more and more adopt the strategy of overall-listing (such as other major steel SOEs and the state banks: see Deng 2004; Ge 2004).

From the perspective of Tanggang's senior management, the state's corporatization initiative aimed at curing the two 'illnesses' suffered by most SOEs. One is *guoqi bing* (literally 'SOE sector illness', or the 'systemic problem') caused by long-run practices generally inherent in SOEs, the major symptoms of which are the social welfare burden, surplus labour, and confusion over who exactly represents the 'state' (that is, the problem of multiple government agencies interfering with a state firm's decision-making function, or in Chinese terms, the '*po po*' – literally 'mother-in-law' – problem). The other 'illness' is that of *qiye bing* (literally, 'enterprise illness'), which refers to the problems faced by specific enterprises in specific industries, and primarily in respect to operations, marketing and fund raising (although the causes of this illness are frequently interwoven with those of the 'systemic problem'). As noted, informants at Tanggang suggest the enterprise's most serious *qiye bing* problem has been shortage of funds, for despite Tanggang's access to relevant natural resources and its cost advantages relative to many of its rivals, in being placed under the supervision of the Hebei provincial government, rather than administered by central government, it has had trouble in obtaining sufficient funds for development. In what follows we will explain the processes through which Tanggang has restructured itself so as to cure its *guoqi bing* and *qiye bing* problems. In so doing we draw upon, among other sources, interview data with senior managers, official statistics, industry journals and enterprise literature to develop our analysis.

## Corporatizing process (1997–2003)

Tanggang started restructuring its steel business in the mid-1990s and proceeded gradually to reform its non-steel business later that decade. More far-reaching changes in the group's structure have been realized since 2000.

### *Setting up TISCO and incorporating Tanggang*

By the end of 2003, Tanggang was considered by its senior management to be only 'partially' restructured. In the mid-1990s it had reorganized its steel assets and created a subsidiary, TISCO of which Tanggang was the holding company. TISCO was formed in June 1994: it was injected with Tanggang's main steel assets, which included 18 steel making and related plants and mills together with 12 other administrative and support departments, such as research and development, machinery and equipment maintenance, quality control, material supply and sales. A full list of TISCO's plants and departments at start-up is presented in Appendix 9.1 (end of chapter). Associated with the injection of steel-making assets were related operational, administrative and managerial personnel plus a pro-rata share of retirees. In early 1996, Tanggang was incorporated and registered as a limited liability company, with in 1997 TISCO being listed on the A-share market of the

Shenzhen Stock Exchange. As of end 2003, TISCO had 24,899 'on-the-job' staff and workers (*zaigang zhigong*) in addition to 7,408 'retirees' on its payroll (TISCO *Annual Report* 2003).

Despite the implication from being classified as 'overall-listed' that Tanggang had moved all of its assets to TISCO, at the time of our data collection (2004–2005) there were still substantial assets remaining at Tanggang. This is common in Chinese SOEs in transition because, in addition to the main operational assets, such enterprises incorporate a range of additional social welfare services and non-core businesses. As shown in Table 9.1, by value TISCO's assets were only about 70 per cent of what Tanggang formally possessed. Moreover, according to our estimate, the 30+ per cent assets remaining at Tanggang had been losing money over the period 1997–2003 and thus had substantially eroded the profitability of TISCO (further details are presented in the section on 'unhealthy' assets below).

### Reorganizing business units into independent subsidiaries

Between 1996 and 2003, Tanggang streamlined its structure by reorganizing its administrative departments and business units (including merging and closing some units). 2,910 employees were 're-settled' in 1998 and a further 355 were transferred to other units in 2000. In 1998, Tanggang commenced the reorganization of the management system of its sub-companies by signing 'asset management responsibility contracts' with nine units. This represented its first step in weaning-off sub-companies from the financial support of the parent.

Table 9.1 describes the changes that took place during 2000–2001 in some of Tanggang's sub-companies. As shown, the ultimate aim of restructuring Tanggang's sub-companies was for them to become independent business units with legal person status. Like their parent, the incorporated subsidiaries were to have their own Board of Directors and supervisory committees. They were expected, eventually, to be both financially and operationally independent and to compete with other like firms in the market. In terms of ownership, the restructured subsidiaries could be wholly owned by the state, or jointly owned with employees and other private parties. The table also shows that Tanggang had 40 per cent ownership in a foreign-domestic joint-venture at this time. As a result, mixed ownership forms appeared in the enterprise group (*jituan*). While Tanggang is wholly owned by the state, subsidiaries are either wholly owned by Tanggang or partially private, and thus incorporated as limited liability companies or shareholding companies.

### Obstacles in restructuring Tanggang's non-steel business

Table 9.2 shows that in 2003 Tanggang still had 14,877 staff and workers and 2,828 retirees in its other non-steel business and social service units. While there are no explicit figures showing the size of Tanggang's non-steel

*Table 9.1* Structural change in Tanggang's sub-companies (2000–2001)

| 2000 | 2001 |
|---|---|
| *Four wholly-owned subsidiaries with limited liability:* | Eight *wholly-owned subsidiaries with limited liability:* |
| Tanggang Fire-resistant Material Ltd Co. | Tanggang Fire-resistant Material Ltd Co. |
| Tanggang Mining Ltd Co. | Tanggang Mining Ltd Co. |
| Tangshan Sanhuang Project Development Supervision Ltd Co. | Tangshan Sanhuang Project Development Supervision Ltd Co. |
| Tangshan Tianchen Investment Ltd Liability Co. | Tangshan Tianchen Investment Ltd Liability Co. |
| | *Tanggang Group Technology Economic Development Ltd. Liability Co.* |
| | *Tanggang Material Storage & Transportation Ltd Co.* |
| | *Tanggang Group Design & Research Ltd Co.** |
| | *Tanggang Group Jiakun Ltd Liability Co. (formerly Tanggang Piping Factory)** |
| *Five subsidiaries without legal person status* | Two *subsidiaries without legal person status* |
| Tanggang Transportation Co. | Tanggang Group Import & Export Co. |
| Tanggang Technology Economic Development Co. | Tanggang Coking Factory |
| Tanggang Material Storage and Transportation Co. | |
| Tanggang Coking Factory | |
| Tanggang Piping Factory | |
| *One shareholding company:* | *One shareholding company:* |
| Tangshan Micro-electronic Shareholding Co. Ltd (22.5% owned by TISCO) | Tangshan Micro-electronic Shareholding Co. Ltd (26% owned by TISCO) |
| *One shareholding company with controlling stake:* | Three *shareholding subsidiaries with controlling stake:* |
| TISCO (67.6%) | TISCO (59.25%) |
| | *Tanggang Group Construction Installation Ltd Co.** |
| | *Tanggang Group Transportation Ltd Liability Co. (employee owned 30%)** |
| *One joint venture:* | *One joint venture:* |
| Capus[†] (China) Coal Chemical Co. Ltd (40%) | Capus (China) Coal Chemical Co. Ltd |

Notes:
Changes are *italicized*.
* Companies were explicitly classified as non-steel subsidiaries.
[†] Our translation from Chinese.
Source: *China Steel Yearbooks* 2001 (276–277) and 2003 (180–181)

*Table 9.2* Tanggang staff, workers and retirees (as of end 2003)

|  | On-the-post staff and workers | Retirees | Total on payroll |
|---|---|---|---|
| TISCO | 24,899 | 7,408 (23%)* | 32,307 |
| Other business units and social service units | 14,877 | 2,828 (16%) | 17,705 |
| Total at Tanggang | 39,776 | 10,236 (20%) | 50,012 |

Note: * Brackets indicate the percentage of retirees relative to the total on payroll.
Source: *China Steel Yearbook* (2004: 24) and TISCO *Annual Report* (2003: 11)

business, it was reported in 2000 that the goal was to have the revenue of non-steel business equivalent to one-third of Tanggang's total, or in other words half of the steel revenue (*China Steel Yearbook* 1999: 193). In 2000, Tanggang's steel revenue was RMB7.1 billion (US$855 million) and thus the target figure should be about US$400 million, implying an intention to develop sizeable non-steel business operations.

In early 2004, Tanggang's senior managers admitted to us that the enterprise's restructuring mission was far from complete, even though Tanggang still planned to realize the process within two years, so as to capture tax savings under the state's reform directives (see *People's Daily* (RMRB), 15 January 2003; State Economic Trade Commission (SETC) SOE reform document no. 859). The two major obstacles that Tanggang faced in restructuring its non-steel business were, first, the satisfactory resettlement of employees, and second the development strategy of robust business strategies for adoption after separation. These two issues were interconnected: if the business units had clear and viable strategies and prospects, and their products had markets, senior management felt it would take little effort to persuade employees to change their employment contracts, for they would welcome the opportunity to become financially independent. In contrast, if a business unit had been operating poorly and employees saw little prospect of their unit surviving after Tanggang terminated its financial support, then the 'big problem' could arise – potentially high levels of resistance from such employees when their unit was forced to separate from the parent.

## How did Tanggang handle the surplus labour problem?

Similar to Wugang, Tanggang's efforts at reducing the level of its surplus labour have not been directed primarily at sacking workers. Rather, it has attempted, on the one hand, to re-deploy surplus workers to other business units within the group (*China Steel Yearbook* 2001) and, on the other, to implement an early retirement programme.

*Surplus labour*

Tanggang senior managers admitted to us that as of end-2003 the enterprise was still massively overstaffed. Applying the industry yardstick for efficiency per worker, production at Tanggang only amounted to around 250 tons in 2003. This was extremely low in comparison to the world standard of 600 tons per employee (International Iron & Steel Institute 2004). Compared with Wugang's productivity at 560 tons per employee, Tanggang thus appeared to have a far worse potential surplus labour problem.

Senior managers interviewed, however, suggested that during the restructuring process, Tanggang actually laid-off relatively few workers. This was due largely to concerns on behalf of both the Hebei provincial government and the central government over social stability. As Tangshan city is only 120 kilometres from Beijing it was felt that if mass demonstrations took place demonstrators could physically march to Beijing and thus promote instability in the capital. As one Tanggang senior manager commented: 'Tangshan is too close to Beijing . . . As an SOE, we have an obligation towards social stability. We cannot help create unemployment. We have a political mission.' As noted, central government and local political leaders have remained highly sensitive to public means for displaying grievance and consistently attempted to suppress mass demonstrations and public rallies (see Chapter 7; also Oi 2005). The Hebei government had thus paid special attention to ensuring that significant demonstrations did not occur in Tangshan.

Despite this concern, Tanggang managers still felt the pace of reform could have been increased if the provincial Party Secretary until 2002, Wang Xudong, had been less politically conservative. Aggressive reform measures were not initiated and hence the non-state economy in Hebei was not developed as rapidly as in other provinces. Without the assistance of the non-state economy to absorb surplus labour, state enterprises such as Tanggang lagged behind others in the reform process. It is perhaps interesting that in 2002, apparently at the behest of central government, the former head of the CCP in Hainan, Bei Keming, with a reputation as a proactive reformer, was transferred to serve as the Party Secretary of Hebei.

*Early retirement programme*

The major means that Tanggang applied to reduce surplus labour was to encourage early retirement. Whereas the existing legal age for retirement was 60 for men and 55 for woman, to reduce headcount Tanggang encouraged female workers of 45 years of age and above and male workers of 50 and above to retire. Those who chose early retirement would receive around RMB800 as a monthly allowance, which was equivalent to about 70 per cent of an average worker's income. Such early retirees would retain their family's rights to subsidized education and medical facilities, but relinquish any bonus entitlement. As for housing benefits, by 2003 all housing units at Tanggang were sold to employees, with almost all retired employees thereby owning their own home. On implementing the early retirement programme Tanggang developed annual targets for reducing headcount. On average, it wanted to see 5 to 8 per cent of the workforce retiring early. However, as our informants suggested, many workers were less than willing to do so.

### Contract employment system

Starting in 2001, all new recruits to Tanggang were hired on three to five year renewable contracts. In addition, from October 2001, Tanggang started gradually to replace all existing employees' life-long contracts with short-term renewable ones. Employees who agreed to make the change were offered incentives, primarily in the form of one-off monetary compensation ranging from RMB20,000 to RMB200,000. The amount varied according to seniority and salary, the formula being – average monthly income for the immediate past 11 months multiplied by the number of years service at Tanggang. According to this formula, a middle/senior-ranking employee with 30 years' service could receive just over RMB100,000. As one experienced middle manager commented: 'Considering the current cost of living in China, that [amount] is acceptable . . . [even though] . . . our first feeling was [there is] no other way' (implying that those targeted could not realistically do anything about the change). The same manager suggested, 'we believe the country should have considered our needs and the level of acceptability when they planned that policy'.

The deployment of short-term contracts now permitted, in theory, both the state firm and the employee to choose if they wanted to continue the employment relationship. Although the creation of short-term contracts now empowered Tanggang to make employees redundant, in practice the enterprise was reluctant to use such a right, a major reason being the traditional contractual entitlement to life-long employment with the enterprise. In addition, there were no specific criteria to guide the determination of whose contract would be renewed and whose would not. Since implementing the short-term contract scheme, Tanggang has, in fact, tended to renew almost all contracts. As one senior manager informed us, the basic principle has turned out to be: 'As long as the position in question is still open and needed, an employee's contract will be renewed.' However, another experienced manager commented ominously that: 'In the past the enterprise did not have such a right [to terminate an employment contract] because of its social responsibility . . . In the future, there may be changes.'

In short, Tanggang did not rush to alleviate its surplus labour problem, and the former Premier Zhu Rongji's call for sacking surplus workers did not seem to have much impact on Tanggang's move towards a leaner organization. Surplus employees were protected by political concerns for stability and, in particular, by the conservativeness of the local political leader. As commented by one senior Tanggang manager: 'Reducing surplus labour is a mission that will take a long time to achieve.'

### Reducing the social welfare burden

Like its experience in reducing surplus workers, Tanggang was relatively slow to restructure its social service units. Indeed, it did not start genuinely separating-off its social units until 2003, and only then after some concrete policy papers were issued. As one senior manager informed us, '[Tanggang] could not have started this separation project sooner because it was not one of the centrally administered state firms that were allowed to experiment with this type of separation'. Therefore, as of early 2004, Tanggang still had over 10,000 workers in its social units, in addition to around 29,000 in steel and non-steel businesses and 10,000 retirees (*China Steel Yearbook* 2004). By the end of 2003, Tanggang had only successfully separated-off its schools, police force and fire brigade.

### *Transferring schools to city government*

In the case of separating-off its schools, our informants suggested that it took a lot of discussion with Tanggang teachers before they agreed to be transferred to the Tangshan city government. What made the transfer difficult was that at the time of negotiating the transfer, in late 2003, some teachers at Tanggang received higher salaries and better benefit packages than government teachers locally. However, all Tanggang teachers were offered the standard government package, no matter what their compensation was at Tanggang. In the beginning, Tanggang teachers requested the city government to raise its remuneration levels, but that proved unacceptable, and in the end all teachers accepted the government offer. The main reason for their acceptance was the stability of income they would receive as civil servants. Although Tanggang teachers could receive a bonus when the enterprise had a profitable year, such as in 2003 and 2004, such performance-linked bonuses were not stable and could fluctuate with the industry's economic fortunes. Ultimately, the teachers weighed up the employment risks of remaining with Tanggang against the security of work and income if they were transferred. Nevertheless, Tanggang also gave the teachers a choice of whether to leave the enterprise or not, suggesting that any who wished to remain would be placed in other units in the group. Ultimately this proved unnecessary as all of Tanggang's teachers accepted the government's offer. In terms of financing, Tanggang ceased funding its schools on paying to the Tangshan city government an annual education tax. This annual contribution to the city's education finances was considered sufficient and thus any additional funding of schools deemed unnecessary. While we have no information as to how much education tax Tanggang has paid, it was reported that TISCO paid 3.5 to 4 per cent of VAT educational tax surcharge, which amounted to RMB29.69 million (US$3.6 million) in 2003 (TISCO *Annual Report* 2003).

*Plan for commercializing hospitals*

In contrast, instead of passing its medical units to the local government, Tanggang saw the possibility for its hospital and clinics to be run on a commercial basis and thus to become financially independent. By the end of 2003, Tanggang had submitted a plan to the Hebei government to allow its medical units to be run as profit-making commercial units (*China Steel Yearbook* 2004: 243).

## Alleviation of the '*po po*' problem

According to Tanggang senior managers, the aforementioned '*po po*' problem in China's SOEs has 'two symptoms': the first is that of multiple government agencies meddling in the business of SOEs; and the second is that of multiple government agencies making claims on SOE output (see Steinfeld 1998). To Tanggang managers, it seemed that the former was more of a concern than the latter, for Tanggang as an enterprise still lacked genuine autonomy over its operations even though, on paper, it had been awarded increased decision-making powers during the reform era.

Although Tanggang is state owned, an enduring problem from the early years of SOE reform has been confusion as to who actually represents the state. In the past, it could be the State Development and Economic Commission (SDEC), SETC or several other government agencies. As one Tanggang senior manager commented:

> As long as it is a state agency, it can claim to represent the state. For some substantial projects, we have identified a good investment project, and yet we still need to put it up for approval. Often such approval can take half a year or even a year. So we have missed many good opportunities, which have negatively affected the development and growth of the enterprise. That is the consequence of the absence of a single representative for the state.

For Tanggang managers, therefore, a direct result of the 'who is the state?' problem was lengthy delays in decision-making, which resulted in slow growth for the enterprise. In early 2004, for example, the provincial SASAC could only approve projects of up to RMB50 million, with any project over that limit requiring higher order government approval. For an enterprise such as Tanggang, with RMB22 billion worth of assets, such a rule implied that the provincial government would need to sanction any change above 0.23 per cent of its asset value. Furthermore, if a project was under the jurisdiction of a number of government agencies, approval was necessary from each. For example, projects related to environmental issues needed prior approval from the State Environmental Protection Administration, whereas ones related to labour required approval from the Ministry of Labour and Social Security. Managers could even find that additional approvals were needed after a proposal had been submitted and agreed. In short, new projects that were above the 50 million yuan budget limit could often take some considerable time to get launched.

Tanggang managers were keen to stress, however, that major projects could receive faster approval if the leader of the enterprise was motivated and able to call upon his or her political connections. Leaders exercising such influence were often able to draw the attention of their contacts in key government agencies to particular strategic developments. It was suggested to us that their own chairman, Wang Tianyi (also the managing director of TISCO) had drawn upon his own considerable political influence in securing the listing of TISCO on the Shenzhen Stock Exchange.

Furthermore, despite views expressed by Tanggang managers that levels of autonomy were insufficient in certain areas, in others they were apparently far in excess of those of the pre-reform period. We were reminded, for example, of the situation in maintenance, whereby before reform the enterprise was only allowed to approve relatively minor and routine projects. In contrast, Tanggang can presently implement significant maintenance projects, such as the change of a furnace or upgrading facilities in a mill, without seeking government approval. Another area over which Tanggang has increasing discretion is the appointment of labour. In the past, labour was centrally planned with authority resting with the state and provincial government. Increasingly the employment of labour rests with the enterprise, although the appointment of senior managers at wholly or majority state-owned enterprises, such as Tanggang, still requires approval from the provincial government.

## Raising equity

Tanggang managers felt that restructuring has helped to solve the historical problem of shortage of funds. They saw restructuring primarily as a way to obtain access to a new source of funds – raising equity by selling shares – with such funds being essential to promote the growth of the firm. Since the creation of TISCO, it has twice raised funds by issuing new shares. Originally Tanggang valued the net worth of TISCO's assets at RMB2.37 billion (US$285 million) against which 2.37 billion shares were issued. It then sold shares of TISCO at a 20 per cent premium (or RMB1.2 per share) over its net asset value to other state and non-state legal persons (14 per cent), and employees (2.67 per cent). Tanggang, itself, thus kept 83.33 per cent of the holding. In total there were 60,369 employee shareholders, implying that almost all workers on the payroll at Tanggang subscribed to shares of TISCO (TISCO *Annual Report* 1997). Prior to public listing, TISCO had a reverse split at the ratio of 1 : 0.285. As a result, the number of total shares reduced while the per share value increased to RMB4.21. In 1997, TISCO was listed on the A-share market of the Shenzhen Stock Exchange by issuing an additional 120 million new shares priced at RMB9.22. At the same time the paper value of the holding of the original shareholders (i.e. Tanggang, other legal persons and employees) increased by 118 per cent in less than a year, this leading analysts to cast doubt on the accuracy of the appraisal of TISCO's assets and suggest that its employees were given a good deal deliberately. However, those original issues were not currently tradeable on the stock market and as such no party could realize the potential gain. The only tradeable shares of TISCO at this time were the 120 million new issues – 15 per cent of the total number of shares – with the four year embargo on trading employee shares not being lifted until 2000 (although legal person shares had been changing hands in private deals). In total, between 1994 and 1997, Tanggang raised about RMB1.4 billion (US$169 million) by selling shares to legal persons, employees and the public. This amount was equivalent to 60 per cent of TISCO's pre-listing net worth.

The second fund-raising activity took place in 2002 when the nation's steel markets started recovering. This new issue raised about RMB890 million (US$107 million) through the sale of an additional 150 million shares at RMB6.06. As of end-2003, Tanggang still owned about 60 per cent of TISCO, with the state's holding and majority of the legal person shares still being non-tradeable. Altogether, about 29 per cent of TISCO shares were now in circulation. Selling shares to the public helped TISCO increase its equity base, which, in turn, allowed TISCO to borrow more without significantly increasing its debt ratio. As shown in Appendix 9.2, TISCO's debt ratio started off at around 40 per cent in 1997 and increased to about 50 per cent in 2003. The total debt increased by RMB5.1 billion from 1997 to 2003, an amount that is more than double its original net worth. This increase in total capital provided the finance for the subsequent growth in TISCO's assets.

## Financial analysis of TISCO and Tanggang

Since TISCO included all the major operational assets of Tanggang, an analysis of TISCO's financial statements will give an indication of its profitability and of the extent the listed subsidiary has efficiently managed Tanggang's steel assets. To do this, we will first provide a trend analysis of TISCO's post-listing performance based upon the data provided in its annual reports. (A list of selected ratios and financial data are presented in Appendix 9.1). Then we will compare a selection of TISCO's ratios before and after its listing, using information for the two years preceding its IPO. This comparison will help us to discern if there was any significant change in TISCO's performance after it became a public company.

However, the trend of TISCO's financial data alone does not tell us exactly how well the enterprise has performed, for the macroeconomic environment and conditions in the domestic and world steel markets also influence performance. A comparative approach is thus appropriate for achieving a more accurate assessment. As per the chapter on Wugang, we have compiled several efficiency and profitability ratios for TISCO and these are presented after the trend and pre- and post-listing analyses. They are exhibited alongside those of Tanggang, Wugang, WSPC, the composite ratios of the four largest listed iron and steel firms in China, and the five largest listed steel firms in the world. (Lists of China's and the world's largest steel makers are presented in the appendices of Chapter 8.)

### Trend analysis of TISCO

The years 2003 and 2004 were truly exceptionally for the steel industry in China, reflecting rapid price rises within a booming market. To describe the trends in TISCO's financial performance, we have therefore divided our analysis into two periods: the five years following the company's listing (1997–2002) and the recent years in which demand has exploded (2003–2004).

### Profitability and efficiency measures (1997–2002)

From 1997 to 2002, TISCO experienced a considerable increase in revenues, with annual growth as high as 21 per cent and an average annual compound growth of 14.3 per cent. However, profit measures showed somewhat mixed results, with most of the measures showing gains, but at a somewhat lower rate of growth than revenues. Earnings before interest and tax (EBIT), a measure of operating profit, showed the highest annual growth, averaging 8.5 per cent between 1997 and 2002, while net income lagged behind, averaging only 4 per cent. Earnings per share (EPS) remained steady from 1997 to 1999 and then began to decline, resulting in a negative annual average growth rate of 5.2 per cent over the entire 1997–2002 period. This decline was mainly in response to stock splits in 1999 and 2000 that increased the number of shares outstanding by 71 per cent, from 793.9 million in 1997 to 1,353.8 million in 2000. Another reason for the decline in EPS, as well as the rather anaemic growth in net income, was the expiration of a significant tax advantage at the end of 2001. This caused the average tax rate to rise to 33 per cent in 2001, more than double the 12–15 per cent in previous years. Also the annual report mentioned that the change in the rate of depreciation and in the method of calculating bad debt negatively influenced the company's profitability in 2002.

Profitability ratios showed a general decline over the five-year period. Operating profit margins of nearly 15 per cent in 1997 and 1998 fell to about 11 per cent in 2002. Net margins showed a similar pattern except for a more dramatic fall-off in 2002 mainly in response to the increased tax rate.

Asset management, however, showed continuous improvement, with both fixed and current assets growing at a significantly slower rate than revenues. Over the five-year period, fixed assets grew at an average annual rate of 11.4

per cent while current assets grew at just 5.5 per cent. This resulted in a rise in total asset turnover from 0.62 times in 1997 to 0.76 times in 2002. In the case of current asset management, the average collection period declined from nearly three months to two, and inventory turnover nearly doubled, from 4.4 to 8.3 times, in the same period.

## *Profitability and efficiency measures (2003 and 2004)*

TISCO's revenues grew by almost 55 per cent in both 2003 and 2004. EBIT also grew at an average of 50 per cent and so did net income. That resulted in high growth in EPS of 15.4 per cent in 2003 and 51 per cent in 2004. High growth in profits was partially attributed to the tax savings obtained by the firm's purchase of other state firms' products. Because of tax savings, effective tax rates were reduced to 23 and 29 per cent, far less than the nationwide rate of 33 per cent. However, growth in profits did not lead to increases in profitability ratios. Net margin continued to decline, albeit at a lower rate than in the previous five-year period. Operating margin declined significantly from 2002 to 2003, but improved to 10.5 per cent in 2004, which was still below the 15 per cent margin in 1997.

Following the trend of the previous five years, asset management continued to improve. Fixed assets grew at a much slower rate than revenues and current assets substantially increased because of cash raised from the new issues in 2003. The combined effect was continuous improvement of total asset turnover, from 0.91 times in 2003 to 1.14 times in 2004. Inventory turnover kept improving from 8.76 times in 2003 to 9.89 times in 2004, which doubled the ratio in 1997. The average collection period kept declining, to 47 days in 2004 compared with 81 days in 2003 and 122 days in 1997. Short-term credit provided by accounts payable and advances together with accrued payroll and welfare continued to play an important role in the firm's financing.

## *Capital structure and return on equity (1997–2004)*

TISCO's reliance on debt financing grew in the seven-year period from 1997 to 2004, with the debt-to-asset ratio rising significantly from 39.4 per cent in 1997 to 56.7 per cent in 2004. Its use of leverage was higher even after it raised 900 million yuan (equivalent to 16 per cent of the total equity in 2001) by issuing new shares in 2002. This was accomplished while pursuing a dividend payout ratio of more than 62 per cent in all but one of the seven years analysed. The average maturity of the liabilities shortened as the current liabilities grew at a slightly faster rate than long-term liabilities. Accrued payroll and welfare together with accounts payable and advances became significantly more important as financing tools.

The combined influence of profit margin, asset turnover and financial leverage produced ROEs that varied from a low of 8.64 per cent in 2002 to a high of 16.01 per cent in 2004. ROE shows the net income earned per dollar of shareholder's equity. This is the profitability ratio that shareholders are most concerned with. However, ROE is difficult to interpret without reference to some benchmark or opportunity rate of ROE. With the relevant data available between 2001 and 2004, the opportunity costs of equity of TISCO, as shown in Table 9.3, are estimated to be about 8.4 per cent. This assumes that the betas of TISCO are about 0.9, risk-free rate is about 2.8 per cent and the market risk premium is 6.19 per cent. Since TISCO's ROEs were significantly larger than its costs of equity, shareholders should be pleased that TISCO was able to generate such a relatively high return over the four-year period of 2001–4.

Another commonly used measure of a company's profitability is Economic Value Added (EVA). EVA is the residual amount after deducting the total cost of capital (cost of equity and cost of debt) from operating income after tax. If a company's EVA is positive, then it creates value or wealth to the shareholder. If the EVA is negative, then the company consumes value. Shareholders of a firm with negative EVA could have made a higher return in another investment that carried a similar level of risk. As shown in Table 9.3, the after-tax weighted average costs of capital range from 5.59 per cent to 6.55 per cent. TISCO's EVAs are thus estimated to have been positive in three of the four years between 2001 and 2004, implying TISCO did create value for its shareholders over that period except in 2003.

### Conclusion of trend analysis

TISCO experienced substantial growth in both its assets and profits during the seven years analysed, although profits increased at a lower rate. Specifically

Table 9.3 After-tax Weighted Average Cost of Capital (WACC) and Economic Value Added (EVA) for TISCO (2001–2004)

| Year | 2004 | 2003 | 2002 | 2001 |
| --- | --- | --- | --- | --- |
| Risk free rate (%) | 2.93 | 2.79 | 2.81 | 2.88 |
| Market risk premium (%) | 6.19 | 6.19 | 6.19 | 6.19 |
| Beta of TISCO | 0.908 | 0.902 | 0.894 | 0.883 |
| Cost of equity (%) | 8.55 | 8.37 | 8.34 | 8.35 |
| Return on equity (%) | 16.01 | 11.59 | 8.64 | 12.97 |
| Debt ratio (%) | 56.68 | 50.78 | 44.20 | 48.90 |
| Effective tax rate (%) | 29 | 23 | 32 | 12 |
| Cost of debt (%) | 4.681 | 4.574 | 4.84 | 5.30 |
| After-tax weighted average cost of capital (After-tax WACC) (%) | 5.59 | 5.91 | 6.11 | 6.55 |
| Net operating profit after tax (NOPAT)/Operating Assets (%) | 10.38 | 5.32 | 8.07 | 9.24 |
| Positive EVA? (Yes, if NOPAT/ operating assets > after-tax WACC) | Yes | No | Yes | Yes |

its assets grew by 360 per cent whereas net income increased by 163 per cent, suggesting a shrinking profit margin. The data suggest that TISCO's managers have done an increasingly better job in utilizing and managing the company's assets. The major asset management ratios on inventory turnover, average collection period and total asset turnover all improved substantially. With regard to financing, TISCO moderately increased its leverage. The combined result of narrower margins, higher asset turnover and higher leverage represented a respectable return to shareholders, with TISCO's ROE reaching a highpoint of 16 per cent in 2004. However, whether such a high ROE is sustainable or not is questionable. Will TISCO be able to increase its margin and asset turnover without increasing its leverage risk? Will competition in both domestic and world markets erode its profitability? These two questions are crucial in determining the future return to TISCO's shareholders. Nevertheless, within the period of 2001–2004, TISCO had created value for its shareholders, fulfilling the mission set for it by the SASAC.

## Connected transactions

As discussed in the previous chapter, overall-listing was deemed a way to reduce connected transactions between listed subsidiaries and their parents and other parents' sub-companies. In the case of TISCO, over the period of 1997–2003, its sales to connected parties remained at about 2 per cent, except for one year, and its purchases from connected parties declined from 24 to 18.5 per cent (see Table 9.4). Compared to WISCO, whose connected transactions amounted to 30 per cent of total sales and almost half of the cost of goods sold in 2004, TISCO's connected transactions were moderate and generally showed improvement. Even though TISCO claimed that market prices were used in those transactions, the substantial amount of purchases should still draw the attention of analysts.

*Table 9.4* Disclosed connection transactions of TISCO (1997–2003) (in million RMB)

| Year | TISCO's sales to parent or other companies in the enterprise group | TISCO's purchase from parent and other companies in the enterprise group |
|------|------|------|
| 1997 | 103 (2.1%) | 897 (24%) |
| 1998 | 251 (5.0%) | 924 (22.7%) |
| 1999 | 100 (1.7%) | 941 (20.0%) |
| 2000 | 153 (2.2%) | 909 (16.6%) |
| 2001 | 156 (1.9%) | 1,017 (15.6%) |
| 2002 | 142 (1.5%) | 1,125 (14.9%) |
| 2003 | 287 (2.0%) | 2,191 (18.5%) |

Note: Brackets indicate the value of connected transactions relative to total sales or purchases.
Source: TISCO *Annual Reports* 1997–2003

### How did TISCO fare before and after listing?

TISCO was incorporated in 1994 and listed in 1997. Comparable financial information of pre-listing years is available for 1995 and 1996. Using the pre-listing information available in the 1997 *Annual Report*, the authors compiled Table 9.5 for three key financial ratios.

With the exception of the positive performance data in 2004, pre-listing ROEs in 1995 and in 1996 were slightly higher than the ROEs in the post-listing period. The trend in ROAs suggests that TISCO's performance in the post-listing years was not materially better than the pre-listing years. TISCO's capital structure remained quite stable over the pre- and post-listing years with debt financing at about 50 per cent. Considering the results in previous sections on trend analysis, we can conclude that TISCO managers had better utilized the company's assets after listing though the company's profitability was slightly squeezed in the post-listing years.

### Comparison with Tanggang, other large domestic steel makers, and the world's largest steel makers

The ratio comparisons in Appendix 9.3 indicate that Wugang's listed subsidiary WSPC was a more profitable company than TISCO. However, like WSPC relative to Wugang, TISCO was much more profitable and efficiently managed than its parent. Mixed results were found when comparing the ratios of Tanggang and TISCO with the global composite ratios. While a consolidated table describing the ratios is presented in Appendix 9.3, for ease of reference, some related ratios are presented in the following sections.

### TISCO versus Tanggang

The data in Table 9.6 confirm that Tanggang did, indeed, transfer its main operating assets to TISCO. Consolidated revenues for Tanggang are only slightly higher than those of TISCO, suggesting that whatever assets were retained by Tanggang did not generate much revenue. Over the period 1997–2003, only about 3 per cent of Tanggang's total sales were generated

*Table 9.5* Selected financial data of TISCO before and after listing

|  | 2004 | 2003 | 2002 | 2001 | 2000 | 1999 | 1998 | 1997 | 1996 | 1995 |
|---|---|---|---|---|---|---|---|---|---|---|
| ROA (%) | 6.94 | 5.70 | 4.82 | 6.63 | 5.78 | 5.75 | 6.09 | 6.63 | 6.7 | 5.6 |
| ROE (%) | 16.0 | 11.59 | 8.64 | 12.97 | 11.06 | 10.32 | 11.63 | 10.93 | 12.79 | 11.74 |
| Total debt to total assets (%) | 56.68 | 50.78 | 44.20 | 48.90 | 47.77 | 44.30 | 47.62 | 39.40 | 47.70 | 51.95 |

Notes: ROA = net income/total asset; ROE = net income/total equity.
Source: TISCO *Annual Reports* 1997–2004

*Table 9.6* Steel revenues and assets of TISCO and Tanggang (1997–2003)
(in million RMB)

| | Revenue | | Total asset | | Net income | |
|---|---|---|---|---|---|---|
| | Tanggang | TISCO | Tanggang | TISCO | Tanggang | TISCO |
| 2003 | 14,866.46 | 14,167.10 (95.3%) | 21,936.95 | 15,507.41 (70.1%) | 591.62 | 884.48 (149.50%) |
| 2002 | 9,565.49 | 9,221.49 (96.4%) | 16,486.29 | 12,089.91 (73.3%) | 159.71 | 582.54 (364.75%) |
| 2001 | 8,317.10 | 8,083.24 (97.2%) | 14,826.81 | 11,055.50 (74.6%) | 135.38 | 732.81 (541.30%) |
| 2000 | 7,121.44 | 6,934.32 (97.4%) | 14,354.38 | 10,255.70 (71.4%) | 90.69 | 592.54 (653.7%) |
| 1999 | 5,726.00 | 5,726.21 (100%) | 14,280.00 | 9,310.13 (65.2%) | n/a | 535.09 |
| 1998 | 5,182.37 | 5,048.89 (97.4%) | 13,248.54 | 8,430.05 (63.6%) | −41.22 | 513.44 |
| 1997 | 4,565.68 | 4,732.67 | 12,162.25 | 7,598.59 (62.5%) | 35.99 | 503.41 (1,400%) |

Notes:
(i) Tanggang does not compile its own Yearbook. Top steel state firms exchange information each year and so Tanggang data appear in Wugang's Yearbooks.
(ii) Brackets indicate the weight relative to Tanggang's total.
(iii) The authors could not obtain the net income of Tanggang in 1999.
Sources: TISCO data derived from *Annual Reports* 1997–2003; Tanggang data derived from *Wugang Yearbooks* (1997–1999 and 2001–2004) and *China Steel Yearbooks* (1997–2004). Note: where Tanggang revenue/asset data is available in both *China Steel Yearbooks* and *Wugang Yearbooks* the figures match, with the exception of Tanggang's revenue of 1997

by non-TISCO steel assets, although those assets represented 30 per cent of Tanggang's total. A more dramatic comparison is shown in the proportion of net income, with TISCO's being several times that of Tanggang, implying that Tanggang's non-listed assets had been losing money and were consuming the value of the company.

The value-consuming assets remaining at Tanggang reflect China's widespread 'unhealthy' asset (*buliang zhichan*) problem (Li 2003; *People's Daily* online, 9 January 2004). Unhealthy assets refer to items with low productivity and efficiency; that is, assets that generally fail to make profit but remain on the balance sheet of the state enterprise (He 2005). In state banks, for example, unhealthy assets refer to NPLs or bad debts. In industrial firms, they refer to, for example: uncollectible accounts receivable; work-in-progress; finished goods and raw materials that have little or no potential to generate sales; investment or income that cannot be recovered; damaged or unusable fixed assets; and fixed assets whose book value is higher than their market value. According to data from China's finance ministry, in 2003 about 10 per cent of the SOEs' total assets were classified as unhealthy (Table 9.7). Put in perspective, 10 per cent of the nation's state assets was equivalent

*Table 9.7* 'Unhealthy' assets of China's SOEs (1998–2003)

|                                              | 1998   | 1999   | 2000   | 2001   | 2002   | 2003   |
|----------------------------------------------|--------|--------|--------|--------|--------|--------|
| Unhealthy assets to equity (%)               | 24.8   | 27.5   | 31.4   | 31.2   | 31.2   | 28.5   |
| Debt ratio (%)                               | 65.5   | 65.4   | 66     | 65     | 64.8   | 65.9   |
| Equity to total assets (%)                   | 34.5   | 34.6   | 34     | 35     | 35.2   | 34.1   |
| Unhealthy assets to total assets (%)         | 8.6    | 7.9    | 10.7   | 10.9   | 11     | 9.7    |
| Total assets of all SOEs (billion yuan)      | 13,478 | 14,529 | 16,007 | 17,924 | 18,022 | 19,971 |
| GDP (billion yuan)                           |        | 7,835  | 8,207  | 8,947  | 9,731  | 10,517 11,731 |

Source: Data from: *Finance Yearbook of China* 2004: 371–373. *Zhongguo Caijzheng Zazhishe, China Industrial Economy Statistical Yearbook*, 2004: 7, plus figures calculated by the authors.

to 2 trillion yuan (US$241 million) or almost 17 per cent of China's GDP for that year. Although analysts may argue about the accuracy of the valuation of such unhealthy assets, 10 per cent nevertheless represents a significant burden for the SOE sector to shoulder.

Another context in which the unhealthy asset issue can be examined is where the ratios of such assets are expressed relative to the equity of locally administered SOEs (see Table 9.8). In this context, the unhealthy asset ratios ranged from 30 per cent in Beijing to 393 per cent in Guizhou. In the three north-eastern provinces (Liaoning, Jilin and Heilongjiang), Jiangxi in the south, and Guizhou in the south-west, unhealthy state assets were valued several times more than the aggregate enterprise equity. That is to say, if one were to write-off the value of those unhealthy assets, all equity in those enterprises including that of the provincial SASACs (i.e. the state) or private parties would be eliminated. As such, the local SOE sector was technically insolvent in those provinces.

Table 9.9 indicates the percentage profitability levels for Tanggang and TISCO in terms of net margin and ROE. Given that 30 per cent of the total assets were non-productive explains why Tanggang's financial ratios were so much poorer than TISCO's.

In terms of asset management (see Table 9.10) Tanggang still lagged behind TISCO, although the difference was much smaller. TISCO carried less inventory and fixed assets relative to sales. However, in collecting receivables, Tanggang was highly efficient and took a lot less time to collect the bills than TISCO.

In 2003 the overall debt ratio of Tanggang averaged 65 per cent while TISCO's averaged 50 per cent (see Table 9.11). Since TISCO's assets are equivalent to 70 per cent of Tanggang's total assets, to make the overall debt ratio at 65 per cent, it appears that the remaining 30 per cent non-TISCO assets were 100 per cent debt-financed. This suggests another reason why the non-listed assets at Tanggang are a significant burden – it costs a lot to service the borrowed funds used to finance the non-productive assets.

*Table 9.8* 'Unhealthy' assets to equity in local SOEs (2003)

| Cities or provinces | Unhealthy assets to equity (%) |
| --- | --- |
| Beijing | 30.3 |
| Tianjin | 38.5 |
| Hebei | 54.3 |
| Shanxi | 42.0 |
| Inner Mongolia | 60.5 |
| Liaoning | 130.5 |
| Jilin | 352.1 |
| Heilongjiang | 196.5 |
| Shanghai | 18.0 |
| Jiangsu | 28.4 |
| Zhejiang | 9.2 |
| Anhui | 53.9 |
| Fujian | 21.5 |
| Jiangxi | 117.2 |
| Shandong | 39.5 |
| Henan | 55.3 |
| Hubei | 90.0 |
| Hunan | 84.3 |
| Guangdong | 40.1 |
| Guangxi | 49.2 |
| Hainan | 52.0 |
| Chongqing | 46.1 |
| Sichuan | 35.8 |
| Guizhou | 392.6 |
| Yunnan | 49.0 |
| Tibet | 30.9 |
| Shaanxi | 87.1 |
| Gansu | 63.5 |
| Qinghai | 40.9 |
| Ningxia | 48.0 |
| Xinjiang | 67.7 |

Source: *Finance Yearbook of China* 2004: 380

*Table 9.9* Profitability – Tanggang versus TISCO

| Year | Tanggang (all steel business) | TISCO |
| --- | --- | --- |
| *Net margin (%)* | | |
| 2003 | 3.98 | 6.24 |
| 2002 | 1.67 | 6.32 |
| 2001 | 1.63 | 9.07 |
| 2000 | 1.27 | 8.55 |
| *Return on equity (%)* | | |
| 2003 | 7.76 | 11.59 |
| 2002 | 2.66 | 8.64 |
| 2001 | 4.59 | 12.97 |
| 2000 | 2.90 | 11.06 |

*Table 9.10* Asset management ratios of Tanggang and TISCO

| Year | Tanggang (all steel business) | TISCO |
|------|-------------------------------|-------|
| *Average collection period (days)* | | |
| 2003 | 5 | 81 |
| 2002 | 13 | 61 |
| 2001 | 29 | 50 |
| 2000 | 54 | 60 |
| *Inventory turnover (times per year)* | | |
| 2003 | 7.3 | 8.76 |
| 2002 | 6.35 | 8.32 |
| 2001 | 4.32 | 5.42 |
| 2000 | 3.48 | 4.63 |
| *Fixed asset turnover (times per year)* | | |
| 2003 | 1.22 | 1.82 |
| 2002 | 0.91 | 1.20 |
| 2001 | 0.89 | 1.17 |
| 2000 | 0.81 | 1.08 |

*Table 9.11* Capital structures of Tanggang and TISCO (total debt/total assets %)

| Year | Tanggang (all steel business) | TISCO |
|------|-------------------------------|-------|
| 2003 | 65.25 | 50.78 |
| 2002 | 63.52 | 44.20 |
| 2001 | 66.97 | 48.90 |
| 2000 | 63.74 | 47.77 |

Tanggang also benefited from the state's assistance in reducing the SOEs' debt burden. In 2000, Tanggang was allowed to swap its debt for equity with three asset management companies. The debt involved amounted to RMB3.53 billion, of which 66 per cent was acquired by Huarong AMC, 33 per cent by Xinda AMC and the remaining 1 per cent by Dongfeng AMC. The agreements with these three AMCs would reduce Tanggang's debt ratio by about 25 per cent. The effect, however, did not show on Tanggang's debt ratio between 2001 and 2003.

## TISCO versus the largest domestic and world steel makers

While TISCO was not considered as one of the most profitable steel makers in China, it had been more profitable than its world counterparts over the period 2000–2003 (Table 9.12). When the top world steel makers started recovering in 2002, TISCO had a net margin over 6 per cent, which was nevertheless behind WSPC and other domestic steel makers. TISCO's ROEs, ranging from 8.64 to 12.97 per cent, were better than the global composites

*Table 9.12* Profitability – TISCO versus domestic and world's largest steel makers

| Year | TISCO | WSPC | PRC composite | Global composite |
|------|-------|------|---------------|------------------|
| *Net margin (%)* | | | | |
| 2003 | 6.24 | 8.36 | 13.14 | 0.37 |
| 2002 | 6.32 | 8.82 | 8.66 | −1.31 |
| 2001 | 9.07 | 11.11 | 6.46 | −2.57 |
| 2000 | 8.55 | 10.21 | 7.14 | 0.60 |
| *Return on equity (%)* | | | | |
| 2003 | 11.59 | 9.7 | 17.85 | 4.11 |
| 2002 | 8.64 | 11.64 | 11.82 | −1.22 |
| 2001 | 12.97 | 15.05 | 8.73 | −35.24 |
| 2000 | 11.06 | 15.53 | 6.46 | 3.8 |

of −35.2 to 4.11 per cent. Again, TISCO's performance was inferior to WSPC in terms of return to shareholders.

Over the period 2000–2003, TISCO's performance in collecting its receivables (Table 9.13) ranged from 50 to 81 days (though it made a remarkable improvement in 2004). The domestic steel makers were generally better at managing their receivables account with an average collection period of about 50 days over that period. TISCO's ratios were, however, generally on a par with the global composites, which ranged from 39 to 91 days.

For inventory management, TISCO's inventory turnover ratios improved from 4.6 to 8.8 times over the four-year period. While TISCO's ratios were still behind those of the largest domestic steel firms they were better than the benchmark of the largest world steel makers.

TISCO's fixed asset turnover was on a par with those of the largest domestic steel makers, with ratios ranging from 1.08 to 1.82. WSPC, however, still performed better with a fixed asset turnover ratio above 2 in three of the four years. In utilizing its fixed assets, TISCO had outperformed its global counterparts, which produced turnover ratios below 1 in three of the four years.

TISCO, like its domestic counterparts, has utilized relatively low debt-financing by world standards, even though its debt ratio has risen slightly, to about 50 per cent, in recent years (Table 9.14). The global composite debt ratio ranges from around 60 to 80 per cent during the period studied. While maintaining a relatively low debt ratio, TISCO could still pay out over 60 and even 80 per cent of its after-tax earnings, which again was very high. The world's largest steel makers retained more and paid out only a small fraction of earnings over the same period.

One issue that has drawn our attention while examining TISCO's financing is a subsidized loan provided by the provincial treasury department. As reported in its 2004 *Annual Report* (p. 38), TISCO received a loan of RMB104.5 million (US$13 million) at an interest rate of 1.9 per cent from the Hebei government. This is substantially lower than other long-term industrial

*Table 9.13* Asset management ratios – TISCO versus domestic and world's largest steel makers

| Year | TISCO | WSPC | PRC composite | Global composite |
|---|---|---|---|---|
| *(A)  Average collection period (days)* | | | | |
| 2003 | 81 | 53.35 | 44.08 | 57.18 |
| 2002 | 61 | 45.84 | 50.24 | 90.77 |
| 2001 | 50 | 50.29 | 53.73 | 42.46 |
| 2000 | 60 | 9.72 | 56.21 | 38.71 |
| Year | TISCO | WSPC | PRC steel industry index | Global composite |
| *(B)  Inventory turnover (times per year)* | | | | |
| 2003 | 8.76 | 14.98 | 12.00 | 4.5 |
| 2002 | 8.32 | 12.27 | 11.47 | 4.27 |
| 2001 | 5.42 | 11.06 | 10.41 | 3.98 |
| 2000 | 4.63 | 9.12 | 12.22 | 3.94 |
| *(C)  Fixed asset turnover (times per year)* | | | | |
| 2003 | 1.82 | 1.81 | 1.53 | 1.59 |
| 2002 | 1.20 | 2.2 | 1.22 | 0.92 |
| 2001 | 1.17 | 2.03 | 1.16 | 0.88 |
| 2000 | 1.08 | 2.54 | 1.45 | 0.87 |

*Table 9.14* Financing – TISCO versus domestic and world's largest steel makers

| Year | TISCO | WSPC | PRC composite | Global composite |
|---|---|---|---|---|
| *Total debt/total assets (%)* | | | | |
| 2003 | 50.78 | 23.84 | 43.17 | 78.28 |
| 2002 | 44.20 | 26.70 | 46.93 | 79.06 |
| 2001 | 48.90 | 30.03 | 45.5 | 69.67 |
| 2000 | 47.77 | 28.09 | 35.31 | 62.12 |
| *Payout ratio (%)* | | | | |
| 2003 | 77.78 | 101.35 | 41.09 | 15.5 |
| 2002 | 64.10 | 17.54 | 60.67 | n/a |
| 2001 | 64.81 | 83.25 | 63.92 | 12.9 |
| 2000 | 79.55 | 82.8 | 63.31 | n/a |

loans provided by the Hebei government, which are generally made at 4.58 per cent, which is already low by the nation's standards. In fact, it is lower than the state banks' borrowing costs (namely, the five-year deposit rate given to depositors). (This seems to lend substance to a comment made by politicians in the US in connection with state-owned CNOOC's (China National Offshore Oil Corporation) abortive attempt to acquire UNOCAL (Union Oil Company of California) that the SOE was unfairly subsidized by cheap loans (via state banks) from the state (*Economist*, 2 July 2005 and 3 September 2005).)

## Evaluating TISCO's and Tanggang's finances

TISCO obviously inherited the best of Tanggang's assets and produced over 95 per cent of the state firm's revenue. Although by domestic standards it has not been that profitable, by world standards it has outperformed the largest world steel makers over the period of 2000–2003. In asset management, TISCO has shown continuous improvement in inventory management, receivables collection and fixed asset utilization, which overall were on a par with, if not better than, the world's largest steel firms. In terms of financing, like other Chinese steel makers TISCO is still relatively under-powered in use of leverage, but at the same time it has consistently paid out over 60 per cent of its earnings to its shareholders. Certainly, Tanggang, which suffered from the losses incurred by the non-TISCO assets, has relied on the cash provided by the dividends from its more profitable subsidiary.

To answer the question, 'Have Tanggang's steel assets been better managed after they were transferred to the listed subsidiary?', the answer provided by our analysis would appear to be 'yes'. However, readers should be aware that this positive picture is influenced by two critical factors: first, Tanggang's restructuring efforts carved out the best assets and transferred them to the subsidiary while keeping the worst, non-productive, value consuming assets in the group company; and second, China's steel market very much bottomed-out in early 2002 and started to recover significantly in the second half of that year, thus contributing to positive sales figures in 2002 and 2003.

Thanks to its listed subsidiary, TISCO, Tanggang as a whole experienced substantial growth in both steel output and revenue over the period 2000–2003. Its revenue tripled, its total assets increased by 80 per cent, and its net income grew by more than 21 times. Tanggang's net income could have been even higher if it had been able to dispose of all its non-listed assets. Thus if Tanggang wished to enhance its profitability it had either to dispose of its value consuming assets and dormant resources or make them more productive, so as to produce returns in excess of its cost of capital.

## Conclusion

In terms of restructuring, Tanggang did not progress as fast as Wugang. By the end of 2003, its accomplishment in restructuring was limited to incorporating TISCO (plus some subsidiaries) and listing it on a domestic stock exchange. In relation to separating-off its social service units, it also failed to make substantial progress. Two reasons for this relatively slow pace of reform became apparent. First, as Tanggang was not a centrally administered enterprise, it was not on the nation's 'priority list'; and second, Hebei's politically conservative former Party Secretary had failed to make reform of the steel industry one of his strategic priorities.

Tanggang, like Wugang, did not apply drastic measures to lay off employees, even though it had a much worse redundancy problem. Its proximity to Beijing reinforced the general stability concerns of political and enterprise leaders, who wished to inhibit any potential expressions of public resistance.

However, allowing surplus workers to remain within the enterprise very much impaired Tanggang's profitability and efficiency, which could have been far higher if it had been allowed to reduce significantly its various loss-making assets. Although TISCO showed significant improvement in asset management (and, in turn, so did Tanggang), in terms of profitability TISCO's ratios were slightly lower in the post-listing years.

As the majority shareholder, however, the state should be satisfied, for the establishment and subsequent listing of TISCO very much fulfilled its central mission of procuring more funds for development. This permitted Tanggang to increase its total crude steel production from 2 million tons in the mid-1990s to over 6 million tons in 2003 and 2004. (Tanggang's recently approved (November 2005) 'consolidation' merger with Chengde Steel and Xuanhua Steel – to form 'New Tanggang' – has now seen its projected tonnage more than double, to over 13 million tons.) Overall, Tanggang's success in securing funding through the sale of shares has helped alleviate some of its *guoqi bing* and *qiye bing* problems, although it retains significant others in respect of high levels of surplus labour and its social welfare burden being far from relieved.

So, are Tanggang's prospects for the future good? TISCO is its money-making engine – if TISCO does well, Tanggang will do well – as it still owns 60 per cent of TISCO. However, much depends upon how soon Tanggang will be able to dispose of its non-productive assets, all of which have added to costs. Recently, Tanggang seems to have been pressured into speeding up its reform. Apart from its approved merger with Chengde and Xuanhua, we have also mentioned the highest profile issue currently affecting the enterprise – the state's proposal to move Shougang, the plant chosen to be the leading steel maker for northern China (and China's third ranking steel firm by output) to Tangshan. Currently situated in west Beijing, Shougang is a major contributor of pollutants to the capital city. As part of the preparation to ready Beijing for the 2008 Olympics, environmentally unfriendly factories such as Shougang are being relocated. The state plans to make Shougang and Tanggang the largest steel maker in the north, similar to Baosteel's position in the east. Currently, Shougang and Tanggang are in cooperation to build a new steel plant with a capacity of producing 8 million tons of crude steel in northern Hebei. This merger development will likely put Tanggang back on the state's SOE priority list, with its reform progress being a key issue in respect of future discussions between itself and Shougang.

So what's next for Tanggang and TISCO? Even though at the time of writing (December 2005) TISCO has been up and running for eight years, we have noted that significant issues of redundancy and social welfare remain. Given recent events it appears that these issues will be dealt with in a context where both the central and provincial governments heighten their involvement. The state has recently expressed its intention to remain the controlling shareholder in state steel makers and ban foreign investors from taking controlling stakes (*China Daily*, 4 August 2005). In all likelihood this will limit the extent of further privatization and the possibility of forming joint-ventures with foreign partners. In addition to Tanggang being required to

merge with two other smaller Hebei steel plants, the Hebei provincial government still intervenes in the firm's main operational decisions and in the provision of low-cost loans. As such, it appears that Tanggang will continue to grow in a direction consistent with the state's industrial policy, with many of its *guoqi bing* and *qiye bing* problems remaining attached to it for some time. However, 2010 is the year by which the state wants to complete the economic reform process and that is not too far away.

## Appendix 9.1: Tanggang production and administration units moved to TISCO

18 factories:

1  Sintering Plant
2  No. 1 Iron-smelting Plant
3  No. 2 Iron-smelting Plant
4  No. 1 Steel-making Plant
5  No. 2 Steel-making Plant
6  Electric Steel-making Plant
7  No. 1 Rolling Mill
8  No. 3 Rolling Mill
9  No. 4 Rolling Mill
10  Medium Section Steel Mill
11  High Speed Wire Rolling
12  Bar Mill
13  Narrow Strip Rolling Mill
14  South District Power Plant
15  North District Power Plant
16  Oxygen Plant
17  Raw Material Preparation Plant
18  Machining Plant

12 administrative and supportive units:

1  Construction and Maintenance Engineering Company
2  Transportation Department
3  Raw Material Purchasing Department
4  Equipment and Material Supply Department
5  Import and Export Department
6  Machinery and Equipment Maintenance Department
7  Quality Control Department
8  Research and Development Centre
9  Construction Management Department
10  Production Coordinating Department
11  Sales Department
12  Measuring Department

Source: TISCO *Annual Report* (1999: 29)

**Appendix 9.2: Selected financial data and ratios of TISCO (1997–2004) (million yuan)**

| Data/ratio | 2004 | 2003 | 2002 | 2001 | 2000[a] | 1999[a] | 1998[a] | 1997[a] |
|---|---|---|---|---|---|---|---|---|
| Revenues | 21,833.97 | 14,167.10 | 9,221.49 | 8,083.24 | 6,934.32 | 5,727.21 | 5,048.89 | 4,732.67 |
| EBIT | 2,291.62 | 1,395.58 | 1,024.56 | 959.97 | 833.61 | 707.99 | 749.94 | 689.87 |
| EBIT/Revenues | 10.50% | 9.85% | 11.11% | 11.88% | 12.02% | 12.36% | 14.85% | 14.58% |
| Net income | 1,325.48 | 884.48 | 582.54 | 732.81 | 592.54 | 535.09 | 513.44 | 503.41 |
| Tax rate | 29% | 23% | 32% | 12% | 15% | 15% | 15% | 15% |
| Net income/revenue | 6.07% | 6.24% | 6.32% | 9.07% | 8.55% | 9.34% | 10.17% | 10.64% |
| Total assets[b] | 19,104.70 | 15,507.41 | 12,089.91 | 11,055.50 | 10,255.70 | 9,310.13 | 8,430.05 | 7,598.59 |
| Total assets turnover (times) | 1.14 | 0.91 | 0.76 | 0.73 | 0.68 | 0.62 | 0.60 | 0.62 |
| Current assets | 10,302.94 | 7,290.48 | 4,065.47 | 4,055.67 | 3,834.39 | 3,324.39 | 3,501.46 | 3,105.11 |
| Fixed assets | 8,205.52 | 7,791.73 | 7,699.24 | 6,914.03 | 6,396.11 | 5,935.87 | 5,321.53 | 4,468.95 |
| Fixed asset turnover | 2.66 | 1.82 | 1.20 | 1.17 | 1.08 | 0.96 | 0.95 | 1.06 |
| Cash and equiv. | 4,285.72 | 1,523.96 | 1,142.99 | 1,284.20 | 1,079.80 | 501.26 | 250.48 | 260.49 |
| Net bills, accts and other receivables | 2,828.22 | 3,126.34 | 1,552.75 | 1,113.29 | 1,147.73 | 1,330.73 | 1,671.16 | 1,575.91 |
| Average collection period (days) | 47 | 81 | 61 | 50 | 60 | 85 | 121 | 122 |
| Inventory, net | 2,207.17 | 1,617.79 | 1,108.44 | 1,490.76 | 1,496.51 | 1,380.01 | 1,477.29 | 1,074.77 |
| Inventory turnover (times) | 9.89 | 8.76 | 8.32 | 5.42 | 4.63 | 4.15 | 3.42 | 4.40 |
| Current liabilities | 6,375.64 | 5,405.54 | 3,441.45 | 3,272.21 | 3,104.08 | 3,472.07 | 3,361.35 | 2,089.28 |
| Current ratio (times) | 1.62 | 1.35 | 1.18 | 1.24 | 1.24 | 0.96 | 1.04 | 1.49 |
| A/P and advances as a % of current liabilities | 70.61% | 75.20% | 41.40% | 26.61% | 40.14% | 29.31% | 26.98% | 28.49% |

| | | | | | | | | |
|---|---|---|---|---|---|---|---|---|
| Accrued payroll and welfare | 579.01 | 526.89 | 439.95 | 426.21 | 419.14 | 335.12 | 46.53 | 44.48 |
| *Total debt to total assets* | *56.68%* | *50.78%* | *44.20%* | *48.90%* | *47.77%* | *44.30%* | *47.62%* | *39.40%* |
| *Equity multiplier (times)* | *2.31* | *2.03* | *1.79* | *1.96* | *1.91* | *1.80* | *1.91* | *1.65* |
| *Return on equity* | *16.01%* | *11.59%* | *8.64%* | *12.97%* | *11.06%* | *10.32%* | *11.63%* | *10.93%* |
| NOPAT (net operating profit after tax)[c] | 1,744.22 | 746.16 | 746.68 | 859.78 | 732.69 | 613.57 | 659.58 | 601.03 |
| Operating assets[d] | 16,802.00 | 14,0109 | 9,253.92 | 9,303.17 | 8,967.74 | 7,887.71 | 7,134.55 | 6,724.18 |
| *NOPAT/Operating Assets* | *10.38%* | *5.32%* | *8.07%* | *9.24%* | *8.17%* | *7.78%* | *9.24%* | *8.94%* |
| Expenditure for fixed assets, intangible assets and other long-term assets[e] | 1,648.65 | 946.45 | 1,400.56 | 993.35 | 936.23 | 961.14 | 1,087.69 | n/a |
| EPS (in RMB) | 0.68 | 0.45 | 0.39 | 0.54 | 0.44 | 0.63 | 0.65 | 0.63 |
| Shares outstanding (millions) | 1,954.98 | 1,954.98 | 1,503.83 (150 million, new issues @RMB6.06) | 1,353.83 | 1,353.83 | 846.14 | 793.9 | 793.9 |
| % of shares owned by holding company | 59.25 | 59.25 | 59.25 | 67.60 | 67.60 | 67.64 | 70.80 | 70.80 |
| Total dividends | 977.49 | 684.24 | 375.96 | 473.84 | 473.84 | none | 476.33 | 309.99 |
| *(Dividend) payout ratio* | *73.53%* | *77.78%* | *64.10%* | *64.81%* | *79.55%* | *0.00%* | *92.30%* | *62.00%* |
| Dividend per share (in RMB) | 0.50 | 0.35 | 0.25 | 0.35 | 0.35 | none | 0.60 | 0.39 |

Notes:
a Substantial discrepancies are found in the figures in accounting years 1997, 1998, 1999 and 2000 between the current year *Annual Report* and those in the subsequent year. For example, the net income of year 1998 was reported as 513.35 million in the 1998 annual report but 413.35 million in the 1999 report, which translates into a 24 % difference. Figures applied and included in the above reflect the data collected in the current year reports.
b Including current, fixed and intangible assets. Intangible assets are negligible.
c NOPAT (net operating profit after tax) = EBIT (earnings before interest and tax) – income tax.
d Operating assets excludes short and long-term investment, construction materials and construction-in-progress. No other adjustments were made, although accounts receivable and the 'monetary fund' sometimes seemed excessive.
e As shown in the cash flow statement.
Source: TISCO *Annual Reports* 1997–2004

## Appendix 9.3: Comparison of financial performance: Tanggang and TISCO versus Wugang, WISCO/WSPC, top listed Chinese steel firms and top steel firms globally (2000–2003)

| Year | Tanggang (all steel business) | TISCO | Wugang (steel business) | WISCO/ WSPC | PRC composite | Global composite |
|---|---|---|---|---|---|---|
| *(A) Profitability – Net margin (%)* | | | | | | |
| 2003 | 3.98 | 6.24 | 6.70 | 8.36 | 13.14 | 0.37 |
| 2002 | 1.67 | 6.32 | 4.31 | 8.82 | 8.66 | −1.31 |
| 2001 | 1.63 | 9.07 | 3.45 | 11.11 | 6.46 | −2.57 |
| 2000 | 1.27 | 8.55 | 3.44 | 10.21 | 7.14 | 0.60 |
| *(B) Profitability – return on equity (%)* | | | | | | |
| 2003 | 7.76 | 11.59 | 9.78 | 9.7 | 17.85 | 4.11 |
| 2002 | 2.66 | 8.64 | 4.16 | 11.64 | 11.82 | −1.22 |
| 2001 | 4.59 | 12.97 | 3.21 | 15.05 | 8.73 | −35.24 |
| 2000 | 2.90 | 11.06 | 3.01 | 15.53 | 6.46 | 3.80 |
| *(C) Asset management – average collection period (days)* | | | | | | |
| 2003 | 5 | 81 | 7 | 53.35 | 44.08 | 57.18 |
| 2002 | 13 | 61 | 38 | 45.84 | 50.24 | 90.77 |
| 2001 | 29 | 50 | 52 | 50.29 | 53.73 | 42.46 |
| 2000 | 54 | 60 | 75 | 9.72 | 56.21 | 38.71 |

| Year | Tanggang (all steel business) | TISCO | Wugang (steel business) | WISCO/ WSPC | PRC steel industry index | Global composite |
|---|---|---|---|---|---|---|
| *(D) Asset management – inventory turnover (times per year)* | | | | | | |
| 2003 | 7.3 | 8.76 | 6.14 | 14.98 | 12.00 | 4.50 |
| 2002 | 6.35 | 8.32 | 3.98 | 12.27 | 11.47 | 4.27 |
| 2001 | 4.32 | 5.42 | 3.80 | 11.06 | 10.41 | 3.98 |
| 2000 | 3.48 | 4.63 | 3.94 | 9.12 | 12.22 | 3.94 |
| *(E) Asset management – fixed asset turnover (times per year)* | | | | | | |
| 2003 | 1.22 | 1.82 | 0.85 | 1.81 | 1.53 | 1.59 |
| 2002 | 0.91 | 1.20 | 0.63 | 2.2 | 1.22 | 0.92 |
| 2001 | 0.89 | 1.17 | 0.61 | 2.03 | 1.16 | 0.88 |
| 2000 | 0.81 | 1.08 | 0.61 | 2.54 | 1.45 | 0.87 |

| Year | Tanggang (all steel business) | TISCO | Wugang (steel business) | WISCO/ WSPC | PRC composite | Global composite |
|------|------|------|------|------|------|------|
| *(F) Financing – total debt/total assets (%)* | | | | | | |
| 2003 | 65.25 | 50.78 | 56.21 | 23.84 | 43.17 | 78.28 |
| 2002 | 63.52 | 44.20 | 48.13 | 26.70 | 46.93 | 79.06 |
| 2001 | 66.97 | 48.90 | 48.05 | 30.03 | 45.50 | 69.67 |
| 2000 | 63.74 | 47.77 | 51.10 | 28.09 | 35.31 | 62.12 |
| *(G) Financing – payout ratio (%)* | | | | | | |
| 2003 | n/a | 77.78 | n/a | 101.35 | 41.09 | 15.5 |
| 2002 | n/a | 64.10 | n/a | 17.54 | 60.67 | n/a |
| 2001 | n/a | 64.81 | n/a | 83.25 | 63.92 | 12.9 |
| 2000 | n/a | 79.55 | n/a | 82.8 | 63.31 | n/a |

# 10  Conclusion

Just as in each new phase of enterprise reform in China, it has been easy to point out the flaws and failings of the previous stage of the programme, so have obvious shortcomings in the performance of SOEs come into focus with the hindsight provided by the People's Republic of China's passage from one era to the next. The judgement most frequently passed on the typical Mao-era, large, heavy-industrial SOE, that it was characterized by chronic inefficiency and low labour productivity and therefore in need of radical reform if the national industrial economy were to develop and modernize, is hard to contradict. However, it is somewhat fairer to measure SOEs' records not against what each new historical era might require of them, but against the role they were originally intended to play. Even though it makes for research findings that often resist strict national or cross-sectoral generalization, specific historical and political context, even down to the level of an individual SOE in a particular year, matters enormously for an accurate understanding of what has happened to China's large SOEs since the launch of the economic reforms.

The tendency to lump together the entire 28 years of the reform period to date as one common policy phase and a uniform environment for SOEs must also be resisted. Baoshan Steel has come into its own in the reform era as China's most successful, efficient and profitable state-owned steel maker and a likely candidate for one of the CCP government's 'global industrial champions' in the near future. But its key advantage – the fact that it was founded in the late 1970s and so has been unhampered by the major pension responsibilities faced by its 1950s-era domestic competitors – only really came into play in the 1990s when divesting SOEs of their welfare responsibilities started to be seriously tackled. This was the specific policy phase in which it took off. Few remember now the company's inauspicious beginnings as a deeply unpopular project, criticized by name in the journals and posters that briefly flourished as expressions of extra-Party opinion during the Democracy Wall Movement of 1978–1981. Baoshan required massive, long-term state investment at a time when citizens' faith in the competence of the CCP government to manage major projects was at one of its lowest ebbs, following the Bohai Gulf incident and a series of admissions by CCP leaders such as Zhao Ziyang that after 30 years of effort, China had still only reached the 'primary stage' of socialism. Before the early 1990s, its Shanghai location was also a marked disadvantage, as that city, punished with neglect and underdevelopment in the Mao era by a CCP suspicious of its pre-1949 cosmopolitanism, was further penalized for having been the main base of the Gang of Four.

On their own terms, as providers of full urban employment as a social good, and as the essential welfare safety net that enabled the low-wage, high-accumulation development model selected by the CCP government to function at all, large SOEs cannot be judged to have failed in pre-reform China. In fact, the slow and patchy progress of the replacement of work-unit welfare with local-government provision since the end of the 1990s has thrown into sharp relief just how successful, well-organized and cost-effective large SOEs' provision often was – and the companies on which these studies are based also managed to make and sell quite a lot of steel while they were doing the job of the urban welfare state. Their effectiveness in preventing the emergence of collective resistance to management and/or the state on the part of their workers has been somewhat exaggerated (Walder 1986; Sheehan 1998), but their record of offering labour enough security to make the absence of democratic participation and managerial respect in industry just about tolerable a lot of the time is still a respectable one when the hyperbole is stripped away from it.

Although managerial autonomy was much more restricted in the Mao era, SOEs essentially were operating then within a network of institutional and political constraints which varied according to their particular status and relationships with local and central government agencies, just as they have been since 1978 as they have undergone reform, and they can only be judged fairly when these constraints are taken into account. For a while in the latest reform phase, in the second half of the 1990s, it did look as if the ambitious aims of the MES and GCS reforms were as far as ever from being realized, but in part this now appears to have been the result of one of the paradoxes of enterprise reform: that the state actually institutionalizes its interference in large SOEs through its crucial role in a reform programme aimed at minimizing that interference in the day-to-day running of companies. SOEs were still looking for special 'policies' from different levels of the state, according to their status, in order to be able to participate in major elements of the corporatization programme, such as the stock-market listing of sub-companies, debt-to-equity swaps, and domestic mergers and acquisitions. To an extent, some SOEs still experience significant restrictions on their operational and strategic decision-making in these areas, but developments in other companies have demonstrated that the paradoxical effects of the state's execution of its own removal from SOE management are generally temporary, with real and significant change in the state–management relationship eventually emerging.

Judged on this basis, gradualism in enterprise reform has been a success story, even though at times change appeared to be not so much gradual as stalled. Gradualism has also had important benefits for large SOEs in dealing with the potentially explosive issue of surplus labour. Large SOEs' resources have enabled them to make massive lay-offs over a relatively long period of time, and to identify particular categories of worker for eventual laying-off, which can be presented to the workforce as a whole as objectively reasonable. For example, including employees on short-term contracts among the first wave of lay-offs while protecting the status of the longest-serving permanently employed was widely accepted as fair, as the last-in, first-out principle generally is in workplaces across the globe. As Cai (2006) has shown, sequential lay-offs, even those involving very large numbers over time, are less likely to generate collective resistance as compared with simultaneous redundancy for the entire workforce of a smaller SOE, since the number of those directly affected in the same way at any given time is minimized. By the time the next batch are laid-off, some of those who lost their jobs earlier will have found new ones, and variation in the terms of lay-offs, with more generous provision for some categories of worker than for others, can also minimize the extent to which the laid-off feel they have common cause for protest. Divide and rule is scarcely an innovative strategy for minimizing labour unrest in the face of severe damage to workers' interests, but it is often an effective one, given the necessary resources to carry it out.

Large SOEs' resources have given them the ability to implement staged programmes of lay-offs and to afford almost indefinite delays on compulsory redundancies where necessary to avoid too powerful a backlash. These have proved to be significant advantages over smaller SOEs, where sudden announcements of job losses affecting, often, the entire workforce have been much more likely to produce protests, sit-ins, traffic blockades, and attempts to take the case to higher authorities. However, in the avoidance of collective resistance to job losses, large SOEs have also experienced one major disadvantage. One of the factors reducing the likelihood of laid-off workers being about to organize themselves for collective resistance or protest is that once they have lost their job, they no longer see each other regularly or have any obvious place to meet and discuss how to do something about their plight. The laid-off from large SOEs, however, are much more likely still to live on-site, or very nearby, in former SOE housing bought cheaply in the housing reforms of the late 1990s. This housing typically cannot be sold on for a period of five years, and by the time this has elapsed, most of the employees affected would either already have been laid off or would be well aware of the insecurity of their employment, and thus would be unable or unwilling to make a move into unsubsidized, market-priced accommodation. Thus there is a risk that, even though lay-offs are done in stages, the disgruntled unemployed from previous batches of the redundant will be ready and waiting to enlist the newly jobless in a joint resistance effort. Shougang, in many respects the major SOE least likely to be troubled with labour unrest given its unique political status and the consequent care taken there to avoid it, has been one of the companies caught out by the fact that the workers it had just sacked were nursing their grievances on the premises and had nowhere else to go.

Labour unrest as a result of the reforms has tended to remain localized, sporadic, and possible for the authorities to control through a mixture of concessions, including delays of the most unpopular reform elements, and repression, including extremely harsh treatment of those judged to be the leaders of any organized, collective resistance. It has, nonetheless, been significant enough in scale, frequency and the ability to articulate damaging political criticisms of the CCP government's treatment of the urban working class, to change the way in which the authorities have approached the whole question of lay-offs and the unemployed. It was laid-off workers' pressure in the late 1990s which made the government take their plight seriously instead of blithely dismissing it as a price well worth paying for the goal of SOE corporatization, as symbolized by the 1998 transformation of the Ministry of Labour into the Ministry of Labour and Social Welfare (Cai 2006). It is also one of the factors driving government promotion of collective bargaining in industry and attempts to reform the official trade unions. The latter is vital for providing an effective mechanism for coping with the conflicts that SOE reform as it affects labour will continue to generate. The fact remains, however, that as the last vestiges of the special status of the traditional SOE in China are removed, with them go the last remaining arguments as to why their workers' interests are so nearly identical with those of managers and the state that they do not require representation fully independent of state and managerial influence. The more that China's remaining large SOEs resemble Western corporations, the harder it becomes to marshal an intellectually and politically respectable case for refusing to allow employees to join organizations of their choice in order to defend their collective interests. This has always been the point at which government willingness to accommodate the social changes brought about by reform has foundered on the CCP's continued attachment to its state-corporatist organizational monopoly in industry. It is an attachment likely to be put under increasingly severe strain by the demands of urban workers in China in the next few years of reform.

# Bibliography

Adams, J. S. (2000) 'Economic reform in China: ethical issues in labour law and human resource management practices', paper presented to the World Congress on the Ethical Challenges of Globalization, New York, July 2000

Aharoni, Y. (2000) 'State-owned enterprise: an agent without a principal', in P. Cook and C. Kirkpatrick (eds) *Privatization in Developing Countries*, London: Harvester Wheatsheaf

Ahlstrom, D., Bruton, G. D. and Liu, S. S. (2002) 'Navigating China's changing economy: strategies for private firms', *Business Horizons*, 43 (1): 5–15

Alchian, A. (1965) 'Some economics of property rights', *Politico*, 30 (4): 816–829

—— and Demsetz, H. (1972) 'Production, information costs, and economic organization', *American Economic Review*, 62 (5): 125–137

Angelucci, M., Bevan, A., Estrin, S., Fennema, J. A., Kuznetsov, B. and Mangiarott, G. (2002) 'The determinants of privatized enterprise performance in Russia', Discussion Paper 3193, CEPR Discussion Papers

Ayub, M. and Hegstad, O. S. (1987) 'Management of public industrial enterprises', *Research Observer* 2 (1): 79–101

Barberis, N., Boycko, M., Shleifer, S. and Tsukanova, N. (1996) 'How does privatization work? Evidence from the Russian shops', *Journal of Political Economy*, 104 (4): 764–790

Barr, N. (1992) 'Economic theory and the welfare state: a survey and interpretation', *Journal of Economic Literature*, 30 (2): 741–803

Basu, S., Estrin, S. and Svejnar, J. (2000) 'Employment and wages in enterprises under communism and in transition: evidence from central Europe and Russia', London Business School Working Paper 440

Baum, R. and Shevchenko, A. (1999) 'The state of the State', in M. Goldman and R. MacFarquhar (eds) *The Paradox of China's Post-Mao Reforms*, Cambridge, MA: Harvard University Press

Beato, P. and Mas-Colell, A. (1984) 'The marginal cost pricing rule as a regulation mechanism in mixed markets', in M. Marchand, P. Pestieau and H. Tulkens (eds) *The Performance of Public Enterprise: Concepts and Measurement* (Studies in Mathematical and Managerial Economics series, Vol. 33), New York, Oxford: North-Holland

*Beijing Review* 'China remains first in GDP growth', 41 (52) 20. 28 December 1998–3 January 1999

——, 22–28 March 1999

Bennett, J., Estrin, S. and Maw, J. (2001) 'Mass privatisation and partial state ownership of firms in transition economics', CEPR Discussion Paper 2895, CEPR Discussion Papers

Benson, J., Debroux, P., Yuasa, M. and Zhu, Ying (2000) 'Flexibility and labour management: Chinese manufacturing enterprises in the 1990s', *International Journal of Human Resource Management*, 11 (2): 183–196

Berglof, E. and Roland, G. (1998) 'Soft budget constraints and banking in transition economies', *Journal of Comparative Economics*, 26 (1): 18–40

Bevan, A., Estrin, S., Angelucci, M., Schaffer, M., Fennema, J. and Mangiarotti, G. (2001) 'The determinants of privatised enterprise performance in Russia', Discussion Paper No. 21, Centre for New and Emerging Markets, London Business School

Bhaumik, S. and Estrin, S. (2005) 'How transition paths differ: enterprise performance in Russia and China', William Davidson Institute Working Papers Series 744, William Davidson Institute at the University of Michigan Stephen M. Ross Business School

Biggart, N. (1991) 'Explaining Asian economic organization: toward a Weberian institutional perspective', *Theory and Society*, 20: 199–232

—— and Hamilton, G. (1992) 'On the limits of a firm-based theory to explain business networks: the western bias of neo-classical economies', in N. Nohria and R. Eccles (eds) *Networks and Organizations: Structure, Form and Action*, Boston, MA: Harvard University Press

Bishop, M. and Kay, J. (1989) 'Privatization in the United Kingdom: lessons from experience', *World Development*, 17 (5): 643–657

Bjorkman, I. and Lu, Y. (1999) 'The management of human resources in Chinese-western joint ventures', *Journal of World Business*, 34: 306–24

—— and —— (2000) 'Local or global? Human resource management in international joint ventures', in M. Warner (ed.) *Changing Workplace Relations in the Chinese Economy*, London: Macmillan

Blanchflower, D. G., Oswald, A. and Stutzer, A. (2001) 'Latent entrepreneurship across nations', *European Economic Review*, 45 (4–6): 680–691

Blecher, M. (2002) 'Hegemony and workers politics in China', *The China Quarterly*, 170: 283–303

Boardman, A. E. and Vining, A. R. (1989) 'Ownership and performance in competitive environment: a comparison of the performance of private, mixed, and state-owned enterprises', *Journal of Law and Economics*, 32 (1): 1–33

—— and —— (1992) 'Ownership vs competition: efficiency in public enterprise', *Public Choice*, 73 (2): 205–239

Boisot, M. (1987) 'Industrial feudalism and enterprise reform – could the Chinese use some more bureaucracy?', in M. Warner (ed.) *Management Reforms in China*, London: Francis Pinter

—— (1994) 'The lessons from China', in M. Boisot (ed.) *East-West Business Collaboration: The Challenge of Governance in Post Socialist Enterprises*, London: Routledge

—— and Child, J. (1988) 'The iron law of fiefs: bureaucratic failure and the problem of governance in the Chinese economic reforms', *Administrative Science Quarterly*, 33: 507–527

—— and —— (1996) 'From fief to clans and network capitalism: explaining China's emerging economic order', *Administrative Science Quarterly* 41: 600–628

Bolton, P. (1995) 'Privatisation and the separation of ownership and control: lessons from Chinese enterprise reform', *Economics of Transition* 3: 1–12

Boycko, M., Shleifer, A. and Vishny, R. (1996) 'A theory of privatization', *Economic Journal*, 106 (435): 309–319

Brinton, M. and Nee, V. (eds) (1998) *The New Institutionalism in Sociology*, New York: Russell Sage Foundation

Broadman, H. G. (1999) 'The Chinese state as corporate shareholder', *Finance and Development*, September, 36 (3): 52–55

Brodsgaard, K.-E. (2002) 'Institutional reform and the *Bianzhi* system in China', *The China Quarterly*, 170: 361–386

Brown, D. and Earle, J. (2001) 'Privatization, competition and reform strategies: theory and evidence from Russian enterprise panel data', CEPR Discussion Papers 2758, CEPR Discussion Papers

Bryman, A. (1988) *Quantity and Quality in Social Research*, London: Unwin Hyman

Buck, T., Filatotchev, I. and Wright, M. (1998) 'Agents, stakeholders and corporate governance in Russian privatised firms', *Journal of Management Studies*, 35: 81–104
——, —— and —— (2000) 'Different paths to economic reform in Russia and China: causes and consequences', *Journal of World Business*, 35 (4): 379–400
——, ——, —— and Zhukov, V. (1999) 'Corporate governance and employee ownership in an economic crisis: enterprise strategies in the former USSR', *Journal of Comparative Economics*, 27 (3): 459–474

Byrd, W. A. (1991) *The Market Mechanism and Economic Reforms in China*, Armonk, NY: M. E. Sharpe
—— (1991) 'Contractual responsibility systems in Chinese state-owned industry', in N. Campbell, S. Plasschaert and D. Brown (eds) *The Changing Nature of Management in China: Advances in Chinese Industrial Studies*, 2, Greenwich, CT: JAI Press

Cai, Fang (1996) *The China Miracle: Development Strategy and Economic Reform*, Hong Kong: Chinese University Press (with Justin Lin and Li Zhou)
—— (2006) *China Growing, yet Greying: Policy Innovations Vital to Sustain Economic Development*, Oxford: Blackwell

Cai, Shi (2001) 'The rapid development of informal sector during Ninth Five-Year Plan', Shanghai Labour & Social Security, No. 1

Cai, Yongshun (2002) 'The resistance of Chinese laid-off workers in the reform period', *The China Quarterly*, 170: 327–344

Campbell, J. and Pedersen, O. (1996) *Legacies of Change*, New York: Aldine

Cao, Y., Qian, Y. and Weingast, B. (1999) 'From federalism, Chinese style to privatization, Chinese style', *Economics of Transition*, 7 (1): 103–131

Carlin, W., Fries, S., Schaffer, M. and Seabright, P. (2001) 'Competition and enterprise performance in transition economies: evidence from a cross-country survey', Working Paper No. 376. The William Davidson Institute, The University of Michigan Business School, USA

Caves, D. W. and Christensen, L. R. (1980) 'The relative efficiency of public and private firms in a competitive environment: the case of Canadian railroads', *Journal of Political Economy*, 88 (5): 958–976

CEF and CESS (2001) 'The SOE reform and management: latest evaluation and suggestions on 1000 SOE managers', China Enterprise Federation and China's Entrepreneurs Survey System

CESS (2000) '2000 report on the growth and development of Chinese enterprise managers', China's Entrepreneurs Survey System

Chan, A. (1993) 'Revolution or corporatism? Workers and trade unions in post-Mao China', *Australian Journal of Chinese Affairs*, 29: 31–61

Chang, H.-J. and Singh, A. (1997) 'Can large firms run without being bureaucratic?', *Journal of International Development*, 9 (6): 865–884

Chen, D. (1995) *Chinese Firms between Hierarchy and Market*, London: St Martin's Press

—— and Faure, G. (1995) 'When Chinese companies negotiate with their government', *Organization Studies*, 16: 27–54

Chen, F. (1995) *Economic Transition and Political Legitimacy in Post-Mao China: Ideology and Reform*, Albany, NY: State University of New York Press

—— (2000) 'The reemployment project in Shanghai: institutional workings and consequences for workers', *China Information*, 14 (2): 169–193

Chen, J. (2002) 'Alternative organising and the ACFTU', *China Labour Bulletin*, 13 February

Chen, M. (1995) *Asian Management System: Chinese, Japanese and Korean Styles of Business*, London: International Homson Business

—— (2000) *The Institutional Transition of China's Township and Village Enterprises: Market Liberalization, Contractual Forms, Innovation and Privatization*, Aldershot: Gower

Cheng, A. T. (2004) 'Labour unrest in growing in China', *Asian Labour News*, 1 November, http://www.asianlabour.org/archives/003017.php

Cheng, Siwei (ed.) (2000) *The Issues and Countermeasures for the Chinese Enterprise Management*, Beijing: Minzhu yu Jianshe Pess

Chevrier, Y. (1990) 'Micropolitics and the factory director responsibility system, 1984–1987', in D. Davis and E. Vogel (eds) *Chinese Society on the Eve of Tiananmen*, Cambridge, MA: Harvard University Press

Chi, Lo (2000) 'China's banking reform – the good, the bad and the ugly', Hong Kong Standard Chartered Bank

Child, J. (1994) *Management in China during the Age of Reform*, Cambridge: Cambridge University Press

—— (1995) 'Changes in the structure and prediction of earnings in Chinese state enterprises during the economic reform', *International Journal of Human Resource Management*, 6: 1–30

—— and Lu, Yuan (1996) 'Institutional constraints on economic reform: the case of investment decisions in China', *Organization Science*, 7: 60–77

—— and Steward, S. (1997) 'Regional differences in China and their implications for Sino-foreign joint ventures', *Journal of General Management*, 23 (2): 65–86

*China Business Weekly*, dates in text

*China Daily*, 19 May 1989, 'Workers rally for students'

——, 19 May 2001, 'WTO entry to greatly boost investment'

——, 13 March 2003, 'Hosing down steel mania'

——, 14 October 2004, 'Steel sector facing reshuffle'

——, 4 August 2005, 'Nation's steel industry ready for change'

*China Economic Net*, 2 Feb. 2005, 'New measure to stimulate SOE reform'

*China Industrial Economy Statistical Yearbook* (2004) Beijing: National Statistical Bureau

*China Labour Bulletin* (1998a) 'On closures, corruption and unemployment' (July–August)

—— (1998b) 'Welfare: more poor people' (May–June)

—— (1998c) 'Protesting against poverty' (May–June)

—— (1998d) 'Letter from Hunan' (July–August)

—— (1998e) 'Labour action: nationwide' (May–June)

—— (1998f) 'Trade unionist detained following house search' (July–August)

—— (2002) 'CLB analysis of the new Trade Union Law' (January–February)

—— (2003) '300 retired iron and steel workers protest in Wuhan' (March–April)

*China Metallurgical News* (2001) 'Key policies of implementing 15th year plan for metallurgical industry', (in Chinese) 27 June

*China Newsletter*, dates in text

*China Reform Daily*, dates in text

China Reform and Development Report – Expert Group (1999) *The Experience of Success: Case Studies of China's Well-performing Large Firms*, Shanghai: Shanghai Far-East Press

*China State Statistics Bureau* (1989) 'China labour & wages statistics manual (1978–1987)', Beijing: China Statistics Publishing House

*China Steel Yearbook* (1999–2004) Beijing: Yejing Zhubanshe

Chow, I. H. S. and Fu, P. P. (2000) 'Change and development in pluralist settings: an explanation of HR practices in Chinese township and village enterprises', *International Journal of Human Resource Management*, 11: 822–836

Chu, Ke-young and Gupta, S. (1998) 'Social safety nets: issues and recent experience', Working Paper, International Monetary Fund, 15 April

Clark, P. and Mueller, F. (1996) 'Organizations and nations: from universalism to institutionalism?', *British Journal of Management*, 7: 125–139

Clarke, E. and Soulsby, A. (1999) 'The adoption of the multi-divisional firms in large Czech enterprises: the role of economic, institutional and strategic choice factors', *Journal of Management Studies*, 36: 535–559

Commander, S. (1998) *Enterprise Restructuring and Unemployment in Models of Transition*, Washington, DC: World Bank

——, Dutz, M. and Stern, N. (1999) 'Ownership, competition and regulation', paper prepared for the Annual World Bank Conference on Development Economics, Washington, DC, 28–30 April, 1999.

Cook, P. (1997) 'Privatization, public enterprise reform and the world bank: has "bureaucrats in business" got it right?', *Journal of International Development*, (6): 887–897

—— (2001) 'Competition and its regulation: key issues', Institute for Development Policy and Management, The University of Manchester, CRC Working Paper No. 2

—— and Fabella, R. (2001) 'The welfare and political economy dimensions of private vs state enterprise', Institute for Development Policy and Management, The University of Manchester, CRC Working Paper No. 1

—— and Kirkpatrick, C. (1988) *Privatization in Less Developed Countries*, London: Harvester Wheatsheaf

—— and —— (1995) *Privatization Policy and Performance: International Perspectives*, New York: Prentice-Hall

—— and —— (1997) 'Privatization: trends and future policy', Working Paper No. 3, IDPM, Manchester University, UK

—— and —— (1998) 'Privatization, employment and social protection in developing countries', in P. Cook, C. Kirkpatrick and F. Nixson (eds) *Privatization, Enterprise Development and Economic Reform*, Cheltenham: Edward Elgar

—— and —— (2000) *Privatization in Developing Countries*, Vol. 1, Cheltenham: Edward Elgar

—— and Minogue, M. (1990) 'Waiting for privatization in developing countries: towards the integration of economic and non-economic explanations', *Public Administration and Development*, 10 (4): 389–403

—— and Nixson, F. (1995) *The Move to the Market? Trade and Industry Policy Reform in Transitional Economies*, New York: St Martin's Press

——, Kirkpatrick, C. and Nixson, F. (1998) *Privatization, Enterprise Development and Economic Reform*, Cheltenham: Edward Elgar

Cooke, F.-L. (2002) 'Ownership change and reshaping of employment relations in China: a study of two manufacturing companies', *The Journal of Industrial Relations*, 44 (1): 19–39

—— (2005) *HRM, Work and Employment in China*, London: Routledge

Cooper, M. (2003a) 'The politics of China's shareholding system', working paper, Walter H. Shorenstein Asia-Pacific Research Centre, Stanford University

—— (2003b) 'Local governments and the Chinese stock markets', working paper, Walter H. Shorenstein Asia-Pacific Research Centre, Stanford University

Cremer, H., Marchand, M. and Thisse, J.-F. (1987) 'The public firm as an instrument for regulating an oligopolistic market', paper presented at the 2nd Congress of European Economic Association, Vienna, 13–17 July

Crew, M. (1975) *Theory of the Firm*, London: Longman

Cyert, R. (1988) *The Economic Theory of Organization and the Firm*, London: Harvester Wheatsheaf

—— and March, J. (1963) *A Behavioral Theory of the Firm*, Englewood Cliffs, NJ: Prentice-Hall

Dabrowski, M., Gomulka, S. and Rostowski, J. (2000) 'Whence reform? A critique of the Stiglitz perspective', CEP Discussion Papers 0471, Centre for Economic Performance, LSE

Damadaran, A. (2005) 'Estimating equity risk premiums and a note on country default spreads and risk premiums', unpublished paper posted on http://pages.stern.nyu.edu/adamodar/

Davey, J. (1995) *The New Social Contract: America's Journey from Welfare State to Police State*, Westport, CT: Praeger

Davies, D. G. (1971) 'The efficiency of public versus private firms, the case of Australia's two airlines', *Journal of Law and Economics*, 14 (1): 149–165

Davis, D. (1988) 'Patrons and clients in Chinese industry', *Modern China*, 14 (4): 487–497

Demsetz, H. A. (1968) 'Why regulate utilities?', *Journal of Law and Economics*, 11 (1): 55–65

—— and Lehn, K. (1985) 'The structure of corporate ownership: causes and consequences', *Journal of Political Economy*, 93 (6): 1155–1178

Deng, Xiaozhuo (2004) 'Comparison of "overall listing" methods', *Theory and Practice of Finance and Economics*, 25 (131): 59–61 (in Chinese)

Denny, C. (2002) 'China is no threat to America – for now', *The Guardian*, 2 April: 21.

Dewatripont, M. and Maskin, E. (1995) 'Credit and efficiency in centralized and decentralized economies', *Review of Economic Studies*, 62 (4): 541–555

Di Maggio, P. J. and Powell, W. (1991) 'Introduction', in W. Powell and P. J. Di Maggio *The New Institutionalism in Organizational Analysis*, Chicago, IL: University of Chicago Press

Ding, D. and Akhtar, S. (2001) 'The organisation choice of human resource management practices: a study of three cities in the PRC', *International Journal of Human Resource Management*, 12: 946–964

—— and Warner, M. (1999) 'Re-inventing Chinese industrial relations at enterprise-level: an empirical field study in four major cities', *Industrial Relations Journal*, 30: 243–260

—— and —— (2001) 'China's labour-management system reforms: breaking the "three old irons" (1978–1999)', *Asia Pacific Journal of Management*, 18 (3): 314–334

——, Fields, D. and Akhtar, S. (1997) 'An empirical study of human resource management policies and practices in foreign invested enterprises in China: the case of Shenzhen special economic zone', *International Journal of Human Resource Management*, 8: 595–613

——, Goodall, K. and Warner, M. (2000) 'The end of the "iron rice-bowl": whither Chinese human resource management?', *International Journal of Human Resource Management*, 11 (1): 217–236

Ding, X. L. (2000) 'The illicit asset stripping of Chinese state firms', *The China Journal* 22: 1–28

Domadenik, P., Prasnikar, J. and Svejnar, J. (2003) 'Defensive and strategic restructuring of firms during the transition to a market economy', William Davidson Institute Working Papers Series 541, William Davidson Institute at the University of Michigan Stephen M. Ross Business School

Douglas, J. (1985) *Creative Interviewing*, London: Sage Publications

Dunleavy, P. (1986) 'Explaining the privatization boom: public choice versus radical approaches', *Public Administration*, 64: 13–34

Earle, J. and Estrin, S. (1997) 'After voucher privatization: the structure of corporate ownership in Russian manufacturing industry', CEPR Discussion Papers 1736, CEPR Discussion Papers

Easterbrook, F. H. and Fischel, D. R. (1991) *The Economic Structure of Corporate Law*, Cambridge, MA: Harvard University Press

Easterby-Smith, M., Malina, D. and Lu, Yuan (1995) 'How culture sensitive is HRM? A comparative analysis of practices in Chinese and UK companies', *International Journal of Human Resource Management*, 6: 31–59

*Economist*, 2 July 2005, 'Leaders: never give a sucker an even break'; 'China and Unocal'

*Economist*, 3 September 2005, 'The myth of China Inc.'; 'Chinese industry and the state'

Ellman, M. and Kontorovich, V. (1998) *The Destruction of the Soviet Economic System: An Insiders' History*, London: M. E. Sharpe

ERDCSETC (Enterprise Reform Division of China State Economic and Trade Commission) (1999) *The Reform of State-owned Enterprises and the Establishment of Modern Enterprise System*, Beijing: Law Press

Erickson, J. and Hsien, D. (1998) 'Sunrises in Shanghai', *Asianweek*, 9 October, 51–52

Estrin, S. (2002) 'Competition and corporate governance in transition', *Journal of Economic Perspectives*, 16 (1): 101–124

—— and Perotin, V. (1991) 'Does ownership always matter?', *International Journal of Industrial Organization*, 9 (1): 55–72

—— and Wright, M. (1999) 'Corporate governance in the former Soviet Union: an overview', *Journal of Comparative Economics*, 27 (3): 398–421

——, Bevan A., Kuznetsov, B., Schaffer, M., Angelucci, M. and Fennem, J. (2001) 'The determinants of privatised enterprise performance in Russia', William Davidson Institute Working Papers Series 452, William Davidson Institute at the University of Michigan Stephen M. Ross Business School

Fama, E. F. and Jesen, M. C. (1983) 'Separation of ownership and control', *Journal of Law and Economics*, 26 (2): 301–352

Fan, Gang (1996) 'The characteristics and trend of China's economic system reform', in Wu Jinglian, Zhou, Xiaochuan and Zhao, Renwei (eds) *Gradualism and Big Bang: The Choice of China's Reform Path*, Beijing: Jingji Kexue Press

Fan, Qimiao (1994) 'State-owned enterprises reform in China: incentives and environment', in Qimiao Fan and P. Nolan (eds) *China's Economic Reform: The Costs and Benefits of the Incrementalism*, London: Macmillan

—— and Nolan, P. (1994) (eds) *China's Economic Reform: The Costs and Benefits of the Incrementalism*, London: Macmillan

*Far Eastern Economic Review*, 11 March 1993: 'Congressional record', 23–25

——, 18 November 1993: 'Model on the rocks', 63–64

——, 23 December 1993: 'Smelted down', 9

——, 9 June 1994: 'Shougang sets goals', 73

——, 2 February 1995: 'The reckoning begins', 16

——, 23 March 1995: 'Goodbye to all that', 46–47

——, 7 December 1995: 'Shougang sheds shares', 83

——, 13 June 1996: 'Teams investigating corruption cases are proliferating in Beijing', 29

——, 27 June 1996: 'Former model enterprise in Beijing is now the target of an anti-pollution campaign', 30

——, 12 September 1996: 'Trials by fire', 62–68

Farazmand, A. (1996) *Public Enterprise Management: International Case Studies*. Westport, CT: Greenwood Press

—— (1997) 'Bureaucracy is alive and well: a critique of the chaos theory and market', *Public Administration Times*, November

—— (1998) 'Building a community-based administrative state', paper presented at the 1998 Annual Conference of the American Political Science Association, Boston, September

—— (1999) 'Privatization or reform? Public enterprise management in transition', *International Review of Administrative Sciences*, 65 (4): 551–567

—— (ed.) (2001) *Privatization Or Reform? Implications for Public Management*, Westport, CT: Greenwood Press

—— (ed.) (2004) *Sound Governance*, Westport, CT: Greenwood Press

Feng, Ming (2000) 'Achieving the targets of net increase of 100,000 jobs', *Shanghai Labour & Social Security*, No. 24

Filatotchev, I., Buck, T. and Zhukov, V. (2000) 'Downsizing in privatised firms in Russia, Ukraine and Belarus: theory and empirical evidence', *Academy of Management Journal*, 43: 286–304

——, Wright, M. and Bleaney, M. (1999) 'Privatization, insider control and managerial entrenchment in Russia', *Economics of Transition,* 7: 481–504

*Finance Yearbook of China* (2004) Beijing: Zhongguo Caizheng Zazhishe

*Foreign Broadcast Information Service Daily Report – China*. Dates in text

Francis, C. (1996) 'Reproduction of Danwei: institutional features in the context of China's market economy: the case of Haidian district's high-tech sector', *China Quarterly*, 147· 839–859

Freund, E. (1998) 'Downsizing China's state industrial enterprises: the case of Baoshan steel works', in G. O'Leary (ed.) *Adjusting to Capitalism: Chinese Workers and the State*, London: M. E. Sharp

Frydman, R., Gray, C., Hessel, M. and Rapaczynski, A. (1999) 'When does privatization work? The impact of private ownership on corporate performance in the transition economies', *The Quarterly Journal of Economics*, 114 (4): 1153–1191

Galal, A., Jones, L., Pankaj, T. and Ingo, V. (1994) *Welfare Consequences of Selling Public Enterprises*, New York: Oxford University Press

Gamble, J. (2000) 'Localising management in foreign-invested enterprises in China: practical, cultural, and strategic perspectives', *International Journal of Human Resource Management*, 5: 883–903

Gao, Congjing (1998) 'Relevant problems in reemployment of layoffs and remedies', *Shanghai Labour & Social Security*, No. 6

Gao, S. and Yang, Qixian (1999) *China State-owned Enterprise Reform (Zhongguo Guoyou Qiye Gaige)*, Jinan: Jinan Press

Ge, Hong (2004) 'Choice of listing models of state commercial banks', *Pioneering with Science and Technology Monthly*, 10: 26–27 (in Chinese)

Gilbert, N. (1993) *Researching Social Life*, London: Sage

Gill, J. and Johnson, Phil (1997) *Research Methods for Managers* (2nd edition), London: Paul Chapman Publishing Ltd

Glover, L. and Siu, N. (2000) 'The human resource barriers to managing quality in China', *International Journal of Human Resource Management*, 11 (5): 867–882

Goldberg, V. P. (1976) 'Regulation and administered contracts', *Bell Journal of Economics*, 7 (2): 426–448

Goldman, M. and MacFarquhar, R. (1999) 'Dynamic economy, declining party-state', in M. Goldman and R. MacFarquhar (eds) *The Paradox of China's Post-Mao Reform*, Cambridge, MA: Harvard University Press

Goodall, K. and Warner, M. (1997) 'Human resources in Sino-foreign joint ventures: selected case studies in Shanghai, compared with Beijing', *International Journal of Human Resource Management*, 8: 569–594

Goodhart, C. and Xu, C. (1996) 'The rise of China as an economic power', *National Institute Economic Review*, February: 56–80

Goodman, D. (ed.) (1997) *China's Provinces in Reform*, London: Routledge

Granovetter, M. (1985) 'Economic action and social structure', *American Journal of Sociology*, 91: 481–510

Grossman, S. and Hart, O. (1986) 'The costs and benefits of ownership: a theory of vertical and lateral integration', *Journal of Political Economy*, 94 (4): 691–720

Groves, T., Hong, Y., McMillan, J. and Naughton, B. (1994) 'Autonomy and incentives in Chinese state enterprises', *Quarterly Journal of Economics*, 109 (1): 183–209

Gu, E. X. (1999) 'From permanent employment to mass lay-offs: the political economy of "transitional unemployment" in urban China (1993–1998)', *Economy & Society*, 28: 281–299

Guan, X. (2000) 'China's social policy: reforms and development in the context of marketization and globalisation', *Social Policy and Administration*, 34 (1): 115–130

Guo, S. (1999) 'Social security issues in SOEs reform and remedies', *Shanghai Labour & Social Security*, No. 22

—— (2003) 'The ownership reform in China: what direction and how far?', *Journal of Contemporary China*, 12 (36): 553–573

Gupta, S., Schiller, C. and Ma, H. (1999) 'Privatization, social impact, and social safety nets', Working Paper No. 99/68. International Monetary Fund, 1 May

Guthrie, D. (1999) *Dragon in a Three-piece Suit: The Emergence of Capitalism in China*, Princeton, NJ: Princeton University Press

Hamilton, G. and Biggart, N. (1988) 'Market, culture and authority: a comparative analysis of management and organization in the Far East', *American Journal of Sociology*, 94: S52–S94

Han, Minzhu (1990) *Cries for Democracy: Writings and Speeches from the 1989 Chinese Democracy Movement*, Princeton, NJ: Princeton University Press

Hannan, K. (ed.) (1998) *Industrial Change in China: Economic Restructuring and Conflicting Interests*, London: Routledge

Hao, Yunhong (2000) 'Entrepreneur motivation: institutional motivation, form motivation and motivation forms', *Economist* (in Chinese), 2: 25–29

Hart, O. D. (1983) 'The market mechanism as an incentive scheme', *Bell Journal of Economics*, 14 (2): 366–382

*Harvard China Review* (1998) 'Unchaining China's SOEs: interview with ten leading economists on SOE reform', Vol. 1 (1)

Hassard, J. and Sheehan, J. (1997) 'Enterprise reform and the role of the state: the case of the Capital Iron and Steel Works, Beijing', in A. Bugra and B. Usdiken (eds) *State, Market and Organizational Form*, Berlin: Walter De Gruyter

—— and —— (2005) 'Chinese state-enterprise reform and the worker representation question', Working Paper, Manchester Business School

——, Morris, J. and Sheehan, J. (1999a) 'Enterprise reform in post Deng China; the fall of the contract responsibility system', *International Studies of Management and Organisation*, 29: 54–68

——, —— and —— (1999b) 'Enterprise reform in post Deng China: the rise of the modern enterprise system', *International Studies of Management and Organisation*, 29: 68–83

——, —— and —— (2004) 'The "third way": the future of work in a corporatized Chinese economy', *International Journal of Human Resource Management*, 15 (2): 314–330

——, ——, —— and Xiao, Yuxin (2002) 'Policing the slow commotion: corporate transformation and its consequences in the Chinese state-owned steel industry', Working Paper, Manchester School of Management, UMIST UK

——, ——, —— and —— (2006) 'Downsizing the danwei: Chinese enterprise reform and the surplus labour question', *International Journal of Human Resource Management*, 17 (8): 1441–1455

——, ——, —— and —— (2006) 'Steeling for reform: Chinese state-enterprise restructuring and the surplus labour question', in G. Lee and M. Warner (eds) *Downsizing China*, London: RoutledgeCurzon

Hay, D. A., Morris, D. J., Liu, G. and Yao, S. (1994) *Economic Reform and State-owned Enterprises in China 1979–1987*, Oxford: Clarendon Press

He, Fuping (2005) 'Some thought on the unhealthy asset problem in state-owned enterprises', *Pioneering with Science and Technology Monthly*, 7: 42–43 (in Chinese)

He, Jun (2000) 'Urban economic transformation in Shanghai, China', unpublished dissertation

He, Zili (1999) 'Models of corporate governance: comparison and lessons', *Nankai Journal: Social Science and Philosophy Version*, 6: 41–50. (Title in Chinese: Gongsi Zhili Moshi: Bijiao Yu Jiejian)

Henderson, D., McNab, R. and Rozsas, T. (2004) 'The hidden inequality in socialism', Development and Comp Systems 0411012, Economics Working Paper Archive EconWPA

Hodgson, G. (1989) 'Institutional economic theory: the old versus the new', *Review of Political Economy*, 1: 249–269

Holmstrom, B. (1982) 'Moral hazard in teams', *Bell Journal of Economics*, 13 (2): 324–340

Holtz, C. (2003) *China's Industrial State-Owned Enterprises: Between Profitability and Bankruptcy*, New York: World Scientific

Hong, Liu, Campbell, N., Lu, Zheng and Wang, Yanzhong (1996) 'An international perspective on China's township enterprises', in D. Brown and R. Porter (eds) *Management Issues in China*, London: Routledge

*Hongkong Standard*, dates in text

Hoskisson, R., Eden, L., Lau, C. M. and Wright, M. (2000) 'Strategy in emerging economies', *Academy of Management Journal*, 43: 249–267

Howard, P. (1991) 'Rice bowls and job security: The urban contract labour system', *Australian Journal of Chinese Affairs*, 25: 93–114

Howe, C. (1992) 'Foreword', in Korzec, M. (ed.) *Labour and Failure of Reform in China*, London: Macmillan

Hu, Angang (1998) 'An analysis of Chinese unemployment conditions', *Management World*, 4: 21–39

Hu, F., Ma, X. (2000) 'Constructing pension system with Chinese characteristics through the combination of social pooling and individual accounts', *Shanghai Wages Information*, No. 5

Huang, Guobo (1994) 'Problems of monetary control in China: targets, behaviour and mechanism', in Fan Qimiao and P. Nolan (eds) *China's Economic Reforms*, London: Macmillan

Huang, Qifan (2000) 'Shanghai industrial development', www. Apcity.org – digital, Shanghai

Huang, Yiping (1999) *Agricultural Reform in China: Getting Institutions Right*, Cambridge: Cambridge University Press

Hughes, O. (1994) *Public Management and Administration*, Basingstoke: Macmillan

Hung, S. and Whittington, R. (1997) 'Strategies and institutions: a pluralistic account of strategies in the Taiwanese computing industry', *Organization Studies*, 18: 551–575

Hung, Yiping (1999) 'Reforms without privatization: Chinese experience in state enterprise reform', paper presented at 'Policy issues on privatization', 22–26 November, Tokyo

Hurst, W. and O'Brien, K. (2002) 'China's contentious pensioners', *The China Quarterly*, 170: 345–360

Hussain, A. (1994) 'Social security in present-day China and its reform', *American Economic Review*, 84 (2): 276–280

—— and Zhuang, J. (1997) 'Chinese state enterprises and their reforms', *Asia Pacific Business Review*, 3 (3): 20–37

IIECASS (Institute for Industrial Economy of the Chinese Academy for Social Science) (2000) *China's Industrial Development*, Beijing: Economic Management Press

IMF (1993) *China at the Threshold of a Market Economy*, Geneva: International Monetary Fund

—— (1997) *People's Republic of China – Selected Issues*, Geneva: International Monetary Fund

*Interfax News* (2004) 'Wuhan Steel secures approval for 2-bln new share placement, Jiusteel Hongxing rejected', 31 May

International Iron & Steel Institute (2004) *World Steel in Figures*. Posted on www.worldsteel.org

ILO (1999) *Good Practices: Re-employment in Reform of State-owned Enterprises*, Geneva: International Labour Organization

—— (2000) *World Labour Report*, Geneva: International Labour Organization

Jeffries, I. (2001) *Economies in Transition: A Guide to China, Cuba, Mongolia, North Korea and Vietnam at the Turn of the Twenty-First Century*, London: Routledge

Jensen, M. (1988) 'Takeovers: their causes and consequences', *Journal of Economic Perspectives*, 2 (1): 21–48

Jiang, Xiaorong (1997) 'An overview of the reform of China's administrative system and organizations and its prospects', *International Review of Administrative Sciences*, 63: 251–256

Johnson, R. (2001) 'Privatization and layoffs: the real story', working paper, Reason Public Policy Institute, www.rppi.org/privsl.html

Jones, L. (1985) 'Public enterprise for whom? Perverse distributional consequences of public operational decisions', *Economic Development and Cultural Change*, 33 (2): 334–347

——, Pankaj, T. and Vogelsang, I. (1991) 'Selling state-owned enterprises: a cost-benefit appoach', in R. Ramamurti and R. Vernon (eds) *Privatization and Control of State-owned Enterprises*, Washington, DC: World Bank

Josephs, H. (1995) 'Labour law in a "socialist market economy": the case of China', *Columbia Journal of Transitional Law*, 33: 561–581

Joshi, G. (2000) 'Privatization in South Asia: minimizing negative social effects through restructuring', working paper, International Labour Organization, Geneva, www.ilo.org/public/english/employment/ent/sed/publ/privatsa.htm

Kang, Yan (2001) *'Understanding Shanghai, 1990–2000'*, Shanghai People's Publishing House

Kato, Takao and Long, C. (2004) 'Executive compensation, firm performance, and state ownership in China: evidence from new panel data', William Davidson Institute Working Papers Series 2004–690, William Davidson Institute at the University of Michigan Stephen M. Ross Business School

Kay, J. and Thompson, D. (1986) 'Privatization: a policy in search of a rationale', *Economic Journal*, 96 (381): 18–32

Ke, L. and Morris, J. (2002) 'A comparative study of career development in state owned and foreign owned financial service companies in China', Chinese Management, Organisation and HRM Working Paper 3, Cardiff Business School, Cardiff University

Kikeri, S. (1998) 'Privatization and labour: what happens to workers when government divests?', Technical Paper No. 396, World Bank

—— (1999) 'Labour redundancies and privatization: what should governments do?', Technical Paper No. 412, World Bank

——, Nellis, J. and Sirley, M. (1994) 'Privatization: lessons from market economies', *World Bank Research Observer*, 9: 241–272

Killick, T. (1983) 'The role of the public sector in the industrialization of African developing countries', *Industry and Development*, 7: 57–88

Kirkpatrick, C. (1987) 'Trade policy and industrialization in developing countries', in N. Gemmel (ed.) *Surveys in Development Economies*, Oxford: Basil Blackwell

Knight, J. and Song, L. (1995) 'Towards a labour market in China', *Oxford Review of Economic Policy*, (11) 4: 97–119

Kolodko, G. (1999) 'Ten years of post-socialist transition: lessons for policy reform', Transition Economies Working Paper No. 2095, World Bank, Washington, DC http://www.worldbank.org/html/dec/Publications/Workpapers/wps2000series/wps20 95/wps2095-abstract.html

Konings J., Van Cayseele, P. and Warzynski, F. (2003) 'The effects of privatization and international competitive pressure on firms' price-cost margins: micro evidence from emerging economies 1', William Davidson Institute Working Papers Series 2003–603, William Davidson Institute at the University of Michigan Stephen M. Ross Business School

Kornai, J. (1990) *The Road to a Free Economy: Shifting from a Socialist System, the Example of Hungary*, New York: Norton

Korten, D. (1995) *When Corporations Rule the World*, West Hartford, CT: Kumarian Press

Kuehl, J. and Sziraczki, G. (1995) 'Employment restructuring at micro-level: results of the Dalian pilot enterprise survey', in Lin Lean Lim and G. Sziraczki (eds) *Employment Challenges and Policy Responses: Chinese and International Perspectives*, Beijing: International Labour Office, (Area Office Beijing)

Laffont, J. and Tirole, J. (1986) 'Using cost observation to regulate firms', *Journal of Political Economy*, 94: 614–641

Lam, K. (2002) 'A study of the ethical performance of foreign-investment enterprises in the China labour market', *Journal of Business Ethics*, 37: 349–365

Lan, Zhiyong (1999) 'The 1998 administrative reform in China: issues, challenges and prospects', *Asian Journal of Public Administration*, 21 (1): 29–54

Lardy, N. (1994) *China in the World Economy*, Washington, DC: Institute for International Economics

—— (1998) *China's Unfinished Economic Revolution*, Washington, DC: Brookings Institution Press

Lau, L. (1998) 'Why economic reform in China worked', in Gungwu Wang and John Wong (eds) *China's Political Economy*, Singapore University Press

——, Qian, Yingyi and Roland, G. (2000) 'Reform without losers: an interpretation of China's dual-track approach to transition', *Journal of Political Economy*, 108 (1): 120–143

Lee, C. (1999) 'From organized dependence to disorganised despotism: changing labour regimes in Chinese factories', *China Quarterly*, 157: 45–71

Lee, G. and Warner, M. (2004) 'The Shanghai re-employment model: from local experiment to nationwide labour market policy', *China Quarterly*, 177: 174–189

—— and —— (2006) (eds) *Downsizing China*, London: Routledge/Curzon

Lee, Keun (1996) 'An assessment of the state sector reform in China: viability of China: viability of "legal person socialism"', *Journal of the Asia Pacific Economy*, 1 (1): 105–121

Lee, P. (1997) 'The political economy of state enterprise relations in Shaanxi Province', *Journal of Contemporary Asia*, 27: 287–314

Lee, V. (2000) 'Unemployment insurance and assistance systems in mainland China', http://legco.gov.hk

Leng, Xiliang (2001) 'The origin of the informal sector theory and development in the world', *Shanghai Labour & Social Security*, No. 6

Leong, Liew (1997) *The Chinese Economy in Transition: From Plan to Market*, Cheltenham: Edward Elgar

Leung, Wing-yue (ed.) (1988) *Smashing the Iron Rice Pot: Workers and Unions in China's Market Socialism*, Hong Kong: Asian Monitor

Levy, B. and Spiller, P. (eds) (1996) *Regulations, Institutions and Commitment: Comparative Studies of Telecommunications*, New York: Cambridge University Press

Li, Feng (1998) 'Creating non-profit labour organisation to set the bottom line for employment protection', *Shanghai Labour & Social Security*, No. 20

Li, Jian Guo (1998) 'A million workers reemployed', www.China.org. cn/China today

Li, J. T., Tsui, A. S. and Weldon, E. (eds) (2000) *Management and Organizations in the Chinese Context*, New York: St Martin's Press

Li, Min (1999) 'The amendment of Shanghai unemployment regulations', *Shanghai Labour & Social Security*, No. 10

Li, Qiang (2004) 'Two female workers in Yancheng, Jiangsu arrested for opposing "buy and cut" severance pay', *Asian Labour News*, 1 Nov. (http://www.asianlabour.org/archives/003016.php)

Li, Wei (1997) 'The impact of economic reform on the performance of Chinese state enterprises, 1980–1989', *Journal of Political Economy*, 105 (5): 1080–1106

Li, Xiaoxi (1996) 'The integration of gradualism and big bang: economy-oriented Chinese reform path', in Wu Jinglian, Zhou, Xiaochuan and Zhao, Renwei (eds) *Gradualism and Big Bang: the Choice of China's Reform Path* (in Chinese), Beijing: Jingji Kexue Press

Li, Xun and Perry, E. (1997) 'Introduction: the changing Chinese workplace in historical and comparative perspective', in Xun Li and E. Perry (eds) *Danwei: The Changing Historical and Comparative Perspective*, Armonk, NY: M. E. Sharpe

Li, Yining (1986) 'Proposal for China's ownership reform' (title in Chinese: *Woguo Soyouzhi Gaige de Shexiang*). *People's Daily*, 26 September

—— (1987) 'Search for China's economic system reform' (title in Chinese: *Jingji Tizhi Gaige de Tansuo*). *People's Daily*, 5 February

Li, Zhang (2003) 'The problems and strategies of current state-owned enterprise reform', *Techno-economics and Management Research*, 2: 61–62 (in Chinese)

Lim, L. L. and Szizaczki, G. (1995) 'Introduction', in L. L. Lim and G. Szizaczki (eds) *Employment Challenges and Policy Responses: Chinese and International Perspectives*, Beijing: International Labour Office.

Lin, C. (1995) 'The assessment: Chinese economic reform in retrospect and prospect', in *Oxford Review of Economic Policy*, 11 (4): 1–24

Lin, Yifu (1997) *Perfect Information and State-owned Enterprise Reform*, Shanghai: Shanghai Sanlian Bookstore and People Press

——, Fang, Cai and Zhou, Li (1994) *The China Miracle: Development Strategy and Economic Reform* (in Chinese), Shanghai: Shanghai Sanlian Shudian

——, —— and —— (1998) 'Competition, policy burdens, and state-owned enterprise reform', *American Economic Review*, 88 (2): 426–431

——, —— and —— (2001) *State-owned Enterprise Reform in China*, Hong Kong: The Chinese University Press

Liu, Guogang (1987) 'Problems in the reform of ownership relations in China', in M. Warner (ed.) *Management Reforms in China*, London: Frances Pinter

Liu, Wei and Gao, Minghua (1999) *State-owned Enterprise Restructuring in the Transitional Period* (Title in Chinese: *Zhuanxingqi de Guoyou Qiye Chongzu*), Shanghai: Shanghai Far-East Press

Lu, Ping (1990) *A Moment of Truth: Workers' Participation in China's 1989 Democracy Movement and the Emergence of Independent Unions*, Hong Kong: Hong Kong Trade Union Education Centre/Asia Monitor Resource Centre

Lu, Yuan and Bjorkman, I. (1997) 'HRM practices in China – western joint ventures: MNC standardization versus localization', *International Journal of Human Resource Management*, 8: 614–627

—— and Child, J. (1996) 'Decentralisation of decision making in China's state enterprises', in D. Brown and R. Porter (eds) *Management Issues in China*, London: Routledge

Lu, Xiaubo and Perry, E. (eds) (1997) *Danwei: The Changing Chinese Work Place in Historical and Comparative Perspective*, New York: M. E. Sharpe

Lui, Guoguang (1987) 'Problems in the reform of ownership relations in China', in M. Warner (ed.) *Management Reforms in China*, London: Frances Pinter

Luo, Bingsheng (1993): 'The Shougang Contract Management Responsibility System: effects, practices and thoughts', Keynote address to International Seminar on the Shougang Contract Management Responsibility System, Beijing

Ma, Jun (1997) *China's Economic Reform in the 1990s*, Washington, DC: World Bank

Ma, Licheng and Ling, Zhijun (1998) *China's Problems*, Beijing: China Today Publishing House

McCourt, W. (2001) 'Towards a strategic model of employment reform in developing countries: explaining and remedying experience to date', *International Journal of Human Resource Management*, 12 (1): 56–75

McCutcheon, D. and Meredith, J. (1993) 'Conducting case study research in Operations Management', *Journal of Operations Management*, 11 (3): 239–256

McKinnon, R. (1994) 'Gradual versus rapid liberalization in socialist economies: the problem of macroeconomic control', in *Proceedings of the World Bank Annual Conference on Developing Economies 1993*, Washington, DC: World Bank

Macmillan, J. and Naughton, B. (1992) 'How to reform a planned economy: lessons from China', *Oxford Review of Economic Policy*, 8 (1): 130–143

——, Whalley, J. and Zhu, Lijing (1989) 'The impact of China's economic reforms on agricultural productivity and growth', *Journal of Political Economy*, 97 (4): 781–807

McNally, C. and Lee, P. (1998) 'Is big beautiful? Restructuring China's state sector under the Zhuada policy', *Issues and Studies*, 34 (9): 22–48

Marris, R. (1964) *Economic Theory of Managerial Capitalism*, London: Macmillan

Martin, S. and Parker, D. (1995) 'The impact of privatization on labour and total factor productivity', *Scottish Journal of Political Economy*, 42 (2): 201–220

—— and —— (1997) *The Impact of Privatisation-Ownership and Corporate Performance in the UK*, London: Routledge

Megginson, W., Nash, R. and Van Randenborgh, M. (1994) 'Financial and operating performance of newly privatized firms: an international empirical analysis', *Journal of Finance*, 49 (2): 403–452

Meyer, M. (2002) 'Decentralized enterprise reform: notes on the transformation of China's state-owned enterprises', in A. Tsui and C.-M. Lau (eds) *The Management of Enterprises in the People's Republic of China*, New York: Kluwer

Mitsuhashi, H., Hyeon, J. P., Wright, P. and Chua, R. (2000) 'Line and HR executives' perceptions of HR effectiveness in firms in the People's Republic of China', *International Journal of Human Resource Management*, 11: 197–216

Mok, Chiu Yu and J. F. Harrison (eds) (1990) *Voices from Tiananmen Square: Beijing Spring and the Democracy Movement*, Montreal: Black Rose Books

Morris, J. and Shen, Y. (2002) 'An employment model with 'Chinese characteristics': a case study of a Chinese SOE', Working Paper, Cardiff Business School, Cardiff University

—— and Wu, Q. (2002) 'Current reform in the Chinese public sector', Chinese Management, Organisation and HRM Working Paper 5, Cardiff Business School, Cardiff University

—— and Yang, Q. (2002) 'Reward management in China: comparative case studies of an SOE and an FIE', Chinese Management, Organisation and HRM Working Paper 6, Cardiff Business School, Cardiff University

—— and Zhang, J. (2001) 'Effective and rational human resource allocation: a study of differing ownership forms in China', China Management, Organisation and HRM Working Paper 1, Cardiff Business School, Cardiff University

—— and Zhang, H. (2002) 'Reforming health care in China: a study of performance related pay in Chinese hospitals', Chinese Management, Organisation and HRM Working Paper 7, Cardiff Business School, Cardiff University

——, Hassard, J. and Sheehan, J. (2002) 'Privatisation Chinese-style: economic reform and the state-owned enterprises', *Public Administration*, 80: 355–369

——, —— and —— (2003) 'From "iron arm chair" to HRM? Managing human resources in China's state owned enterprises', working paper, Cardiff Business School, Cardiff University

——, Sheehan, J. and Hassard, J. (2001) 'From dependency to defiance? Work-unit relationships in China's state enterprise reform', *Journal of Management Studies*, 38: 697–718

Movshuk, O. (2004) 'Restructuring, productivity and technical efficiency in China's iron and steel industry, 1988–2000', *Journal of Asian Economics*, 15: 135–151

Mueller, M. (1998) 'China's telecommunications sector and the WTO: can China conform to the telecom regulatory principles?', in James Dorn (1998) (ed.) *China in the New Millennium: Market Reforms and Social Development*, Washington, DC: CATO Institute

Naughton, B. (1994) 'What is distinctive about China's economic transition? State enterprise reform and overall system transformation', *Journal of Comparative Economics*, 18: 470–490

—— (1995a) *Growing Out of Plan: Chinese Economic Reform 1978–1993*, New York: Cambridge University Press

—— (1995b) 'China's macroeconomy in transition', *China Quarterly*, 144: 1083–1104

—— (1996) 'China's macro economy in transition', in Andrew Walder (ed.) *China's Transitional Economy*, Oxford: Oxford University Press

—— (1999) 'China's transition in economic perspective', in M. Goldman and R. MacFarquhar (eds) *The Paradox of China's Post-Mao Reforms*, Cambridge, MA: Harvard University Press

Nee, V. (1992) 'Organizational dynamics of market transition: hybrid forms, property rights, and mixed economy in China', *Administrative Science Quarterly*, 37: 1–27

—— (1998) 'Sources of the new institutionalism', in M. Brinton and V. Nee (eds) *The New Institutionalism in Sociology*, New York: Russell Sage Foundation

—— and D. Stark (eds) (1989) *Remaking Three Economic Institutions of Socialism: China and Eastern Europe*, Stanford, CA: Stanford University Press

Nellis, J. (1989) 'Contract plans and public enterprise performance', World Bank Discussion Paper No. 48, Washington, DC

—— (1999) 'Time to rethink privatization in transition economies?', IFC Discussion Paper No. 38, Washington, DC: World Bank

Nixson, F. (1995) 'Enterprise reform and economic restructuring in transitional economies: Mongolia, Vietnam and North Korea', in P. Cook and C. Kirkpatrick (eds) *Privatization Policy and Performance: International Perspectives*, London: Harvester Wheatsheaf

Nolan, P. (1993) 'China's post-Mao political economy: a puzzle', *Contributions to Political Economy*, 12: 71–87

—— (1995a) *China's Rise, Russia's Fall: Politics, Economics and Planning in the Transition from Stalinism*, Basingstoke: Macmillan

—— (1995b) 'From state factory to modern corporation? China's Shougang Iron and Steel Corporation under economic reform', Department of Applied Economics, Working Paper, Amalgamated Series, No. 9621, Cambridge: Cambridge University

—— (1996) 'Large firms and industrial reform in former planned economies: the case of China', *Cambridge Journal of Economics*, 20 (1): 1–29

—— (2001) *China and the Global Economy: National Champions, Industrial Policy and the Big Business Revolution*, London: Palgrave

—— (2003) *China at the Crossroads*, Cambridge: Polity Press

—— and Dong, Fureng (1990) *The Chinese Economy and Its Future*, London: Polity Press

—— and Wang, Xiaoqiang (1999) 'Beyond privatization: institutional innovation and growth in China's large state-owned enterprises', *World Development*, 27 (1): 169–200

—— and Yeung, G. (2001) 'Two paths to the reform of large firms in China', *Cambridge Journal of Economics*, 25 (4): 443–465

——, Buck, T. and Filatotchev, I. (2000) 'Different paths to economic reform in Russia and China: causes and consequences', *Journal of World Business*, 35 (4): 379–400

OECD (1998) 'Labour market aspects of state enterprises reform in China', Technical Paper No. 141, OECD Development Centre, http://www.oecd.org/

OECF (1998) 'State-owned enterprise reform in East Asian transitional economies (China and Vietnam)', Overseas Economic Cooperation Fund Research Paper No. 24, Tokyo

Oi, J. (1999) *Rural China Takes Off: Institutional Foundations of Economic Reform*, Berkeley, CA: University of California Press

—— (2005) 'Patterns of corporate restructuring in China: political constraints on privatization', *The China Journal*, 53: 116–136

—— and Walder, A. (eds) (1999) *Property Rights and Economic Reform in China*, Stanford, CA: Stanford University Press

O'Leary, G. (1998) 'The making of the Chinese working class', in G. O'Leary (ed.) *Adjusting to Capitalism: Chinese Workers and the State*, Armonk, NY: M. E. Sharpe

Olivia K. M. Ip (1995) 'Changing employment systems in China: some evidence from the Shenzhen special economic zone', in *Work, Employment & Society*, 9, (2): 269–285

Orru, M., Biggart, N. and Hamilton, G. (1997) *The Economic Organization of East Asia Capitalism*, Thousand Oaks, CA: Sage

Parker, D. and Hartley, K. (1991) 'Do changes in organization status affect performance?', *Strategic Management Journal*, 12: 278–296

—— and Pan, W. (1996) 'Reform of the state-owned enterprises in China', *Communist & Economic Transformation*, 8 (1): 109–127

Peltzman, S. (1971) 'Pricing in public and private enterprises: electric utilities in the United States', *Journal of Law and Economics*, 14 (1): 109–147

Pendleton, A. (1997) 'What impact has privatization had on pay and employment? A review of the UK experience', *Relations Industrielles*, 52: 554–582

——— (1999) 'Ownership or competition? An evaluation of the effects of privatization on industrial relations institutions, processes and outcomes', *Public Administration*, 77 (4): 769–791

Peng, M. (1997) 'Firm growth in transitional economies: three longitudinal cases from China, 1989–96', *Organization Studies*, 18: 385–413

——— (2000) *Business Strategies in Transition Economies*, London: Sage

——— and Heath, P. (1996) 'The growth of the firm in planned economies in transition: institutions, organizations and strategic choice', *Academy of Management Review*, 21: 492–528

Peng, Q. (1951) *A Political Textbook for Workers (Gongren Zhengzhi Keben)*, Beijing: Workers' Press

*People's Daily Online*, 9 January 2004, 'China's "iron belt" readies financial revival'

———, 11 May 2004, 'Pro-active fiscal policies added millions of jobs in six years'

Perry, E. (1994) 'Shanghai's strike wave of 1957', *China Quarterly*, 137: 1–27

——— (1997) 'From native place to workplace: labour origins and outcomes of China's *danwei* system', in E. Perry (ed.) *Danwei: The Changing Historical and Comparative Perspective*, Armonk, NY: M. E. Sharpe

——— and Li, Xun (1997) *Proletarian Power: Shanghai in the Cultural Revolution*, Boulder, CO: Westview Press

Pollard, V. (2003) 'Revolutionary aspirations, state capitalist detour and democratisation in the Philippines', paper presented at International Studies Association 44th Annual Convention, Portland, Oregon, 27 February

Putterman, L. (1995) 'The role of ownership and property rights in China's economic transition', *China Quarterly*, 144: 1047–1064

——— (1996) 'The role of ownership and property rights in China's economic transition', in A. Walder (ed.) *China's Transitional Economy*, Oxford University Press

——— and Dong, X.-Y. (2000) 'China's state-owned enterprises: their role, job creation and efficiency in long-term perspective', *Modern China*, 26 (4): 403–447

Pyle, D. (1997) *China's Economy: From Revolution to Reform*, London: Macmillan

Qi, Zhaodong (2000) 'The evolution of the development of the Chinese corporate theories', *Journal of the Capital University of Economy and Trade*, 2: 29–34 (in Chinese: 'Zhongguo Gonsi Lilun Fazhan de Yanbian' in *Shoudou Jingji Maoyi Daxue Xuebao*)

Qian, Yingyi (1999) 'The institutional foundations of China's market transition', paper presented at the Annual Bank Conference on Development Economics of the World Bank, 28–30 April, Washington, DC

——— (2000) 'The process of China's market transition (1978–1998): the evolutionary, historical and comparative perspectives', *Journal of International and Theoretical Economics*, 156 (1): 151–171

Rawski, T. (1994) 'Chinese industrial reform: accomplishments, prospects and implications', *American Economic Review*, 84 (2): 271–275

——— (1995) 'Implications of China's reform experience', *China Quarterly*, 144: 1150–1173

Redding, G. (1990) *The Spirit of Chinese Capitalism*, Berlin: De Gruyter

RMRB, 2 June 2003, 'How does SASAC innovate its supervision function?' p. 5 (in Chinese)

———, 15 January 2003, 'Important measure of SOE reform; separated auxiliary business units to restructure as mixed ownership economic entities', p. 2 (in Chinese)

Ros, A. (1999) 'Does ownership or competition matter?', *Journal of Regulatory Economics*, 15 (1): 65–92

Sachs, J. (1993) *Poland's Jump to the Market Economy*, London: MIT Press

—— and Woo, Wing Thye (1994) 'Structural factors in the economic reforms of China, Eastern Europe, and the former Soviet Union', *Economic Policy*, 18 (1): 102–145

——, Zinnes, C. and Eilat, Y. (2000a) 'Patterns and determinants of economic reform in transition economies: 1990–1998', Consulting Assistance on Economic Reform II, Discussion Paper 61, http://www.geocities.com/capitolhill/senate/8539/paradtansitnew.htm

——, —— and —— (2000b) 'The gains from privatization in transition economies: is "change of ownership" enough?', Consulting Assistance on Economic Reform II, Discussion Paper No. 63, http://www.cid.harvard.edu/caer2/htm/content/papers/confpubs/bns/dp63bn.htm

Samuels, W. (1995) 'The present state of institutional economics', *Cambridge Journal of Economics*, 19: 569–590

Sappington, D. (1991) 'Incentives in principal-agent relationships', *Journal of Economic Perspective*, 5 (2): 45–66

Schueller, M. (1997) 'Liaoning: struggling with the burdens of the past', in D. Goodman (ed.) *China's Provinces in Reform*, London: Routledge

Selden, M. and Lai, Yin You (1997) 'The reform of social welfare in China', *World Development*, 25 (10): 1657–1668

SETC (2002) 'Method to implement settlement and transfer of surplus workers in restructuring and separating auxiliary business units in large and medium sized SOEs', SOE Reform Document no. 859. 18 Nov. Posted on http://www.sasac.gov.cn/

Shanghai Economic Commission (1996) 'Materialising social security and promoting reemployment', *Shanghai Labour*, No. 14

Shanghai Labour & Social Security Bureau (2000) 'The first group of loans materialised'

—— (2001) 'Training guidance'

Sheehan, J. (1995) 'Conflict between workers and the Party-state in China and the development of autonomous workers' organizations, 1949–1984', unpublished doctoral dissertation, University of London

—— (1996) 'Is there another Tiananmen uprising in the offing?', *Jane's Intelligence Review*, 8 (12): 554–556

—— (1998) *Chinese Workers: A New History*, London: Routledge

—— (2000) 'From client to challenger: workers, managers and the state in post-Deng China', working paper, ICCS, University of Nottingham

——, Morris, J. and Hassard, J. (2000) 'Redundancies in Chinese state enterprises: a research report', *Industrial Relations*, 39 (3): 486–501

——, ——, —— and Xiao, Y. (2003) 'The surplus labour problem in large/medium SOEs: experiences from the steel industry', Paper presented at SOE Reform and Privatization in China conference, Australian National University, Canberra, July

Shenkar, O. and Chow, I. (1989) 'From political praise to stock options: reforming compensation systems in the People's Republic of China', *Human Resource Management*, 1: 65–85

Shieh, S. (1999) 'Is bigger better?', *China Business Review*, May–June: 50–55

Shirk, S. (1993) *The Political Logic of Economic Reform in China*, Berkeley, CA: California University Press

Shirley, M. (1983) 'Managing state-owned enterprises', World Bank Working Paper No. 577, Washington, DC

—— (1997) 'The economics and politics of government ownership', *Journal of International Development*, 9 (6): 849–864

—— (1999) 'Bureaucrats in business: the role of privatization versus corporatization in state-owned enterprise reform', *World Development*, 27 (1): 115–136

—— and Walsh, P. (2000) *Public versus Private Ownership: the Current State of the Debate*, Washington, DC: World Bank

Shleifer, A. and Vishny, R. (1994) 'Politicians and firms', *Quarterly Journal of Economics*, 109 (4): 995–1025

—— and —— (1997) 'A survey of corporate governance', *Journal of Finance*, 52 (2): 737–783

'Shougang reforms', Editorial Committee (1992) *The Reforms at Shougang*, Beijing: Beijing Municipal CCP Propaganda Department, Beijing Municipal Research Group on Ideological and Political Work, and the Shougang Iron and Steel Works (3 volumes)

Smith, C. and Meiskins, P. (1996) 'System, society and dominance effects in cross-national organizational analysis', *Work, Employment and Society*, 9: 241–267

Smyth, R. (1998) 'New institutional economics in the post-socialist transformation', *Journal of Economic Surveys*, 12 (4): 361–398

—— (2000) 'Should China be promoting large-scale enterprises and enterprise groups?', *World Development*, 28 (4): 721–737

Solinger, D. (1993) *China's Transition from Socialism: Statist Legacies and Market Reforms, 1980–1990*, Armonk, NY: M. E. Sharpe

—— (1996) 'Despite decentralization – disadvantages, dependence and ongoing central power in the inland: the case of Wuhan', *China Quarterly*, 145: 34

—— (1999) 'China's floating population', in M. Goldman and R. MacFarquhar (eds) *The Paradox of China's Post-Mao Reforms*, Cambridge, MA: Harvard University Press

—— (2001) 'Why we cannot count the unemployed', *The China Quarterly*, 167: 671

—— (2002) 'Labour market reform and the plight of the laid-off proletariat', *China Quarterly*, 170: 304–326

—— (2003) 'Chinese urban jobs and the WTO', *The China Journal*, 50: 36–48

—— (2005) 'China is no worker's paradise', *Asian Labour News*, 12 February, http://www.asianlabour.org/archives/003384.php

Song, Jingsong (2000) *Contemporary Theory and Practice of the Firm*, Beijing: China Economic Press. (Title in Chinese: *XianDai Qiye Lilun yu Shijian*)

*South China Morning Post*, 9 March 1990, 'Cases of industrial unrest in 1989 viewed'

——, 17 February 1993, 'Retired workers in daring Beijing pensions protest'

——, 20 May 2004, 'China Telecom cashes in on rebound'

——, 15 June 2004, 'Wuhan Steel seeking to raise 9b yuan'

——, dates in text; Internet edition used unless otherwise stated

State Council, Document No. 10, 1998

SSB (State Statistical Bureau of China) (1993–2000) 'China Statistical Yearbooks'

—— dates of yearly reports in text

*Statistics Yearbook of Shanghai* (1999–2000) Shanghai Municipal Statistics Bureau, China Statistics Publishing House

Steinfeld, E. (1998) *Forging Reform in China: The Fate of State-owned Industry*, Cambridge: Cambridge University Press

Stiglitz, J. (1988) *Economics of the Public Sector*, (2nd edition), London: W. W. Norton and Co.

——— (1993) 'Some theoretical aspects of the privatization: application to eastern Europe', in M. Baldassarri, L. Paganetto and E. S. Phelps (eds) *Privatization Processes in Eastern Europe*, New York: St Martin's Press

——— (1994) *Whither Socialism?* Cambridge, MA: MIT Press

——— (1999) 'China: forging a third generation of reforms', World Bank Keynote speech, Beijing China, 23 July 1999. Website: www.worldbank.org.cn/english/content/34316160684.shtml

Sun, Ping (1997) 'Initial discussion on redundancy problem in large and medium-sized SOEs', ('Guoyou dazhongxing qiye rongyuan wenti chutan'), *Guangli Jiaoyu Xuekan (Management Education Academic Journal)* 6: 38–40 (in Chinese)

Sun, Qinghai and Sun, Shangqing (1990) 'China's economic development and reform: achievements, problems and prospects', in D. Kemme and E. Gordon (eds) *The End of Central Panning? Socialist Economics in Transition*, Boulder, CO: Westview Press

Sutherland, D. (2003) *China's Large Enterprises and the Challenge of Late Industrialization*, London: Routledge/Curzon

Tan, C. (1996) 'Some issues of reform of the state-owned enterprises', in Tao Song and Xinhua Wei (eds) *Multi-Dimensioned Thinking on Promoting State Enterprise Reform by 40 Economists*, Beijing: Economics Science Press

Taylor, B. (2002) 'Privatisation, markets and industrial relations in China', *British Journal of Industrial Relations*, 40 (2): 249–272

Thayer, F. (1995) 'Privatization: carnage, chaos and corruption', in S. Albert Hyde and J. Shafritz (eds) *Public Management: The Essential Readings*, Chicago, IL: Lyceum Books/Nelson Hall

Thoburn, J. (1997) 'Enterprise reform, domestic competition and export competitiveness: the case of China', *Journal of the Asia Pacific Economy*, 2 (2): 166–177

Thys, W. (2000) 'Gender and informal sector', www.europrofem.org

Tian, G. (2001) 'State shareholding and the value of Chinese firms', paper presented to Chinese Accounting, Finance and Business Research Unit seminar, Cardiff University, 14 March

TISCO (Tangshan Iron and Steel Company Limited) *Annual Reports, 1997–2004*

Tsang, E. (1998) 'Can Guanxi be a source of sustained competitive advantage for doing business in China?', *The Academy of Management Executive*, 12 (2): 64–73

Tsui, A. and Lau, C.-M. (eds) (2002) *The Management of Enterprises in the People's Republic of China*, New York: Kluwer

Tung, R. and Worm, V. (2001) 'Network capitalism: the role of human resources in penetrating the China market', *International Journal of Human Resource Management*, 12 (4): 517–534

Uehara, Kazuyoshi (1999) 'State-owned enterprise reform and the labour force in China', http://www.Chinaonline

Unger, J. and Chan, A. (1995) 'China, corporatism and the east Asian model', *Australian Journal of Chinese Affairs*, 33: 29–53

UNIDO (United Nations Industrial Development Organisation) (1996) *China: Managing-Investment-Led Growth*, London: Economist Intelligence Unit

Van De Walle, N. (1989) 'Privatization in developing countries: a review of the issues', *World Development*, 17 (5): 601–615

Van der Hoeven, R. and Sziraczki, G. (1998) *Lessons from Privatization: Labour Issues in Developing and Transitional Countries*, Geneva: International Labour Organization, www.brook.edu/press/books/clientpr/ilo/privatiz.htm

Verburg, R. (1996) 'Developing HRM in foreign-Chinese joint venture', *European Management Journal*, 14 (5): 518–525

Vickers, J. and Yarrow, G. (1988) *Privatization: An Economic Analysis*, Cambridge, MA: MIT University Press

—— and —— (1991) 'Economic perspectives on privatization', *Journal of Economic Perspectives*, 5 (2): 111–132

Walder, A. (1986) *Communist Neo-Traditionalism*, Berkeley, CA: University of California Press

—— (1989) 'The political sociology of the Beijing upheaval of 1989', *Problems of Communism*, 38 (5): 30–40

—— (1991) 'Workers, managers and the state', *The China Quarterly*, 127: 467–492

—— (ed.) (1996) *China's Transitional Economy: Interpreting its Significance*, Oxford: Oxford University Press

—— and Gong, Xiaoxia (1993) 'Workers in the Tian'anmen protests: the politics of the Beijing Workers' Autonomous Federation', *Australian Journal of Chinese Affairs*, 29: 1–29

Walter, C. and Howie, F. (2003) *Privatizing China: The Stock Markets and their Role in Corporate Reform*, John Wiley & Sons

Wang, Gungwu and Wong, J. (1998) *China's Political Economy*, Singapore: Singapore University Press

Wang, Mingqiang (1999) 'Construction of the critical component of labour market', ('Gou Jian Lao Dong Li Shi Chang de Zhong Xin Huan Jie'), *Shanghai Labour & Social Security*, No. 18

—— (2001) 'Implementing "4050" programme, creating jobs for difficult group', *Shanghai Labour & Social Security*, No. 10

—— and Xin, Wu (2001) 'Upgrade the skills of labour force' ('Ti Sheng Bai Wan Lao Dong Zhe Su Zhi'), *Shanghai Labour & Social Security*, No. 1

Wang, Shaoguang (1993) 'From a pillar of continuity to a force for change: Chinese workers in the movement', in R. Des Forges, Luo Ning and Wu Yen-bo (eds) *Chinese Democracy and the Crisis of 1989*, Albany, NY: State University of New York Press

Wang, Xiaodong (1993) 'A review of China's economic problems: the industrial sector', in R. Des Forges, Luo Ning and Wu Yen-bo (eds) *Chinese Democracy and the Crisis of 1989*, Albany, NY: State University of New York Press

Wang, Zhuo and Wen, Wuhan (eds) (1992) *An Evaluation of Guangdong's Opening and Reform (Guangdong gaige kaifang pingshuo)*, Guangzhou: Guangdong People's Press

Warner, M. (1992) *How Chinese Managers Learn: Management and Industrial Training in China*, Macmillan: London

—— (1993) 'Human resource management with Chinese characteristics', *International Journal of Human Resource Management*, 4: 45–65

—— (1995a) *The Management of Human Resources in Chinese Industry*, London: Macmillan

—— (1995b) 'Managing China's human resources', *Human Systems Management*, 14: 239–248

—— (1996a) 'Human resources: the People's Republic of China: the "three systems" reforms', *Human Resource Management Journal*, 6 (2): 153–202

—— (1996b) 'Chinese enterprise reforms, human resources and the 1994 labour law', *International Journal of Human Resource Management*, 7: 779–796

—— (1996c) 'Managing China's enterprises reform: a new agenda for the 1990s', *Journal of General Management*, 21 (3): 1–18

—— (1996d) 'Chinese enterprise reform, human resources and the 1994 labour law', *International Journal of Human Resource Management*, 7 (4): 779–796

—— (1996e) 'Economic reforms, industrial relations and human resources in the People's Republic of China: an overview', *Industrial Relations Journal*, 27 (3): 195–210

—— (1996f) 'Beyond the iron rice bowl: comprehensive labour reform in state owned enterprises in northeast China', in D. Brown and R. Porter (eds) *Management Issues in China*, London: Routledge

—— (1997a) 'China's HRM in transition: towards relative convergence', *Asia Pacific Business Review*, 3 (4): 19–33

—— (1997b) 'Management–labour relations in the new Chinese economy', *Human Resource Management Journal*, 7 (4): 30–43

—— (1999) 'Human resource management in China's "hi-tech" revolution: a study of selected computer hardware software and related firms in the PRC', *International Journal of Human Resource Management*, 10: 1–20

—— (2000a) 'Introduction: the Asia-Pacific HRM model Revisited', *International Journal of Human Resource Management*, 11: 171–182

—— (2000b) 'Society, Organisation and Work in China', in M. Maurice and A. Sorge (eds) *Embedding Organisations*, Amsterdam: John Benjamins Publishing Company

—— (ed.) (2000c) *Changing Workplace Relations in the Chinese Economy: Beyond the Iron Rice Bowl*, London: Macmillan

—— (2001a) 'Human resource management in the People's Republic of China', in P. Budhwar and Y. A. Debrah (eds) *Human Resource Management in Development Countries*, London: Routledge

—— (2001b) 'The new Chinese workers and the challenge of globalization: an overview', *International Journal of Human Resource Management*, 7: 134–141

—— and Ng, S. (1999) 'Collective contracts in Chinese enterprises: a new brand of collective bargaining under market socialism?', *British Journal of Industrial Relations*, 37: 295–314

Waterbury, J. (1993) *Exposed to Innumerable Delusions: Public Enterprise and State Power in Egypt, India, Mexico, and Turkey*, Cambridge: Cambridge University Press

Wei, Jie (2001) *Frontier Issues of the Firm: Management Proposals for Modern Firms* (Chinese title: *Qiye Qianyan Wenti: Xiandai Qiye Guanli Fangan*), Beijing: China Development Publishing

Weller, R. and Li, J. (2000) 'From state-owned enterprise to joint venture: a case study in the crisis in urban social services', *The China Journal*, 43: 83–99

West, L. (1999) 'Pension reform in China: preparing for the future', *Journal of Development Studies*, 35 (3): 153–202

White, G. (1987a) 'The politics of economic reform in Chinese industry: the introduction of the Labour Contract System', *China Quarterly*, 111: 365–389

—— (1987b) 'Labour market reform in Chinese industry', in M. Warner (ed.) *Management Reforms in China*, London: Frances Pinter (Publisher) Limited

White, L. III (1989) *Policies of Chaos: The Organizational Causes of Violence in China's Cultural Revolution*, Princeton, NJ: Princeton University Press

White, S. and Liu, X. (2001) 'Transition trajectories for market structure and firm strategy in China', *Journal of Management Studies*, 38 (1): 103–124

Whitley, R. (1991) 'The social construction of business systems in east Asia', *Organization Studies*, 12: 1–28

—— (1992) *Business Systems in East Asia: Firms, Markets and Societies*, London: Sage

—— (1994) 'Dominant forms of economic organization in market economies', *Organization Studies*, 15: 153–182

—— (1999) *Divergent Capitalisms*, Oxford: Oxford University Press

—— (ed.) (2002) *Competing Capitalisms*, London: Edward Elgar

—— and Czaban, L. (1998) 'Institutional transformation and enterprise change in an emergent capitalist economy: the case of Hungary', *Organizational Studies*, 19: 259–280

——, Henderson, J. and Czaban, L. (1997) 'Ownership, control and the management of labour in an emergent capitalist economy: the case of Hungary', *Organization*, 4: 409–432

Whyte, M. (1999) 'The changing role of workers', in M. Goldman and R. MacFarquhar (eds) *The Paradox of China's Post-Mao Reforms*, Cambridge, MA: Harvard University Press

Wildsmith, J. (1973) *Managerial Theories of the Firm*, London: Martin Robertson

Wilkinson, B. (1995) *Labour and Industry in East Asia*, Berlin: De Gruyter

Williamson, E. (1990) 'A comparison of alternative approaches to economic organisation', *Journal of Institutional and Theoretical Economics*, 146: 61–71

Williamson, O. (1963) 'A model of rational managerial behaviour', in R. Cyert and J. March, *A Behavioural Theory of the Firm*, Englewood Cliffs, NJ: Prentice-Hall

—— (1967) *Economics of Discretionary Behaviour: Managerial Objectives in A Theory of the Firm*, Chicago, IL: Markham Publishing

—— (1975) *Markets and Hierarchies: Analysis and Antitrust Implications*, New York: Free Press

—— (1976) 'Franchise bidding for natural monopolies – in general and with respect to CATV', *Bell Journal of Economics*, 7 (1): 73–104

Willig, R. (1985) 'Corporate government at the product market structure', Mimeo; Princeton University

Wilson, J. (1990) 'Labour policy in China: reform and retrogression', *Problems of Communism*, 39 (5): 44–65

WISCO (Wuhan Iron and Steel Company Limited) (2004) *Annual Report*

Wong, A. and Slater, J. (2002) 'Executive development in China: is there any in a western sense?', *International Journal of Human Resource Management*, 13: 338–360

*Workers' Daily* (*Gongren Ribao*) dates in text

World Bank (1983, 1990) *World Development Report*, Washington, DC: World Bank

—— (1995) *Bureaucrats in Business: The Economics and Politics of Government Ownership*, New York: Oxford University Press

—— (1996) *From Plan to Market*, Washington, DC: Oxford University Press

—— (1997a) *China's Management of Enterprise Assets: The State As A Shareholder*, Washington, DC: World Bank

—— (1997b) *World Bank Development Report*, Oxford: Oxford University Press

—— (2000) *The World Bank and China*, Washington, DC: World Bank, www.worldbank.org

—— (2002) *World Bank Report 2002: Building Institutions for Markets*, Oxford: Oxford University Press

Wright, M., Buck, T. and Filatotchev, I. (1998) 'Bank and investment fund monitoring of privatized firms in Russia', *Economics of Transition*, 6: 361–387

Wright, P., Mitsuhashi, H. and Chua, R. (1998) 'HRM in multinational's operations in China: business, people and HR issues', Center for Advanced Human Resource Studies Working Paper, Ithaca, NY: Cornell University

——, Sizato, F. and Cheng, T. (2002) 'Guanxi and professional conduct in China: a management development perspective', *International Journal of Human Resource Management*, 13: 156–182

WSPC (Wuhan Steel Processing Company Limited) *(2000–2003) Annual Reports*

Wu, Jinglian (1993) *Reform of Large and Medium-Sized Enterprises: The Establishment of Modern Enterprise System*, Tianjin: Tianjin People's Press. (Title in Chinese: *DazhongXing Qiye Gaige: Jianli Xiandai Qiye Zhidu*)

—— (1994) *Modern Corporation and Enterprise Reform*, Tianjin: Tianjin People's Press. (Title in Chinese: *Xiandai Gongsi yu Qiye Gaige*)

—— (1996) *Gradualism and Big Bang: The Choice of China's Paths to Reform*, Beijing: Economic Science Press (Title in Chinese: *Jianjin yu Jijin: Zhongguo Gaige Daolu de Jueze*)

—— (1999) *Contemporary China's Economic Reform: Strategy and Implementation*, (in Chinese), Shanghai: Shanghai Far-east Press (Title in Chinese: *Dangdai Zhongguo Jingji Gaige: Celue yu Shishi*)

—— et al. (1993) *General Conception and Scheme Proposal for Building Market Economy*, Beijing: Zhongyang Bianyi Press (Title in Chinese: *Jianshe Shichang Jingji de Zongti Gouxiang yu Fangan Sheji*)

Wu, Wenwu and Wang, Wubin (1996) 'Education and employment in China', Asia Pacific Centre for Human Resources & Development Studies – Papers on HRD/Labour Market Issues

*Wugang Yearbooks*, 2001–2004 (in Chinese)

Xiao, G. (1998) 'Reforming the governance structure of China's state-owned enterprises', *Public Administration and Development*, 18: 273–280

Xiao, J. and Dahya, J. (2000) 'The grounded theory exposition of the supervisory board in China', Paper presented to the ESRC Economic Reform in China: New Forms of Corporate Governance conference, Cardiff

Xiao, Yanshun (1997) Jinxing guoyou zichan cunliang fenjie – fenli guoyou qiye shehui gongneng (Decomposing state-owned assets – separating enterprise's social functions), *Jingji Yanzhao Cankao (Economic Research Reference)*, 6: 25–31 (in Chinese)

Xing, Q. (2000) 'Housing reforms and the new governance of housing in urban China', *International Journal of Public Sector Management*, 13: 519–525

Xinhua News Agency (2004) 'China axes redundant operations of state enterprises', 30 April. Re-printed on China.org.cn (http://www.China.org.cn/english/BAT/94471.htm)

*Xinhuanet* (2005a) 'Regrouping of SOEs to speed up – official', 1 September

—— (2005b) 'Foreign investors able to buy large SOEs', 16 September

Xu, Lixin Colin (2000) 'Control, incentives and competition: the impact of reform on Chinese state-owned enterprises', *Economics of Transition*, 8 (1): 151–173

Yang, M. M. (1989) 'Between state and society: the construction of corporateness in a Chinese socialist factory', *Australian Journal of Chinese Affairs*, 22: 31–60

—— (1994) *Gifts, Favors, and Banquets: The Art of Social Relationships in China*, New York: Cornell University Press

Yang, X. (1998) *Contemporary Economics and Chinese Economy*, (*Dangdai Jingjixue He Zhongguo Jingji*) Beijing: Publishing House of China's Social Sciences

Yarrow, G. (1986) 'Privatization in theory and practice', *Economic Policy*, 1 (2): 323–377

——— (1999) 'A theory of privatization, or why bureaucrats are still in business', *World Development*, 27 (1): 157–168

——— and Jasinski, P. (1996) *Privatization: Critical Perspectives on the World Economy*, Vols I–IV, London: Routledge

Yi, Chu (2001) 'Enhancing the safety net of labours', Shanghai Labour & Social Security, No. 3

You, Ji (1998) *China's Enterprise Reform: Changing State/Society Relations After Mao*, London: Routledge

Yu, Ching and Luo, Chongwei (2005) 'Daxing guoyou qiye gaizhi hou cunxu qiye de gaige yu fazang yanjiu' (The reform and development of the subsidiaries in restructured large state-owned enterprises), *Jingji Yanzhao Cankao (Economic Research Reference)*, 4: 2–40 (in Chinese)

Yu, Linghe (1998) 'The development of informal sector in Shanghai', Shanghai Labour & Social Security, No. 10

Yuang, Zhigang and Fang, Ying (eds) (1998) *The Evolution of China's Employment System, 1978–1996*, Shanxi: Shanxi Economic Publishing House

Zhang, Chengyao (2000) *Case Studies of the Reform and Development of China's Enterprises*, Beijing: Economic Management Press (Jingji Guanli Chubanshe)

Zhang, Dezhi (1999) 'Increasing urban employment in Shanghai: active labour market programmes and other initiatives', Paper presented at the Manila Social Forum, 1999, www.aric.adb.org/conference

Zhang, Guoyun (1997) 'Rongyuan: Jiuqi qiye yige chenzhong de huati', (Redundancy: A serious topic to enterprises in 1997), *Xingzheng Renshi Guanli (Administrative and Personnel Management)*, 2: 17–18 (in Chinese)

Zhang, Leyin (2004) 'The roles of corporatization and stock market listing in reforming China's state industry', *World Development*, 32 (12): 2031–2047

Zhang, Weiying (1995) *Entrepreneurs of Enterprises: A Contract Theory*, Shanghai: Sanlian Bookstore and Shanghai People's Press (Title in Chinese: *Qiye de QiyeJia: Qiyue Lilun*)

——— (1997) 'Decision rights, residual claims and performance: a theory of how Chinese state enterprise reform works', *China Economic Review*, 8 (1): 67–82

——— (1999) *Enterprise Theories and China's Enterprise Reform* (in Chinese), Beijing: Beijing University Press

——— and Zhong, Hongjun (2000) 'Corporate governance', in Siwei Cheng (ed.) *Problems and Counter-measures for the Management of Chinese Enterprises*, (*Zhonguo Qiye Guali Mianlin de Wenti ji Duice*), Beijing: Minzhu yu Jianshe Press

———, Hu, X. and Pope, M. (2002) 'The evolution of career guidance and counselling in the People's Republic of China', *The Career Development Quarterly*, 50: 226–234

Zhang, Xunhai (1992) *Enterprise Reforms in a Centrally Planned Economy: A Case of the Chinese*, New York: St Martin's Press

Zhang, Yichi (1996) 'Insider control and corporate governance in state-owned enterprise reform', *Economics*, 6 (Title in Chinese: 'Shilun Guoyou Qiye Gaige de Neiburen Kongzhi Yu Gongsi Zhili Jiegou')

Zhang, Yunqiu (1997) 'An intermediary: the Chinese perception of trade unions since the 1980s', *Journal of Contemporary China*, 6 (14)

Zhao, M. (2002a) 'Globalisation and Chinese labour: case studies of the Chinese shipping and textiles industries', paper presented to the CAFBRU Second Symposium on Marketisation and Accounting, Finance and Business in China, Cardiff University

—— (2002b) 'The consequences of China's socialist market economy for seafarers', *Work, Employment and Society*, 16: 171–183

—— and Nichols, T. (1996) 'Management control of labour in state owned enterprises: cases from the textiles industry', *The China Journal*, 36: 1–25

—— and —— (1998) 'Management control of labour in state-owned enterprises: cases from the textiles industry', in G. O'Leary (ed.) *Adjusting to Capitalism: Chinese Workers and the State*, Armonk, NY: M. E. Sharpe

Zhao, Yaohui (2001) 'Earning differentials between state and non-state enterprises in urban China', working paper, Centre for Economic Research, Beijing University

Zheng, Hongliang (1998) 'Theory on corporate governance and the Chinese state-owned enterprise reform', *Economic Research*, Vol. 10 (Title in Chinese: 'Gongsi Zhili Lilun Yu Zhongguo Guoqi Gaige')

—— and Wang, Fengbing (2000) 'Study on the reform of Chinese corporate governance: a theory overview', *Management World*, 3: 119–125 (Title in Chinese: 'Zhongguo Gonsi Zhili Jiegou Gaige Yanjiu: Yige Lilun Zongshu')

Zheng, Q. and Zhang, J. (1986) 'Shareholding system is not a correct way to vitalize state enterprises', *Economic System Reform*, 3 (Title in Chinese: 'Gufenhua Bu Shi Gaohao Quanmin Suoyouzhi Qiye de Zhengque Fangxiang')

Zhu, Cherrie Jiuhua and Dowling, P. (1994) 'The impact of the economic system upon human resource management practices in China', *Human Resource Planning*, 17 (4): 1–21

—— and —— (2000) 'Managing people during economic transition: the development of HR practices in China', *Asia Pacific Journal of Human Resources*, 38 (2): 84–106

Zhu, Junyi (2000) 'Achieving the overall transition to the labour market by the year 2000', *Shanghai Labour & Wage Information*, No. 3

Zhu, Ying (1995) 'Major changes under way in China's industrial relations', *International Labour Review*, 134 (1): 37–49

Zweig, D. (2001) 'China's stalled "fifth wave": Zhu Rongj's reform package of 1998–2000', *Asian Survey*, 16 (2): 231–248

# Index